MW00861101

The Science of Trust

A Norton Professional Book

The Science of Trust

Emotional Attunement for Couples

John M. Gottman, PhD

W. W. Norton & Company

New York · London

"For Love in a Time of Conflict" from TO BLESS THE SPACE BETWEEN US:
A BOOK OF BLESSINGS by John O'Donohue, copyright © 2008 by John O'Donohue.
Used by permission of Doubleday, a division of Random House, Inc.

Copyright © 2011 by John M. Gottman

All rights reserved
Printed in the United States of America
First Edition

For information about permission to reproduce selections from this book, write to
Permissions, W. W. Norton & Company, Inc., 500 Fifth Avenue, New York, NY 10110

For information about special discounts for bulk purchases, please contact
W. W. Norton Special Sales at specialsales@wwnorton.com or 800-233-4830

Manufacturing by Maple Press
Production manager: Leeann Graham

Library of Congress Cataloging-in-Publication Data

Gottman, John Mordechai.
 The science of trust : emotional attunement for couples / John M. Gottman.
     p. cm. — (A Norton professional book)
 Includes bibliographical references and index.
 ISBN 978-0-393-70595-9 (hardcover)
 1. Marriage. 2. Married people—Psychology. 3. Trust. 4. Betrayal.
 5. Man-woman relationships. 6. Communication in marriage. I. Title.
 HQ734.G71358 2011
 155.6'45—dc22
                           2011000432

ISBN: 978-0-393-70595-9

W. W. Norton & Company, Inc., 500 Fifth Avenue, New York, N.Y. 10110
                       www.wwnorton.com
W. W. Norton & Company Ltd., Castle House, 75/76 Wells Street, London W1T 3QT

     6 7 8 9 0

This book is dedicated to my mother, Lina, who really should have been running a small country. Her insight into people, her huge sense of humor (once, when angry with me, she called me a "son of a bitch," paused a beat, and then immediately started laughing), her strong moral sense, her loyalty, her great capacity to love without conditions, and her courage have been a model for my life.

This book is also dedicated to John Thibaut, Hal Kelley, and Caryl Rusbult. These three pioneers in interdependence theory will be gravely missed.

Contents

The subtitle of chapter 2 was thought of by Jim Davis
(August 2010), who kindly gave me permission to use it.

Acknowledgments

Almost all of my work for the past four decades has been made possible by a miraculous lifelong collaboration with my best friend, Robert W. Levenson, who was also the best man at my wedding. Nothing can compare with this great blessing of friendship, love, and camaraderie that has endured and enriched our lives for so many years. Based on learning and laughter, Bob and I have enjoyed the great gift of deep and lasting friendship. At every talk I give, I acknowledge Bob's contribution. This book, however, was written without Bob's careful and insightful eye, so if there's anything wrong with it, I take all the blame.

I want to thank my good friend Rafael Lisitsa for reading a draft of this book and being totally honest with me. Rafael has been a great source of wisdom and advice, and a great traveling companion over the years. Together we try to figure out how our world has gotten into such a mess and what to do about it. I also want to thank my two closest colleagues and friends in the couples therapy area. Both of them read an early draft of my manuscript and gave me extremely valuable feedback and support. Sue Johnson and Dan Wile are amazing thinkers and great teachers. I keep learning from their wisdom and their tireless search for truth about couples. I don't know what I would do if I didn't have them to talk to and learn from.

I would like to acknowledge the important interactions I have had over the years with my dearest colleagues Steve Asher, Carolyn and Philip Cowan, Paul Ekman, Jean Goldsmith, Mavis Hetherington, Susan Johnson, James Murray, Bill Pinsof, Ross Parke, Steve Porges, Ed Tronick, Dan Wile, and Jeff Zeig.

I would like to acknowledge the work of my many talented students, laboratory staff, and colleagues over the years. They have all made this work possible. They are: Julia Babcock, Guy Bodenmann, Renay Bradley, Kim Buehlman, Sybil Carrere, Jim Coan, Julian Cook, Jani Driver, Sharon Fentiman, Dan Friend, Bill Griffin, Carole, Hooven, Dirk Jager, Vanessa Kahen-Johnson, Neil Jacobson, Lynn Katz, Itziar Luzarraga, Tara Madhyastha, Howard Markman, Kim McCoy, James Murray, Eun Young Nahm, Cliff Notarius, Jennifer Parkhurst, Regina Rushe, Joanne Wu Shortt, Cathryn Swanson, Kristin Swanson, Amber Tabares, and Dan Yoshimoto. It's been a long and a very great ride, and I am grateful for all their hard work and creative energy. I have been very lucky.

I would like to acknowledge the vast contributions of my wife and long-time collaborator in work, and in life, Dr. Julie Schwartz Gottman. I actually finally got to have a great relationship, instead of just studying them. Thankfully, after a while it became hard to recall who invented what in our collective work trying to help couples and train clinicians. Her strength, intuition, imagination, and keen intellect have been so vastly enriching. I cherish her.

The Gottman Institute, which we founded with our good friend and trusted colleague Etana Kunovsky about 16 years ago, has been a vital fountain of sustained support. Etana has been the spinal cord and brain of our organization for all these years, and she has bailed us out many times. Whenever I present at a talk or workshop, I think about how lucky I am to have Etana's steadfast support. What professor has an entire energetic company and an enthusiastic, hardworking staff to support him? For all their tireless work and dedication I would like to thank Zoya Bhan, Jaime Bradley, Kristi Content, Lee Culverwell, Belinda Gray, Allie Guerrero, Kyle Morrison, Beverly Parnell, Michelle Plackett, Kate Ramsburgh, Ann Scranton, Carol Snyder, Stacy Walker, Cynthia Williams, and Linda Wright.

Our therapists have been also been a source of understanding and inspiration. I would like to thank and acknowledge our Gottman-Certified Therapists and colleagues Lisa Baker-Wilson, Christina Choi, Peck Cho, Connie Foits, Ken Fremont-Smith, Marcia Gomez, Andy Greendorfer, Barbara Johnstone, Bob Navarra, Dave Penner, Michael Rediger, Trudy Sackey, Ruth Saks, Maureen Sawyer, John Slattery, Olea Smith-

Kaland, Terry Sterrenberg, Lawrence Stoyanowski, Mirabai Wahbe, Darren Wilk, Pat Worthy, Lynda Vorhees, and Ray Varlinsky.

I would also like to thank my steady sources of research funding, the National Institute of Mental Health, for grants and a 20-year Research Career Scientist Award, The Kirlin Foundation, The Talaris Research Institute, Mathematica, and the Federal Administration of Children and Families.

Research is an expensive and slow enterprise, and these friends and patrons make it all possible.

So many people contribute to make an effort like this possible, and the greatest of all these contributions are those of our valiant research subjects, who volunteered for the sake of science and helping others. I am forever grateful.

John Gottman
Deer Harbor, Orca's Island, WA

For Love In A Time of Conflict

When the gentleness between you hardens
And you fall out of your belonging with each other,
May the depths you have reached hold you still.

When no true word can be said, or heard,
And you mirror each other in the script of hurt,
When even the silence has become raw and torn,
May you hear again an echo of your first music.

When the weave of affection starts to unravel
And anger begins to sear the ground between you,
Before this weather of grief invites
The black seed of bitterness to find root,
May your souls come to kiss.

Now is the time for one of you to be gracious,
To allow a kindness beyond thought and hurt,
Reach out with sure hands
To take the chalice of your love,
And carry it carefully through this echoless waste
Until this winter pilgrimage leads you
Toward the gateway to spring.

John O'Donohue, *A Book of Blessings*, (2008).
New York: Doubleday, p. 32.

The Science of Trust

The Sound Relationship House

Create Shared Meaning
Legacy, Values and Rituals of Connection

Make Life Dreams Come True

Manage Conflict
Dialogue for Perpetual Problems
Six Skills for Managing Conflict

The Positive Perspective

Turn Towards
Build the Emotional Bank Account

Share Fondness and Admiration

Build Love Maps
Know One Another

Figure 1.1   The Sound Relationship House

Why a Book
on Trust?

This chapter is a review and update of our findings on relationships since the publication of my book The Marriage Clinic *more than 10 years ago. It explains why solving the problems of defining and understanding trust, trustworthiness, and betrayal is an essential next step in the development of the "Sound Relationship House" theory.*

In the first chapter of Malcolm Gladwell's blockbuster book *Blink*,[1] I was portrayed as an amazingly wise expert on relationships—someone who could see the secrets of a relationship after just a moments' glance. He called it "thin slicing" a relationship in conflict.

Because of his bestseller, I was suddenly catapulted to the international stage. That turned out to be a mixed blessing. Many people subsequently called my lab to have their relationships evaluated and "thin sliced." They wanted me to tell them if their relationship was doomed or if it was going to survive. I tried to tell these people that although our studies had allowed us to predict and understand relationships, our prediction was only statistical, and we couldn't predict accurately in every single case. Still, people were desperate for advice about their relationships. They wanted both understanding and hope.

Another outcome of Gladwell's book was that I, along with my wife Dr. Julie Schwartz Gottman, was invited to do a series of articles for *Reader's Digest*. This project involved having couples come into my lab once a month for "thin slicing" analysis *and* brief interventions designed to help them transform their marriages.[2] I want to start this book with an example of two people who came to my lab to examine their relationship and get advice about improving their communication.

"You Used to Have a Cute Ass"

Following is an excerpt of this couple's 15-minute conflict conversation, which I have named "you used to have a cute ass" because of a comment by the husband. Segments of the transcript are followed boxed text that indicates what I think the partners were thinking.

After their conversation, we were able to pinpoint some simple things the couple could do to improve their style of dealing with conflict.

HER: Our problem is that we need to get closer. I feel so distant from you. You've disappeared since the baby came.

He thinks	She thinks
She's talking about sex. Good. We really need to improve our sex life. I'm not getting any.	We are so distant, we hardly know each other. Now at last I've said it.

HIM: I agree that we should get closer, have more sex, have more fun. Like we used to when we were dating, before the baby came. Make love every day at least. Go for hikes, ride bikes, work out, get healthier together. I ride my bike a lot. But you've stopped working out.

He thinks	She thinks
We hardly have any fun anymore. She's gained weight. She's probably really depressed. She used to work out a lot so that's part of the problem.	Once again he's thinking about everything in terms of sex. He feels neglected. I don't blame him. I have no interest in sex anymore.

HER: You ride your bike *alone*. You always want to do everything alone these days.

HIM: I'd like to ride with *you*. You and me, each on a bike. We'll get you a bike. Then we'll both be on bikes. Then maybe everything will be back to the way it once was.

HER: I know you felt neglected after I got pregnant.

HIM: Yes, totally. We never had *any* sex after that.

He thinks	She thinks
Now we're getting somewhere.	I feel really guilty. But he has no idea what I went through having a baby. He just disappeared. He has no idea! I'm so angry.

HER: Actually, we've had sex twice a month. That's how much sex we have and have had for a long time now, except for when we first met. But you have to understand that when I was pregnant I felt like a cow, pumping milk, still working. Balancing everything at home, *alone*. No time for myself.

HIM: Wow, is that right? Twice a month, is that it? I was gonna say *never*. But anyway, twice a month is still nothing for a guy like me. I could have it once a day. Twice a day even. That would suit me better. Because I am so attracted to you, honey. And nowadays I feel these huge financial pressures. And the job has suddenly become very challenging. Three people have been laid off and I have to do the work of four people now.

He thinks	She thinks
We are really getting somewhere. She has no idea how much pressure I'm under with this new job. More sex would help a lot to relieve some of that tension. No doubt about it.	Now it's suddenly all about him. No chance he will listen to me now. It'll be about his job stresses and how I have to listen to him.

HER: Here's what actually happened. I gained weight when I was pregnant. It freaked you out. I also freaked out too, pumping all that milk and still having to work, to be away from the baby. I felt as attractive as a potato. I had no time to take care of myself. I have no sex drive at all anymore.

HIM: I think that the thing is you need time for yourself. You by yourself. See, that's where I say, just take time for yourself, go to the gym, get on a bike, work out, lose all that extra weight. That's my solution. It'll do you good. You'll soon look great and feel great. I feel great when I work out.

He thinks	She thinks
I never would have brought up the weight thing. It's a minefield. I'm glad she brought it up. I've now encouraged her to lose weight. That's probably gonna be a really good move.	Can he begin to understand how unattractive I feel after gaining all that weight? I felt like a big cow pumping all that milk.

HER: So now it's all *my* problem? It's all about me, my fault? That's not the solution for me to work out. You're missing the point.

HIM: Why does everything have to become a fight with you? Why can't you be more positive? If you're not happy, find a solution. What is your solution? Go ahead.

He thinks	She thinks
Gotcha! If my solution makes me the bad guy, let her solve this problem. One more negative word out of her and I'm out of here!	Now he's going to start criticizing me. I'm just not going to put up with that!

HER: I don't know what the solution is.

HIM: Okay, see, now listen to me. If you say, "I don't know what the solution is," I say, why not go along with *my* solution? At least then we don't go round in circles. It gives us a handle on the problem. A place to start. Take some time for yourself. Try that. Do whatever you want. Read a book, go for a walk, see some friends. Don't you see that it's a starting point?

He thinks	She thinks
She doesn't have a solution, so I will think logically for both of us. That's gotta be helpful.	I give up. Doesn't he see it's not about me, it's about us?

HER: That's not our solution, for me to have time alone. Don't you see the problem is about *us*?

HIM: Just try it my way for a while. Start working out. You'll feel better. In no time you will be happier. That will be about *us*. I want to encourage you here—you know you used to have a cute ass.

He thinks	She thinks
That ought to be encouraging. She really did have a great ass before she let herself go, and I haven't paid her a compliment in a while.	I'm going to kill him.

HER: That's just great, that's real nice. Now I'm unattractive, is that it? I have a big fat ass now? I put on a little weight and now you are not attracted to me anymore?

HIM: I *am* attracted to you. Totally. I was trying to pay you a compliment. You'll get that cute ass back real fast if you just work out a bit more. I do. I know that inside you, in your nature, there is still a cute ass lurking inside of you.

HER: That's our problem right there.

He thinks	She thinks
This is going badly. Time to get an aerial view of this problem. Back up a bit.	The problem is that he is so distant and he keeps judging me.

HIM: Okay, let's stop. This is what we do with an impasse at work. Tell me, what do you want? What would make you happy? Just tell me. What's your goal?

He thinks	She thinks
This is what we do at work when we arrive at an impasse and it works there. We have to think about what our big-picture vision is here—our goals, and our plan.	I think my goal is for him to just go away, but I can't say that. Now there's the baby to think of.

HER: I just don't really know anymore. (*long sigh*)

HIM: (*ignoring the sigh*) Okay, so I say if you "don't really know"—that's what you said, right?—why not give my solution a try? If you don't get time for yourself, you can't feel happy. You're so frazzled, pulled in so many directions. It only makes sense. Listen, I need time for myself, too, and I can generate a million excuses for not going to the gym.

He thinks	She thinks
I can lay out a plan here and finally solve this problem.	How am I going to tell him that I don't want sex because sex isn't that good with him anymore?

HER: When we have sex, it's so brief. It's not satisfying for me. Or for you, probably. (*Now I have said it.*)

HIM: (*I come too fast—I knew it. Now I'm in big trouble.*) I know it's mostly brief, and I agree that it's not romantic enough, but my point is that it's not often enough. So I'm all pent up with frustration, so I come real fast. Let's have more of those romantic dates you like. We can do that. Let's make that our objective. Why don't we work toward that? That makes sense. Romantic dates and you going to the gym, or us both biking together. That will be our solution.

He thinks	She thinks
Now this is finally going well. We're finally getting somewhere.	He's so logical about everything. Can't he see how lonely I feel?

HER: I don't know. I'm just so lonely. (*There, now I've finally said it.*)

HIM: (*Another negative emotional reaction from her. I'll ignore that and things will become more positive on their own. If I respond to her negativity, I'll just reinforce it and she'll become even more negative.*) There you go saying, "I don't know" again. If romance is our objective, then we set ourselves to that course, and then we accomplish that. Take it one step at a time. At least we'll be doing something positive.

HER: The problem is that you never understand how I feel.

HIM: Am I not being very tactful?

HER: Not really. It's not about tact. It's about listening.

HIM: Okay. I will listen tactfully.

HER: That'd be great.

He thinks	She thinks
I have to say everything just the right way, perfectly, or I'm sunk. I am almost ready to leave the house.	Now he's being less defensive.

HIM: So, okay, I'll work on being more tactful. Tell me what would make you happy and I'll be more tactful. Tact can be our goal, too.

HER: Time for myself is not the solution. Maybe time with *you* is a part of the solution. It's about you being there for me. You are not there for me.

HIM: What does that even *mean*? You keep saying I'm not there for you. I am "there for you" every day when I go to work for our family, when I mow the lawn, or play with the baby, or clean up the kitchen. I come home on time every day, or I call when I can't. I'm there for you. Just how much time do you need from me anyway? You have to remember I have a lot more work now, so what's the right balance? What would we even do together?

HER: It's not just *time*, it's you *being there* for me when I need to talk. I am too tired for biking anyway. I am not sleeping well.

HIM: But see, biking or working out would *give* you more energy.

HER: The green light is on. I think we're done.

He thinks	She thinks
She has some nerve saying I'm "not there for her." I am working my butt off at work and that's being there for her and the baby both. What the hell does that mean, anyway? She is being so negative. I just know that Gottman is going to point out to her how illogical she is and how logical I am.	I thought he was going to listen to me. Too much hope to hope for. What's it going to take to get through to him? This lab's got to see that he just can't listen to me. Gottman is going to say we're getting a divorce. Great, then I'll have that to deal with that, too.

These two people were both frustrated and puzzled by their conflict. He was trying to listen to her as he would listen to coworkers at a staff meeting at work. He thought he was being encouraging and optimistic. He was trying to find a sensible solution to all their problems at once. He was apparently unaware that she did not see his "cute ass" comment as complimentary, encouraging, or optimistic. He didn't understand what she meant by his "being there" for her. She was frustrated that he couldn't just listen to her and respond with empathy to her feelings.

My wife and I talked to this couple about the impasse we saw in their conflict discussion. We summarized each of their hopes and their positions so that they could better listen to each other. We explained that listening and understanding each other was the central issue that had to be addressed *before* they could problem-solve, and we translated for each of them what we thought they were trying to say in each of their messages. We specifically got her to tell him what "being there" meant to her, and we explained how unappreciated they both felt by each other. We also noted that their heart rates had exceeded 100 beats a minute and that they were both highly physiologically aroused, which made listening very difficult. We explained to them what we know about relationships and what they needed to do to improve their own relationship. They then got to go to our 2-day Art and Science of Love workshop.[3] This couple's communication had improved dramatically by the end of their time with us.

What Do We Know?

So, just what *do* we know about relationships? And why have I written this new book on the science of trust? I am going to start by reviewing what we know from over three decades of research in my laboratory and in Robert Levenson's laboratory (together with our collaborators and students). Then I will explain why trust is the missing element of my previous work.

How Have We Studied Relationships?

When I was an assistant professor 38 years ago, I decided that I would help children without friends to make a friend. A famous behavior therapist had already designed a program like this, so I called him up to ask about its inception. The therapist said that he and a few of his graduate students had sat in his office and tried to remember how they made friends at age 4. Their program encouraged kids to go up to other kids and say things like, "Hi! My name is Harold. What's your name? Isn't this a great day? I would like to play with you."

Later, when I went to the library to do research for my program, I was surprised to find that developmental psychologists didn't yet know how children made friends. So I started making tapes of children making friends and children talking to their best friends. I thought my study of how children make friends and talk to their friends would take a year or so, and then I would get back to the intervention. I wound up studying children from age 3 through the college years, and had to design a new observational coding system. All in all, it took 13 years to find out how children make friends, as well as how that changes them developmentally and why.

As my students and I did the basic research, it became increasingly clear that that the approach suggested by the famous behavior therapist was *exactly* the way to get rejected if you are a preschool child. Young children do not start a play session with strangers by introducing themselves. Calling attention to yourself is also guaranteed to get you rejected. My former student Professor Martha Putallaz of Duke University did some classic research on children entering groups that demonstrated the validity of these facts.[4]

The point of this story is that one cannot know how to design intervention programs for target populations in trouble by *imagining* what they need, or even by imagining it according to some abstract theoretical position. The early, descriptive, observational phase of science is crucial if one is to find out how people who are doing well with the same problems manage to do these tasks competently. It's not a very hard concept, but it's not how social scientists think, because we are typically trained to go from theory to experiment.

However, I did my graduate work at the University of Wisconsin, where there was a primate research center and the very famous work of Harry Harlow had taken place. Description was "king" in the Midwest, and there was even a dirt-filled urn outside the primate center library labeled "the center of Midwest dust-bowl empiricism." There was also a very talented primate researcher there named Jim Sackett. Lots of monkey researchers were observing primates in the wild, or in more controlled labs, at the time. Sackett developed a new method for detecting *sequences of interaction*, called "lag sequence analysis," that I wound up using with couples to discover the patterns of interaction that were different in the "masters" of relationships compared to the disasters.

Of course, there is a hidden assumption in this dust-bowl empirical approach. That assumption is that if we learn how couples normally go about the business of being in a lasting and satisfying relationship, we will discover a set of principles that can be used to help relationships that are ailing. The assumption is that these will be the same. In other words, the principles at work in good relationships can be applied to ones that are unhappy to fix them. But this could be wrong. There might be a different set of principles for fixing ailing relationships. Just like orthopedics requires knowledge not only of how healthy bones work but also of how to set bones that are broken, couple therapy may require some new principles for healing broken relationships. Even if this hypothesis is wrong, it's not a bad place to start. So far it's worked as an approach.

Happiness and Stability in Relationships: The Facts

In his novel *Anna Karenina*, Leo Tolstoy said that all unhappy families are different in their distinct miseries but all happy families are essentially the same. It turns out that the exact opposite is true.

Jay Haley, a talented researcher in family therapy, has shown that there is more rigidity in distressed families than in happy families. In happiness there is the possibility for much greater diversity and randomness. Unhappiness creates more constraints upon interaction patterns and therefore more sequences that could be detected through Jim Sackett's lag sequence analysis.

It turns out that all unhappy couples have the same general dysfunctions. So what makes happy and unhappy families different? And what's the secret to relationship happiness? We can discover these differences by observing sequences hidden in couples' interactions.

Despite the basic truth in the Beatles' refrain "all you need is love," we know that being happy in love is only part of being a happy person. It may, however, be a big part of the happiness life has to offer us. It is certainly the main subject of thousands of poems, novels, songs, plays, and films. The secrets of happiness in love appear to have remained a mystery for many millennia. Can a scientific approach to love provide the answers that poets have dreamed of for centuries? That is still an open question.

We Were Never Relationship Gurus

It's important to question why you should read what I have to say. I raise this question in every public talk I give. I am certainly not a "love guru"; instead, I offer a scientific view of happiness in relationships. I am a scientist, but I am also a clinician, with a unique goal for scientific investigation—namely, trying to be helpful to people.

About 40 years ago, when Robert Levenson and I began doing research about relationships, what we brought to this field was our profound ignorance. Truthfully, our own relationships with women were not going very well. They were interesting but often painful. So because we weren't naturally endowed with relationship wisdom, we began without hypotheses. One morning at coffee Bob said, "John, you can either *have* relationships or *study* them, and we're studying them." I'm happy to be able to report that since then, both of us have had considerably more success with our relationships than we did at that time. I think our research has helped us. At least a little.

Like the ancient astronomers, who began by simply describing the motions of the stars and planets, we thought that a good scientific beginning needed to start with description. So we began with the basics. We built a lab we thought was very cool, and we created a paradigm for collecting data, which, with minor variations, has served us well for nearly four decades. We observed couples in our laboratories as they talked about how their day had been, talked about their real conflicts, and enjoyed their time together hanging out for 24 hours in an apartment laboratory. We also studied couples in their own homes. We interviewed them and collected all sorts of physiological measures like heart rate and blood velocity, all synchronized to the video time code by Bob's huge PDP-11 computer. We showed couples their videotapes and asked them to tell us what they were thinking and feeling using our numerical rating dial which ranged from "very positive" (plus 9) to "very negative" (minus 9). The rating dial tapped into their moment-to-moment perception of how they were feeling on a wide-ranging numerical scale. We were therefore studying physiology, behavior, and perception, all synchronized to the video time code.

For the first 24 years of this research, we never tried to help anyone. In fact, we asked the people who participated in our research if they were getting therapy, and we discovered that there was a reasonably high correlation between getting therapy and getting a divorce. It was more likely that couples would get a divorce if they had therapy than if they had no therapy. This was especially true for individual therapy, but it was also true of couple therapy. We were worried that we would do just as badly as everyone else if we tried to help anyone.

Over time we simply tried to describe the differences between happy, stable couples, whom we called "the masters" of relationships, and unhappy couples (stable or unstable) whom we called "the disasters" of relationships.

Over the years we studied couples from every major ethnic and racial group in the U.S. We studied married and unmarried heterosexual couples and, for a dozen years, we also studied committed gay and lesbian couples. I also spent 10 years with the late Neil Jacobson studying couples plagued by domestic violence.

In our two labs, Bob and I have studied couples from the newlywed stage to the late 80s, studying some older couples for as long as 20 years. My students and I watched newlywed couples get pregnant and have babies, and we watched them with their babies. We followed the children of our couples, studied parent-child interaction, and discovered a process I called "emotion coaching." We studied the relationships of children with their friends as well. In some studies I have observed children and watched how the children grew up and made friends with other children.

We studied couples going through major life transitions, from having babies to facing retirement. At every second of their interaction in our labs we scientifically described couples' voice, gestures, movements, speech, and emotional and facial expressions, and we scored how they made decisions and how they used humor and affection. We scored their videotapes and classified what they said in specific interviews. I designed and validated a set of questionnaires created to give a profile of strengths and weaknesses in relationships.

To our great surprise we found that, with just the knowledge we collected in a few hours with a couple, we could predict what would happen to a relationship with reasonably high accuracy. I recall a landmark phone call in my life from Bob asking me if I had ever obtained high correlations (in the .90s), and him reporting that we had obtained such high correlations in our first 3-year follow-up study, using only physiological data in predicting relationship happiness, controlling for initial levels.[5]

For over 20 years we got paid by our universities just to watch people deteriorate, or not. Then, in 1994, I began working with my wife, Dr. Julie Schwartz Gottman, to develop methods to prevent relationship meltdown and to help couples and therapists turn the disasters into masters. It was out of this work that our Sound Relationship House theory developed.

The research evidence does indeed suggest that all relationships, happy or unhappy, seem to have to deal with the same "tasks" of being in a lasting relationship, and that these tasks change with life-span development. For example, it is well known that the severity of problems across happy and unhappy couples is the same, and people in all kinds of relationships argue about essentially the same stuff. Even predictors of divorce occur in relationships that are stable and happy; except for contempt, they just occur less often. So there really may be a set of "tasks" or milestones that all relationships have to deal with, particularly in their early stages. As we will see, most of these issues have to do with establishing trust.

Repair

The therapy we designed focuses heavily on *repair*. Every couple, in their daily life together, messes up communication, and every relationship has a potential "dark side." It is a misconception that communication ought to be the norm in relationships. What may matter most is the ability of couples to repair things when they go wrong. That idea has turned out to be the basis of my theory building. In this book I finally am able to report on excellent data that my former students Jani Driver and Amber Tabares collected on repair in newlywed couples (Chapter 8).

I contended that what we needed was a real theory of how relationships work and fail to work, and that that theory ought to emerge from basic research of what real couples do to accomplish the everyday "tasks" of being in a stable, satisfying relationship. As a clinical field so far we have done the reverse: We have started with a theory and constructed a therapy. For example, Bernard Guerney decided that partners should communicate with each other the way therapists and clients communicate, following Carl Rogers's client-centered therapy. That is how his "relationship enhancement therapy" was born.[6]

My point is that our field had not generated a theory of relationships by studying the various ways that people go about the business of being in a good relationship—that is, going from the data to build the theory. All the ideas I present in this book have been developed in light of real data about everyday couple interactions.

One advantage of this basic descriptive approach to describing natural variability is that we no longer have to rely on our fantasies of what good relationships are like. We studied them, longitudinally for as long as 20 years, and we have come to believe that all relationships are basically the same soup.

Myths About What Is "Dysfunctional" When a Relationship Is Ailing

Whole books have been written about what is dysfunctional in relationships. Most of these books are not based on real data, and many have turned out to be totally wrong. One example is George Bach and Peter Wyden's *The Intimate Enemy*.[7] Bach suggested that the problem in relationships is when people suppress their resentments. So he had partners take turns airing their resentments and hitting each other with foam-rubber bats called "batakas." We now know from hundreds of studies that anger has no cathartic effect, and, in fact, doing what Bach called "therapy" actually builds resentment (see Carol Tavris's terrific book *Anger: The Misunderstood Emotion*[8]). Yet when it was written, Bach's book became a bestseller and influenced many therapists.

So what should couples decide needs fixing in their ailing relationships? That's an important question. Let us first look at what research has revealed about the correlates of couple unhappiness.

Truths About What Is "Dysfunctional" When a Relationship Is Ailing

Following are nine predictors of divorce or continued couple misery that are characteristic of relationships when partners are attempting to resolve conflict. They hence describe what is "dysfunctional" when a relationship is ailing.

1. *More negativity than positivity.* The ratio of positive to negative affect during conflict in stable relationships is 5:1; in couples headed for divorce, it is 0.8:1 or less. That said, negativity *is* necessary in relationships. For example, it potentially can eliminate interaction patterns that don't work, and it may

also create a cyclical dance of emotional distance and close-ness necessary for renewing courtship over time. As thera-pists and couples we should not declare war on negativity. On the contrary, my idea is that a relationship without nega-tivity would be a living hell. In a close relationship we get *all* the emotions, not just the happy ones. I agree with Charles Darwin that all emotions have adaptive value.[9] I also agree with psychologist Haim Ginott,[10] who said that all emotions and all wishes are acceptable, but that not all behavior may be acceptable.

However, positive comments are the major means for estab-lishing a good relationship. Imagine a salt shaker filled not with salt but with all the ways to say "yes!" (things like: "good point"; "I see"; "yes"; "that makes sense, tell me more"; "you're starting to convince me"; "I never thought of it that way"; "if that's so important to you let's find a way to make that hap-pen"; "say more about how you feel and what you need"; and so on). Use that salt shaker throughout your interactions, and you'll instantly become a master. Conversely, imagine a salt shaker filled not with salt but with all the ways to say "no!" (things like: "that's ridiculous!"; "no"; "that is so stupid"; "you're stupid"; "you're making no sense"; "be logical"; "shut up!"; "stop talking"; "you're an idiot"; "you're a jerk"; "how can you be so insensitive?"; "you never have cared about me"; "you're so selfish"; and so on). Use that salt shaker throughout your interactions and you'll instantly become a disaster. Of course, we all use the second salt shaker some of the time. But the disasters do it much more often. With the masters, there is far more positive emotion, warmth, affection, being there for each other, interest, humor, understanding, and empathy. Masters say "yes" in the various ways more often than they say "no" through anger, hostility, insult, disgust, contempt, sarcasm, sadness, disappointment, belittling, disagreement, and emotional withdrawal.

The bottom line is that relationships need to have at least a 5 to 1 ratio of positivity to negativity during conflict—that is, the relationship has to be much more positive than negative, even when the couple is disagreeing.[11]

2. *Escalation of negative affect: The "four horsemen of the apocalypse."* Criticism, defensiveness, contempt, and stonewalling—what we call the "four horsemen of the apocalypse" in relation-ships—are dysfunctional in relationship conflict. These are part of a pattern of escalation of negativity. In the 1970s many therapists believed that anger and hostility in a relationship were dysfunctional, but we discovered that even in happy, stable relationships, when one person gets angry and hostile, the other person reciprocates in kind. It is the *escalation* of negativity, marked particularly by criticism, defensiveness, contempt, and stonewalling, that predicts divorce. We found that couples who escalated conflict divorced an average of about 5.6 years after their wedding.[12]

3. *Turning away.* Later we discovered that this pattern of escala-tion was related to a negative style in everyday interaction that we called "turning away" from bids for emotional connection. In that pattern, one partner ignores the other's attempts to connect or get the partner's attention, interest, humor, affec-tion, or support.[13]

4. *Turning against: Irritability, emotional disengagement, and with-drawal.* Another negative, dysfunctional pattern emerged from our research. When we first studied them, some couples didn't escalate conflict. They just had little positivity at all during conflict (no affection, shared humor, question asking, active interest, excitement, joy, support, empathy). These couples divorced an average of 16.2 years after their wedding. Subsequent research discovered that this pattern was related to a negative style in everyday interaction that we called "turn-ing against" bids for emotional connection. People responded to their partner's bids for emotional connection in a crabby, irritable manner.

5. *Failure of repair attempts.* Our goal is not to get couples to avoid fights, even ones that are painful and alienating. Nor is our goal to get couples to avoid hurting each other's feelings,

or avoid times when they do not respond to each other's needs for emotional connection. Instead, our goal is to help people process their inevitable fights and moments of miscommunication or hurt feelings, and to enable them to repair the relationship. Regrettable incidents in interaction are simply par for the course. The goal is to be able to heal the emotional wounds created by those incidents.

6. *Negative sentiment override.* Robert Weiss defined the concepts of positive and negative "sentiment override."[14] In negative sentiment override, observers would say that a message was sent in a neutral or even positive way, but the partner sees it as negative. (Hence, negative sentiment *overrides* positive interaction.) In positive sentiment override, even messages an outsider would see as negative are not interpreted as particularly negative by the partner, or at least they are not taken personally. In negative sentiment override, a negative perception is the "subtext" that accompanies all interactions, and people start seeing their partner as having negative traits, such as being selfish, insensitive, or mean. Robinson and Price had observers go into married couples' homes to look for positive behavior; they also trained the partners to observe positivity from their spouse.[15] When couples were happy, the observers and the partners were in complete agreement with one another regarding the number of times the partners' behavior was positive. But when the married couples were unhappy, the partners saw only 50% of their spouse's positive behavior toward them (as determined by the observers).

Psychologist Fritz Heider described "fundamental attribution errors,"—a tendency in people to minimize their own errors and attribute them to temporary, fleeting circumstances, but to maximize the errors of others and attribute them to lasting, negative personality traits or character flaws.[16] It's an "I'm okay, but you're defective" pattern. That's what happens for unhappy couples. We found that these negative traits people see in their partner are also related to retelling the history of their relationship in negative terms.

In the beginning of research on marriage, psychologist Louis Terman attempted to find a personality profile that was ideal for marriage, a kind of "emotional intelligence."[17] Terman was also one of the developers of the I.Q. test. However, research on "personality" in marriages only really paid off when one partner was asked to describe the personality of the other partner: In distressed relationships, people endorsed all sorts of negative traits for the partner, whereas in happy relationships they minimized negative traits and endorsed positive traits for the partner.

7. *Maintaining vigilance and physiological arousal.* A fairly universal finding is that after an argument men are more likely to rehearse distress-maintaining thoughts than women. This is related to becoming diffusely physiologically aroused. When our heart rates become high we also start secreting adrenaline, and we can't process information very well. We also don't have access to our sense of humor, or our creativity. We tend to repeat ourselves and become aggressive, or we want to run away. What we call the "distance and isolation cascade" accompanies this physiological arousal. Physiological arousal may accompany feelings of being overwhelmed by the way one's partner raises issues, but not always. But we think that after many experiences of diffuse physiological arousal, people develop a state we call "flooding." This state is measured with a questionnaire. Flooding is the experience that leads people to want to flee, aggress, or become defensive. We have discovered (as I report in this book) that it is very important to take breaks and self-soothe when flooded. We now use structured breaks, relaxation instructions, and biofeedback devices that give feedback on heart rate variability to help teach self-soothing.

8. *Chronic diffuse physiological arousal.* General activation of many physiological systems activates the "general alarm system" that spells danger to us. There is a natural cascade of physiological events called "diffuse physiological activation" (DPA). DPA is very adaptive for dealing with many kinds of danger, and it has developed over millions of years in our evolution. DPA

involves increased heart rate, an increase in how hard the heart contracts, an increase in constriction of the arteries, increased blood volume, reduced oxygen concentration in the blood, decreased blood supply for nonessential functions like those of the gut and kidney, removal of glycogen from the liver and conversion of it into the glucose our body needs for energy, secretion neurotransmitters and hormones like adrenaline and cortisol, increased brain amygdala activation for the early detection of danger, decreased frontal lobe activation (which controls planning and complex processing of information), immunosuppression, and so on. In the context of relationship conflict, DPA has big psychological effects. It decreases one's ability to take in information (reducing hearing and peripheral vision and making it difficult to shift attention away from a defensive posture). It can also create increased defensiveness and what we call the "summarizing yourself syndrome," which is repeating one's own position in the hope that one's partner will suddenly "get it" and become loving again. DPA can reduce the ability to be creative in problem solving, it eliminates access to one's sense of humor and to affection, and it reduces the ability to listen to one's partner and empathize. This is no one's fault. It is simply an adaptive mechanism that sometimes goes haywire. In Malcolm Gladwell's *Blink*, he described examples in which DPA had led soldiers to see everyone as the enemy, and frightened rookie cops to pump 41 bullets into Amidou Dialou, an innocent man who was in fact reaching for his ID, not a gun as the rookie cops thought they saw.

9. *The failure of men to accept influence from their women.* This is manifested in one of two patterns of rejecting influence: (1) male emotional disengagement (which eventually becomes mutual emotional disengagement), or (2) male escalation (belligerence, contempt, defensiveness) in response to their wives' low-intensity negative affect (complaining). The master men don't reject influence from their women as often. They tend to say things like "okay," or "good point," or "you're making perfect sense, really," or "you're starting to convince me." This

is not compliance; it is lively give and take. To be powerful in a relationship we must be capable of accepting influence on some things our partner wants.

What Is "functional" When a Relationship Is Going Well?

Following are seven signs of happy, stable relationships.

1. *Matches in conflict style.* In 1974, an important book by Harold Raush was published.[18] It described the first observational longitudinal study of the transition to parenthood; the study was also the first to analyze sequences of interaction. Raush divided his couples into three groups: "harmonious," "conflict-avoiding," and "bickering." He suggested that the two extreme styles of conflict (conflict-avoiding and bickering) were dysfunctional. However, in our own research we found that all three styles (which we called "validators," "avoiders," and "volatiles") were actually functional (stable and happy) if the ratio of positive to negative interaction during conflict was greater than or equal to 5:1. It was *mismatches* between conflict styles that predicted divorce. These mismatches were rooted in one person's wanting change and the other person trying to avoid it, which psychologist Virginia Satir had previously called the "pursuer-distancer" pattern[19] and psychologist Andy Christensen later studied as the "demand-withdraw" pattern.[20] An avoider paired with a validator was the most common mismatch we found. Because we didn't see any avoiders paired with volatiles we speculated that those couples would never get beyond the courtship phase to the phase of commitment. Susan Johnson also identified this mismatch as a basic contributor to attachment injuries.[21] More specifically, we think that mismatches in how people feel about emotion (which we call "meta-emotion mismatches") are at the heart of these conflict-style mismatches. I will say more about those mismatches later in this book.

2. *Dialogue with perpetual issues.* By studying couples repeatedly over many years and asking them what their unresolved prob-

lems were at each time, we learned that only 31% of couples' major area of continuing disagreement was about a resolvable issue. Much more frequently—69% of the time—it was about an unresolvable perpetual problem. These *perpetual problems* arose because of lasting personality differences between partners. All couples have those differences. There was also enormous stability in couples' interaction over time in our data. Some couples can talk about these perpetual problems with positive affect (which I call "dialogue") while others have only negative affect (which I perhaps call "gridlock").[22]

On the other hand, functional problem solving about *resolvable issues* had the following characteristics:

a. The much-touted active listening model of functional relationship received no support in our research in discriminating happy from unhappy couples. We also found that people rarely naturally engaged in active listening during conflict, even in stable, happy relationships, and even when they *did*, it wasn't predictive of positive outcomes for the relationship.[23] Furthermore, in Kurt Hahlweg and Dirk Revenstorf's Munich marital study, extensive training in active listening (using Bernard Guerney's intensive method) was essentially ineffective, with a low effect size and high relapse.[24] We now believe that the problem with active listening is that in order for it to be effective, the speaker needs to be "down-regulated" (so that he or she is not in attack mode) which rarely happens in conflict. More often, the speaker begin the instruction with hostility and anger, and studies show that very few people can be constructive as listeners in these situations. We found this to be true even in stable, happy relationships: When conflict begins with hostility, defensive sequences result (although happy, stable couples go through these negative sequences but less often). In other words, although active listening seems like a good idea in theory, in actual practice it seldom works, except on the rare occasions when the speaker employs neutral affect in beginning the interaction. That said, our initial reaction against active listening has been tempered over time by the success of Markman and Stanley's PREP psychoeducational program for couples, in which they consider active listening effective.[25] Clearly active listening may have some positive effects. We suspect that when it works at all, the speaker has been down-regulated to be much gentler. Later in this book I discuss modifying the active listening model by substituting what I call "the Gottman-Rapoport blueprint" for constructive conflict discussions (Chapter 6).

b. *Softened startup rather than harsh startup.* The woman's role here is usually critical, as in heterosexual relationships (in most Western culture) it is the woman who brings up the issues 80% of the time, according to research by Philip and Carolyn Cowan at Berkeley.[26] Again, the findings suggest that starting with attack is less likely to result in nondefensive or empathic listening. In one study in which couples talked about the events of their day before the conflict discussion, Bob Levenson and I discovered that harsh startup by the wife during the conflict discussion was predictable by a lack of interest or irritability by the husband during the events-of-the-day conversation.[27] I recall one husband who was totally disinterested in his wife's excited report about their one-year-old's 30-minute concentration on a flower. He looked at his watch and acted bored and she lost all her enthusiasm and eventually just stopped talking. Then he talked excitedly about a pump for his truck coming in that week, mentioning that he was looking forward to finally fixing the truck this coming weekend. She reciprocated being bored and he eventually lost all his enthusiasm for *his* topic. Their conflict discussion began very harshly. In another case, a husband said to his wife, in a hostile manner, "Why don't you talk about your day? It won't take *you* very long." That was our first inkling that friendship and conflict are strongly correlated. Later, Janice Driver and I went on to discover that positive responses to a partner's requests for interest and attention during dinner time in our apartment lab (which we called "turning toward bids") were related to gentler startup, as well as to affection and a shared sense of humor during conflict.[28]

  c. *Accepting influence rather than "batting in back."* The pattern of saying "no" to every request by a wife was characteristic of characterologically violent men in my research with Neil Jacobson.[29] Jim Coan and I then discovered that in newlywed nonviolent heterosexual relationships, the man's role was critical in not rejecting influence from his wife. An important negative finding was that negative reciprocity *in kind* (anger being met with anger, for example) was generally unrelated to anything bad in couple outcomes. It was the *escalation* of negativity—that is, when a partner responds to sadness or anger with criticism or contempt—that was predictive. That was a very new finding, and it has been controversial in the literature, with authors differing on how to define anger.[30] In this book we will reexamine negative-affect sequences and explore why some negative-negative exchanges in unhappily married couples become what I call an "absorbing state," meaning that it is easier to enter than it is to exit.

  d. *Effective repair attempts.* In one study we looked at repair attempts by newlywed couples a few months after their wedding. Those who were still married 6 years after the wedding repaired at a less negative threshold than those who wound up being divorced (this was discovered with the Gottman-Murray math model).[31]

e. *Deescalation of negativity.* This was usually done by the male partner, but only with low-conflict situations. In general, men seem to be socialized to try to calm things down when they start becoming a little negative. However, once the negativity reaches a certain point, men simply withdraw (stonewall).[32]

f. Anger was not a dangerous emotion by itself, but when the four horsemen and belligerence were coupled with it, anger suddenly became dangerous. However, we did discover that for emotionally disengaged couples, anger when we first started studying the couples (at "Time 1") was a predictor of later divorcing. So the final word is not yet in on the ways that anger hurts relationships.[33]

g. *Positive affect.* This was the only variable that predicted both couple stability and happiness in our newlywed study.[34] Furthermore, the positive affect was not distributed evenly or randomly during the conflict conversation—rather, it was used precisely—it was in the service of conflict deescalation. Positive affect and deescalation were used in the service of physiological soothing, particularly of the male in heterosexual relationships. That's why even small amounts of positive affect during conflict predicted positive outcomes in the relationship. Bob Levenson's lab has also found that humor is effective at reducing physiological arousal.[35]

h. As I mentioned, 69% of the time, a couple's conflict was shown to be about perpetual issues in the relationship that never got resolved. These lasting issues were due to lasting personality differences between partners. Often the very qualities in our partner we find most attractive during courtship become irritating later on, and these become the seeds of the perpetual problems. These perpetual problems have led family therapist Salvador Minuchin to proclaim that "all marriages are mistakes" (personal communication). Minuchin then added, "But what matters most is what one does with the mistakes." We found that what mattered most was not resolution of these perpetual problems but the affect that occurred around discussion of them. The goal of happily married couples seemed to be establish a "dialogue" around the perpetual problem—one that included shared humor and affection and communicated acceptance of the partner and even amusement. In this way happy couples actively coped with the unresolvable problem rather than getting trapped in "gridlock." Therapist Andy Christensen has also emphasized this idea of the importance of accepting each other's personalities.

3. *Happy couples presented issues as joint problems, and specific to one situation.* Unhappy couples, on the other hand, presented issues as if they were symptoms of global defects in the partner's personality. As previously noted, Bob Levenson and I discovered that the ratio of positivity to negativity in a conflict discussion was predictive of what would happen to the relationship later.[36] But we wondered if all negativity was equally corrosive. Studies showed that, indeed, there were four behaviors that were more corrosive than other negative behaviors: the aforementioned "four horsemen of the apocalypse" (criticism, defensiveness, contempt, and stonewalling).[37] Partners in unhappy relationships saw it as their responsibility to help their partners become better people. They acted as if they believed that the problem in relationships is that we pair with people who aren't as perfect as we are. Then it becomes our responsibility to point out to our partners how they can become better human beings. They need us to point out their mistakes. We expect them to be grateful to us for our great wisdom. In miserable relationships our habit of mind

is to focus on our own irritability and disappointment, and to explain to our partners how they are responsible for these miserable feelings we have.

Happy couples, on the other hand, presented issues by talking about what they felt and what they needed. They were gentle in the way they talked about their negative emotions (this was particularly true of women in happy relationships). For both men and women there was a positive recipe for the partner to be successful with them. Their habit of mind was opposite of that of unhappy couples: They were not involved with the partner's mistakes but rather noticed what was going right and appreciated it. These differences can appear small, but their implications are vast. Here's an example: If I am upset that my wife took up the whole dinner conversation talking about herself, I could say, "Julie, what is wrong with you?"(a question people rarely answer by saying, "Oh I am so glad you asked; let me take a look. Oh, there is something wrong with me—you're right!") and continue by saying, "You are so self-centered and selfish. You never think about others. You always just think about yourself." Or I could act like a master and say, "Honey, this isn't a big deal, but I was upset about the conversation at dinner. I need you to ask me about my day." Her response might then be, "Sorry, how was your day?"

4. *Successful repair attempts.* Even the masters of relationships disagree, get defensive, and hurt each other's feelings at times. But they are able to repair, even *during* the conflict discussion (see Chapter 8). This suggests that the goals of couple therapy ought not be to avoid fights, avoid hurting each other's feelings, or attempt to stay close at all times. Rather, a goal of couple therapy should be to help couples fully process these inevitable regrettable incidents that happen in all relationships, and to be able to repair the relationship. Relationship happiness relies on the ability to talk fully with each other about negative affect, a process we will talk about extensively in this book. Dan Yoshimoto found a way to study these processes in

his couples' "meta-emotion" or "attunement" interview. In this book I will call this process "emotional attunement." It is the major mechanism through which couples build trust.[38]

5. *The ability to remain physiologically calm during conflict.* Physiological arousal and feeling overwhelmed by negativity make it very difficult to listen well or be understanding and empathetic. The ability to create peace and the ability to self-soothe and soothe one's partner are central to relationship happiness.[39]

6. *The ability to accept influence from one's partner.* As noted earlier, this was especially true in the case of men. Men's acceptance of influence from their female partner was critical for well-functioning heterosexual relationships. The inability to accept influence from women was a stable predictor of relationship meltdown.

7. *Active building of friendship, intimacy, and the positive affect systems.* In relationships that were happy, people continued courtship and intimacy and nurtured emotional connection, friendship, fun, adventure, and playfulness.

Are Checklists Enough?

These checklists are critical in discerning what is dysfunctional when a relationship is ailing and what is going right when a relationship is stable and happy, but this ability to predict the outcome of a relationship is only the beginning of scientific knowledge. Prediction isn't the same as understanding.

For example, you can't say to an unhappy couple, "Please have more positive emotion when you disagree." Or, "Just laugh the next time you talk about his mother." The response you'd get is "Sorry. His mother's just not that funny." How does one create more positive affect during conflict? To accomplish goals like that, you need not just prediction but also understanding.

And for understanding, you need a theory. Our theory of why relationships wind up as masters or disasters is called the Sound Relationship House theory. The theory is like a house with seven levels (Figure 1.1, see first page of this chapter).

The Sound Relationship House Theory[40]

The first three levels of the Sound Relationship House describe friendship in relationships. Now here's part of the great thing about being a scientist: You can't just say, "Friendship is important in relationships," or "Yes, congregation, let's now have a moment of silence, for we all know how sacred a golden friendship is." That's okay for the clergy, or for Oprah or Dr. Phil. But as a scientist you actually have to measure things reliably, so you have to be able to *define* what you mean, and that automatically provides a recipe for success.

So here's what we mean by "friendship" in the Sound Relationship House. One needs to be able to do three things.

1. *Build Love Maps.* A love map is a roadmap you create in your mind of your partner's inner psychological world. It is the most basic level of friendship. It's about feeling known in the relationship. It's about feeling like your partner is interested in knowing you, and your partner feeling that you are interested in knowing her or him. What are your partner's worries and stresses at the moment? Do you know? What are some of your partner's hopes and aspirations? What are some of his or her dreams, values, and goals? What is your partner's mission statement in life? The fundamental process in making a love map is asking questions and remembering the answers—keeping them in working memory. These should be open-ended questions that you want to know the answer to, not closed questions like "Did the plumber come?" People rarely ask questions.

But when they do, it's an invitation, as opposed to a statement, which is like "take that." Again, there are three parts to love maps: (1) ask questions you're interested in, (2) remember the answers, and (3) keep asking new questions.

2. *Share Fondness and Admiration.* This is about building affection and respect in the relationship. There are two parts to nurturing fondness and admiration. First, we need a habit of mind that scans our world for things to admire, be proud of in our partner, and appreciate. This is the opposite of a critical habit of mind that scans for our partner's mistakes. Then the appreciation or admiration needs to be expressed verbally or nonverbally—it can't stay hidden. The idea is to catch your partner doing something right and say, "Thanks for doing that. I noticed you did this and I really appreciated that." Actively build a culture of appreciation and respect.

3. *Toward (rather than away).* When people are just kind of hanging out, they actually are often letting their needs be known to each other nonverbally or verbally. They're making what we call "bids" for emotional connection. This is a fundamental unit of emotional connection. They are asking for attention, interest, conversation, humor, affection, warmth, empathy, assistance, support, and so on. These tiny moments of emotional connection form an emotional bank account that gets built over time. For example, suppose your partner says, "There's a pretty boat!" If you don't respond, that's turning away. A crabby response— "Will you be quiet? I am trying to read!"—would be turning against. Conversely, "Huh!" would be turning toward—not a *great* turning toward, but sometimes that's as good as it gets. A more enthusiastic turning toward would be: "Wow that *is* a beautiful boat. Hey, baby, let's quit our jobs and get a boat like that and sail away together, what do you say?" All this builds an emotional bank account.

In our studies we found that couples who were divorced 6 years after their wedding turned toward each other only 33% of the time; ones still together after 6 years had an 86% turning-toward rate. We discovered that turning toward was related to more affection and humor during conflict.

The fundamental process of turning toward involves increasing your awareness and mindfulness about how your partner makes bids, and seeing the longing behind a bid that may be a bit negative or unclear. Gary Chapman has called these bids "love languages."

The fundamental law of turning toward is that it leads to more turning toward. Because there's a positive feedback loop, one can start with small steps, and turning toward will build over time.

What's the test of a good theory? It should be able to be disconfirmed and it should be supported by experiment. A good theory also should make unexpected new predictions that turn out to be true. What were our unexpected results?

We discovered, much to our surprise, that love maps, fondness and admiration, and turning toward were the basis for humor and affection during conflict. They were also the basis for romance, passion, and good sex. To convince yourself of this latter result, begin by asking yourself, "How could I make my relationship more romantic in the next 2 weeks? What could I do?" In his book *1001 Ways to Be Romantic*, Gregory Godek recommends "getting your wife a golden locket with your picture in it." Sounds like a good idea, right? But suppose that: (1) You haven't asked your wife a question in 10 years, so you fail love maps. (2) When you were at a recent dinner party and your wife was telling a story, you said, "Don't tell that story. You don't know how to tell a story. Let me tell it." So you fail fondness and admiration. And (3) You never notice her bids, so you fail turning toward. Now reconsider the golden-locket idea—is that going to be the romantic event Godek suggested it would be? I don't think so. She'll probably throw it on the ground and drive the S.U.V over it a few times for good measure. Love maps, fondness and admiration, and turning toward are far more romantic than golden lockets.

A further discovery was that these first three levels of the Sound Relationship House are also the basis for effective repair when you do have a regrettable incident. This is because the basis for effective repair is not *how* you make the repair but rather how much money in the emotional bank you have, as this is what predicts how the repair will be received. We will explore this connection in Chapter 8.

So these three components of friendship affect the way people behave and feel when they disagree. Couples with a strong friendship have a lot more access to their humor, affection, and the positive energy that make it possible to have disagreements or to live with them in a much more constructive and creative way. It's about earning and building up points. These three levels of the Sound Relationship House are fundamental for accessing positive emotions during times of disagreement.

The next level of the House determines whether Repair Attempt during conflict will work. That is our hypothesized link between friendship quality and the management of conflict.

4. *The Positive Perspective.* What happens when friendship isn't working? People go into negative sentiment override. Recall that in 1980 Robert Weiss suggested that couples are in one of two states:

- *Negative sentiment override.* In negative sentiment override, the negative sentiments we have about the relationship and our partner override anything positive our partner might do. We are hyper-vigilant for putdowns. We tend not to notice positive events. As I already mentioned, Robinson and Price (1980) discovered that unhappy couples don't see 50% of the positive things that objective observers see. We tend to distort and see neutral, or sometimes even positive, things as negative. We are overly sensitive.
- *Positive sentiment override.* Here the positive sentiments we have about the relationship and our partner override negative things our partner might do. We don't take negativity personally; we see it merely as evidence that our partner is stressed. We may notice negative events but we don't take them very seriously. We tend to distort toward the positive and see even negative as neutral. We are not overly sensitive.

  This is the one level of the House that's a noun, not a verb. We suggest you can't make it happen. People are in negative sentiment override for good reason—the friendship isn't working. We see our partner as our adversary, not as our annoying friend. Thus, the Sound Relationship House theory does not try to apply cognitive-behavioral modification to move people from negative to positive sentiment override. Rather, we believe that it won't work unless fundamental friendship processes are working. If friendship is working, you automatically get positive sentiment override. If friendship isn't working, you automatically get negative sentiment override, because you are "running on empty" in the friendship. Research that has attempted to simply move people from negative to positive sentiment override has failed. We think that's because you can't change it except by altering the quality of the friendship.

5. *Manage Conflict.* We use the term "manage" conflict rather than "resolve" conflict because relationship conflict is natural and has functional, positive aspects. For example, it helps us learn how to better love and understand our partners, deal with change, and renew courtship over time. So how do the masters of relationships do this?

One important way the masters of relationship manage conflict is by remaining gentle toward each other. They soften startup (including preemptive repair), they accept influence, they self-soothe, they repair and deescalate, and they compromise. This is the opposite of Bach and Wyden's approach, discussed earlier, in which couples were asked to take turns airing resentments and even hit each other with foam-rubber bats. This doesn't mean we need to expurgate anger from our emotional repertoire, as some writers have claimed—rather, we need to make it constructive from the outset.

It is also important to remember that not all conflict in relationships is the same. Conflict around perpetual issues differs from conflict around resolvable issues. As I noted previously, our research revealed that when couples were asked to talk about an area of continuing disagreement, 69% of the time what they discussed was a perpetual issue. These are problems that have to do with fundamental differences between partners—differences in personality or needs that are fundamental to their core definitions of self. These are issues without resolution that the couple has often been dealing with for many years. They continue to talk about the same issues, occasionally making some progress, or at least improving the situation for a short time, but then, after a while, the problem reemerges. In each case, the discussion is an attempt to establish a dialogue about the problem, which, admittedly, will never go away or be fully resolved.

Our research supports the view of Dan Wile, who wrote, in his book *After the Honeymoon*, that "choosing a partner is choosing a set of problems" (p. 12).[41] He noted that problems would be a part of any relationship, and that a particular person would have some set of problems no matter whom that person married. For example:

> Paul married Alice, who tends to get loud at parties. Paul, who is shy, hates that. But if Paul had married Susan, he and Susan would have gotten into a fight before they even got to the party. That's because Paul is always late and Susan hates to be kept waiting. She would have felt taken for granted, which she is very sensitive about. Paul would have seen her complaining about this as an attempt to dominate him, which he is very sensitive about. If Paul had married Gail, they wouldn't have even gone to the party because they would still be upset about an argument they

had the day before about Paul's not helping with the housework. This lack of help would have made Gail feel abandoned, which she is sensitive about. And Paul would have interpreted Gail's complaining as an attempt at domination. The same is true about Alice. If she had married Steve, she would have had the opposite problem, because Steve gets drunk at parties and Alice would have been so angry about his drinking that they would have gotten into a fight about it. If she had married Lou, she and Lou would have enjoyed the party, but trouble would have begun after they got home, when Lou would have wanted sex because he always wants sex when he wants to feel closer, whereas Alice only wants sex when she already feels close.

Wile also wrote: ". . . there is value, when choosing a long-term partner, in realizing that you will inevitably be choosing a particular set of unsolvable problems that you'll be grappling with for the next ten, twenty, or fifty years" (p. 13). I therefore suggest that relationships work to the extent that you have wound up with a set of perpetual problems you can learn to live with.

To live with perpetual problems, couples need to turn their focus away from attempts at solutions and instead learn how to "dialogue" about their different subjective realities. This avoids "gridlock" on the perpetual issue. The masters of relationships seem to be able to come to some acceptance of their problem. They are able to simultaneously communicate acceptance of the partner and the desire to improve the problem, often with amusement, respect, and affection. However, if partners cannot establish such a dialogue, the conflict may become gridlocked, and gridlocked conflict eventually leads to emotional disagreement.

As Andy Christensen has noted, the masters of relationships are able to express a fundamental acceptance of their partner's personality as they ask for change.[42] They soften the importance of the change request. Here are the differences between gridlock and dialogue about a perpetual issue:

- *Gridlock conflict.* The topic of the conflict is of no help in knowing if the conflict is in gridlock or dialogue. The perpetual conflict can be about anything. To an outsider it may seem like a very small issue. But within the relationship it seems quite big. A good *visual image* for gridlock is two fists in opposition. In gridlocked conflicts, people feel basically rejected by their partner. They are probably feeling like their partner doesn't like them when talking about the gridlocked issue. They will have the same conversation over and over again. It seems like they are spinning their wheels and not making any headway. There is no possibility of compromise. Over time, people become more and more entrenched in their positions and even more polarized, Conversations on the issue lead to frustration and hurt. There's very little shared humor, amusement, affection, or giving of appreciation when they talk about this problem. Nor is there much positive affect. That's the key to measuring gridlock.

Over time with gridlock people start vilifying one another. They start thinking negative thoughts about their partner, especially when they talk about the gridlocked issue. Researchers have found that thinking of your partner as selfish is common in vilification. That finding is essential in our analysis of gridlock as a loss of trust.

- *Dialogue about a perpetual issue.* Dialogue about a perpetual issue is different from gridlock in one major way. In dialogue there is a lot of positive affect (amusement, laughter, affection, empathy), whereas in gridlock there is almost no positive affect. Couples dialoguing about a perpetual issue seem to be trying to arrive at a better understanding of the issue, or arrive at some temporary compromise. They have an amused "oh, here we go again" attitude that involves a lot of acceptance, taking responsibility, and amusement, as well as a serious attempt to make things better and accommodate their personalities and need differences.

Why are people in gridlock? Previous clinical writing has suggested that these gridlocked couples have some kind of psychopathology that keeps them from taking the partner's perspective, such as an inability to empathize or a deficit in "theory of mind." Perhaps, various clinical writers have suggested, these gridlocked folks are narcissistic, borderline, or have a personality or character disorder.

However, our research revealed that there is a very good reason most people cannot yield on their gridlocked problems. We used to call the reason the "hidden agendas." But now we understand hidden agendas existentially.

We now realize that behind each person's gridlocked position lies something deep and meaningful—something core to that person's belief system, needs, history, or personality. It might be a strongly held value or perhaps a dream not yet lived. These people can no more yield and compromise on this issue than they can give up "the bones" of who they are and what they value about themselves. Compromise seems like selling themselves out, which is unthinkable.

But when a relationship achieves a certain level of safety and one partner clearly communicates that he or she wants to know about the underlying meaning of the other partner's position, the other partner can finally open up and talk about his or her feelings, dreams, and needs. Persuasion and problem solving are postposed. The goal is for each partner to understand the other's dreams behind the position on the issue. For example, one partner may wish to save for retirement, and the other may want instead to spend that money and travel now. We call this intervention the "Dreams Within Conflict" intervention. It is based on the realization that not all relationship conflicts are the same or require the same skill set. Existential conflicts are fundamentally different.

6. Make Life Dreams Come True. A crucial aspect of any relationship is creating an atmosphere that encourages each person to talk honestly about his or her dreams, values, convictions, and aspirations, as well as feel that the relationship supports those life dreams. We are back to love maps in a deeper way here. One of my favorite films is *Don Juan DeMarco*. In that film, Johnny Depp plays a mental patient who thinks he is Don Juan. He transforms the life of his psychiatrist, played by Marlon Brando. Brando's character is about to retire. One day, after Depp talks to him about women, Brando converses with his wife, played by Faye Dunaway, in their garden. He asks her what her life dreams are. After a silence she says, "I thought you'd never ask." Making life dreams come true is about asking, and remembering the answer.

7. *Create Shared Meaning.* A relationship is also about building a life together—a life that has a sense of shared purpose and meaning. Victor Frankl said that the pursuit of happiness is empty.[43] He suggested that we find happiness along the way as we pursue deeper meanings in life. So, finally, we come to the "attic" of the Sound Relationship House, where we build a sense of shared purpose and meaning. I believe that everyone is a philosopher trying to make some sense out of this brief journey we have through life. This level of the Sound Relationship House is about creating *shared* meaning in the relationship. People do that in many ways, including creating formal and informal rituals of connection, creating shared goals and life missions, supporting each other's basic roles in life, and agreeing on the meaning of central values and symbols (like "what is a home?"). Once again we return here to building love maps, but on a deeper level. So the seventh level of the house loops back to the first level. (It should probably be called the "Sound Relationship Bagel"!)

Trust: The Missing Element in the Sound Relationship House Theory

Like all good theories, the Sound Relationship House was essentially a "cookbook" with practical recipes about how to create friendship, turn toward bids for emotional connection, nurture love, and build romance, passion, and a sense of respect and affection. It described how to have intimate conversations, talk about emotions, have constructive conflict, heal old wounds, repair conflict, nurture positive affect systems (play, fun, sensuality, adventure), and create shared meaning.

However, the implicit suggestion of the Sound Relationship House theory was that by following its seven principles, *any* two people in the world could create a stable, happy relationship. We had misgivings about those implications. Were we really claiming that every relationship failure was simply due to the inability to apply the principles of the Sound Relationship House? And that every stable, happy relationship worked because people *were* applying the seven principles? So it seemed.

Yet, we can ask, as I often was by astute reporters, "What about 'magic'? What about 'love'? What about 'passion'? And 'chemistry'?"

For many critics of this research, something fundamental, mysterious, and basic was apparently missing from our analysis. Skills didn't seem to capture the essence of what made love relationships work. It all felt too mechanistic—not mysterious, dramatic, poetic, artful, or musical enough.

Something about these criticisms felt right. And as we worked with couples in therapy, we found that indeed something might be missing in the seven principles conceptualization. For example, although the social skills we outlined for constructively dealing with conflict were crucial in any relationship, many couples seemed to be unable or unwilling to make their conflicts constructive. Some couples resisted learning the skills. They would come to therapy sessions not having "practiced" intimacy. What was going on for these couples? Had there simply been "too much water under the bridge"? Had their fights and betrayals done too much emotional damage? Had we simply arrived too late for these couples? Or was there something missing from the Sound Relationship House theory?

There seemed to be some truth in the "too much water under the bridge" hypothesis, because our preventive interventions resulted in much larger effect sizes and less relapse than our interventions with distressed couples.

It also seemed possible that perhaps some of these couples simply never "belonged together" in the first place. Was there was some fundamental mismatch between them that we should be able to identify in the early phases of their relationship? What was the mismatch? Was there a mysterious missing ingredient for some couples?

I therefore began searching for the missing ingredient for these couples—the "magic" absent in the seven principles. The answer came during the course of building a program for lower-income couples expecting a baby. My wife, Julie, and I conducted focus groups with these low-income couples throughout the U.S.; they represented the social and ethnic diversity of our country. What we found was that all the couples talked about the importance of "trust." As we interviewed partners in these focus groups about the emotional fabric of their lives and the stories of their relationships, many told us that the central missing ingredient was the ability to build and maintain trust with each other. Many distressed couples complained that their partners simply couldn't be counted on to "be there" for them when they needed them most. Over time, they said, the emotional injuries they sustained from a lack of trust built a huge gulf of emotional distance between them, leading to eventual betrayal or the quiet whimper of the demise of love.

Happier couples, for whom trust was *not* missing, described the concept of "trust" as the mysterious quality that somehow created safety, security, and openness for both of them. Trust was that seemingly indefinable condition that made their relationship safe, that made it possible for them to be vulnerable with each other, and that thereby deepened their love beyond the first passionate infatuations and illusions of courtship. As love matured, these couples told us that trust ripened to a sense of mutual nurturance and moral responsibility for building a life together. For them, love and trust were intertwined and grew together into a lasting relationship. Friendship and intimacy blossomed. People accepted each other despite perpetual personality issues. Romance and sexual intimacy also seemed to be part of this ingredient of trust. In several studies we discovered that trust and acceptance were key features of relationships between partners whose sex lives stayed good over time, compared to those in which the sex life deteriorated.

So it appeared that the missing ingredients of the Sound Relationship House were all about trust and betrayal. After all, trust and safety in a relationship are also the theoretical pillars of John Bowlby's attachment theory[44] and Susan Johnson's[45] creative and effective use of Bowlby's ideas in designing emotionally focused couples therapy.

As my research embraced these "mysterious" and "elusive" qualities of trust and betrayal, I also discovered how to define them precisely and mathematically using the mathematics of game theory. I learned how to create a "trust metric" and, with my former graduate student Dan Yoshimoto, discovered the dynamics for building or eroding trust through what we came to call "emotional attunement." The mathematics of game theory also made it possible to define a "betrayal metric." Using that metric we began understanding the dynamics of betrayal, the "absorbing state" of negative affect for unhappily married couples. Using precise and insightful coding of how couples repair negativity during conflict (developed by two of my former graduate students, Janice Driver and Amber

Tabares), we began studying the dynamics of repair. Applying Carol Rusbult's brilliant measurement[46] of Thibaut and Kelley's "Comparison Level for Alternatives" (CL-ALT)[47] to our therapy with and research on lower-income couples' decision making, we began understanding the dynamics of betrayal, along with how one might help couples heal from betrayal. That's what this book is about.

Nothing was actually wrong with the Sound Relationship House theory. It didn't say anything that wasn't true. The problem was that it hadn't considered that the processes that build a strong relationship house are simultaneously building a strong *foundation of trust* as well. Knowing about the processes that control trust and betrayal therefore deepens the levels of the Sound Relationship House theory.

That foundation is now no longer elusive. It's all about (1) trust instead of distrust, (2) loyalty instead of betrayal, and (3) an optimal balance of power. In this book I will talk about what trust is, what betrayal is, how to conceptualize and measure them, how to help people build trust as a strong foundation within the Sound Relationship House, the dynamics of betrayal, and how to heal from betrayal. Then I will talk about the role of power imbalance in building trust.

Chapter 2

The Trust Metric: The Declaration of Interdependence

This chapter explains why trust is such an important concept in all social relationships and why it has been studied in many fields of science and philosophy. It then discusses how game theory can be used in conceptualizing and mathematically measuring trust in any single interaction. Then I show that the "rationality assumption" of traditional game theory is wrong and explain why.

Social Capital Research

In what has come to be called "social capital research," sociologists typically ask survey questions like "Do you think that people can be trusted?" Respondents' answers are based on a 4-point rating scale.[1] It turns out that there are high and low trust regions in the U.S., as well as internationally. For example, the deep South and Nevada are very low-trust states, whereas Minnesota has a high trust rating. Internationally, only 2% of Brazilians trust people, compared to 65% of Norwegians. Why does this question matter so much?

Low-trust geographical regions tend to have significantly greater income disparity between the rich and the poor; worse health and social services available to the poor; lower political participation rates (for example, the percent of people who vote); lower participation rates of volunteering with neighborhood, social, and philanthropic groups; lower levels of philanthropic giving; and less sense of neighborhood and community. Lower social trust in a geographical region is also associated with overall poorer physical and mental health of the populations, lower longevity, greater crime, and lower child achievement in schools and on standardized tests. Also, interventions (such as reducing class size in schools) are generally far less effective in low-trust states.

What an amazing and provocative body of findings!

These results have been reflected in international research as well.[2] Hence, there are vast implications of low trust for the entire world. The classic book that defined this field was *Bowling Alone* by Robert Putnam. Putnam's goal was to demonstrate the dramatic decline in trust and community in the U.S. over the last 50 years. His conclusions seem incontrovertible, but they are still somewhat controversial. Other sociologists have claimed that social participation isn't the active ingredient that has declined in low-trust states. They suggest that the problem is rather the increasing income disparity between the rich and the poor, which is indicative of neglect of the most needy, greater xenophobia, less willingness to help people who are different from the people doing the charitable giving, and more giving within homogenous groups (like giving within a church). Also, scholars wonder what the many new Internet communities, like Facebook, will mean for this generation. Will they mean less community, more community, or just a different kind of community?

Some of this social capital work has also been extended to organizational work teams. In this research the total amount of positive emotion is compared to the total amount of negative emotion in one interaction, and the ratio of positive to negative is computed. This research shows that work teams with high social capital—which also have higher positive-to-negative ratios, less social exclusion, greater social density, and less isolation—are more effective.

A large body of literature on trust has developed since Putnam's classic book. This work is very exciting and it has shown that the implications of trust are profound for the fabric of a society. Questions of the benefits of the mistrust of government by the larger society have been raised, and political issues regarding regulating government and dealing with corruption have been discussed within the concepts of trust and mistrust. Recall that Brazilians had very low trust in people whereas Norwegians had very high trust, which has huge implications for vast differences between these cultures.

Can we account for these differences in trust? Empirical research has made considerable headway in understanding these differences. For example, studies have shown that just three factors—(1) income disparity between the rich and the poor, (2) legal enforcement of contracts, and (3) social similarity across the culture (large differences are related to distrust)—account for an amazing 76% of the variance in trust across nations.[3]

Trust and Betrayal Are Popular Themes

The previous work on trust is enormous. Wiktionary lists "trust" as the 848th-most frequently used word in English ("love" has a frequency rate of 179; "desire" comes in at 563). "Trust" was listed as number 999 out of 86,800 words on the website Wordcount. So, if use is any indication, we apparently tend to think and talk about trust a great deal. In one study, scientists asked the question, "What do people desire in others?"[4] They concluded: ". . . across different measures of trait importance and different groups and relationships, trustworthiness was considered extremely important for interdependent others" (p. 208). Hence, the most widely desired characteristic of a potential partner was that the person be trustworthy.

We also write about trust and study trust a great deal. Recently I searched the PsycInfo database and it yielded 30,184 results on "trust." Amazon.com yielded an astounding 95,193 books on the subject (though a small number of them were referring to building financial trusts, not to trust in the way I am using it). Countless songs have been written about trust and betrayal, and many plays, films, poems, and stories have been created based on these two themes.

The Science of Trust

The idea of turning to science for answers about how to have a high-trust, low-betrayal love relationship—and about how to heal from betrayal—is relatively new. The good news is that science can now say a great deal about these important questions.

Obviously, it isn't possible for me to do a complete review of all the writings and scientific work on trust and betrayal. But a broad overview of this work may give you a sense of the scope of this vast field and help contextualize my own approach to trust in couple relationships.

Literature on trust appears in many fields—sociology, economics, psychology, political science, and philosophy, to name a few. In each discipline, the word "trust" has multiple meanings, and it is common for scholars in each field to periodically decry the lack of an agreed-upon or precise meaning for the term. These multiple meanings aren't necessarily a problem, but they do make scientific progress and measurement difficult. Let's look at a few of them.

Sociology. According to Wikipedia, in sociology the word "trust" measures "a belief in the honesty, fairness, or benevolence of another party." This is a cognitively based view. James Coleman's four-part definition of trust[5] is often cited. One of the four parts involves the function of trust as allowing one to interact with incomplete information. A second function of trust is that it makes the "trustor" better off than if he or she had not trusted. A third iteration of trust involves the voluntary transfer of resources (as in when one hands money over to a trusted financial advisor). A fourth aspect of trust involves the extension of trust over time in a continuing long-term relationship. Coleman's definition offered a behavioral view of trust, as opposed to the cognitive definition of trust as a belief or expectation of reliability or dependability of another.

A central aspect of sociological research also involves discussions of power. Power asymmetries and their relationship to trust are part of sociological analyses of the power relationship between different social groups. This book will also address trust and its relationship to power (Chapter 11).

Economics. Economists have studied trust at the individual level as well as at the level of societies. Initially this field was influenced by the classic 1944 work by John von Neumann and Oscar Morgenstern, *The Economic Theory of Games.*[6] The field began studying "solutions" to various games, or structures of interaction and payoffs (costs and benefits), and searching for "equilibria," the most common of which were the von

Neumann-Morgenstern equilibrium and the Nash equilibrium. I'll talk about game theory later in this book.

In economics, trust is often thought of as reliability in economic transactions that makes it possible to ease their potential complexity. Trust is seen as essential for an economy to function well. Of course, there is a difference between trusting a business partner and trusting Wall Street or the banking system, especially in light of the recession that began in 2007. Initially economists saw trust as based on a rational model, which assumed that people in a transaction acted rationally. However, a new field of "behavioral economics" or "neuroeconomics" has subsequently emerged.[7] This field describes the systematic ways in which economic transactions are *irrational* and based on the *emotions* and functioning of the brain.

Psychology. Erik Erickson suggested that trust is the essential first stage of children's psychological development, occurring or failing to occur in the first 2 years of life.[8] In Erickson's thinking, the consequences of failing to develop trust had profound implications for the development of psychopathology. The idea of establishing trust early in life is also an essential part of the work of attachment theorists such as John Bowlby and Mary Ainsworth.[9] Harry Harlow's work with infant rhesus macaque monkeys showed that Bowlby's theorizing had wide experimental validity.[10] Harlow demonstrated that the ability of the infant rhesus to deal with fear and the quality of the infant's attachment were highly influenced by the amount of contact comfort the infant received, not by the mere obtaining of milk, as had been suggested by Freud. More recently, this work on attachment has included the search for a biological basis for trust and attachment security.

In psychology, trust has been also defined as a set of traits. Julien Rotter's Interpersonal Trust Scale gave rise to a large body of literature on trust and gullibility.[11] For a review, see Yamagishi,[12] who has argued that trusting is a form of social intelligence, pointing to evidence suggesting only trusting people are also able to spot untrustworthiness in others. This hypothesis relates to literature that has evolved on loneliness. John Cacioppo's book *Loneliness* reviews research suggesting that lonely people may be unable to trust others and therefore expect rejection when they meet strangers.[13] In this book I will discuss loneliness as partly a result of an inability to trust people.

Many new scales of trust have been developed and validated since the inception of Rotter's trait scale. For example, in 1985 three investigators defined three aspects of trust in a relationship.[14] They said that (1) trust evolves as a relationship matures; (2) attributions are made about the partner, who is seen as reliable, dependable, and concerned with providing expected rewards to the partner; and (3) trust implies "a willingness to put oneself at risk, be it through intimate disclosure, reliance on another's promises, sacrificing present rewards for future gains, and so on" (p. 96).

Trust has also been defined from a *transactional* perspective—rather than in terms of lasting traits—in what has come to be called "interdependence theory." This definition of trust focuses on the rewards and costs of various kinds of behavioral exchanges in actual interaction and decision making. Here we are not examining trust within an entire relationship but rather within just one *interaction*. Interdependence theory was introduced in 1959 by John Thibaut and Harold Kelley, who wrote the classic work *The Social Psychology of Groups*. Thibaut and Kelley applied game theory to social psychology.[15] Their work was seminal, and it led to a large body of experimental and theoretical literature in social psychology that has continued to remain relevant. I will review the groundbreaking research of the late Caryl Rusbult and her colleagues[16] in Chapter 9.

In interdependence theory, trust is an essential part of the development of commitment, effective dependency, investment in the relationship, and stability of the relationship. It is also an essential part of social influence—the idea being that it is easier to influence those who trust us. The interdependence field is now also becoming very specific about critical choices that people make in relationships. For example, Sandra Murray and John Holmes used interdependence theory to investigate the parameters of the "if . . . then" choice to either increase dependency by risking being vulnerable and trusting a significant other, or to operate out of the fear of rejection and pursue purely selfish goals.[17]

In addition to interdependence theory and attachment theory, social psychological work on creating trust and cooperation has been very important for my thinking. Primarily spearheaded by Anatol Rapoport in his classic book *Fights, Games, and Debates*,[18] this work was continued by Robert Axelrod in *The Evolution of Cooperation* and *The Complexity of Cooperation*.[19] Like Thibaut and Kelley, Rapoport and Axelrod applied game theory to the study of social conflict, social influence, cooperation versus selfishness, and social interdependence. They were particularly interested in international conflict, but I'm going to apply their ideas to couples. Rapoport and Axelrod used a game called the "Prisoner's Dilemma" as a model in which the essential choice is between self-interest and cooperation. They applied this game as a model for group functioning and international cooperation.

Sociobiologists have also written about the development of cooperation and altruism as a fundamental human survival aspect of social groups. For example, Donald Pfaff's *The Neuroscience of Fair Play* suggests that altruism is hardwired into the human brain and prompts us to treat others as we would treat ourselves, a neural Golden Rule.[20] In *The Neurobiology of We*, Dan Siegel also suggested that mirror neurons in the brain form the basis of cooperation and empathy, and that the search for secure attachment is hardwired into the human infant's brain.[21] These analyses seek to link the social behavior of cooperation and trust (or their absence) to neural mechanisms. Perhaps the most profound attempt at a theoretical and empirical integration of research along these lines on all mammals is Jaak Panksepp's brilliant book *Affective Neuroscience*.[22] Emotions are very central to my thinking about the dynamics of trust and betrayal.

Political science and philosophy. There is a large body of literature on the role of trust in organizations, managerial leadership, and effectiveness in work teams. There is also extensive research literature on political systems and trust and distrust in government.[23]

My Perspective on Trust

I have been influenced by all the perspectives I have reviewed. However, I am primarily interested in the precise measurement of trust in single *interactions* within a relationship (for example, conflict, dinnertime, talking about the events of the day, having sex). Thus, I have been primarily influenced by John Thibaut and Harold Kelley's interdependence theory,

John Bowlby's and Susan Johnson's uses of attachment theory, and Caryl Rusbult's investment and trust model of commitment.

What am I trying to accomplish? I am trying to combine three measurement domains in my work on trust: (1) the behavioral coding of social interaction, particularly emotions, (2) the perception of that interaction by the couple, and (3) physiology, with all three measurement domains synchronized in real time. That will make it possible to measure trust within any single interaction.

One problem with the research and scholarly writing is that the concept of "trust" hasn't been precisely defined and measured within *one interaction*, such as within one conflict discussion. I believe this lack of precision has stymied our study of the correlates of trust and our building of a theory of what affects high or low levels of trust. In what situations should we define and measure trust? Is trust the same in the dining room as it is in the bedroom? Are the processes involved the same or different? How should we help people build trust? What situations and processes are involved in betrayal and healing from betrayal?

It is my view that the lack of specificity of situation and lack of precision in defining trust specific to interactions in any specific situation are likely to be a problem in creating usable theory. I think we need a usable theory if we are to build trust and reduce betrayal. For example, because trust is not well defined in social-capital research, we do not know how one should go about *building* trust in a state or country, or minimizing mistrust, or helping communities heal from betrayal. A good theory might come from an increased precision that focuses on the situations in which building trust is important.

Harold Kelley, John Holmes, Norbert Kerr, Harry Reis, Caryl Rusbult, and Paul Van Lange attempted to deal with this issue of precision by contextualizing trust within specific types of social situations in their massive book *An Atlas of Interpersonal Situations*.[24] Their set of situations and review of interdependence theory may prove useful. However, I thought that it would be a contribution to define trust precisely and to validate such a definition empirically within *any interaction* in a couple's relationship. In that way the overall trust in a relationship could be built "bottom up" instead of "top down"—from the specific interactions up to the relationship in general. In a similar manner, I will be very specific about contexts.

Game Theory and Trust

A look at game theory provides this opportunity for specificity. As Camerer wrote:

> Because the language of game theory is both rich and crisp, it could unify many parts of social science. For example, trust is studied by social psychologists, sociologists, philosophers, economists interested in economic development, and others. But what is trust? The slippery concept can be defined precisely in a game: Would you lend money to somebody who doesn't have to pay you back, but might feel morally obliged to do so? If you would, you trust her. If she pays you back, she is trustworthy. This definition gives a way to measure trust, and has been used in experiments in many places.[25] (p. 3)

Using these game-theory ideas, we can expand the crisp discussion of the question "What is trust?" to other situations. An alternative, the *Atlas of Interpersonal Situations*, may then be provided by the many contexts for the measurement of trust, naturalistic contexts for interactions, and the development of those contexts over the entire life course in a relationship. That was my initial idea in outlining the contexts in a couple's relationship where trust would be most important. Trust, then, isn't just about confidence that a stranger will pay back a loan; in a committed, loving relationship, trust represents a spectrum, like a fan that opens up to reveal areas in which the question "Are you there for me?" is asked in different contexts.

As we will see among newlyweds, that fan reveals areas of trust that every new relationship tests. For example: "Can I count on you to help with the housework?" "To be on time?" "To earn money for our family?" "To choose me over your friends?" "To choose me over your parents?" "Can I count on you to stay interested in me sexually?" "Will you cheat on me?" These contexts are all important in a loving, long-term, committed relationship.

The Evolution of My "Trust Metric"

In episode 401 of the popular television show *Numb3rs*, math professor Charlie Eppes introduces the idea of a "trust metric" to help solve
a crime. He and his colleagues are trying to identify and capture a network of terrorists before they strike with the deadly gas sarin. I have
been fascinated with this highly successful television series, in part
because it has helped me "come out of the closet" as a mathematician.
I started off as an undergraduate mathematics student before I went to
MIT for graduate work in math and was randomly assigned a roommate, William Bruce, who happened to be studying psychology. I soon
switched from mathematics to psychology for a Ph.D. at the University
of Wisconsin.

I love *Numb3rs* in part because all the math is right. Dr. Gary Lorden,
math consultant to the *Numb3rs* show, wrote a book called *The Numbers
Behind Numb3rs* that explains this fact.[26] So you can imagine my excitement when I saw the episode on the trust metric. After the show I looked
up the website of Steven Wolfram, (another math consultant for *Num-
b3rs,* as well as for other shows) hoping to find out more about the trust
metric. I was very disappointed to learn that in this case, the featured
major mathematical concept was not real.

Further online research, however, revealed that the search for a trust
metric was not just the subject of television fiction. The need for a trust
metric has arisen because of the concern with Internet security, identity
theft, and invasions of privacy. Unfortunately, these trust metric ideas
were not yet actually real mathematics, nor did they have real measurement behind them.

However, I was inspired by the idea, and I sat down at my computer
to look at my data and see if I could develop a real trust metric that
could be used to measure trust and also the potential for betrayal in real
human relationships.

I thought: What exactly do we usually mean by trust? Can we define
it with mathematics, and can we measure it precisely? The answer to
these questions, I thought, must lie in the "mathematics of trust," which
I discovered can be measured using a branch of mathematics called

"two-person Game theory." Harold Kelley and John Thibaut also began at this starting point.

Two-Person Game Theory

Two-person game theory is a way of examining strategies between two people playing a game, like rock-paper-scissors.[27] However, amazingly, the ideas of two-person game theory can be generalized to include any set of interactions between two people, or even used to describe an entire relationship.

How is this possible? Imagine a table with rows and columns, called a "matrix." All the major strategies of one player are listed in the rows of the matrix, and the strategies of the opponent are listed in the columns. In the cells of the matrix are the "payoffs" or rewards to each for person for each transaction or type of move using the combined strategies of the two players.

A "game" can be thought of as a rationally conducted conflict. Both people are assumed to search for the best strategy so that they can win the game. That's all very logical. Both people have to play by the same rules or constraints. The constraints may be agreed upon as the "rules of the game," as they are in parlor games like chess or bridge, or imposed by circumstances, such as the rules of war imposed by the Geneva convention. However, in a relationship the rules may be hidden and unspecified.

In the game theory we usually assume that our opponent wishes to win, which probably means the opponent seeks to minimize our payoff and maximize his or her payoff. That is the logic of most games. However, some games are manipulated by changing the payoffs so that cooperation is a more likely result than competition or winning.

Games in which one person wins and the other loses are called "zero-sum" games. However, the goal of most games in life, except perhaps some games of warfare, is not to destroy or eliminate the "opponent" but rather to outwit him or her. The goal usually is for gain (payoffs) to be maximized for our side and minimized for the opponent's side. Game theory has been used to model economies, competition between nations, and warfare. Let us now turn to the problem of applying game theory to personal relationships and defining a trust metric.

The Deadly Zero-Sum Game

As I just explained, games in which one person wins and the other loses are zero-sum games. But even games where there is no winner or loser can be considered zero-sum if the sum of the opponents' payoffs is a constant, because one person's gains are still the other person's losses. (Think of it as being like a see-saw: When one person goes up—even if it's just slightly—the other person must go down.) In a zero-sum game, once we know the payoffs for one person, we automatically know the payoffs for the other person.

In the context of a love relationship, a zero-sum game could be seen as betrayal or the fertile ground for betrayal. In a zero-sum game each partner sees his or her own interests as *preeminent*: the interests of the partner do not count at all. The very notion of trust is directly opposed to the notion of the zero-sum game. In fact, we could define trust by claiming that *in a trusting relationship we take as a given that our partner has our best interests at heart*, rather than *just* self-interest.

It's not necessary that our partners be selfless for us to trust them, just that our interests are important to them. That idea will be the basis for the mathematical definition of trust, as well as for the following three metrics: (1) the trust metric, (2) the trustworthiness metric, and (3) the betrayal metric.

Behavioral Game Theory in Relationships

As I have said, in game theory a table, or matrix, is used to represent the two players and their strategies. The strategies of each player form the rows and columns of the table. In the cells of the table are the payoffs for each player of choosing the combined strategy.

Figure 2.1 represents the possible strategies of a man and a woman in a love relationship with each other. The late social psychologist Harold Kelley actually did this study with 100 couples.[28]

The data in this table are real, averaged over 100 couples. Harold Kelley asked each partner to evaluate the positivity or negativity of each of four possible choices: (1) only he cleans the apartment, (2) only she cleans the apartment, (3) they both clean the apartment, or (4) neither cleans the apartment. The couple might not know it, but they could actually be using game theory to make a decision about who will and who will not clean their apartment. They could have evaluated the payoffs of all four alternatives for each of them. These payoffs need not be a zero-sum game, and we will need two matrices to fully describe the payoffs for both people.

Figure 2.1   **A game-theory matrix for couples.**

Female's Payoffs

	Female cleans	Female doesn't clean	Row Totals
Male cleans	8.3	−2.6	5.7
Male doesn't clean	0.2	−4.0	−3.8
Column Totals	8.5	−6.6	1.9

Male's Payoffs

	Female cleans	Female doesn't clean	Row Totals
Male cleans	6.8	−1.1	5.7
Male doesn't clean	0.9	−3.1	−2.2
Column Totals	7.7	−4.2	3.5

These tables are what two-person game-theory matrices look like when there are payoffs for each player. In general, in relationships the "payoffs" (the numbers in the boxes) are presumed to be determined by some unknown complex computation of a mathematical "utility function." The utility function is presumed to determine the payoffs for each combination of actions. The utility function is not unique, but it needs to satisfy some general properties that reflect each person's preferences. Therein lies one of the major problems of applying game theory—finding a "utility function" that really works. That has turned out to be no easy task.

Let's walk through the numbers in the tables above. Take your time doing this. It's not very complicated, but it's a good idea to go through these numbers slowly. Looking at the payoffs of both people, mutual cooperation (in which they both clean the apartment) wins the most points for both partners in this decision. Neither of them cleaning is somewhat less odious for the male than the female (his payoff is –3.1 and hers is –4.0; for both this option is negative, but it's more negative for her). Her cleaning when he doesn't is also somewhat more acceptable to the male than to the female (his payoff is 0.9 and hers is 0.2, so he favors this option a bit more than she does; is this male chauvinism?). His cleaning when she doesn't is actually less acceptable to *her* than to him (his payoff is –1.1 whereas hers is –2.6, so she finds this option far more odious than he does). This is probably because women tend to have higher standards for cleaning than men.

Game theory tries to use tables like this one to predict the likely outcomes of conflict, and to also ask what arrangement of payoffs might facilitate any of the four outcomes. If we add up the rows and the columns of the table for each partner, we find out something very interesting.

Let's look first at her payoff matrix. The two columns represent two different behavioral options for her—cleaning and not cleaning. Together they can be seen as representing a change in her behavior, from cleaning to not cleaning. (The same goes for the male's behaviors, in the rows.) Notice that there is much more variability in the payoffs resulting from *her* changing *her* behavior than in those resulting from *his* behavior. In her either cleaning or not (look at column totals here) she goes from 8.5 to –6.6, for a total change in payoffs of 15.1 points. Now look at the row totals. She goes from 5.7 to –3.8 for *him* changing his behavior, a spread of only 9.5 points. In other words, she gets more bang for the buck by her changing than by him changing. That means that in the area of cleaning, she pretty much has to rely on herself to better her situation rather than relying on him. Remember this table is the average across 100 couples, so this may be true of the cleaning situation for all couples.

Let's now look at his payoff matrix, and do the same computations. Notice that once again there is more change in payoffs resulting from *her* changing *her* behavior than in those from his changing his behavior. For her changing her behavior (column totals) his payoff goes from 7.7 to –4.2, a total of 11.9 points. For him changing his behavior (row totals) he goes from 5.7 to –2.2, a mere 7.9 points. So he pretty much has to rely on *her* to better his situation. He gets more bang for the buck by getting *her* to change.

Those differences were my first clue about how to mathematically define trust. I thought, maybe we can trust our partner if our partner's changing his or her behavior gives *us* the most gain in changing *our own* payoffs. That's equivalent mathematically to the idea that we can trust that our partner will act in a way that demonstrates caring about how *we* fare—that is, that our partner is working for our best interests. Our partner "has our back," or acts like he or she cares a great deal about our outcomes, our payoffs. Mutual trust would make these gains symmetric. We could say that our partner is "there for us," and we are "there for" our partner. (I define more precisely what "being there for me" means in Chapter 6).

What I am proposing about defining and using a trust metric is a somewhat complex idea, but it can be computed directly from the payoffs in the game-theory matrices. It is computed by examining the variation in one person's payoffs as the partner changes behavior.

Equilibrium Points (or "Solutions") of a Game

How do we analyze the game-theory tables mathematically? We try to find the "best" outcomes for the game, or the "best" strategies for each player of the game. There are lots of ways to accomplish this analysis. I'll explain two—the von Neumann-Morgenstern method and the Nash method. In analyzing game theory tables, von Neumann and Morgenstern defined what they called the "saddle point" equilibrium of a game. They called it a "saddle point" because, like a saddle, it is the lowest with respect to the horse's horizontal plane and highest with respect to the horse's vertical plane. They arrived at this equilibrium point in a game theory matrix by computing the most conservative strategy, with a no trust situation, for each player. Here's what a saddle point is, in brief. Since this is a competitive situation, Player A knows that Player B will only let him or her win the minimum in each row of the matrix. Then, within that limitation, he hopes to get the maximum of these minimums. This is called Player A's "mini-max" point.

In the matrix above, he takes the sum of his rows, and the best he can hope for is to win is 5.7 points by his cleaning, versus the minimum sum of -2.2 points that he gets by his not cleaning. He knows she won't let him get his maximum payoff, so he settles for the minimum. That's the saddle point for him. The von Neumann minimax is -2.2. It's the "best of the worst" of the payoff outcomes for him. According to von Neumann he will take this maximum of the minimum, the best of the worst, so he therefore decides not to clean. That point is his saddle point. Similarly she computes the minimum of each column and is willing to take the maximum of those numbers. The minimum she get is -6.6 by not cleaning so she takes the minimum and decides not to clean. That's her saddle point, or Player B's "maxi-min." When his mini-max and her maxi-min are equal, the game is said to have a "saddle point solution." That is the case for the matrix above—there is a saddle point. In the matrix above the von Neumann-Morgenstern saddle point is for neither of them to clean. Notice that this is not at all the most satisfactory outcome of the game, but it's the most conservative strategy in a win-lose concept of the game. It's a logical solution to the game if we assume that each person's goal is to win, and we also assume that *they do not trust one another at all*. That's what interests me about the von Nuemann and Morgenstern saddle point. This saddle point represents the best each player can hope to get with the most conservative combination of strategies in a win-lose (no trust) type of game, which is what von Neumann and Morgenstern assumed. Note that neither player may be very happy with the saddle point solution because it is so conservative. It's a kind of mathematical "solution" to the game theory matrix, but, as we can see from the situation above, it is not a very satisfying solution. That solution is called an *equilibrium point of the game*.

There is an alternative, the Nash equilibrium. If you saw the movie "A Beautiful Mind," you have heard of the famous Princeton mathematician John Nash,[29] who struggled with paranoid schizophrenia his whole life. Nash was played by academy award winner Russell Crowe. John Nash later won the Nobel Prize by defining another equilibrium point in the game-theory matrix, or solution to a two-person game, which has come to be called "*the Nash equilibrium*." Nash's equilibrium, when it exists, is that point where neither player can do any better, or have no regrets, given what the opponent has done. Neither can have regrets because of how the other person played the game. It may not be the best option for either player, but it's the best under the circumstances. There isn't always an equilibrium in a game, or a Nash equilibrium in a game theory matrix. However, if it exists, in many cases the Nash equilibrium is a far better outcome for both players than the von Neumann saddle point.

In the Kelley apartment cleaning game-theory matrices above, the Nash equilibrium is for them both to clean. Consider *his* payoffs. He does much better if he cleans no matter what she decides to do (because 5.7 is much greater than -2.2). Now consider *her* payoffs. She also does better if she cleans no matter what he does (because 8.5 is much greater than -6.6). So they have a stable Nash equilibrium at the joint strategy = (Male Cleans, Female Cleans). Then neither of them can have regrets about that choice because with that choice neither of them can do any better, regardless of what the partner does. With the Nash equilibrium their strategy is to maximize one's own gains even if it means maximizing the partner's gains (as well as one's own). This is in contrast to the von Neumann strategy of minimizing one's losses, which assumes one's opponent will do his or her worst as well. In some senses, we can think of the Nash equilibrium as expecting the best (high trust) while the von Neumann-Morgenstern equilibrium expects the worst (low trust).

Defining Trust in any Relationship Transaction

The problem with Kelley's study was that couples had to *imagine* a situation in which one or another decision might be made, like cleaning the apartment or not cleaning it. Because of the complexity of real life, and the fact that not all interaction involves decision-making, it is hard to generalize from this approach to the entire natural life a couple. However, if we focus just on the context of couples' conflict, we can develop what psychologists call an "observational coding system." Such a system categorizes everything of interest that each person might do in a particular situation. For example, it might describe all the ways that people behave during conflict. We then assume that what people actually do represents the "strategies" they choose in playing the "game" of their interaction. This gives us the rows and columns of our game-theory table. Now all that is needed are the numbers to put in the cells of the table.

To get these numbers, we separate the partners and show each of them a videotape of their previous interaction. While they watch the tape, they turn a dial with a set of numbers ranging from "extremely positive" to "extremely negative." This is not unlike a skit that *Saturday Night Live* once did. In the skit, a panel of "Olympic" judges scored the zero-sum game interaction of a combative married couple having breakfast. First, she sleepily appeared in the kitchen in her bathrobe and poured herself a cup of coffee. The SNL judges gave her 3 points for not pouring another cup of coffee for him. So far, 0 for him and +3 for her. Then he arrived and poured himself a cup of coffee. The judges gave him 3 points for not greeting her affectionately. Now the score was tied: +3 for him and +3 for her. He then sat down and opened his newspaper. One of the SNL judges remarked, "A great move by the husband. He has totally shut her out." The other SNL judges agreed. "Nine points for him." Final score: +12 for him and +3 for her. Our work is really no more sophisticated than this SNL skit, except the partners do their own rating, not judges.

If we average the rating dial numbers on a second-by-second basis, we arrive at 900 numbers for each person, which we can plot on a graph. If we line up these numbers on the same graph, we can get an idea of whether the couple has interacted in a zero-sum game strategy or not. A zero-sum game strategy would be indicated by lines that move in opposite directions so that they essentially add up to a constant. In other words, when her line goes up, his goes down, and when her line goes down, his goes up. His gain is her loss and her gain is his loss.

Conversely, if both lines follow the same pattern of ups and downs in time, the graph indicates a cooperative game strategy for their inter-action: His gain is her gain and his loss is her loss. If the two lines are unrelated, we could call their interaction a "mixed" game strategy.

In the 20-year study of couples in their 40s and in their 60s that that Levenson and I conducted, our breakdown was: 50.7% cooperative game strategy, 8.6% zero-sum game strategy, and 40.7% mixed game strategy. In this very crude way we were starting to zoom in on how trust might be quantified mathematically in conflict interactions. As discussed in Chapter 4, this classification may have huge implications for health and longevity in later life.

To recapitulate: The observational coding system gives us categories of behaviors or actions. These form the rows and columns of our game-theory matrices. The payoffs are determined by the rating dial numbers for the particular combination of behaviors by her and by him. These go in each cell of the matrix. But how do we know if the categories we are using have validity, and how do we determine whether the rating dial is valid as well?

The observational coding system I developed, called the "Specific Affect Coding System" (SPAFF), has repeatedly demonstrated great validity in predicting the future of relationships, both heterosexual and same-sex.[30] It is able to predict divorce and stability with significantly high accuracy, and it is also able to predict how happy people will be if they stay together. Additionally, this observational coding system can predict how long a relationship will last based solely on specific interaction patterns during conflict. Therefore, in our decades-long program of research in both my laboratory and Robert Levenson's laboratory, these observational-coding categories have demonstrated a great deal of validity, as well as reliability over time within couples. They have also been used in a study that I conducted with the late Neil Jacobson in discriminating between unhappy violent couples, unhappy nonviolent couples, and happy nonviolent couples.[31] The rating dial ranges from 1 to 9, with 1 being extremely negative and 9 being extremely positive.

Amazingly, the rating dial has also produced numbers that have been remarkable in predictive power.[32] As simple a device as it is, the rating dial has been used to accurately predict the long-term success or failure of relationships, even over long periods of time. Also, Robert Levenson and his student Anna Reuf used the rating dial to find an astonishing physiological substrate for empathy.[33] Partners were asked to rate their own payoffs (as usual), but then they also tried to guess how their partner had rated the videotape. Levenson and Reuf discovered that people were accurate guessers of their partner's payoffs on the rating dial to the extent that, as they were watching the videotape, they relived not their own physiology but rather their partner's physiology. Hence, the rating dial has performed admirably in many research studies and has demonstrated its validity as a measure of payoff.

To simplify matters, my programmer Dr. Tara Madhyastha and I reduced the SPAFF observational system to just three categories: negativity, neutrality, and positivity, which I will call here "nasty," "neutral," and "nice." By "nasty" I mean all the categories of negative affect and behavior on the SPAFF, which includes, among others, anger, belligerence, domineering, sadness, disappointment, fear, whining, disgust, and contempt. By "nice" I mean all the categories of positive affect and behavior on the SPAFF: interest, amusement, humor, laughter, excitement, joy, validation, empathy, and so on. Everything else is considered "neutral." These categories can be mapped on matrices such as those in Figure 2.2.

Figure 2.2   Title A general game theory matrix of a couple.

Husband Payoffs

	Wife Nasty	Wife Neutral	Wife Nice	Totals
Husband Nasty	H_{11}	H_{12}	H_{13}	H_{1-}
Husband Neutral	H_{21}	H_{22}	H_{23}	H_{2-}
Husband Nice	H_{31}	H_{32}	H_{33}	H_{3-}
Totals	H_{-1}	H_{-2}	H_{-3}	H_{-}

Wife Payoffs

	Wife Nasty	Wife Neutral	Wife Nice	Totals
Husband Nasty	W_{11}	W_{12}	W_{13}	W_{1-}
Husband Neutral	W_{21}	W_{22}	W_{23}	W_{2-}
Husband Nice	W_{31}	W_{32}	W_{33}	W_{3-}
Totals	W_{-1}	W_{-2}	W_{-3}	W_{-}

The letters in each cell of the two tables are symbols for the numbers we might get for any conflict conversation that a couple might have in our lab. What we put in each cell in the table is the average of all the rating dial numbers in each combination of SPAFF categories. For example, suppose that her rating dial numbers for when both of them were nasty was 1, 2, 1, 1, 3 and 2 for the six times out of 150 six-second time blocks that they were both nasty. In the wife payoff table we'd put the average of those numbers, 8/6 = 1.33. We would expect her rating dial numbers for when both of them were nice to be higher, so maybe the two times they were both nice her ratings were 9 and 6. So her average in the nice-nice cell would be 15/2 = 7.50. Actually, with the SPAFF we could compute the same payoff matrices for *any* conversation the couple had, such as sharing the events of their day, preparing dinner, or making love. The letters in the table represent the husband or wife payoffs for that combination of behaviors. For example, W_{11} is her payoff when they were both nasty (row 1, column 1). W_{12} is her payoff when he was nasty and she was neutral (row 1, column 2). For the totals, the minus sign in the subscripts denotes what we are averaging across. Hence W_{1-} means we are averaging across all columns to get her average payoff when the husband was nasty. W_{-1} is her average payoff, across all husband behaviors, where *she* was nasty.

We also computed a third matrix, which told us how *often* people did each of these behavior exchanges. That matrix is shown in Figure 2.3.

Figure 2.3 Nasty/Neutral/Nice Matrix

	Wife Nasty	Wife Neutral	Wife Nice	Totals
Husband Nasty	F_{11}	F_{12}	F_{13}	F_{1-}
Husband Neutral	F_{21}	F_{22}	F_{23}	F_{2-}
Husband Nice	F_{31}	F_{32}	F_{33}	F_{3-}
Totals	F_{-1}	F_{-2}	F_{-3}	F_{-}

The Fs in this matrix represent the *frequencies* with which each of the mutual events occurred. For example, F_{11} is how often Husband Nasty–Wife Nasty occurred within a 6-second time block. The reason we needed this third matrix was that it allowed us to test the rationality assumption which suggests that people do more of whatever provides the highest payoffs. We could compare happy and unhappy couples and see if their payoffs could allow us to predict the frequencies of their behavior in each cell.

Why was this last matrix necessary? In their classic book on inter-dependence theory, Thibaut and Kelly wrote about this matrix of behavioral frequencies, but they rejected the idea of actually measur-ing behavior and computing the probabilities of specific behavior exchanges.[34] Instead, they said: "In this book we limit ourselves to the use of reward-cost matrices on the grounds that in ordinary social relationships the two sets of values [probabilities and payoffs] ultimately tend to correspond fairly well." They actually never tested that claim. That assumption has become etched in stone as an underlying but untested assumption of the couple behavioral-therapy literature. We are finally able to test that assumption.

I would like to tell you now about the startling results that my colleague Tara Madhyastha and I obtained by applying these ideas to a sample of 100 couples in one of our major studies in my laboratory, and also to the study that Robert Levenson and I did together in his laboratory on two groups of couples, one group in their 40s and one group in their 60s (a total of 140 couples).

Under What Conditions Is Couple Conflict Rational?

As I have mentioned, all of game theory is based on the assumption that we always have two rational players who want to maximize their own payoffs. That's the idea behind people's behavior being predictable by the payoffs in their game-theory matrix. That assumption has recently been questioned as part of the evolution of the field of behavioral economics, but it has yet to be directly tested.

Tara and I were now finally able to test this assumption. As usual, we divided our sample of couples into happy and unhappy couples using a measure of relationship satisfaction. The rationality assumption predicts that people will fall into whatever cell of the matrix has the highest payoffs. We were able to test this assumption in each cell of the matrix by assessing the extent to which payoffs matched behavior in happy and unhappy couples.

1. *Positive-affect exchanges: The nice-nice cell of the matrices.* The nice-nice cell is all about mirroring positive interaction. This is probably the very engine that makes the world of love go round. It is often called the "quid pro quo," or something positive in exchange for something positive. In their 1968 book, *The Mirages of Marriage,* family therapist Don Jackson and William Ledever suggested that the implicit contract in any marriage was that if you do something nice for your partner, it will be reciprocated by your partner.[35] Your partner will respond by doing something nice for you. They suggested that this reciprocity is the basis of trust in relationships. They claimed that marriages go bad when that implicit contract is violated.

We get into relationships, they argued, expecting that during courtship our affection, passions, humor, attention, interests, compliments, and excitement will be reciprocated by our lover. We seek the reciprocation of pleasure, interest, security, trust, affection, and love.

Let's test whether this cell of our game-theory table fits the rationality assumption. Admittedly, this reciprocation of positivity may be very rare during conflict, and, therefore, perhaps unimportant. However, long ago, in my study of 130 newlywed couples in Seattle, I discovered that positivity during conflict predicted not only the newlyweds' relationship stability over a 6-year period after the wedding, but happiness as well.[36] That was no small feat of prediction, because it meant we could distinguish between couples who would divorce and those who would stay together but be miserable. Most other studies had trouble telling these two kinds of unhappy couples apart. So positive affect during conflict was very important.

We also discovered that positivity during conflict among newlywed couples was not sprinkled randomly, liberally, and evenly throughout an interaction, without conditions. Rather, it was used very precisely, like a scalpel, for the express purpose of physiological soothing of the partner. In another study, Robert Levenson and his students have also been looking at moments of physiological soothing, and they have found that positive affect, such as humor, was effective in physiologically soothing one's partner.[37] So positive affect during conflict is very important.

It also turns out that positive exchanges are entirely rational. In our study of middle-aged and older couples, the payoffs in this nice-nice cell of the game-theory matrix were significantly higher for happy couples than for unhappy couples. Also—and *this is the ultimate test*—the couples who had higher payoffs in the nice-nice cell did these nice-nice exchanges more frequently than couples who had lower payoffs in that cell of the matrix. Those results are consistent with the rationality assumption of game theory.

That's wonderfully logical, and it's a big effect. For example, we found that couples who experience more positive payoffs for both nice and neutral behaviors have twice as many positive behaviors as those who do not value these codes as highly (i.e., have lower payoffs). We observed that 35.1% of the non-neutral emotions of happily married men are positive, compared to 21.9% of positive non-neutral emotions among unhappy men. That's a big difference. For women these figures were even more dramatic. The positive non-neutral emotion of happier women was 33.9%, whereas for unhappy wives it was only 16.3%. So being nice to your partner during conflict is a very good idea. Not easy to do, but still a very good idea.

So, everything works in totally logical fashion in this nice-nice cell of the game-theory matrix. But what about the neutral-neutral cell of the matrix?

2. Unemotional exchanges: The neutral-neutral cell of the matrices. It turned out that the neutral-neutral cell of the matrices was also entirely rational. Psychological theory tells us almost nothing about neutral interaction, but Levenson and I have known for years that neutral affect is a good thing during conflict. There isn't a single couple therapy that we know of that lauds and celebrates neutral, nonemotional interaction, even during conflict. Empathy, yes, but not emotion. Can you imagine a couple therapist saying: "What a great therapy session I had with that couple! During their conflict today they showed *absolutely no* emotion throughout the session. I am so pleased!"

This neutral-neutral cell of the game-theory matrix is the "Cinderalla" cell. It's the ignored stepsister, the one who gets short shrift in any theory about relationships and any theory about emotion. In discussions of therapy, the nonemotional part of conflict is usually shunned as a big waste of time.

Most lay people, as well as therapists and researchers of relationships, see neutral-neutral interaction as "boring." It's the footage in reality TV shows that winds up getting cut in the editing. It is, by definition, *not* emotional; *therefore*, many TV producers who have come to my lab conclude that it must be devoid of any interest. They are so wrong. But their view nevertheless matches that of both the layman and the professional. The typical therapist thinks: "Let's spend hours and hours of therapy examining and understanding the nasty-nasty cell. That's where the real power is. When we do, and real change occurs in therapy, the couple will simply naturally drift from the nasty-nasty cell into the nice-nice cell."

They are absolutely wrong about the neutral-neutral cell! Even if we were able to magically understand the nasty-nasty exchanges, couples might become less nasty, but that's it. To get from nasty-nasty interaction to nice-nice, we may first have to take the shuttle to the neutral-neutral cell of the game-theory matrices. It's a two-step process.

Here's a great story about this point. Robert Levenson and his student Rachel Ebling did a very clever study.[38] They created a videotape of the first 3 minutes of a conflict discussion for 10 couples, 5 of whom eventually divorced and 5 of whom stayed married. They then asked people from all walks of life—pastors, researchers, therapists—to guess which couples were in which group. Their finding was that no one did very well guessing—almost everyone they tested was at a chance level. I think that one of the reasons almost everyone did so badly was that they typically underestimated the importance of neutral affect during conflict. Neutral affect seems boring, and it *is* boring. People are far more fascinated by Jerry Springer moments of hostility in doomed marriages and tender, tear-jerking Oprah Winfrey moments in happy, stable marriages. No one thinks that in the context of conflict, just being nonemotional is an asset.

But think about the relationship fights you have had. You'd probably agree that a neutral presentation of your partner's point of view by your partner would probably be an enormously welcome relief. That's exactly what we found. Neutral-neutral interaction was much more common among happier couples, and it was also rated higher.

When we examine this cell of the matrix, we are, in part, also asking whether there is any validity to John von Neumann's dream of the unemotional computer making the best decisions. To me, this means that this cell ought to be the most helpful in discriminating happy from unhappy couples.

If it's true that these neutral-neutral exchanges are so important, then perhaps they also ought to become more frequent with age, as the couples who stay together long-term get more and more happy with their relationships. We examined our 20-year longitudinal data and found that that was indeed the case! Over time in our middle-aged and older couples who stayed together, more and more of their interaction moved *away* from non-neutral discussion during conflict and *toward* greater and greater neutrality. Couples who stayed together over the long haul became more neutral during conflict in later life, and behavior goes along with the rating dial payoffs.

This means that couple therapists should work toward moving couples into a less emotional exchange during conflict, not just on getting them out of the nasty-nasty cell of the matrix or on increasing positive affect. That goal would currently seem to many therapists to be a violation of their training in most couple therapies, which tend to celebrate an emotional life for a good relationship. Neutral affect is meant to exclude people suppressing the expression of negativity.

To summarize, both the nice-nice and the neutral-neutral cells of the game-theory matrices operate on the rationality assumption: *People do more of what provides higher payoffs and less of what provides lower payoffs.* That is totally logical.

But what about the nasty-nasty cell of these matrices?

3. Negative-affect exchanges: The nasty-nasty cell of the matrices. It turns out that the nasty-nasty cell is *not* rational. Nasty-nasty is obviously a state most of us probably assiduously avoid. It is the cell of negative reciprocity and conflict escalation. More than any other cell of the game-theory matrix, this is where couple therapists expend most of their energy. They start here, identifying the negative cycles the couple engages in. For example, stage 1 of Susan Johnson's effective emotionally focused couple therapy is called "identifying the negative cycles."[39] We therapists are fascinated by negative-negative states and patterns of interaction in those states.

Once we have focused on identifying a couple's nasty-nasty cycles, we then typically try to "understand why" these patterns happen, hoping to gain insight into what's going on in these negative exchanges. We ask questions like: "What starts them?" "What maintains them?" "Has injury been caused by these nasty-nasty exchanges?" "Is one person most at fault?" "If so, does that person have a psychopathology?" "Are there any emotional-attachment injuries caused by the negative cycles?"

"Are there psychopathologies of one or both people that have created and maintained these exchanges?" "Do they come from the partners' primary families?" "Are these negative and dysfunctional patterns being replicated over generations?" "How can the couple arrive at insight about these destructive cycles?" "Are unconscious processes like projection involved?" And so on—we just can't stop asking questions about negative exchanges.

The nasty-nasty cell of the matrix is also where the couple's love and fun goes to die. So this cell is probably very important. To understand it, let's go back to the lab. What do our analyses tell us about this cell of the matrix?

We are in for a very big surprise here, but Tara and I actually predicted that surprise. The data about this nasty-nasty cell show that unhappy couples' behavior in this cell is totally illogical. How so? It turns out that unhappy couples rate this negative-negative exchange far more negatively than happy couples do, *and yet they do it more often than happy couples.* According to rational game theory, if they rate it more negatively, they should do it *less* often, not *more* often!

The data also suggest that as couples stay together happily for longer and longer periods, they simply aren't as disturbed by these nasty-nasty exchanges as they used to be. We discovered that happy couples just don't get as upset about these nasty-nasty exchanges as unhappy couples do, perhaps precisely because they don't happen as often. You may say that seems "sort of" logical. But it's not really logical, according to the major assumption of game theory! If your payoff is terrible in this cell, rational game theory would say that you would therefore not choose this "strategy" as often. The explanation I provided makes sense because you are filling in the missing "logic of the emotions," which isn't very logical at all.

So the answer to why people do these nasty-nasty exchanges when they hate them so much cannot lie in any rational game-theory explanation. To understand our results in this cell of the matrix, we need to examine this state further. Again, mathematics will help us.

"Hidden Markov" analysis. Mathematical and statistical analysis can shed some light on unhappy couples' illogical behavior in the nasty-nasty cell of the matrix. Further statistical analyses were done in our lab

by computer scientist Tara Madhyastha using a method called "Hidden Markov models." These models are very popular in the study of languages and in analyzing DNA sequences. They reveal an underlying hidden structure in the data that may not be obvious at first glance. The Hidden Markov Analysis revealed that these nasty-nasty exchanges were what is called an "absorbing" state for unhappy couples, but not for happy couples. An absorbing state is one that is easier to enter than it is to leave. It's like the roach hotel motto: "They check in but they don't check out."

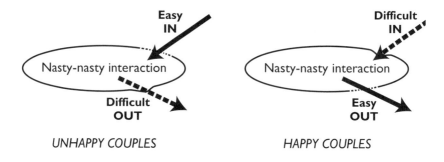

Figure 2.4   Absorbing Versus Nonabsorbing States

Figure 2.4 shows how it is easier for unhappy couples to enter the nasty-nasty state than it is for happy couples. Also, it is easier for happy couples to exit the nasty-nasty state than it is for them to enter it. The dotted exit line for unhappy couples illustrates the fact that it's a lot easier for unhappy couples to enter the nasty-nasty state than it is to leave it. Once unhappy couples enter the state of nasty-nasty exchanges, they have trouble exiting it because they are in some senses trapped in that state. It's as if they have stepped into a bog of quicksand. There's no equivalent quicksand bog for happy couples in nasty-nasty exchanges.

Behavioral Game Theory

A new field called "behavioral game theory" has recently emerged. This new field widely admits that real behavior need not be rational at all. In his book *Behavioral Game Theory,* Colin Camerer wrote that behavioral game theory "expands analytical theory by adding emotions, mistakes, limited foresight, doubts about how smart others are, and learning . . . behavioral game theory is one branch of behavioral economics, an approach to economics which uses psychological regularity to suggest ways to weaken rationality assumptions and extend theory" (p. 3).[40] The goals of this new field seem ideally suited to our discovery of the limits of the rationality assumption for nasty-nasty interaction during couple conflict.

Camerer's book described what I think is a brilliant research strategy using game theory to build theory. One picks a game in standard game theory that makes a clear and bold prediction, or a vague prediction that can be sharpened. Camerer said that simple games may be the most useful because they have very few assumptions. If the prediction is wrong, we then know which principles are at fault and need to be modified so that the prediction can be improved. The question in behavioral game theory then changes from "Does game theory predict actual behavior?" Even if game theory is not accurate, the very failure can become a prescriptive opportunity for discovering the game-theory rules of actual behavior. Of course, it takes a great deal of insight to select a simple game as a model for a complex process, but that's part of the fun of science.

Two illustrations show exactly why this research strategy is so brilliant. Camerer described two simple games. In a simple game he called "ultimatum bargaining," one player has something the second player wants. Camerer gave the example of a photographer who has taken a picture of a couple on a cruise. He offers them a copy of the picture for $5. They wish to bargain, but the photographer has pictures of other passengers, and, if he cuts his price, he runs the risk that no one will pay his $5 price. So his price may be his ultimatum. In repeated ultimatum bargaining experiments, it turns out that there are two possible outcomes. In one outcome, proposers are given $10. They offer whatever they wish to the responder. On average, they offer between $4 or $5. Low offers are often rejected in this outcome. However, in a second version of the game, surprisingly, even substantial sums are rejected. Camerer wrote:

> . . . such surprising rejections are examples of "negative reciprocity":
> Responders reciprocate unfair behavior by harming the person who treated

them unfairly, at a substantial cost to themselves (provided the unfair proposer is harmed more than they are). Negative reciprocity is evident in other social domains, even when the monetary stakes are high—jilted boyfriends who accost their exes, ugly divorces that cost people large sums, impulsive street crimes caused by a stranger allegedly "disrespecting" an assailant, the failure of parties in legal "nuisance cases" to renegotiate after a court judgment even when both could benefit, and so on. (p. 11)

This game illustrates that the negative absorbing state is easily a potential outcome of a very simple game. Thus, this simple game *explains* how negative reciprocity emerges.

The second game that Camerer discussed was called the "continental divide" game. This game highlights why there are just two adaptations to relationship conflict, which we discovered through the Hidden Markov analysis. He called the game "continental divide" because the repeated play of the game can asymptote toward either one of two *very* different outcomes, much like happy and unhappy couples during conflict.

At the geographical continental divide in the U.S., half of the waters spilled wind up in the Pacific Ocean and half wind up in the Atlantic Ocean. The continental divide game is a 7-member group tug-of-war game in which rewards depend also on picking where to build and invest, but the payoff also depends also on being close to what the group chooses. There are two possible outcomes in this game, one that is 3 and another that is 12. Camerer presented an example of the game with specific payoffs and medians. He wrote:

> . . . the game is called the continental divide game because medians below 7 are a "basin of attraction" (in evolutionary game theory terms) for convergence toward the equilibrium of 3. Medians above 8 are a basin of attraction for convergence toward 12. The "separatrix" between 7 and 8 divides the game into two regions where players will "flow" toward 3 and players will flow toward 12. (p. 14)

What this means is that unkown to the players of the game, they will drift toward not one solution, but two very different solutions. Yet it is just one game, with just one set of payoffs. Behavioral game theory therefore can explain how couples might asymptote into one of *two* states during nasty-nasty exchanges in conflict discussions. One model can result in two very different outcomes.

Two Kinds of Couple Conflicts

Amazingly, there are two kinds of conflict discussions: (1) those with absorbing-state nasty-nasty conflict, and (2) those with effective repair. We have two things to explain to fully understand these results. First, why is it so much harder for unhappy couples to *exit* the nasty-nasty state than it is for happy couples? Second, why is it so much easier for unhappy couples to *enter* the nasty-nasty state than it is for happy couples?

Maybe unhappy couples get into an absorbing state more easily because their negativity is different from that of happier couples. Or maybe unhappy couples are unable to *repair* their interaction and get out of the nasty-nasty cell for some reason like high levels of physiological arousal. Perhaps happy couples are more likely to do successful repairs because they are calmer. We are now able to test these and other hypotheses of repair.

In fact, in our most recent study, our mathematical modeling with James Murray and his students (see Chapter 11) revealed that the husband's payoff in the nasty-nasty cell of the matrix was higher to the extent his wife was able to repair the interaction effectively and move it, like a switch after passing a critical threshold, to a more positive state. That result gave us some hint about what our trust metric ought to be. In that sample of couples, the wife's ability to repair the nasty-nasty exchange effectively made it possible for them to exit the nasty-nasty state. So we have discovered that unhappy couples can't exit the nasty-nasty state because they can't repair very well.

Understanding more about repair took a great deal of additional work. Later in this book I will examine what repairs work, when in the conflict discussion they work best, and why they work at all when they do. That analysis took 7 years of work by my students Janice Driver and Amber Tabares. That work is described in Chapter 8.

But so far we can exclaim, "No wonder unhappy couples in conflict can't get out of the absorbing state of nasty-nasty reciprocal exchanges where they were not behaving rationally!" Only unhappy couples can't repair effectively. Unhappy couples are trapped in the hell of reciprocally nasty-nasty and escalating conflict, even though they had more negative payoffs for that exchange than happy couples. As I wrote in my book *What Predicts Divorce?*, I also discovered that for unhappily married couples this negative state becomes more pervasive than it does for happily married couples; it spills over into more supposedly nonconflict interaction as well.

Now for the second question. Why is it so much harder for unhappy couples to exit a nasty-nasty state? Let's try to explain that one also. Is it possible that these couples were also caught in a zero-sum game? Let's explore that possibility. To explore that hypothesis, we will need Robert Weiss's concept of *sentiment override*.

Positive and Negative Sentiment Override

As I mentioned earlier, in 1980 Robert Weiss of the University of Oregon came up with the inspired idea that people in a couple are in one of two states: negative sentiment override or positive sentiment override. In negative sentiment override a person has a tendency to see the partner's behavior as negative, even when objective outside observers see the behavior as neutral or even positive. The negative sentiment overrides anything positive. In negative sentiment override it is as if the person has a "chip on their shoulder" and is hypervigilant for negativity from the partner. Some psychologists have called this "oversensitivity." It's as if that person's cost-benefit analysis of the relationship and the partner's personality were tilted toward the negative. In positive sentiment override, the person has the opposite tendency, giving the partner the benefit of the doubt and assuming that the partner's intentions are generally positive. The positive sentiment overrides anything negative. There is no hypervigilance for negativity from the partner. On the contrary—it's as if that person's cost-benefit analysis of the relationship and the partner's personality were tilted toward the positive.

For example, a wife says to her husband, "You're not supposed to run the microwave when there's no food in it." In negative sentiment override the husband would perceive the comment as nasty (even if it was made neutrally or even nicely)—as if the wife had said something like,

"You idiot. You're not supposed to run the microwave when there's no food in it." On the other hand in positive sentiment override that comment is heard and perceived as neutral (even if it was made with some nastiness)—as if the wife had actually said something like, "I'm so sorry to have to say this to you, you sweet honey of mine, but I need to tell you something small, not really important. Don't take this personally, but I read somewhere that you're not supposed to run the microwave when there's no food in it. Okay, baby?" Weiss's idea was that when people are in negative sentiment override it's very hard to change perceptions.

I have added to Weiss's idea, suggesting that people are in negative sentiment override for very good reason. I suggest that people are in negative sentiment override because they are "running on empty" in the friendship parts of the relationship. They feel unappreciated, unloved, or disrespected. They don't feel that their partner is their friend, but instead that their partner is their adversary. That is the cause, I suggest, of why it is easier to enter the nasty-nasty cell of the matrix. Because a person is running on empty, trust has begun to erode, and he or she is in negative sentiment override. Psychologists Cliff Notarious and Jane Vanzetti were the first to demonstrate the truth of Weiss's hypothesis empirically,[41] and we have replicated the result in our laboratory as well.

Negative and positive sentiment overrides give us our answer to both of our questions. Unhappy couples have a bias—they are more likely than happy couples to *enter* the nasty-nasty state because they are in negative sentiment override. They are also more likely to construe neutral and even positive events as if they were negative, whereas happy couples—who are in positive sentiment override—are more likely to construe negative events as neutral or even positive. Therefore, unhappy couples may be more likely to also see even a positive repair attempt in the nasty-nasty state as another negative act. Hence, they are more stuck in the nasty-nasty absorbing state. Weiss was right. Perhaps it is also the case that for unhappily married couples the nasty-nasty state is a state of eroded or low trust.

The Trust Metric

I am now ready to define the trust metric mathematically. First, let's make everyday language more precise to define trust. We will use the he-she language of heterosexual relationships, although this language is easily modifiable for gay and lesbian couples; I mean no disrespect to same-sex relationships.

Her Trust. By "her trusting him" we mean that, without regard for his own gains, he acts to—and hence can be counted on to (and will)—look out for her interests by changing his behavior to increase her payoffs out of nasty-nasty interaction.

His Trust. By "him trusting her" we mean that, without regard for her own gains, she can be counted on to (and will) look out for his interests by changing her behavior to increase his payoffs out of nasty-nasty interaction.

That is, trust means that in a particular interaction we can rely on our partner to *behave* in such a way that our own payoffs are maximized, especially in getting out of nasty-nasty exchanges. This is a behavioral definition of trust, not a cognitive definition. It is therefore different from previous definitions of trust as either a personality trait or a way one person *thinks* about another. My trust metric is about *action*, not just thinking. Also, my trust metric can be defined in any interaction. It is therefore a characteristic of an interaction, not necessarily of a relationship or a person. It reflects cooperation with one's partner's interests in mind, probably important in any lasting relationship.

Notice also that I am *not* mentioning consideration for one person's gains over and above consideration for the other partner's gains. Trust, in this view, does not require sacrifice of one's own interests in the conflict for the partner's interests or gains. I am suggesting one definition of trust in which it is altogether possible that we can expect our partner to also be bargaining for his or her interests (payoffs). However, my suggestion is that trust means that our partner, perhaps in considering his or her own interests, is also considering our interests in the way he or she *acts*.

Now let's translate this everyday language into the language of mathematics. We do this in two steps. First, in terms of our game-theory matrices, for him we can measure how much variability in her actual behavior moves him out of the negative-negative cell's payoffs into the generally higher neutral-neutral cell's payoffs. Second, for him we can also measure how much her variability in actual behavior moves him out of the negative-negative cell's payoffs into the generally much higher positive-positive cell's payoffs. We can think of these like two possible jumps for escaping from nasty-nasty interaction (Figure 2.5). It assesses how much he can count on her to change her behavior for his interests.

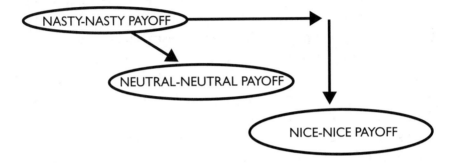

Figure 2.5   **Moving From Nasty-Nasty to Neutral-Neutral or Nice-Nice**

Of course, we do similar computations for her. Thus we arrive at two numbers for each partner, one for each potential advancement out of nasty-nasty interaction. To simplify matters for our first look at the trust metric, purely in the service of data reduction, I will multiply these two potential jump numbers together to get one estimate of the trust metric. See the appendix for the exact formulas for computing the trust metric in this manner.

Validity of the Trust Metric

Am I done once I have defined a trust metric? No, not at all. Even if the trust metric makes conceptual sense, we have to go back to the lab. The *validity* of the trust metric *must* be tested, and this has to be accomplished empirically in the laboratory, or we have accomplished nothing at all. A model of reality is only as good as the empirical results that fit the model's predictions.

When we do these computations we discover that—for married couples—when he trusts her, her relationship satisfaction is significantly higher, and there is: (1) significantly less wife negativity when the couple tells the story of their relationship in our oral history interview, (2) significantly greater expansiveness and openness in her telling the story of their relationship in our oral history interview, (3) significantly greater husband emotional attunement, and (4) significantly lower husband skin conductance (less physiological arousal) during conflict. We also know when she trusts him, there is (by her report) significantly less aggressive language by him toward her during arguments, significantly less emotional abuse by him, significantly less physical violence by him, and significantly less degradation, sexual abuse, and threat of violence and property damage or damage to pets. When she trusts him, she expresses less disappointment in the relationship during our oral history interview; he expresses significantly less disgust, contempt, and domineering during the conflict discussions; she is significantly less depressed (on the Beck Depression Inventory[42]); she has significantly fewer thoughts of divorce and separation (on the Weiss-Cerreto Marital Status Inventory[43]); and she is significantly less flooded during conflict. Thus, the trust metric has demonstrated validity.

Furthermore—and this is critical—the data suggest that the nasty-nasty absorbing state for unhappily married couples during conflict is a state of a significantly lowered trust metric. So trust is low when unhappy couples enter the absorbing state of negativity. These validity indices bode well for trust being important in predicting the future of the relationship, and they tell us that our reasoning about trust makes some sense empirically. They do not suggest that this is the *only* trust metric we might compute within an interaction, just that the one I *have* computed makes some empirical sense.

That's enough for me.

The Advantages of Trust

There is a basic dynamic pattern of the ratios of balance of positivity-to-negativity in couples' relationships that I have observed in our current culture. Once couples establish a stable equilibrium of positivity-to-negativity greater than or equal to 5.0 during conflict, they tend to take on more challenges in their lives. In the beginning years of a new relationship, couples work to see if they can trust each other in various areas of their lives. They are setting up a secure relationship as a base for building a life together.

Once they have established this security, they work harder, or they decide to remodel the kitchen, or they decide to change jobs, or they decide to have a baby. In fact, with regard to the decision to have the first baby, it was the newlyweds who were doing better in their marriages who "progressed" to that decision.

In taking on these new challenges there is invariably a new perturbation to their functional dynamic equilibrium. With this perturbation there is potentially a decrease in the ratio of positivity-to-negativity that follows this dynamic change, one that requires effective repair so that negativity does not become an absorbing state.

What determines if the couple will be able to effectively repair and restore their previously functional set point? The Sound Relationship House theory says it is determined by the quality of their friendship, and we will see that this turns out to be supported by the data.

The overall life pattern is that people in our culture continually increase complexity in their lives until many live at what mathematicians call the "cusp of a catastrophe." That word "catastrophe" doesn't mean disaster; rather, it has a precise meaning for mathematicians.[44] A catastrophe state means that people keep slowly increasing the complexity of their lives until they are at risk for entering a new qualitative state. Mathematically, catastrophe means that small increases in a parameter (like complexity, or stress) can suddenly, once a precise threshold of stress is passed, completely alter the *qualitative* nature of their relationship. The classic example of catastrophe is the straw that broke the camel's back. The parameter that gradually increased was the weight of the load the camel was asked to bear. The camel appeared to be fine, until the last straw was added to its load. Then its back broke and it was suddenly a very different camel. What's important about the catastrophe state is that we gradually change a continuous variable—like complexity—and, after we cross a particular threshold, our lives may change qualitatively, suddenly, and in very big ways.

Usually that qualitative change will be that things will fall apart, and entropy will increase. Chaos in our lives multiplies. Small events suddenly have huge consequences. Resiliency has suddenly evaporated. It is likely that we all have our own individual and finite "carrying capacity" for stress, and most of us gradually increase the amount of stress we are bearing, thinking we can handle it because our relationship is balanced at a functional level of positivity-to-negativity.

Yet, dynamically the result can be that many of us are just barely coping, and we are in danger of inadvertently reaching the cusp of that catastrophe that awaits us. That pattern explains why, in our transition to parenthood study, even though the newlywed couples who became pregnant had higher marital satisfaction than the ones who didn't, two-thirds of these couples had a precipitous drop in marital satisfaction in the first 3 years of the baby's life.

Now we can see why trust might be so important. High levels of the trust metric may make this dynamical progression toward increased complexity give couples more resilience—that is, because of trust there is a higher threshold for the catastrophe's cusp. In other words:

- Trust increases the relationship's resilience as we naturally increase the complexity of our lives over time.

In addition to this increased resilience, there are three other important advantages of trust.

- Trust permits action with incomplete information.
- Trust reduces the complexity of all transactions.
- Trust minimizes transaction costs.

That means that trust simply makes interaction easier and less costly. We don't need to be continually testing our partner to see if this time we can trust him or her to tell the truth, keep promises, and think of our interests. We just assume we can, even with incomplete information about the facts. Therefore, interaction becomes simpler, and complexity is reduced. As with studies of the Orthodox Jewish diamond-merchant communities,[45] jewels and vast sums of money can be exchanged on a handshake, with complete confidence. The community system has made transaction less costly. No lawyers are needed for these very risky transactions. In close personal relationships the risks are equally high: We are trusting our very hearts to the relationship. Betrayals result in a broken heart. As we will see when we discuss the physiology of trust and betrayal, these metaphors have a great deal of truth in them. Betrayals and an inability to trust can cost us our health and many years of life.

When we are making decisions, we need to estimate the probabilities of various alternatives, and evaluate both the probability of risk and the probability of success for each alternative. Mathematically the difference in complexity is expressed as the difference between "unconditional" and "conditional" probabilities. In a conditional probability we always have to make our estimate the chances, conditional on various prior factors and considerations. In an unconditional probability we don't need to consider these prior factors. Trust means that we can compute our probabilities of success and risk for each alternative with considerably less qualification; we can ignore many factors that have to do with not fully trusting our partner. Also, trust makes transaction easier. We don't have to worry, we don't have to look over our shoulder, we don't have to be wary.

Conversely, a high potential for betrayal seems to turn people into private investigators, or prosecuting attorneys, constantly looking for evidence of potential violations of trust. People become detectives, often interrogating their partners as a test, looking for verification that their insecurity is justified by reality. For example, one mistrustful man put chalk marks on his wife's rear tires and on the driveway when he left home one morning. He came home and saw that the car had been moved. He questioned his wife: "Where did you go today?" She couldn't recall having gone out for an errand to the grocery store, so she replied, "Nowhere." He immediately flew into a jealous rage. Mistrust increases suspicion, so people multiplex the amount of information they ordinarily need to gather for a decision. The uncertainty becomes extremely painful, and people become frozen with inaction. There was a famous cartoon by Jules Feiffer that illustrated the pain of this insecurity. A woman asks a man, "Do you love me?" He replies, "Yes, I do." She then asks, "But do you really love me?" He replies, "Yes, I do." She then asks, "But do you really, really love me?" He replies, "Yes, I do." She then asks, "But do you really, really, really love me?" He replies, "Yes, I think do." She then asks, "But do you really, really, really, really love me?" He replies, "Well, I don't know." She responds, "I thought so!"

Summary and Conclusions

When we go into the laboratory to observe actual human conflict, we find that some of the assumptions of two logical players of game theory are validated, but some of them are actually disconfirmed. In my longitudinal study with Robert Levenson of older couples, we found that payoffs were highest in nice-nice exchanges and lowest in nasty-nasty exchanges. Therefore, in our first analyses we were confirming Thibaut and Kelley's ideas about payoffs. We also found that happy couples rated nice-nice exchanges significantly higher than unhappy couples did. They also did these nice-nice exchanges more often. So the probabilities matched the payoffs. That finding also confirmed the rational model of game theory. That finding supported Kelley's idea that people would naturally do the things that gave them the highest payoffs most frequently. That effect replicated across both studies. In fact, when we examined the matrices for both happy and unhappy couples, the Nash equilibrium turned out to be the nice-nice cell of the matrix. So far so good.

We were confirming rational-choice game theory. We were very happy to be extending Kelley's theorizing about interdependence in relationships. In looking at the neutral-neutral symmetry, once again a rational game-theory model held. In addition to increasing nice-nice interaction and decreasing both the frequency and the negative impact of nasty-nasty interaction, a very important goal needs to be to increase the reciprocity of *unemotional exchanges* during conflict. That's a new idea for couple therapy, because the entire field seems to be opposed to discussing conflict with neutral affect. But, like Robert Levenson and Rachel Ebling, we found that neutral affect during conflict was a good thing, and it followed the rational assumption of game theory.

But then a very funny thing happened. Tara and I discovered a very strange effect for the nasty-nasty cell, one that also replicated across both of our studies. The unhappy couples were doing nasty-nasty exchanges far more often than the happy couples were, but they were *rating it far lower* than the happy couples were rating it. Wait a minute! That supports an irrational model! The unhappy couples should be doing nasty-nasty exchanges *less often* if they were rating it lower. That's what Thibaut and Kelley's assumption implied. What was going on here?

What was going on was that we had discovered the true limitations of game theory for what Anatol Rapoport called the "debate mode" of conflict, where logical persuasion is possible. That's our couples' conflict discussion. We found that in actual debate mode, in relationship conflict people did *not* always act rationally! When it came to the more highly charged negative emotional exchanges, for unhappy couples the payoffs and the probabilities were *opposite* of what they were predicted to be by a rational game-theory model. We had just discovered the limitations of rational game theory!

What explained these limitations in the nasty-nasty cell? The answer is that we saw that negativity was an "absorbing state," a virtual quicksand bog for unhappy couples, but not for happy couples. Unhappy couples have an easier time entering nasty-nasty exchanges and a more difficult time exiting them than happy couples do. We also saw that the positivity that the couple brought to the table before influence processes began, as well as the way they influenced each other toward stable amounts of positivity made a significant difference in how they rated the nasty-nasty cell. It was easier for unhappy couples to enter the nasty-nasty state because they were in negative sentiment override, and it was harder for them to exit the nasty-nasty state because repair was more likely to fail for them, because they were running on empty in the friendship part of the relationship. The nasty-nasty state was also an absorbing state for unhappy couples because it turned out to be a state of low trust, one in which negative sentiment override was operating to distort partners' perceptions so that almost any repair seemed to be an extension of negativity.

As Dan Wile said so eloquently in commenting on this quicksand bog of the nasty-nasty absorbing state, "the bog is the self-reinforcing quality of the adversarial cycle—how each partner feels too unlistened-to to hear, too misunderstood to be understanding, and too stung by what the partner just said to do anything other than sting back" (personal communication, 2010). So the cycle continues and the hurts escalate.

Once we defined and measured the trust metric, it also turned out that the absorbing state during conflict—the quicksand bog—is also a state of low trust. No wonder conflict escalates for unhappy couples in nasty-nasty exchanges during conflict and repair fails!

Chapter 3

The Metrics of Untrustworthiness and Betrayal

This chapter reviews the cloak-and-dagger history of game theory during the Cold War and the work of two very different personalities, John von Neumann and Anatol Rapoport. It then extends my work on the trust metrics to develop valid metrics of untrustworthiness and betrayal in any interaction. Finally, it illustrates these metrics in the interaction of two very different older couples.

Okay, so we now have a trust metric. I now want to go further and define two additional metrics, a metric of untrustworthiness and a metric of betrayal. The basis for understanding untrustworthiness and betrayal lies in continuing the application and investigation of game theory. Let's first take a look at the fascinating story of game theory, because in the lives of two very different people, two of game theory's great thinkers, we will see clues to the dynamics of untrustworthiness and betrayal.

The Cloak-and-Dagger History of Game Theory

I want to tell you the story of two brilliant and highly successful men, John von Neumann and Anatol Rapoport, and the issues that their work raises about the nature of human conflict. The two men were very nearly opposites of each other in temperament, character, and life goals.

Rapoport, a Jewish Russian-American, was a strong advocate for peace, whereas von Neumann was an advocate for an unprovoked nuclear strike against the Soviet Union during the Cold War. The men met each other on only one occasion. Rapoport found von Neumann charming and "an excellent conversationalist." He later wrote, "All the greater was the shock I experienced when I found out that he seriously and persistently advocated a preventive war against the Soviet Union."

John von Neumann was a Jewish Hungarian-American physicist and mathematician who designed and built one of the world's first electronic computers at Princeton. His ideas are responsible for huge innovations that we now take for granted, like the internal architecture of the computer, the idea of a computer "program," and the ideas of software and computation both being in a computer's memory. Von Neumann initially designed and built his electronic computer for the computations of the Manhattan project, the U.S. project that built the first two atomic bombs that ended the war with Japan in 1945. Through the efforts of brilliant scientists, we beat the Germans and the Japanese in a dramatic life-or-death struggle for existence.

The Manhattan project was inspired by a presumed race with Nazi Germany. The Nazi nuclear-bomb program was led by the brilliant Nobel-prize winning physicist Werner Heisenberg. The British made secret tape recordings of post-war conversations between captured German scientists without their knowledge. These tape recordings show that, despite his desperate lies to the contrary, Heisenberg was indeed trying to win the race for an atomic bomb for Hitler. It is therefore fortunate that the Hungarian-American physicist Leo Szilard persuaded Albert Einstein to write a personal letter to President Roosevelt urging him to authorize the rapid creation of an atomic-bomb project before Germany could develop its own bomb.

The Manhattan project actually developed two very different atomic bombs. One of the bombs was largely built to von Neumann's original design. It was known as "Fat Man." Von Neumann used his computer to calculate exactly how to detonate the nuclear core of the first atomic bomb using an implosion method. The other atomic bomb was known as "Little Boy," and it used a gun trigger. Fat Man was the one used on Nagasaki. Little Boy was used on Hiroshima.

Von Neumann's contributions do not begin or end with the creation of the atomic bomb. Before the war, in the 1930s, physicists were searching for a theoretical explanation of the new science of quantum mechanics. Von Neumann applied the ideas of the mathematician David Hilbert and wrote a breakthrough formal theoretical version of quantum mechanics using Hilbert's mathematics. His formulation and Paul Dirac's work succeeded in integrating two seemingly different formulations of quantum mechanics, one formulated by Erwin Schrödinger's wave equation, and the other formulated by Werner Heisenberg's uncertainty principle.[1] It was a monumental accomplishment that has stood the test of time. Many other derivations have emerged since von Neumann's and Dirac's, but theirs were the first.

Both Rapoport and von Neumann were innovators in the use of game theory for deriving a mathematical understanding of human conflict. Von Neumann invented much of the mathematics of game theory. He applied game theory to no less a problem than understanding world economies. In addition to making monumental contributions to science, warfare, and computer technology, von Neumann and Oskar Morgenstern tried to understand world economies using game theory.

As you already know from the discussion of the trust metric in the previous chapter, in a "game" there are two "opponents," each of whom has a set of strategies. Player A has strategies A1, A2, A3, . . . , AP. A1 is player A's strategy #1, A2 is player A's strategy #2, and so on. Player B has strategies B1, B2, B3, . . . , BQ. Every combination of strategies has a "payoff," say "H" for player A and "W" for the other player. This creates a familiar table like that shown in Figure 3.1.

Figure 3.1   **Opponents, Strategies, and Payoffs**

	Strategy B1	Strategy B2	Strategy B3	...	Strategy BQ
Strategy A1	H11, W11	H12, W12	H13, W13	...	H1Q, W1Q
Strategy A2	H21, W21	H22, W22	H23, W23	...	H2Q, W2Q
Strategy A3	H31, W31	H32, W32	H33, W33	...	H3Q, W3Q
...	...	...	...	...	...
Strategy AP	HP1, WP1	HP2, WP2	HP3, WP3	...	HPQ, WPQ

Recall that von Neumann and Morgenstern talked about an equilibrium solution to some games. They proved a famous theorem called the "minimax" theorem. To simplify things, the theorem states that for every zero-sum competitive game like Rock-Paper-Scissors, there is an optimal strategy for minimizing loss, which is the expected gain for the other player. Steve Heims, von Neumann's biographer, wrote that this theorem "turned out to be so profound that it opened up new areas and manifested new connections within mathematics" (p. 84).[2] First von Neumann and Morgenstern proved the minimax theorem for a situation where both players have total knowledge of the joint strategies of both players and their utilities (outcomes for each player). In their second minimax theorem they tackled games with incomplete information and proved that the theorem holds only on the average; there is no best strategy for playing only one round. Von Neumann and Morgenstern also developed a rational game-theory strategy for a version of stud poker.

Because he distrusted human emotions so much, it was von Neumann's dream that one day computers could eliminate emotion from decisions central to human survival, and pit alternative strategies of international conflict and military tactics against one another, simulate potential outcomes, and make the best automated, rational choice for our side.

As I have mentioned, the von Neumann-Morgenstern equilibrium point in game theory (when it exists) is a search for a combination of strategies between two opposing players that is "the best of the worst." That means it minimizes each player's potential losses. Even in its conceptualization, this equilibrium point can be considered a pessimistic viewpoint about human relationships. The point of this solution is to cut your losses.

It is very different from the equilibrium point of John Nash.[3] The Nash equilibrium (when it exists) is that point at which neither player can do any better. Hence, it can be considered an equilibrium point that is more optimistic.

Von Neumann and Morgenstern's book definitely put game theory on the map. It eventually led to a series of Nobel prizes in economics, including John Nash's prize. Always connected with military applications, the new von Neumann game theory inspired a new generation of

Cold War warriors, who contemplated using von Neumann's computer to compute the advantages and disadvantages of nuances of diplomacy, brinksmanship, and fundamental nuclear strategy. The mathematical recommendations of game-theory analyses were not always apparent and did not always lead to obvious solutions to problems.

Game theory often comes up with surprises. For example in a "truel," which is a duel fought by *three* people, suppose one of three is the best shot, another the second-best shot, and a third a terrible shot. In many situations of this sort the *weakest* shot will survive, because logically the other two would rather eliminate the better shots.

As mentioned, the design of the electronic computer was another of von Neumann's great contributions. He built one of the world's first computers, called "EDVAC." He designed the "architecture" of the modern computer with what he called four "organs," the arithmetic logic unit, the control unit, the memory, and the input/output unit. Von Neumann's enormous insight was to encode instructions in numerical form, with no distinction in memory between data and programs.

Von Neumann's hope was that the logic and mathematics of game theory, using the electronic computer, could solve even the more complex games of nuclear, political, and military strategy. Rapidly the real problems become too complex for ordinary computations. That computational need led to the development of faster and faster electronic computers. This development was supported by the U.S. military.

Why would game theory have been so appealing to the military and political thinking after World War II? The games that any civilization plays usually tell us a lot about the values of the culture. For example, the ancient Chinese game of "Go" reflected a model of war, and chess was thought to have originated in India, where the pieces were originally the Elephant, Horse, and Chariot, instruments of war.

Even today the very language of a game tells us a great deal about the culture that loves the game. The late comedian George Carlin compared the language of baseball and football. He said that baseball is a 19th century pastoral game that played on a "diamond" in a "park," whereas football is a 20th century technological struggle that is played on a "gridiron." In football, he said, the players wear a helmet; in baseball they wear a cap. In football there are "downs"; in baseball "you're up." In football the specialist comes in to kick the ball; in baseball the specialist comes in to "relieve someone." In football there is hitting, spearing, clipping, blocking, piling on, personal fouls; in baseball there is "the sacrifice." Football is played in hail, rain, sleet, snow, ice, and mud, but baseball cannot be played if it is raining. In football the objective is for "the quarterback to be on target with his aerial assault, riddling the defense by hitting his receivers with deadly accuracy in spite of the blitz even if he has to use the shotgun. With short bullet passes and long bombs he marches his troops into enemy territory balancing his aerial assault with a sustained ground attack as he punches holes in the enemy's defensive wall."[4] In baseball the objective is to "come home and be safe."

Games have a long and venerable history, and mathematics has been interested in games of chance for literally hundreds of years. In the 17th century, the French mathematician and philosopher Blaise Pascal developed the mathematics of probability to advise his friend, a gambler and philosopher named the Chevalier de Méré, about dice. Pascal was famous for his suggestion to weight the probability of an event with how much "utility" the outcome (the benefit, or the disaster) has for the player.[5] In particular, he applied his advice in creating a famous argument about whether or not to believe in the existence of a personal God. His argument was that even though the probability that God existed might be low, the payoff of belief was potentially so high in the comfort it gave people—so the product of low probability and high benefit gave a high number for the payoff for belief—that it made sense to believe. Whether you agree or not, it was an interesting argument.

As rational as Pascal was, he was also, gratefully, a true Frenchman to the core. Pascal was famous for his saying that "the heart has its reason whereof reason knoweth not," by which he meant that the emotions have their own logic.[6] That important point of Pascal's was lost on later game theorists, who assumed that all players of games must be totally logical and all players of the game must be operating with high levels of logical self-interest. Was it possible for von Neumann's computer to eliminate emotion from decision making? Or do the correct representations of how humans deal with conflict of necessity follow Pascal's famous saying?

A central part of early probability applied to games of chance was the assumption that the opponent was totally intelligent and rational. French mathematician Emil Borel was the first to begin developing the mathematics of game theory in the 1920s. Game theory, even from its inception, was closely tied to military strategy. In fact, it's no accident that in 1925 Borel became minister of the Navy. The struggle for survival and the goal of winning were part of the development of game theory.

In the 18th and 19th centuries the idea of individuals in a species competing in the struggle to survive was in the air. It was critical in the formulation of Darwin's "survival of the fittest" competitions for food, mates, and territory. Competition and self-interest were also central to Adam Smith's theory of free markets, which identified self-interest and economic again as the universal motive in civilized society, with the individual's pursuit of his own ends providing maximum benefit to society, the foundation of a capitalist system. Smith believed that self-interest and greed were good and an unregulated economy was enough to create a regulated market when people also had a strong moral responsibility.[7] Marxist politics were instead presumably built on the alternative of only communist cooperation for the "common good" as a way of regulating human greed. Some writers have suggested that the 20th century saw the failure of both types of extreme societal structures (unregulated capitalist and communist) and the emergence of a balance of both types in capitalist-welfare or socialist states.

From childhood, von Neumann was an admirer of businessmen and he was himself a very successful capitalist. In contrast, Rapoport was an avid socialist. There is a history of Rapoport's preoccupation with cooperation. His father ran a grocery store. In his autobiography Rapoport wrote that all the grocery stores were open about 16 hours a day, 7 days a week, and his father was exhausted. So were the other grocers. Rapoport's father got the grocers to agree collectively to close their stores at 7 P.M. on Mondays, Wednesdays, and Fridays, and also on Sundays from 1 P.M. to 5 P.M. However, the agreement lasted only a short time once one grocer defected. Rapoport wrote, "Years later I read about Adam Smith's 'invisible hand'—the regulatory function of the free market—which insures that pursuit of individual advantage by each participant results in the collective good. Thinking back to the neighborhood grocers, I envisage 'the invisible back of the hand'—situations in which pursuit of individual advantage by everyone results in a collective 'bad.' Much of my research in the psychology of decision making centered on this effect, illustrating the dichotomy between individual and collective rationality" (p. 41).[8] Rapoport never forgot that experience. His later social psychological research was designed to find strategies that maximized cooperation even in conditions of potential self-interest.

Game Theory and the Cold War (This Ought to Scare You)

With a great faith in both game theory and in the lightning-quick genius of von Neumann, the U.S. Air force created the first military "think tank," the Rand Corporation. The Rand Corporation was initially designed primarily to use the mathematics of game theory of military strategy during the Cold War. Von Neumann was a central consultant to the Rand Corporation. In any military game, von Neumann argued, it is necessary to know all possible strategies, and to be able to estimate the "payoffs"—that is the rewards and costs for each combination of strategies played by both opponents. With cold rational, emotionally detached logic, the Rand Corporation strategists designed the matrices of U.S.-Soviet nuclear strategy and the utility functions that would determine the computerized solutions to the U.S. democratic, capitalistic life-and-death struggle with Soviet communism.

To give you some idea of how influential von Neumann's thinking was, in June 1959 the U.S. Joint Congressional Atomic Energy Sub-Committee coldly estimated that a moderate attack on 70 key cities and 154 military bases with 263 nuclear bombs would kill 23 million people outright, fatally injure 25.9 million, inflict burn injuries on 7.3 million, and subject 12.7 million to harmful radiation dosages. They estimated the deaths for New York City as 6.10 million, or 47%; for Boston as 2.14 million, or 75%; and for Baltimore as 1.06 million, or 79%. They coldly stated that the lower end of the death rate would therefore be one in four U.S. persons. They estimated that in a moderate attack approximately 50 million Americans would die. The Russians were estimated as losing 100 million, so they argued that this was a clear win for the U.S. Imagine that.

Military strategists claimed that they were using game theory to "think about the unthinkable" in terms of these estimated casualties. It was a tough-minded form of thinking. A new era of military strategy and warfare had begun with this use of game theory, and von Neumann was the central player in and architect of this Cold War strategy. He strongly supported the strategy of a preemptive first nuclear strike against the Soviet Union. His influence on international relations at the start of the Cold War was enormous.

Furthermore, von Neumann didn't stop with the development of the atomic bomb. Whereas most physicists from the Manhattan project withdrew in horror back into the halls of academia, shocked at the human suffering of the people of Hiroshima and Nagasaki, von Neumann remained a central player in the Truman and Eisenhower administrations and an active and respected advisor to the military. With Lewis Strauss (former secretary of the Navy) and Edward Teller, von Neumann helped launch the breakneck-speed project that led to the hydrogen bomb, and the breakneck-speed project that led to its potential deployment with long-range intercontinental ballistic missiles.[9]

The hydrogen bomb was so powerful that von Neumann thought it could beat the Soviet Union's estimated stockpile of atomic bombs (which we grossly *over*estimated, thanks to the KGB's misinformation campaign). Von Neumann's goal was to destroy the Soviet Union in an unprovoked attack, the goal being to "win" even if it was at the cost of 50 million American lives and untold numbers of Soviet families. President Eisenhower awarded von Neumann the Congressional Medal of Honor, and he seriously considered von Neumann's ideas. Thankfully he ultimately didn't take his advice.

Von Neumann, who was in a wheelchair late in his life, was the model for the Peter Sellers film *Dr. Strangelove*, in which a scientist is portrayed as an insane advocate for unprovoked nuclear war. As amusing as the film was, it was no exaggeration. It was fact, not fiction. The U.S. military took von Neumann's ideas very seriously. We came very close to following his advice, and if that doesn't scare you, nothing will.

Anatol Rapoport, on the other hand, became a very different kind of game theorist. Unlike the Hungarian-born von Neumann, who grew up hating Russia, Rapoport loved both the Russian and the American spirits. In fact, in his major book,[10] Rapoport wrote two sympathetic accounts of a Russian and an American worldview that he hoped would increase empathy of both peoples for each other. Unlike von Neumann, Rapoport's major interest in life was figuring out how to create the conditions for peace during the Cold War. He was a peace warrior.

Rapoport differed from von Neumann in other ways as well. Where von Neumann had no use for music, Rapoport started his career as a concert pianist. Where von Neumann had two marriages, with the latter and longer of the two filled with suspicion, conflict, and mistrust, Rapoport's only marriage was long and his family life was harmonious. Where von Neumann died early at the age of 53, probably from a cancer created by closely observing an atomic bomb explosion at the Bikini atoll, Rapoport lived to the ripe old age of 96. Where von Neumann served in the Eisenhower administration and received the nation's medal of honor, Rapoport became an expatriate Canadian citizen who resigned his post at the University of Michigan because he could not accept the zero-sum-game military strategy that was embraced by von Neumann and the U.S.

Where von Neumann used game theory to emphasize winning and self-interest in the Cold War, Rapoport wound up dedicating his life to the empirical and mathematical study of a game called Prisoner's Dilemma. All about trust and betrayal, Prisoner's Dilemma is a simple game that pits self-interest against cooperation. Rapoport's life was dedicated to scientifically learning how to maximize understanding and cooperation in international relations, and how to minimize the zero-sum of extreme self-interest.

Military strategy and its use of game theory spurned such a cooperative mentality as "weak." The hydrogen bomb has the power of 10,000 Hiroshima bombs. Even with an inaccurate intercontinental ballistic missile (ICBM), an entire set of Russian cities could be destroyed even by a multiple warhead missile (MIRV) because the hydrogen bomb was so extremely destructive: The long-range ICBMs could hit anywhere near a city and still destroy most of it. That recommendation led to the Atlas program.

The Rand Corporation's Herman Kahn had written a book called *On Thermonuclear War*, in which Kahn explored the unthinkable choice of thermonuclear war.[11] This was the time of Senator Joseph McCarthy's frenzied national witch-hunting of communists among the U.S. artist community. It was portrayed as a life-or-death world struggle between capitalism and communism.

The dialectic between von Neumann and Rapoport was to have dire consequences for Rapoport's life. It also had dire consequences for the research and teaching on peace and cooperation that Rapoport was spearheading. As noted, Rapoport eventually gave up his professorship at the University of Michigan, moved to Canada, and relinquished his American citizenship. His decision to leave the U.S. was based on a moral choice. He wrote, "What I found impossible was to continue business as usual, while the country to which I owed at least formal allegiance made the slaughter of civilians (which is what counter-insurgency and nuclear warfare entail) a component of its role in the international arena."[12] He talked these things over with his wife, Gwen, and she agreed. They initially moved to Denmark, and from there to Toronto.

Both Rapoport and von Neumann spent a great deal of their intellectual and emotional energy on game theory, but, as you can see, they approached it from opposite perspectives. Von Neumann came at game theory from the perspective of competition, mistrust, and a fight for survival, and he had the goal of maximizing self-interest. Rapoport's approach to game theory was to search scientifically for the strategy that would maximize cooperation in the face of distrust.

It's really no wonder that von Neumann was so persuasive and so attractive to the U.S. military. His intellectual powers were truly spectacular. Known as "Johnny," he was a child prodigy who went on to startle and amaze the world with his intellectual gifts. He had a photographic memory and a brilliant, encyclopedic, lightning-fast mind. He had memorized vast quantities of nonfiction, including Gibbon's *Rise and Fall of the Roman Empire*, and could quote vast passages of the books he had memorized. On his deathbed his friend read to him from Goethe's *Faust*. Once, as his friend paused, von Neumann recited the next page from memory. He also had a vast collection of off-color jokes and loved to tell these jokes and stories at parties. Von Neumann was a very likeable party animal—an extrovert at ease in conversations and cocktail parties. He also loved rubbing shoulders with the rich and powerful.

The two men also differed greatly in their personal lives. Unlike Rapoport, von Neumann had relationships with women that tended to be pragmatic, strategic, and superficial. Von Neumann's biographer, Steve Heims, described his relationships with women as follows: "Johnny believed in having sex, in pleasure, but not in emotional attachments. He was interested in immediate pleasures but had little comprehension of emotions in relationships and mostly saw women in terms of their bodies."[13] His wife Klara once asked him to get her a glass of water. He was gone for a long time and then returned to ask her where the glasses were kept. They had lived in that house for 17 years. Von Neumann was not a man with clear love map of his home.

Rapoport, on the other hand, was shy and introverted. He was a confirmed socialist who shunned the material side of life and instead emphasized intimate relationships, trust, commitment, and family in his life.

Von Neumann's ability to solve mathematical problems at rapid speed was legendary. He would appear at the Rand Corporation, where "unsolvable" problems would be presented to him. He would put his head in his hands for several minutes and come up with the answer. For example, he was once presented with the following problem: Two bicycles are approaching each other at different speeds and a fly is traveling back and forth from one bicycle to the other at a speed of 15 miles an hour. How far will the fly travel before the bicycles collide in one hour? A quick way to solve the problem is to realize that since the bicycles will collide in an hour, the fly travels 15 miles before the impact. A slower way to solve the problem is to add the almost infinite series of shorter and shorter trips the fly makes. Von Neumann solved the problem nearly instantly and the person at Rand who presented it to him said he must have realized the shortcut. "No, I simply added the infinite series," said Johnny.

Rapoport was a slower, more ponderous thinker than von Neumann. Whereas von Neumann made stunning contributions to at least five different areas (computers, economics, weapons, quantum mechanics, and pure mathematics), Rapoport spent his entire life trying to understand one thing: how to maximize cooperation in human conflict and build trust within a potentially untrusting world where self-interest sometimes has bigger payoffs than cooperation.

Rapoport's major book was called *Fights, Games, and Debates*. It was published in 1960. In that book he attempted to describe what he decided were *the* three forms of human conflict. One mode of human conflict he called "fights." Fights involve threats, escalation, brinksmanship, and violence, with war a prime example of a fight. The second mode of human conflict Rapoport called "games." He defined games as having a structure that involves two (or more) opponents finding a strategy that has particular payoffs for each player. In a zero-sum game, one player's gain is the other player's loss. In a cooperative game, strategies of cooperation may produce the best option of joint payoffs. Rapoport thought that the most interesting cooperative games occur in a climate of mutual suspicion and distrust, where self-interest may at times logically trump cooperation. Diplomacy and international relations were gamelike arenas in which very structured and strategic communications dominate. Games, Rapoport noted, invite deception and secrecy, and in a gamelike context, he argued, agencies like the KGB and the CIA would have to spring up. These secret organizations must be created and expected in these forms of win-lose human conflict.

Rapoport called the third model of human conflict "debates." By "debates" he meant conflicts that have the possibility of being resolved by persuasion. These are presumably conflicts that are established in continuing relationships where cooperation is presumably a highly valued state. Debate-mode conflicts include things like labor-management negotiations, and also negotiations in love or marriage relationships. In fact, as we will see, Rapoport's insights have significant application to couples' relationships.

Rapoport's View of War

Unlike von Neumann, Rapoport didn't think game theory was the appropriate way to study war. Rapoport conceived of war as one example of "fight" mode, a physical contest, a mode without the logic of games. He viewed war as a sequence of interacting stimuli and reactions, like a dog fight, escalating from growls to grimaces to bared teeth to postures resembling a coiled spring, finally exploding into violence. He wrote, "A quarrel escalating to a feud can also be described this way."

The reason Rapoport's view of war was so different from von Neumann's was not because of the moral point of difference between the two men but rather a mathematical point of difference. The mathematical difference had to do with the work of a mathematician named Lewis Richardson. Rapoport knew that mathematically, war was best modeled as the *unstable* case of an arms race, which had been described earlier by Richardson in his seminal work on violent conflicts and war.

Richardson's modeling was based on extensive data. He modeled the military buildup before World War I with amazing accuracy. His model also succeeded in modeling many other wars and violent conflicts fought in Europe. Rapoport was personally influential in getting Richardson's book republished and disseminated.

Because of Richardson's impressive modeling, Rapoport, instead of classifying war as a branch of game theory, placed it in the class of violent "fights." He wrote:

> The common feature [of violence] is the "systemic" nature of a fight-like conflict. It is neither planned nor conducted "rationally." It can be described without reference to available means and pursued goals. To the extent that one can speak of a "goal" at all in the context of a physical fight, one could say that it is confined to eliminating the opponent, perceived as simply a noxious stimulus, which one tries to remove by reacting to the irritation. In contrast a "game" is a "rationally" conducted conflict. It is characterized by clearly specified constraints governing the means employed in pursuit of goals. The constraints may be agreed upon "rules of the game" as in parlor games (chess, bridge, etc.) or imposed by circumstances, taken into consideration in planning a course of action. "Rationality" in this context means ascribing "rationality" to the opponent. The goal of a game is not to eliminate the opponent but to outwit the opponent. (p. 48)[14]

As a category of a "fight," war and military conflict could be modeled by the unstable states of Richardson's amazingly powerful model of arms buildup preceding World War I. Richardson, who was a Quaker, conducted mathematical analyses of all wars and other deadly conflicts on the planet from 1820 to 1929. His book *Statistics of Deadly Quarrels* asked and answered many basic questions about war and deadly quarrels.[15] His analyses were based on actual hard data about warfare and other deadly quarrels. Many of his empirical conclusions busted myths about the nature of war. For example, here are a few of Richardson's conclusions: Wars have a periodicity of about 5 and 15 years; deadly quarrels and wars have not become more frequent over the century he studied; the frequency of wars is unrelated to the world's population; the

U.N. Charter was supposed to be made up of the world's "peace loving nations," but an examination of the record of wars reveals that the only nations that can be called "peace loving" are Switzerland and Sweden; Prussia and Germany have not been more aggressive than England and the United States; there appears to be a continuum between war and deadly quarrels, such as feuds; the frequency of war was related to the number of frontiers a country had with other nations (if the number of frontiers was five or lower, there were far fewer wars—1.4 on average between 1830 and 1929—than if there were eight or more frontiers—10.3 on average between 1830 and 1929); more destructive wars do not lead to less retaliation.

Richardson categorized wars into seven groups using the logarithm of soldier-casualty figures. The scale is like a Richter scale of war. The casualties get much worse with every jump. A class 2.5 war had casualties in the range of 4 to 315 deaths; a class 7 war had casualties in the range of 3,162,278 to 31,622,777 deaths. Richardson couldn't get his book published because it was so academic and thorough, filled with detailed statistical analyses, so he published it himself and gave away 35 copies to friends. Then he was done with his work.

The book would have languished in obscurity were it not for Rapoport, who helped resuscitate Richardson's book and used his own money to get the book published. The book answered many questions about war, most of them going counter to prevailing intuition. More importantly, Richardson also created the first mathematical model of an arms race, the buildup that preceded World War I. He had used two differential equations in this modeling. In these equations, constants called "parameters" estimated how the arms expenditures of each nation influenced the arms expenditures of the other nations. The parameters were the extent of each nation's permanent grievances toward the others, and the extent of the limiting brake that each country put on its military budget. With these equations and estimated parameters, a balance of power point could be computed. By suitably altering these parameters either an unstable arms race leading to war or a disarmament was modeled. Through Richardson, mathematics made dramatic headway into the analysis of war and violence. It turned out that violent forms of conflict were not that hard to describe accurately, precisely, and mathematically.

Like Richardson, Rapoport considered "fights," violence, and the escalation of war and deadly quarrels to be easily modeled without requiring the rationality of game theory. That distinction is a major difference between von Neumann and Rapoport.

Because of Richardson's work, Rapoport differed from the game theorists of the Cold War, who viewed war as a means through which violence gets an opponent to submit to one's will, which could be modeled as a zero-sum game, with a winner and a loser. Thomas Schelling's *The Strategy of Conflict*[16] appeared the same year as Kahn's "thinking the unthinkable" zero-sum game nuclear strategy approach to the Cold War. Contrary to Kahn, Schelling, who lavished praise on Rapoport's book, suggested that the Cold War could be modeled as a non-zero-sum game, in which cooperation and strategic negotiation were options, and understanding the enemy was part of the strategy.

Rapoport's contention was that in a thermonuclear war there are no winners, and strategic thinking of nuclear war should be rejected on moral grounds. He also contended that in the thermonuclear zero-sum game approach, the analysis was not fully rational either, because it had never computed the benefit of surrender by one of the players, nor had it computed the benefits of losing 50 million U.S. citizens and 100 million Russians to either side. Surrender had never been considered in the Rand Corporation's game theory. Hence, the Rand Corporation's thinking was patriotic and chauvinistic, not fully rational.

Despite his proposal of game theory as a basis for thermonuclear strategy, von Neumann was well aware of Rapoport's mathematical arguments and Richardson's work. He understood the mathematical simplicity of the escalating arms buildup he himself helped to provoke. In November 1951, von Neumann even wrote:

> . . . the preliminaries of war are to some extent a mutually self-excitatory process, where the actions of either side stimulate the actions of the other side. These then react on the first side and cause him to go further than he did "one round earlier," etc. . . . . Each one must systematically interpret the other's reactions to his aggression, and this, after several rounds of amplification, finally leads to "total" conflict. . . . I think, in particular, that the USA-USSR conflict will probably lead to an armed

"total" collision, and that a maximum rate of armament is therefore imperative. (p. 25)[17]

That statement shows that von Neumann did know about Richardson's mathematical model for the arms buildup before World War I, but publicly, as a consultant for the military and the Rand Corporation, he avoided mentioning it. Instead, he advocated a game-theory logic for the Cold War arms race. No one knows why von Neumann did this. Perhaps it was because he thought that morality and emotions had no place, whereas morality and emotions were central for Rapoport.

Nonetheless, the *appearance* of rationality and the game-theory logic of nuclear strategy was to have profound implications for Rapoport's life. Once, a Rand Corporation strategist came to the University of Michigan to give a defense of military strategic thinking in the nuclear age. Following his talk, Rapoport asked the speaker "whether he would agree to a definition of 'genocide' as a deliberate slaughter of helpless populations for political goals." He later wrote:

> I was bringing up the subject only because he himself had mentioned it in his talk. The speaker accepted my definition. I then asked him whether he realized that in view of the several precedents set at Nuremberg, Warsaw, Jerusalem, and elsewhere, genocide was a hanging offense, and, if so, how he would defend himself if at some time in the future he were a co-defendant in a genocide trial. . . . After the meeting I learned that many of my colleagues thought my questions inappropriate. The feeling was shared, I was told, by the chairman, a convinced and active pacifist. . . . I had violated the standards of academic discourse . . . questions of morality, while possibly crucially important in themselves, were altogether taboo. (p. 76)[18]

Rapoport is also rumored to have asked the Rand Corporation consultant whether they had considered all the options. The consultant said they had, and that nothing was unthinkable, even unprovoked first-strike thermonuclear war. "What about unconditional surrender?" asked Rapoport. "Now *that's* really unthinkable," the consultant was rumored to have answered.[19]

Rapoport was attacking the very assumption that game-theory "rationality" could be applied to an analysis of war. He said that he was attempting to demonstrate "the ambiguity of the very concept of rationality." "Once one starts to cast conflict situations in game-theoretic terms, one must examine the structure of non-zero-sum games," Rapoport wrote. "Since most conflict situations (including those leading to war) can be realistically modeled only in terms of games in which the interests of the players are only partially opposed, one sees how the concept of rationality inevitably splits into at least two concepts—'individual rationality' and 'collective rationality'" (p. 35). Rapoport called the refusal to step out of this dual framework "the intellectualization of war." He wrote: "To be sure my repugnance of this process stemmed from moral outrage, but my critique was constructed on the strategist's own ground" (p. 52).[20]

Rapoport was pointing out that what *appeared* to be the "hard-headed rationality" of von Neumann was actually a misapplication of the mathematics. He wrote:

> . . . the appearance of the theory of games on the intellectual horizon was enthusiastically welcomed in the defense community, and research in the field was generously funded by the U.S. military establishment. For here was a highly sophisticated treatment of "rational" conflict. However, only two-person zero-sum game models fit naturally into the "classical" framework of military thought: what one side gains, the other naturally loses. (p 104)[21]

If Kahn's estimate of 60 million dead were accurate, Rapoport asked, where is the estimate of gain? According to Rapoport, no evidence suggested that such calculations had ever been made. Rapoport's critique of Kahn's game-theory analysis of the possibility of thermonuclear war was based on the irrationality and subjectivity of the utility function (rewards and costs) from the perspective of both opponents in the conflict.

Steve Heims, one of von Neumann's biographers, also attacked the rationality of von Neumann's game theory in the international nuclear context. Heims wrote: "Von Neumann *would much rather err on the side of mistrust and suspicion* [my italics] than be caught in wishful thinking about the nature of people and society" (p. 296).[22] He pointed out that one fly in the ointment in the presumed rationality of game theory was the objective computation of the "utility functions" that formed the mathematical basis of the game-theory decision matrix. For von Neumann the dream was that a computer could rapidly make these game-theoretic decisions, that computation could eliminate philosophical and moral bases for these important life-and-death decisions between opposing nations. Heims wrote:

> . . . in game theory ends and means are neatly separated: the outcomes are judged by their desirability, while the "strategies" are judged solely by their efficaciousness in bringing about the desired ends . . . however, the separation of ends and means, of strategies and outcomes, does not permit us to characterize the sense in which game theory is related to human rationality and irrationality. . . . Rationality enters into a game through the method, not the purpose—it is only a narrow, technical, instrumental kind of rationality, which can be made to serve irrational ends. (p. 297)[23]

The von Neumann-Morgenstern equilibrium is a "cut your losses" strategy, one inspired by a negative view of how much one may trust one's opponent. This insightful critique of the rationality assumption of game theory echoed the wisdom of Blaise Pascal several centuries later.

In his discussion of his "fight mode" of conflict, Rapoport began by talking about the Richardson mathematical modeling of war. He argued that arms buildups, wars, and deadly conflicts with the potential for the escalation of extreme violence were not difficult to understand and even model mathematically with the precision Richardson had obtained with real data.

After discussing fights mathematically, Rapoport turned his attention to the study of his second mode of conflict, games. Rapoport pointed out that game theory made it possible to theoretically analyze political and economic behavior in terms of strategic patterns of interaction. As explained earlier, game theory assumed that there were two rational players of any game. The players were assumed to want to select the best combination of strategies to maximize their own payoffs and minimize their losses, or perhaps to also maximize their opponent's losses and minimize their opponent's gains. Or, depending on the arrangement of payoffs, they might choose to cooperate under some conditions and compete in others. In game theory a matrix is used to represent the two players and their strategies. The strategies of each player form the rows and columns of the matrix. In the cells of the matrix are the payoffs for each player of choosing the combined strategy. See the example in Figure 3.2.

Figure 3.2   Game-Theory Matrix

	Strategy 1: Nation B Cooperates (Capitulates)	Strategy 2: Nation B Threatens War
Strategy 1: Nation A Cooperates (Capitulates)	20, 20	0, 100
Strategy 2: Nation A Threatens War	100, 0	–10, –10

In this game-theory matrix, the payoffs for Nation A come first and the payoffs for Nation B come second. Mutual cooperation wins a smaller number of points for each country. If country A threatens and country B cooperates, then country A wins 100 points while country B gets zero points. Conversely, if country B threatens and country A cooperates, then country B wins 100 points while country A gets zero points. If they both threaten war, they both stand to lose 10 points. Game theory tries to use this matrix to predict the likely outcomes of the conflict, and to ask what arrangement of payoffs might facilitate any of the four outcomes. We will have occasion to study this game theory matrix again as the Prisoner's Dilemma.

Von Neumann saw the Cold War as a zero-sum game. In a zero-sum game, the payoffs of the two players in each cell of the matrix add up to a constant of zero, so it is necessary to write only one number in each cell; the other number is automatically determined by the game being zero-sum. Von Neumann believed either Russia or the U.S. would survive, and he dedicated his energy to seeing to it that the U.S. came out the survivor. Although he thought that only the U.S. had atomic weapons, he was an avid supporter of a surprise atomic attack on the Soviet Union, dubbed euphemistically as "preventive war."

However, in September 1949 the U.S. detected that the Soviet Union had exploded an atomic bomb of its own. Later one of the scientists at the Los Alamos Manhattan Project, a physicist named Klaus Fuchs, was arrested in London as a Soviet spy. Fuchs knew everything that the U.S. then knew about nuclear weapons. Four days after his arrest, President Truman initiated an accelerated program to build a hydrogen bomb. Fuchs was eventually turned over to East Germany and became a physicist at an institute near Dresden. Von Neumann then wrote that he thought that there now should no longer be any hesitation on building the H-bomb. An obituary for von Neumann in *Life* magazine quoted him as saying, "With the Russians it is not a question of whether but of when."[24] A hard-boiled strategist, von Neumann was one of the few scientists to advocate preventive war, and in 1950 he remarked: "If you say why not bomb them tomorrow, I say why not today? If you say today at 5 o'clock, I say why not one o'clock?" (p 247).[25]

The Mathematics of Cooperation

In stark contrast to von Neumann, Rapoport's life work attempted to increase the American understanding of the Russian mind and Russian understanding of the American mind. In his book he wrote two chapters on "the case for collectivism," and "the case for individualism." His goal was to move the Cold War away from the conflict mode of a fight, which could potentially end the world, and also away from the status of a game, which had the potential to erupt into fights because of brinksmanship like the 1960 Cuban Missile Crisis. Rapoport wanted international relations to be elevated to the mode of *debate*, where persuasion was possible for resolving conflicts.

As noted earlier, a great deal of Rapoport's research centered on a game called "Prisoner's Dilemma."[26] That game was invented in 1949 by Merrill Flood of the Rand Corporation and later popularized by A.W. Tucker. It is a game in which we imagine that two people are apprehended by the police and charged with the same crime. The police do not have enough evidence to convict them, so they separate the prisoners. They can be convicted only if either one of them, or both, confess. Figure 3.3 shows a matrix of this game. The upper left cell of the matrix shows what happens if neither prisoner confesses. In this case they both receive a payoff of +1, which means they both get a light sentence. If one prisoner confesses, he is let go and turns state's evidence, but the other prisoner gets a more severe sentence, so the payoff for the prisoner who confesses is +2, and for the prisoner who does not confess is –2. The –2 means that the sentence received by the nonconfessing prisoner is twice as severe as if neither confesses; the +2 means that the confessing prisoner gets an even lighter sentence than if they both fail to confess. If they both confess, they receive the sentence for their crime, payoffs denoted by –1.

Figure 3.3   Prisoner's Dilemma Matrix

	Strategy 1: Prisoner B Doesn't Confess	Strategy 2: Prisoner B Confesses
Strategy 1: Prisoner A Doesn't Confess	1, 1	–2, +2
Strategy 2: Prisoner A Confesses	+2, –2	–1, –1

It is in the best self-interest of each of them to confess, but it is in their collective interest to hold out and not confess. That's the dilemma. Prisoner's Dilemma attracted great interest from social psychologists because it could be used to represent the general conflict between one's own interests and the collective good. In many Prisoner's Dilemma experiments, the experimenter controlled the payoffs and asked under what conditions people would be more likely to confess (self-interest) or not (cooperation). Rapoport and Chammah's 1965 book, *Prisoner's Dilemma: A Study in Conflict and Cooperation*, reported the results of experiments in which people played the Prisoner's Dilemma game hundreds of times with the same partner. Amazingly, Rapoport discovered that most people eventually adopted a mutually cooperative strategy over time. Over time trust develops. In his 2007 book *The Neuroscience of Fair Play: Why We (Usually) Follow the Golden Rule*, Donald Pfaff described how the ethics of cooperation may be wired into the human brain in mirror neurons that may be the basis for the evolution of empathy.[28]

In 1984 Robert Axelrod reported the results of a computer simulation using Prisoner's Dilemma in which game theorists submitted computerized strategies designed to maximize a player's earnings. Rapoport submitted a strategy he called "Tit-for-Tat." In that strategy no matter what Player A does, the first move of Player B is to cooperate (not confess or defect). Thereafter Player B mirrors Player A's move. So in Tit-for-Tat Player B makes an initial move toward cooperation. If Player A confesses, then in the next move Player B confesses. Among all the strategies submitted, Tit-for-Tat did the best. This was a complete surprise in this literature, and mathematicians love surprises.

Applying Game Theory to Rapoport's Debate Mode of Conflict

Rapoport actually never applied game theory to his third mode of conflict, the "debate" mode. Yet that's precisely the situation I am most interested in, because in arguments couples are trying to persuade each other. Rapoport thought he saw in Prisoner's Dilemma the potential for games transmuting into the laws for establishing cooperation over self-interest in the game mode of conflict. His interest was always fixed in international relations and he saw the Prisoner's Dilemma as a perfect example of the fundamental problem in international relations: when to operate in one's own self-interest and when to cooperate.

In actual application, game theory was never applied to any study of real-life conflict in couple relationships. So ultimately game theory failed as an analysis of real human conflict in couple relationships. It stayed with the paradigm of selected games. Part of the reason for the ultimate failure of game theory is that in any game more complex than Tic-Tac-Toe, the number of alternatives (rows and columns) rapidly becomes astronomical. No computer von Neumann designed was large enough to analyze even the simplest of parlor-game-theory situations. The Rand Corporation experiment with game theory for international political and military strategy turned out to be a failure. Game theory was largely abandoned as a scientific study for insight into conflict, military strategy, diplomacy, or international relations.

However, with our extension of game theory to the debate mode, we are ready to tackle the definition of trustworthiness in the debate mode.

The Mathematics of Untrustworthiness in Any Interaction

Just as we are able to quantify the mathematics of trust in any interaction, we can also quantify the mathematics of untrustworthiness in any interaction using the same game-theory matrices. The principle is as follows:

The ideal fertile ground for untrustworthiness occurs when people act for their own self-interest (or payoffs), independent of their partner's interests (payoffs).

This is merely an assessment of untrustworthiness, or self-interest behavior and thinking. Now we will focus on this idea to create a behavioral definition of the metric of untrustworthiness.

Her Index of His Untrustworthiness. She believes that he can be counted on to (and will) look out for his own interests, without regard for her interests, by changing his behavior to increase his own payoffs.

His Index of Her Untrustworthiness. He believes that she can be counted on to (and will) look out for her own interests, without regard for his interests, by changing her behavior to increase her payoffs.

(See the appendix for a translation of untrustworthiness from "everyday language" into the language of mathematics.)

Validity of the Metric for Untrustworthiness During Conflict

Just as we had to empirically validate the trust metric, we also have to empirically validate the metric of untrustworthiness. I computed these metrics during couples' conflict interactions by examining how much one's partner was behaving to maximize his or her own payoffs. That might or might not be an index of interest. That's why again I need to validate that index.

In fact, when I go back to the lab to test the untrustworthiness metric,

I find that for high husband untrustworthiness, she reports significantly more abuse, degradation, sexual abuse, and total physical violence by the husband on the Strauss Conflict Tactics Scale. With her high untrustworthiness of him, she has significantly more thoughts of divorce and separation on the Weiss Cerreto Marital Status Inventory, there is significantly less husband attunement based on our coding of interviews with both the husband and wife, and there is significantly more positive affect during conflict. That latter finding was a bit of a surprise, but we have often observed that in volatile relationships there is a lot of positive as well as negative affect during conflict.

Using our mathematical modeling of couples' conflict interaction (see Chapter 11) for high wife untrustworthiness, we find greater wife negativity when she starts the conflict (uninfluenced negativity) and greater influence on him with negative affect (negative slope). On our oral history interview the couple expresses significantly less sense that conflict is worth it, less sense of purpose in their struggles as a couple, significantly less wife vagal tone during conflict (measured by the eyes closed interbeat interval standard deviation), significantly higher wife heart rate during conflict, and significantly less husband skin conductance during the eyes closed baseline. That physiological pattern suggests that when the wife is untrustworthy, the husband is relaxed during conflict, but that she is far from relaxed. Is he more comfortable with her self-interest than she is? From these data, in general we can conclude that there is sufficient evidence to suggest that the untrustworthiness metric has validity.

Trust and Untrustworthiness Metrics are Independent

It is interesting to note that empirically the trust and untrustworthiness metrics are statistically independent. That means that any combination of trust and untrustworthiness metrics are statistically permissible. The implications are that, for example, it is possible to have a high-trust and high untrustworthiness relationship. What would such a relationship be like?

I predicted that in such a relationship there would be a great deal of volatility around trust and betrayal, perhaps related to jealousy. I was totally wrong. In fact, when I compared high-trust and low-untrustworthiness relationships to high-trust and high-untrustworthiness relationships, the high-trust and high-untrustworthiness relationships were indeed different, but in a surprising way. They were characterized by being *newer* relationships, with more tension during conflict and a lower tolerance for nastiness, particularly a lower tolerance by the wife for her husband's nastiness—she was more likely to retaliate in response to his nastiness than in high-trust and high-trustworthiness relationships.

These high-trust and high-untrustworthiness relationship couples appeared to be in the process of testing whether there would be no betrayal, but they weren't there yet. I was surprised that there was no evidence of issues of jealousy in these high-trust and high-untrustworthiness relationships.

The Seattle Newlywed Study

These surprising findings led me to return to our longitudinal study of 130 newlywed couples in Seattle, conducted in the 1990s. In going back to our study of these newlyweds, I was amazed to discover that almost all of the conflict discussions were about establishing trust in different aspects of the relationship.

Couples appeared to be discussing issues like: "Can I trust you to chose me over your friends when I need you?" "Can I trust you to be there for me when I am upset?" "Can I trust you to help with the housework?" "Can I trust you to back me up even if it's against your mother?" "Can I trust you to keep your promises?" "Can I trust you to not lie to me?" "Can I trust you to be sexually faithful?" And so on. I had never noticed before that almost *all* of these conflict discussions cycled through a large number of "if . . . then" contexts for testing trust. I believe that for many couples these arguments (and not the wedding ceremony) provided the foundation for trust and for real commitment.

Trust and untrustworthiness metrics appear to be the substance of conflict in newer relationships.

The Metric of Betrayal: Indexing the
Zero-Sum Game in Any Interaction

The only business left is to find a metric of betrayal. A metric of betrayal is easily obtained by mathematically computing the correlation of the rating dial time series. Here's the logic. If the payoffs of partners are negatively correlated, then the interaction is like a zero-sum game. This is a veritable definition of a betrayal metric, because what he does in his self-interest implies an equal *cost* to his partner, and vice versa. I suggest that betrayal in any interaction occurs when this self-interest *is at the partner's cost*—that is, when the interaction resembles a zero-sum game. Although the metric for untrustworthiness meant that one's partner is looking out for his or her own interests and changing behavior with the goal of increasing *his* or *her* payoffs, that is not the same as real betrayal.

Hence, for real betrayal we need to look to the zero-sum game metric. If our partner is acting so that his or her gain is our loss, and vice versa, then I would argue that the untrustworthiness metric graduates to an actual betrayal metric. This actual betrayal metric is easily quantified mathematically as a negative cross-correlation between the partners' rating-dial payoffs over time. That metric was significantly related to the nasty-nasty cell of the conflict discussion becoming an absorbing state that is easy to enter and difficult to exit. It was also related to the husband having significantly more negative payoff in the nice-nice and neutral-neutral cells of the matrix.

I will illustrate what I mean by examining two contrasting conflict conversations. The first couple (#438) was extremely low in trust, and high on untrustworthiness and the betrayal metric. Their interaction was a true zero-sum game. Their marital satisfaction was extremely low (42.75), three and a half standard deviations below the population mean of 100. Their rating-dial graphs are represented in Figure 3.4. Notice that the two rating-dial curves are oppositely sloped for this couple, indicative of a pure zero-sum game. Their total payoff over time is essentially a constant. Also notice that their conflict conversation (which follows) centers on their low trust of each other, particularly the wife's low trust of her husband. She immediately began the conversation by explaining why she doesn't trust him and why she thinks he is totally unfair.

Here is part of their conflict discussion:

W: Okay, ah—I want you to try to understand why I feel the way I do, because evidently you don't. It's not so much as what you did. To me it is what you did without involving me. Now we gotta go back to the beginning. You know that you had your money and I had mine.

Rating Dial

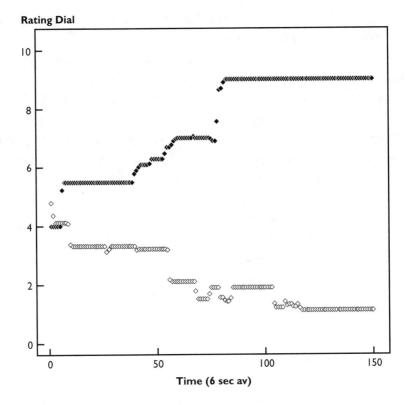

Time (6 sec av)

Figure 3.4   Rating Dial Data Over Time, Duo-Old Couple #438

You also know that when you purchased this home, it was *my* money that put the down payment on this home.

H: (*sighs*)

W: We also know that the improvement that was done on this home—like building a room and another bath—it was *my* money who did that. You also know that—the furniture and everything else in the house—it was *my* money who did that. But when it got time for *you* to pay the bill on the house, what was it—a hundred and seventy-seven dollars a month?—somehow or another, you let get that out of hand and you refinanced the house so many times without my knowledge until it was impossible to save it. That is what bothered me. The idea of you not even coming to me to see if there was some way *we* could get out of this mess before we didn't have anything, and that's what it had come to.

And that's the reason I am so angry. I feel like I wasn't even a part of it when it came to that part, and it shouldn't have been like that. . . . It . . . wasn't togetherness—I mean we, we could have done anything together! But you didn't—I just can't figure out how it ever got in that situation. I'll never be able to figure it out. Because your responsibility for a house note just shouldn't have gotten us into the fix that we're in today. I know what you're doing with your money, now, but I didn't know then. Now you're struggling trying to pay a nine-hundred-dollar house note every month. When the house should be paid for, and we should be paying only a hundred dollars a month. *That's* my problem. If you can tell me why I should be able to understand. . . .

The longstanding betrayal she feels had to do with the finances. It's an old story.

H: (*deep sigh*)

W: . . . why all of this happened, then help me to understand it.

H: Ah . . . you won't—you know, we've been over this before, and you don't believe me.

W: But I don't—I don't unders—I don't understand what it is to believe. What is it to believe?

H: Y-y-l-leave it the way—okay.

W: Try to make me believe it.

She is belligerently daring him to explain his betrayal.

H: All right, I'm gonna try to make you believe it.

W: Okay.

H: (*swallows*) And follow me all the way. . . . The big problem started . . . just before Richard got out of the Navy. Somehow or another, now I'm talking about the early 70s. Now you have to follow me all the way back. And I'm—I'm gonna say things to see if I can make you remember. (*swallows, small sigh*) The first thing—when I realized I didn't have any credit, was—when we tried to get Frank's car.

W: What does credit have to do with any of this?

H: If I had had credit, I wouldn't have had to go to people like—the people that's been ri-ri, that been ripping me off. See, I had to go to these people, because I missed the house note.

W: Yeah, but *why?*

She is never going to believe that the financial problems are not his fault.

H: I missed the house note because I didn't ah . . . ah . . . I didn't— first place about it—I always felt that I could make it up the next month. And I—we needed the money.

W: For what? For what purpose did we need the money?

He has no remorse. Instead he becomes defensive.

H: We needed the money! We needed . . . the money!

W: No, no! I want to know for what purpose now, 'cause I was scrambling everything, the only thing you ever had to—

H: We needed the money to live on now. That's all I can tell you. Now, you—you can't expect me to keep a computer in my head.

W: You only had a house note and you took—

H: You can't tell me what I only had.

W: Oh, I mean for the house that's all you had.

H: No! You can't tell—well, now you don't try and insinuate that I had anything else!

The conflict escalates as he feels attacked and accused. She is looking for remorse.

W: I'm not insinuating anything.

H: 'Cause you only had one family.

W: I do know that in that household, and all those children.

H: Okay, I'll tell you what I'll do—I got every check stub that I ever drew and—

W: You're playing games—

An interesting choice of phrase, suggesting she doesn't believe him at all.

H: No, I'm not—

W: Now, we're here for real. Come on, now, come on! You had no . . .

H: I don't know what else I can say.

W: . . . responsibility but the house—

She knows that he has no excuse for what he did.

H: No. You—you're not gonna make me feel . . .

W: Okay.

H: . . . I'm not gonna a-agree to that.

Clearly this couple was stuck in the absorbing nasty-nasty cell of conflict. The major content of their discussion is about *her* loss of trust in
him. In fact, the probability of them being in the nasty-nasty cell in this
conversation was an enormous 0.88, which means 88% of the time. The
probability of them being in the neutral-neutral cell was 0.01, or 1% of
the time. The probability of them being in the nice-nice cell was 0.00,
or 0% of the time. They have hit rock bottom.

Now let's look at the second couple (#458). This couple had a high-
trust, low-betrayal metric. Their marital satisfaction was 160.0, four
standard deviations *above* the mean of 100. Figure 3.5 illustrates their
rating dial curves, which move in synch. This is a highly cooperative
interaction pattern.

Following is an excerpt from couple 458's conflict discussion. They

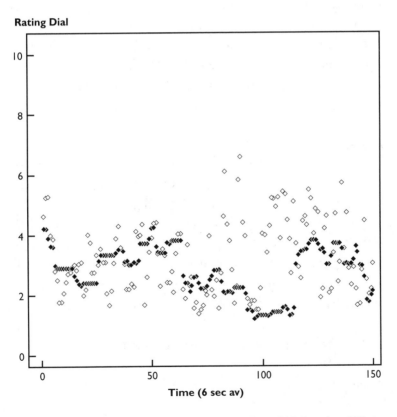

Figure 3.5   Rating Dial Data Over Time, Duo-Old Couple #458

are dealing with what many aging couples find to be a tough issue—his getting a hearing aid. They raise this issue and discuss it sensitively, with humor and laughter sprinkled in. The discussion illustrates how much they trust one another, how much their affect is not negative, and instead how generally neutral they are to each other. As we have seen, neutral interaction during conflict is a strength. This is a cooperative, not zero-sum, game.

She begins gently bringing up the issue of his hearing loss.

W: Well, for the most part, we don't do this in the family, either. We don't jump in, but, ah, there are times, and . . . and I . . . I will say that in our recent experience in Alexandria, that we were referring to earlier, where, where you were putting your hand up to stop me from talking, ah, one of the reasons and I know it—I remember it well— is that you were asking things that had been answered earlier and because you were having trouble with your hearing, I felt you weren't hearing, and so I was repeating what had been said instead of letting them say it. I shouldn't have—I should have let them say it. But there were things that you hadn't heard, and maybe you were reading . . .

H: Uh-huh.

W: . . . and didn't notice they'd been discussed in that room that we were in, the living room. And this didn't have a—

H: Well, th-the reason I was pursuing it because I th—I was hearing something different from Scott than what you were saying. And I'm not sure you were right. Sometimes you were, and then sometimes you weren't. And—and it was Scott that was laying out the plans and so . . .

He is a bit defensive, and he's minimizing the hearing loss.

W: Um-hmm.

H: . . . I, I wanted to hear it directly from him.

W: Yeah, so—

H: And, and I recognize with my hearing problem, w-we frequently run into it in restaurants, and you, you have to . . . ah . . . I can't use the word "translate," but you have to tell me what the waitress said, because I have a hard time with the higher frequencies. And, and I appreciate your helping me out of that, and, and I don't—

Even in minimizing his hearing loss, he still expresses appreciation to his wife.

W: Yeah.

H: 'Til I get a hearing aid, I'm, I'm not gonna get around that one. An-and so that doesn't bother me. I don't let my ego get in the way of that. B-but—but answering for somebody else, as I explained the other day when, when we were discussing it, after we got home, I really think that a person does that because they want to either overtly or inadvertently—I'm not sure those are opposites—any-how, I—and show off that they know the answer. And when I related the other day that I'd hit a situation, I believe it was at work, where I thought I knew the—knew it, and I—I could have shown off that I knew the answer, but—the instructor was there—oh, it was on that new printer that we got—and one of the other guys being taught asked a question and I knew the answer to it. And I just about spoke up and then I bit my tongue. Well, we got an instructor up there to answer it, not me. And if I answer it, all I'm doing is showing off that I know the answer. I'm not helping the group one iota. All I'm doing is disrupting the group, as a matter of fact, 'cause I'm throwing the instructor off, and there's a chance that I'll, I'll answer wrong. So I, I answer for other p—other people at times, but I try not to, 'cause I don't think that it's the right thing to do. Now sometimes, things have to be interpreted. Almost all of us at times have trouble communicating. You hear two people talk, an-and they aren't getting through to each other. And a third party is hearing both sides, understands both sides, and can explain—either side—and in that case, I think it's very proper for a third person to jump in. There may be some social situations where it would be bad, but (*clears throat*) gets the thing off dead center and gets the two communicating at the same wavelength.

He is starting to admit and to recognize that he needs a hearing aid. She is being very gentle with him, but also firm.

W: That—that brings in another aspect of this is that for many years, I as the mother, you know, of our family have been an interpreter [for you]. (*laughs*)

H: (*laughs*) Yes, you have.

W: And, as a former teacher, too, I-I've—you have told me you think I understand what's going on and what people are saying a lot, and I think it's encouraged me to do that, and I'm trying now in these years. . . .

H: Um-hmm.

W: . . . more recently, to back away, and I'm telling family members—they'll say would you let so and so know—and I'll say, you can let him know. You can phone him and let him know, too. I, I'm trying not to be the, the matriarchal interface for everything, and this, this stood I think, because I was, ah, close with the children—my orientation, ah, was in communications, and I think that it just seemed like a natural thing for family.

In her role as "communications expert" she confronts him, very gently.

H: Well, and you're a role model! (*clears throat*) Your mother loves that role of, of, of being i-i-like a-an octopus at all the parts of the computer system. Where you got—where you got the mother—I mean, the main frame an-an-an-and you have all the ah-slaves ah-terminals outside, and everything has to go through the main frame. You-your mother loves that particular thing. She-she takes great joy in it, and-and she does it, I'd say, as much as physically possible. But she just loves to do what y-what you're describing that you don't want to do. Sh-she loves to convey a message from A to B, by people having to go through her—rather than going directly from A to B.

W: I think when the children were tiny, ah, it made sense that I would—I would need to let you know, 'cause th-they were shy of you. It went through me to you then.

H: Oh.

W: Ah, when they were little. An-and I would try to encourage them to talk to you about things. Let's, let's say, well, they'd say you "Tell Daddy," and I'd say, "You tell Daddy." And—often they didn't do that. And I think that, that was—and you didn't feel as comfortable with little children. You'd tell people when they get old enough . . .

Again, she minimizes the issue, explaining she's been playing this role forever. He accepts that.

H: (*laughs*)

W: . . . to reason with . . . (*laughs*)

H: Yes.

W: . . . and, and that you'd feel comfortable, and that meant when they were, like in junior high school—

H: Yeah, then, how do you reason with a teenager? (*laughs*)

W: (*chuckling*) And, and I know that—I think our daughter, you've— h-had even more trouble when she got older, 'cause she was usually more difficult for you to—

H: Yeah.

There was a great deal of gentleness, intimacy, and trust in this conversation, even over the delicate subject of his needing a hearing aid. In fact, the probability of them being in the nasty-nasty cell was a very small number: 0.03, or just 3% of the time. The probability of them being in the neutral-neutral cell was 0.62, or 62% of the time. The probability of them being in the nice-nice cell was 0.02, or 2% of the time. You will recall that the neutral-neutral cell is a very useful one and entirely rational.

The examples of these two conversations were quite general. What do these results mean? They mean that for unhappy couples the nasty-nasty absorbing state is not just an absorbing state and a state of low trust but also *an index of betrayal*, because for unhappy couples the nasty-nasty absorbing state interaction has suddenly turned into a zero-sum game. People are no longer looking out for their partner's interests, or looking out for their own interests, but for their own *instead of* their partner's interests. Trust has not only suddenly evaporated but also been replaced by betrayal. One's ally and friend has turned into one's adversary. Our partner is out to beat us, and we are out to beat our partner. The conflict discussion has become a fight to the finish. No wonder it causes so much pain for unhappy couples. No wonder the nasty-nasty state is a quick-sand bog absorbing state. We have now learned that it is like entering a fight-to-the-finish war zone. In Chapter 4, I will present new data that show that the betrayal metric has validity in predicting the early death of husbands.

Chapter 4

The Physiology of
Trust and Betrayal

Betrayal, low trust, and the negative absorbing state in conflict have very clear physiological implications for happiness, health, recovery from disease, and longevity. This chapter reviews research on the physiology of trust and betrayal and proposes mechanisms that attempt to explain these powerful effects.

What Else Explains the Nasty-Nasty Interaction Becoming an Absorbing State?

We still have a bit of a mystery on our hands. What else could possibly explain these irrational differences in payoff and frequency in the nasty-nasty cell of the game-theory matrix for unhappy couples? So far we know that nasty-nasty interaction becomes an absorbing state for unhappy couples. We now also know that this is a state that resembles a zero-sum game, where trust is low and betrayal has replaced untrustworthiness. But what else is going on that explains why this nasty-nasty cell is an absorbing state?

What is happening in the minds of each person in an unhappy relationship? In a study conducted in my laboratory in Seattle, we very carefully measured a number of things about the everyday emotional experience of couples. One thing we measured was how emotionally "flooded" couples were during conflict. Flooding is an idea originally suggested by my friend Paul Ekman, the man who, with Wallace Friesen, conducted groundbreaking research in studying emotion in the human face.[1] What Ekman meant by "flooding" is the emotional equivalent of what happened to some people in New Orleans when Hurricane Katrina struck: They felt safe in their homes even when water slowly started seeping in. There was National Public Radio report of one New Orleans sheriff who reassured his wife that everything would be okay. People didn't initially panic. They didn't panic until the waters reached a suddenly terrifying threshold. Then they finally realized they weren't even safe in their own home. Eventually many were outside swimming for their lives, separated from their loved ones, fearing that they had been lost and that they might die in the flood.

Something like this sense of being overwhelmed and unsafe happens to people in the face of strong negative emotion in reciprocally nasty-nasty escalating exchanges when they become an absorbing state. They are in a psychological state of insecurity. They are feeling flooded and there is no escape.

We measured flooding using a questionnaire I invented that measures the extent to which people feel overwhelmed emotionally by their conflicts with their partner. It basically assesses the perceived threat value of the conflict for each person.

That perceived threat value tends to be related, but is not always reliably related, to the measures of peripheral autonomic physiology that we gather in our lab. Our species has evolved a physiological defense response that Hans Selye called the "general alarm response."[2] This response takes over when we perceive danger. Flooding is an even more sensitive measure than our physiological measures that the general alarm system has been triggered. Flooding measures the extent to which people's defenses are up when they fight. If unhappy couples were significantly more flooded than happy couples, it would explain why the nasty-nasty interaction was an absorbing state for unhappy couples. When people are threatened, they operate in the ultimate stage of self-interest. Their interest becomes self-preservation. It doesn't seem to matter that they are in a comfortable lab sitting down talking to their partner. There are no predators about to kill and eat them. Still, the alarm has gone off and there might as well be a tiger about to leap at their jugular. Heart rates go up in our lab to as high as 168 beats a minute.

Indeed, Tara Mahdyastha and I discovered that the more flooded people were, the more often they did these nasty-nasty interchanges, and also the more negatively they rated them. That meant that flooding was correlated with nasty-nasty exchanges, potentially transforming them into an absorbing state. What that meant was that when people became flooded, once they passed a critical threshold, dysregulated negative emotions intervened to cause the absorbing state—the irrational game-theory behavior of these couples in the nasty-nasty cell of the game-theory matrix.

That finding gave us a very important clue. It suggested that if we were to understand actual conflict interaction in unhappy relationships, we also needed to study the emotional worlds of these couples. We thus conclude that in our findings of the limits of rational game theory, in the cell where during actual conflict unhappy people couldn't act rationally, they were flooded by the intensity of the negative nasty-nasty emotions. That explains the higher payoffs for happy couples in that cell: They were less flooded than the unhappy couples. This is the kind of "logic to the emotions" that Pascal may have been talking about, even if at first, from a game-theoretic perspective, things do not appear to be logical at all.

Not All Nasty Interaction Is Equally Nasty

We know from our previous research that some nasty interactions are more toxic than others. One thing we learned about predicting divorce is that we can do it effectively with about 85% accuracy in a discriminant function analysis. There were four SPAFF-coded nasty behaviors often present during conflict that dramatically escalated the nature of the conflict. Our consistent finding is that unhappy couples do these four things more than happy couples. These are the "four horsemen of the apocalypse"—criticism, defensiveness, contempt, and stonewalling.[3] Here are their definitions:

- *Criticism.* A person using criticism is suggesting that the conflict issue is caused by a personality flaw in the partner. A global attack will do for criticism—for example, "This problem would never happen if you weren't so selfish." The "selfish" attribution is usually the first attribution made in unhappy relationships, and it has been observed repeatedly in many laboratories. Notice that the word "selfish" suggests a violation of trust in exactly the way we have defined the trust metric. Blaming one's partner for the problem is one example of criticism. Criticism is a type of complaining that is designed as a global attack on the partner's personality. Criticism is not necessarily about being global. A long list of very specific complaints will appear global, so people shouldn't save up those requests. Complaints that begin with "you always" or "you never" are criticisms. So are questions that are rhetorical accusations of negative motive, such as "Why don't you care about me?" or "Why can't you be nice to me?" or "What is wrong with you?" "Why" questions are usually taken as criticism, even if they aren't intended that way. The complaint has direct implications that there is something wrong with the partner's character. Criticisms are most harmful at the start of an interaction. Women in heterosexual relationships characteristically exceed men in this behavior. We have found that the way a discussion begins in the first 3 minutes determines the remainder of the discussion in 96% of cases. Criticisms are usually a part of what we call "harsh startup."

- *Defensiveness.* Defensiveness is defending one's own innocence, warding off a perceived attack, meeting an attack with a counterattack (a righteous stance of indignation), or whining (an innocent-victim stance). There are many ways to do this, such as denying responsibility for a problem (it is all the partner's fault), cross-complaining, or whining. The denial of responsibility fuels the escalation of conflict, probably because it suggests one's partner is totally at fault for the issue.

- *Contempt.* Contempt is typically a statement made to put one's partner down by taking a superior higher plane than one's partner, like maintaining the high moral ground. It usually arises from sense that one is better than one's partner on any dimension, such as neatness or punctuality. People are very creative with contempt and snobbery; the usual method is an insult or calling one's partner an unflattering name (for example, "you're a jerk"). One of my favorites is interrupting to correct someone's grammar when that person is angry with you. Ekman and Friesen have identified a cross-culturally universal facial expression of contempt called "the dimpler," which results from the unilateral action of the left buccinator muscle that pulls the left lip corner aside laterally and creates an unflattering dimple on the left side of the face. Contempt may be accompanied by belligerence, which is a provocative form of anger.

- *Stonewalling.* Stonewalling is the listener's withdrawal from interaction. The listener does not give the speaker the usual listener-tracking cues (eye contact, open body, head nods, brief vocalizations), or move the face, or look continuously at the speaking partner (the listener may use brief "monitoring" gazes). In heterosexual relationships men exceed women in this behavior. This behavior indexes emotional withdrawal.

Are these differences in nasty-nasty behavior between happy and unhappy couples enough to cause the differences between these two groups of couples in flooding? We believe that the evidence suggests they are. Contempt is our single best predictor of divorce. We also found that a husband's contempt predicts the number of a wife's infectious illnesses in the next 4 years. It is interesting to note that the frequency of contempt among happy couples is nearly zero.[4]

Perhaps we now have another way to interpret our finding that only unhappy couples' conflict is illogical in nasty-nasty interaction. That interpretation is that happy couples were not as nasty to each other because they were far less flooded than unhappy couples. This was particularly true for men.

Flooding and Physiology

One stable finding about flooding that replicates across studies is that in heterosexual relationships men are reliably more flooded than women. We discovered that both unhappy men and women in the nasty-nasty cell were more physiologically aroused than happy couples in these same nasty-nasty exchanges. Particularly, we find that unhappier husbands have higher skin conductance than happy husbands. That means that they are sweating (from their psychologically sensitive eccrine sweat glands) more during conflict than happy husbands.

In one study that Robert Levenson and I conducted, we found that physiological arousal was able to almost perfectly predict declines in marital satisfaction over a 3-year period, while a calmer physiology during conflict predicted increases in marital satisfaction. That relationship held regardless of the initial level of marital satisfaction of the couple.[5]

This raises the question of whether this relationship between physiology and marital happiness is just correlational or also causal. The real question is: Can we change interaction during conflict simply by changing physiology? We got the answer to this question in a recent experiment we conducted for a dissertation done in our lab by Amber Tabares.[6] We asked couples to stop their arguments and take a break. They then did one of two simple psychological exercises, or they simply read magazines for half an hour. Then they resumed their conflict discussion. We looked at the couples who were able to lower their heart rates during any of the three break conditions, and we compared the beginning of the second conversation for those who had significantly lowered their heart rate to that for people whose heart rate hadn't significantly dropped. What we were interested in was whether the lowered heart rate would make a difference in the conflict interaction once the couple started talking again.

The answer turned out to be a qualified "yes." Reducing heart rate changed the interaction, but it did so only for men. In the second conflict discussion, those men who had effectively lowered their heart rates were far lower in using the four horsemen in the continuation of their conflict discussion, and so were their wives. But in that study reducing women's heart rates was not associated with women using the four horsemen less.

That difference between men and women in heterosexual relationships is a puzzle. It is reminiscent of a finding that Lowell Krokoff and I once reported that being agreeable was associated with increasing marital satisfaction over a number of years, but only for men.[7] We speculated that being agreeable for women was not a good thing for the long-term happiness of the relationship. Agreeability for women is all about compliance, whereas agreeability for men is associated with being nice and sharing power. We also reported that anger expressed by women during conflict was associated with greater marital unhappiness of the couple at the time, but with greater marital happiness of the couple years in the future. We are clearly living through a time when women's assertiveness in a conflict discussion is not a bad thing at all, and men have to learn how to deal with this fact.

The Antidote for Flooding

Flooding impairs our access to important social processes like our sense of humor, creativity, creative problem-solving, empathy, and nondefensive listening. So, what's the cure for flooding? There are two possible cures. Self-soothing is one. The other is what University of Virginia psychologist Jim Coan calls "co-regulation." Co-regulation is when our partner helps soothe us. When our defensive fear-based system takes over, we often lose the ability to down-regulate our own physiological arousal. Psychiatrist Daniel Siegel calls this "flipping our lids,"[8] because the frontal cortex (our brain's "lid") has relinquished its ability to control our limbic alarm physiology. Coan thinks that when we flip our lids, the most efficient soothing we can get is by in effect borrowing our partner's cerebral cortex. We need to feel safe enough to allow our partner to do the soothing that we are incapable of at the moment.

We now know that taking breaks and creating a way of saying, "Stop, I'm flooded," is very important for couples. Nothing else will do. Couples who are in a nasty-nasty interchange have to stop talking immediately when one person claims to be flooded and asks for a break. In my clinical practice I see couples who can't do this because they have to finish what they are saying before they can leave. But then the other person has to respond to that last statement, and they never take the break. Taking the break once one person is flooded is crucial. Neil Jacobson and I discovered that physically violent couples had no ritual for withdrawing from conflict when one of them was flooded.[9] Often the break seemed like abandonment to one or both of them, so they stayed with each other, interminably arguing while flooded, a context that is a high risk for violence.

But it's not enough to just take a break—it has to be a certain kind of break. The break must be at least 20 minutes long because the major sympathetic neurotransmitters epinephrine and norepinephrine don't have enzymes to degrade them (as opposed to the neurotransmitter acetylcholine, which is the parasympathetic nervous system's major neurotransmitter) so they have to be diffused through blood; this takes 3 minutes or more in the cardiovascular system (for myocardial contractility and sympathetic nervous system increases in rate). Because of the slow decay of these sympathetic neurotransmitters (e.g., adrenaline), we think that a good break must be at least 20 minutes long.

Also, it cannot be a break that gives people time to rehearse "distress maintaining" thoughts like, "I don't have to take this" or "I'm going to get even." It must be truly relaxing, like a pleasant walk around the block. That's not an easy thing to accomplish.

Also the break cannot be an excuse to avoid talking. People need to set a time to get back together again and continue talking, like making an appointment to talk again when they are both calmer. They need to schedule a precise time to get together again so the request for a break doesn't seem like an excuse for avoiding the issue or avoiding the partner.

So what was happening for those men who couldn't lower their heart rates when they read magazines between the two conflict conversations? It turns out that a physiological variable called "vagal tone" is the key to self-soothing. Vagal tone is an important concept in physiology. The vagus is the tenth cranial nerve. It is the largest nerve in our body. Its name comes from the Latin for vagabond. It innervates a great deal of smooth muscle, including the heart, gut, and lungs. Vagal tone is a variable that anesthesiologists monitor when you're having surgery to make sure you're doing okay. The "tone," or tonic firing, of the vagus nerve is what is being measured. Vagal tone measures how active the largest nerve in our body is. Its major role is calming things down in the body, slowing the heart, speeding digestion, and restoring calm after we have had to mobilize energy for emergencies. Vagal tone is not genetic; it's something that we can build, somewhat like muscle tone. It is effectively built with biofeedback about heart rate variability.

One established way of measuring vagal tone is to examine the variability in heart period—that is, the time between heartbeats. There is a respiratory rhythm in the heart period, because the time between heartbeats decreases when we inhale and increases when we exhale. My colleague

Steve Porges has shown that it is possible to compute "how much" power this respiratory rhythm has by computing a function called the "spectral density" of the heart period time series. That power is a measure of vagal tone. It also turns out that there is evidence that the amount of power in rhythms below the respiratory range is a measure of sympathetic nervous system drive to the heart.[10] A company called "HeartMath" makes a small device called an "emWave." About the size of a cell phone, it gives feedback about heart-rate variability. Another company makes a similar device called "Respirate." Its continual use for at least 6 months has been shown to significantly reduce systolic and diastolic blood pressure (an average of 15 points for systolic blood pressure and 10 points for diastolic blood pressure). I use these devices with my clients to help them build vagal tone.[11] We are now doing research with the emWave device, testing whether it helps change the nature of flooding during conflict and helps control low levels of symmetrical domestic violence.

I already referred to a study that Robert Levenson and I conducted when we first studied physiology during conflict discussion with 30 couples. We found that we predict with high accuracy what would happen to couples' relationships in the next 3 years. Basically our results were very straightforward. The faster partners' hearts were beating, the faster their blood was flowing, the more their hands were sweating, and the more they jiggled around in their uncomfortable chairs, the more their marital happiness declined in the next 3 years. The calmer they were, the more their marital happiness increased. The most important concept for organizing these results is what we call "diffuse physiological arousal," or DPA. Here's what that means. Our bodies have a *general alarm mechanism* that we have inherited from our hominid ancestors, who developed it through natural selection. The adaptation is what happens to mobilize your body so that it can effectively cope with emergencies that might injure you. The way this works is that in situations you perceive as "dangerous" (this perception can be very rapid and require very little complex or cortical thought), a series of things happens in your body. It can even happen without your awareness.

For example, suppose you are driving down the highway at night and suddenly see headlights in your lane coming right at you. You swerve onto the shoulder and narrowly avert a collision. If we examined your physiology at that moment, we would find that your heart was beating fast and contracting hard, that your blood pressure was up, that you were secreting adrenaline, that blood flow had shut down to "nonessential services" (your gut and kidney), that your liver had changed some of its supply of glycogen to glucose (sugar) in your blood, that the renin-angiotensin system was conserving blood volume in anticipation of hemorrhage, and that you were sweating, particularly on your palms and the soles of your feet. You would be in a state of high alertness and arousal as well, a state psychologists call "tunnel vision." Your limbic system, particularly the amygdala, the hypothalamus, connections to the cingulate gyrus, the hippocampus, and connections to the prefrontal lobes, would have been activated. Your blood pressure would be up, and blood would have been drawn in from your arms and legs into your trunk.

We call this state *diffuse* physiological arousal because many systems are simultaneously activated. Most of us experience this state as very aversive. You would feel what we call "flooded," a state that, in couples' relationship interaction, begins the "distance and isolation cascade." The distance and isolation cascade refers to avoiding one's partner and feeling hopeless about the relationship, and becoming increasingly more lonely over time.

At the same time, there are neural pathways in our bodies that mediate calming and health and immune-system enhancement. Unlike the sympathetic nervous system, the parasympathetic nervous system has a major nerve—the aforementioned vagus nerve. The vagus nerve affects all the same organs that the sympathetic nervous system affects, and it primarily acts antagonistically, to slow things down, restore calm, and focus attention.

The physiological events of DPA start with the inhibition of the vagus nerve, which releases the parasympathetic brake on the heart. With the vagal brake off, the heart speeds up rapidly, within one heartbeat. When the heart speeds up to beyond about 100 bpm, the "intrinsic" pacemaker rhythm of the heart, your body starts secreting adrenaline. Now the heart increases its contractility as well as its rate. Blood flow changes in your body. Blood flow to the gut and kidneys is shut down. The peripheral arteries constrict and blood is drawn in from the periphery to the trunk to minimize the potential damage to the body from hemorrhage. The kidneys activate the renin-angiotensin system, which increases blood pressure and attempts to conserve fluid volume, again in the event of hemorrhage. The pituitary-adrenal complex is activated and the body's adrenal cortex secretes cortisol. Your body begins getting fuels into the blood stream from the liver—glycogen is converted to glucose. Blood flow to the brain is maintained. Fight or flight routines become more likely to become engaged as the cortex begins judgment of the stimulus conditions so that the associative cortex of your brain can mount a plan for coordinated action. There is a perceptual narrowing and focused attention. These patterns are part of the DPA response. It was hardest to calm down during a break for husbands who had been suppressing the expression of negative emotion during the conflict discussion.

The amazing thing is that all these things can, *and do,* happen during relationship conflict. But whereas the DPA response can be adaptive in dealing with emergencies, in relationship conflict it has consequences that are quite negative. With DPA there is a reduced ability to process information. It is harder to attend to what your partner is saying. Peripheral vision and hearing may actually be compromised. As much as you want to listen, you just cannot do it. There is less access to new learning and greater access to over-learned behavior and thought. Fight and flight routines become more accessible. The sad result for relationship conflict is that creative problem-solving, active listening, empathy, and your sense of humor go out the window.

In our research, couples who eventually divorced had husbands with heart rates 17 beats a minute higher than those in stable marriages (even in the condition where we asked people to just close their eyes and relax), and wives with faster blood flow, evidence of the general alarm reaction. Kiecolt-Glaser and colleagues found that negative marital conflict codes were related to greater secretion of all kinds of stress-related hormones into the blood stream in newlywed couples.[12] They took blood from these couples as they discussed a marital conflict. Their tapes showed that it didn't take much negativity to make this whole host of physiological events take place.

Physiology Interacts With Behavior and Perception

Why is the relationship between flooding and physiology so crucial? Just as there is an optimal heart rate for aerobic exercise, there is also an optimal level of heart rate for relationship interaction, and it should be well below 100 bpm. That is called the "intrinsic rate" of the heart because it is the rate at which a healthy heart's natural pacemaker cells fire. The research of stress physiologist Loring Rowell has shown that when the heart rate exceeds 100 bpm, the body starts secreting adrenaline and the sympathetic nervous system responses of fight or flight begin to activate.[13] Also, physiology is crucial for the couple because of the importance of soothing. Couples need to learn how to help restore calm in each other, to reduce stress. In this way, the relationship becomes a port in the storm instead of the source of flooding. Couples need to learn to do this on their own, not have the therapist do it for them. So the antidote for flooding and the distance and isolation cascade is soothing. The partners need to learn how to *soothe each other*. To use any recently acquired learning when in a state of DPA, a couple needs either rehearsal of the new behavior while they are in those states of DPA, or the ability to recognize DPA in themselves when it occurs and be able to *soothe* each other.

When your heart rate exceeds the intrinsic rhythm and adrenaline is secreted, your perception changes to what is called "tunnel vision." You begin perceiving stimuli as dangerous and focus only on becoming safe, either by fleeing or aggressing, and have little access to social processes like a sense of humor, creativity, or empathy. The ability to listen accurately or with compassion becomes inaccessible to the physiologically aroused person. The therapist who is unaware of this physiological arousal and asks a person to be a good listener or express empathy is setting this client up for failure. Perceiving threat and danger, the partner seems like the enemy, and it becomes impossible to listen with empathy.

Taking a Break From Conflict as Soothing

In a randomized clinical trial, we interrupted the conflict discussion of 40 couples with one of two types of breaks. In the first type, half of the couples were asked to do a video recall before reading magazines for 20 minutes and then resuming the conflict discussion. In the second type, the remaining 20 couples spent the entire 20-minute break reading magazines; these couples did the video recall rating after the second conflict discussion. The first break condition was designed to simulate a "damaged break" with rumination about what had happened in the previous conflict. Viewing the videotape before the break was designed to activate thoughts about what went wrong in the first interaction, thereby increasing rumination. Not seeing the videotape before the break, on the other hand, was designed to simulate a good break that suddenly terminates the previous conflict interaction. Hence, the second condition was designed to simulate a real break with relaxation.

Our results showed that both conditions were successful in significantly lowering both partners' heart rates. However, it was of great interest that only in the second relaxation break did the reduction in heart rate also result in significantly less use of the four horsemen and more neutral affect when the conflict discussion resumed. Furthermore, the effect was only obtained for husbands, not for wives, suggesting that women may have a greater propensity toward rumination than men.

Measuring the Degree of Flooding

As I have mentioned, Ekman's concept of "flooding" can be extended to couples. In the context of couples' conflict, "flooding" refers to (1) an internal state of feeling overwhelmed by one's partner's negative emotions and one's own emotions as the partner brings up issues, (2) an inability to avoid becoming defensive, (3) an inability to avoid repeating oneself, and (4) a wish to flee. This internal state is only weakly related to autonomic physiology measures, because it probably represents the cumulative cognitive and emotional effects of repeated experiences with DPA during many absorbing-state conflict interactions.

Flooding is assessed by a 51-item questionnaire that I designed. Examples of items are: "When my partner gets angry I feel attacked"; "I just don't understand why he/she has to get so upset"; "After a fight I just want to keep away from him/her"; and "My husband's/wife's feelings are too easily hurt."

In previous research Bob Levenson and I suggested that flooding might be a variable behind why some couples get increasingly more distant and isolated from each other in reaction to their conflicts. They grow more distant and hopeless over time, live their lives more in parallel, and become increasingly more lonely. We called that the "distance and isolation cascade."

We also know that men become more flooded during conflict than women. That's just an empirical fact. But what does that mean? What are its implications? Our flooding questionnaire also includes items like: "Suddenly small issues become big ones and we're in a big argument"; "I feel like it's my fault when she gets upset"; "Her blowups seem to come from out of nowhere"; and "The smallest thing can lead to a big fight." As we will see later, flooding during absorbing-state relationship conflict—or even during a fun task (like building a paper tower together)—contributes to people's evaluation of their relationship as less desirable than potential alternatives, which starts a cascade toward betrayal. When people become flooded, their ability to accurately process information is seriously compromised. They really need to calm down before they can interact constructively.

Brain Physiology and Trust

There are now many ways to understand and measure trust and betrayal. We now have the science to measure trust by looking at brain and autonomic nervous system physiology. The following is an example of one landmark study that illustrates that point. A married couple arrives at the University of Virginia's Psychology Department. They have come to Charlottesville to visit the laboratory of Professor James Coan.[14] There they will experience the beautiful campus first designed by Thomas Jefferson, with its stately, graceful, Southern architecture.

They will be met by an affable, enthusiastic, and easy-going young professor, who will chat with them and escort them to his laboratory. First they will fill out questionnaires that essentially ask them how much they trust their relationship with their partner. Coan will eventually place the woman in a functional magnetic resonance imaging (fMRI) tube, where she will experience random electrical shocks delivered to one of her big toes. That aversive experience is designed to activate brain centers that signal danger and alarm. (These parts of our limbic system deep in the brain light up in response to increased metabolism of sugar, which the brain lives on, when these centers become activated. When parts of these limbic areas of the brain are activated, the body responds in the fight or flight ways I discussed earlier.)

During this mildly scary experience, either the husband or a stranger is holding the wife's hand. Coan has discovered that when a woman is happily married, and her husband is holding her hand, there is almost a total shutdown of the physiological pattern signaling alarm and danger in the brain. When she's less happily married, there's more activation of these centers of the brain. If a stranger is holding her hand, the centers are totally activated. Coan has replicated the same results with gay and lesbian relationships, so the effect is not just about women being soothed by a man. We can surmise from Coan's work that perhaps trust has a physiological benefit that helps all of us cope better with fear.

The Hormones of Trust

Bernie Madoff, probably one of the most successful liars in history, was arrested in 2008 for a Ponzi scheme in which he swindled about 13,000 innocent people (and the entire U.S. government oversight apparatus) out of approximately 50 billion dollars. There were many moving tragedies in this story. People's entire life savings were lost; the capital of benevolent foundations evaporated. People trusted Bernie Madoff, but they shouldn't have. Many people wondered how so many individuals could have trusted such an evil crook for so many years.

In the 1730s a Bostonian named Tom Bell, who was kicked out of Harvard University for stealing some chocolate, posed as a member of the Boston Hutchinsons, a prominent family in Massachusetts. Bell conned Benjamin Franklin out of a fine ruffled shirt and an embroidered handkerchief.[15]

In 2008, the *Boston Globe* reported a story about a man named Christian Karl Gerhartsreiter, who sat in a Boston jail after many people trusted his lies and gave him their money. Two women married him, and social clubs in San Marino, California, Greenwich, Connecticut, and Boston vouched for him and believed him to be Clark Rockefeller, heir to the Standard Oil fortune. He was handsome, wore beautiful clothing, approached people at high-society events, was modest, and hinted at a storied lineage.[16]

New research may shed some light on the physiological basis of this phenomenon. A Swiss research team had volunteers play an investment game in a research study.[17] The volunteers earned various amounts of actual cash. Six of the 29 volunteers received a placebo nasal spray and the other subjects received a nasal spray of the hormone oxytocin. The volunteers knew that they could make a hefty profit if they trusted a investment trustee with their money, but they were also told that there was a risk that the trustee could decide not to give them any of their money back. People who had received the hormone oxytocin were far more likely to trust the fake investor. When the trustee was replaced by a computerized random-number generator, the effect disappeared.

Sue Carter is one of the pioneers of research on what have been called "trust hormones" (oxytocin and vasopressin in males).[18] She has found that oxytocin is indeed the hormone of pair bonding and also of maternal attachment. She has studied a small rodent called the prairie vole. These creatures are interesting because they mate for life. It is very hard to get the prairie vole female to be interested in the advances of any particular male. However, if you inject these females with oxytocin, they will readily and rapidly mate with just about any experienced male. And these creatures mate for life! Gobrogge, Liu, Young, and Wang discovered that virally injecting a single gene for the vasopressin receptor (V1aR) into the brain's reward center makes a promiscuous male meadow vole monogamous.[19] How do these things happen?

The major effect of oxytocin is that it reduces high levels of stress hormone activity that result in the secretion of adrenaline and cortisol axes.[20] This sounds a lot like the effects that Jim Coan saw in his hand-holding experiment. Oxytocin contributes in some cases to a shutdown of the brain circuits of fear in the amygdala. It may contribute to suspending judgment when we ought not to.

Further evidence of the "trust hormones" shutting down the fear-producing mechanism in the brain was provided by a collaborative study between researchers at the National Institute of Mental Health and a university in Germany.[21] Using fMRI recording, they found that viewing frightful faces triggered a dramatic reduction in amygdala activity for subjects who had sniffed oxytocin. Their study followed the report by a British research group that increased brain amygdala activity in response to threatening faces was related to a decline in the perception of trustworthiness.[22] The British researchers were interested in studying a group of people who have a genetic brain disorder that renders them overly trusting of others.

Another interesting clinical application of oxytocin and the shutdown of the fear response in the amygdala comes from research conducted by Davidson and colleagues at the University of Wisconsin.[23] These researchers found an overactivation of the amygdala in autistic people who were looking at threatening faces. Oxytocin dampened the amygdala's response, as well as its communication with other sites in the upper brainstem that telegraph the fear response. If oxytocin plays a role in down-regulating the fear response in the brains of people suffering from the autistic disorders, it could become part of an important method of treatment for autism.

Recently, another very exciting Swiss study conducted by Beate Ditzen and colleagues found that intranasal oxytocin had very positive effects on marital interaction. There were 94 heterosexual couples in the study. Half received the oxytocin spray and half received a placebo spray. In a standard conflict discussion, the couples' behavior was coded for verbal and nonverbal behavior, and the stress hormone cortisol was measured repeatedly throughout the experiment. Oxytocin significantly increased positive relative to negative behavior and significantly reduced salivary cortisol levels as well.[24]

The word *oxytocin* comes from the Greek for "swift birth." It is a hormone that facilitates birth and triggers the milk letdown response in lactating women. Oxytocin has also been called the "cuddle" hormone. It is produced by a part of our brain called the "hypothalamus." It also stimulates uterine contractions. It can be stimulated by nipple stimulation in lactating women, by uterine or cervical stimulation during sexual intercourse, or by a baby going down the birth canal. If new mother rats are deprived of oxytocin, they will reject their young, whereas virgin female rats given oxytocin will fawn over these newborns, nuzzling the pups and protecting them.[25] Oxytocin and vasopressin appear to be the hormones of trust in all relationships.

During orgasm achieved through masturbation, researchers have discovered that both men and women secrete oxytocin, although the amount of oxytocin secreted was greater for stronger orgasms, as measured by the strength of anal muscle contractions.[26] There is also evidence reported by Ahern and Young of Emory University that oxytocin stimulates dopamine activity in the reward centers of the rodent brain by 50%, making the manic ecstasy of falling in love a highly pleasurable experience, apparently not unlike a cocaine high.[27]

At the University of California, San Francisco, researcher Rebecca Turner and colleagues studied 26 nonlactating women.[28] She had the women remember a negative and a positive relationship experience and receive 15 minutes of Swedish massage to their neck and shoulders. The results were of borderline significance. Relaxation increased oxytocin release slightly, recalling a negative relationship experience decreased oxytocin slightly, and recalling a positive relationship event had no effect across all subjects. However, she noticed large individual differences that proved interesting and provocative. The women whose oxytocin levels fell significantly during the recall of a negative relationship experience had considerably more difficulty in their own relationships (assessed with questionnaires) than the women who did not have as large a drop. Also, the subsample of women in committed relationships experienced a greater oxytocin increase when recalling a positive relationship than single women.

There is a drug company, Vero Labs, that actually markets the oxytocin nasal spray as "liquid trust."[29] A "weekly supply" costs $29.95 and a "2-month supply" costs $49.95. They claim that the spray can be used as a kind of love potion to increase attraction when dating, and they also recommend that companies have their employees spray the stuff up their noses before attending staff meetings to facilitate cooperation. Unfortunately, a study done at the University of Haifa used the oxytocin nasal spray in a competitive zero-sum game and found that oxytocin-treated subjects *gloated* significantly more often when they won, and were *sore losers* who envied their partner (who was actually a computer) more often when the partner beat them, compared to placebo subjects.[30] The researchers suggested that nasal-spray oxytocin may be the hormone of either trust or mistrust, or even aggression, depending on the situation. In a zero-sum game even the hormones of trust may have an uphill battle in producing the normal trusting effect. That has implications for our thinking about the zero-sum game absorbing state of nasty-nasty interaction for unhappy couples. In such a context, the secretion of oxytocin may not build trust, but rather further build suspicion and mistrust. These couples are indeed caught in a negative spiral.

There is some evidence among 24 females given testosterone or a placebo that testosterone down-regulates interpersonal trust—particularly among those women who trusted more easily—and up-regulates social vigilance.[31] As testosterone is widely considered the hormone of sexual desire, these findings are somewhat counterintuitive; one would think that sexual desire in women might cloud good judgment, but perhaps that is only true for men. More research is clearly needed.

Trust and Living or Dying

There is now strong scientific literature about the physiological and health benefits of trusting relationships. Researcher James House reported that there is a group of people—spread around the planet—who reliably die young.[32] They are the lonely, the socially isolated, and the disconnected people. They are usually men.

In the last 30 years the costs of loneliness in the general population have also been examined carefully by social epidemiologists. Epidemiologists first noticed that some immigrant populations had much better health than nonimmigrant Americans. They examined factors such as diet and exercise. For example, Chinese-Americans, who seemed to have better health than other Americans, maintained a very different diet—one that was much lower in fat. Subsequent research showed that immigrant groups who had the best health were those who created a trusting community and had trusting family ties. The strong factors in the greater health of some of these immigrant groups were not diet or exercise, but rather trusting relationships in community and family. In recent years those findings have been replicated with Mexican immigrants. Strong loyalties and trusting family networks trump the poverty, enormous stress, separations, and hard work for low wages that are familiar to recent immigrants from Mexico.

Were these findings true in general? In Alameda County, Lisa Berkman and Len Syme studied over 9,000 people over a 9-year period to determine what the major causes of living or dying were.[33] When they controlled factors such as diet, exercise, and serum cholesterol, they found that the people who were still alive had friends or were married. Subsequent work by epidemiologists showed that for both men and women, it was not merely being married or having friends, but the *quality* of those relationships that was health-giving. It turned out that enormous health and longevity benefits were conveyed by a trusting marriage and good friendships. Therefore, this study, and many other subsequent studies on social epidemiology, reveal the health-giving and longevity-giving benefits of trusting people who are trustworthy. So what about the other part of trust—that is, what are the psychological and physiological costs of *not* trusting people who are trustworthy? The psychological consequences have been studied extensively in the research literature on loneliness.

Loneliness As (in part) the Inability to Trust

Research on loneliness shows that lonely people crave attention and connection with other people, but they are more negatively judgmental and rejecting of new people they meet than are non-lonely people. Part of their disorder, then, is that they fail to trust people they should trust. Therefore, they miss the potential betrayal that people who trust sometimes experience, but they also miss the enormous benefits of trust placed in the trustworthy.

Loneliness has been shown to be enormously stressful,[34] and it doesn't get better on its own, just with the passage of time. Lonely people tend to be deficient in social skills, deficient in reading other people, and deficient in empathy. They tend to have an activated fear system about meeting new people, and they have trouble regulating their sourness and hostility. They focus on the potential threat in social situations and expect rejection. Their ability to detect treachery is also greatly compromised. Although they are more attentive to social cues than non-lonely people, they tend to *misread* these cues. Lonely people tend to let themselves be treated unfairly in order to be liked, but they also react with extreme suspicion about potential unfairness. Lonely people are therefore caught in a spiral that keeps them away from others, partly because they withdraw to avoid the potential hurt that could occur from trusting the wrong person. So they trust nobody, even the trustworthy.

There is a distinct physiology that accompanies loneliness. University of Chicago social psychologist and psychophysiologist John Cacioppo used fMRI brain studies to show that lonely people get less of a positive pleasure boost in brain reward centers in response to happy faces, and also report that they tend to enjoy positive interactions with people less than non-lonely people.[35] Lonely people tend to have higher blood pressure than non-lonely people, and the cause of the higher blood pressure is peripheral constriction of arteries. High blood pressure is determined by many physiological systems, like the kidneys' renin-angiotensin system, and the actions of the oxytocin-like arginine vasopressin, the male hormone of trust and bonding (as well as aggression). One mechanism through which blood pressure is elevated is arterial vasoconstriction, or how open or closed arteries are. That is controlled by what is called the "alpha branch" of the sympathetic nervous system. Another mechanism through which blood pressure is elevated is myocardial contractility, or how hard and how fast the heart beats. How hard and fast the heart beats (past its intrinsic rhythm) is controlled by what is called the "beta branch" of the sympathetic nervous system, which primarily innervates the left side of the heart. These are two (of many) mechanisms for creating high blood pressure.

Trust and Blood Velocity

When I multiplied my trust metric by the amount of time that the couple spent in the nasty-nasty cell of interaction during conflict, I was surprised to discover an almost perfect correlation between the *wife's* trust metric and the slower blood velocity of both partners. The correlation was 0.85; the highest the correlation coefficient can get is 1.00, so that was a very high correlation. Blood velocity is the time from the big R-spike on the electrocardiogram to the arrival of the blood either at the ear or the finger. The ear pulse transit time is determined almost purely by the amount of beta-sympathetic neural drive to the heart. The beta-sympathetic nerves innervate the left ventricle, so they are major determiners of myocardial contractility. There was no relationship between blood velocity and the *husband's* trust metric. So how much *she trusts him* is what matters physiologically to both.

We obtained the two blood velocity measures during the conflict discussion, but also in two *baseline* conditions before the conflict discussion—an eyes-closed baseline (they were not looking at their partner), which was followed by an eyes-open baseline (they were looking at their partner). If the relationship held between wife trust and blood velocity in the baselines, it would tell us that the elevated blood velocity in low wife trust relationships was *chronic*, not merely a function of the conflict discussion. That was indeed the case. The relationship also held for baseline ear pulse transit time (as well as finger), so the mediating neural factor is beta-sympathetic. Hence, both partners in relationships of low trust by the wife in her husband are likely to develop high blood pressure as a result of chronic high myocardial contractility, due to high activation of the beta branch of the sympathetic nervous system. Low trust is also related to the higher baseline skin conductance of husbands.

Of course, we do not know yet if any of these relationships are causal. If they were, we could theoretically improve trust by lowering beta-sympathetic drive to the heart. This might be accomplished with a beta-blocker, or with biofeedback devices that reduced systolic blood pressure. As I mentioned previously, there are promising biofeedback devices on the market that might accomplish this reduction in systolic blood pressure.

When They Open Their Eyes and See Each Other

In the study I have been talking about we designed two baselines for obtaining physiology. In one baseline, couples closed their eyes and relaxed for 5 minutes. This was followed by a second baseline in which the couples opened their eyes and looked at each other, but could not speak. These two baselines were followed by their first 15-minute conflict discussion. These two baselines made it possible for me to ask the question, "Is there anything interesting that changes in their physiologies when they go from the first to the second baseline that might relate to trust?" It turned out that this was indeed the case. Couples whose blood velocities increased when they opened their eyes during the second baseline had lower trust metrics than the couples whose blood velocities decreased or did not change. The physiological arousal when they open their eyes and see who it is they are soon about to be in conflict with is related to a low trust metric, particularly her trust levels. One of my favorite questionnaire items is "My partner is glad to see me at the end of a day." It has always seemed very sad to me when people answer "false" to that item. Now I suspect that the gladness is accompanied by a physiological calming in blood velocities.

Does oxytocin work the same blood-pressure wonders for men as well as women? It is interesting that researcher Kathleen Light developed a method for couples to create a warm support by having partners sit close to each other with their thighs touching.[36] If the couples were happy with their relationship, both men and women secreted oxytocin during this experience. It doesn't take much, apparently, for happily married couples to secrete the hormone of trust. However, Light found that there were decreases in blood pressure *only* for women. Noradrenaline is a stress hormone that operates in the brain and is the equivalent of adrenaline in the periphery. Oxytocin, in her study, decreased noradrenaline levels for women, but not for men. Hence, this research would suggest that men are more vulnerable to DPA as well as the raised blood pressure effects of a wife-low-trusting relationship.

There are therefore serious implications of low trust on health and longevity.

The Zero-Sum Game, Illness, and Early Death of Men

In the 20-year study that Robert Levenson, Laura Carstensen, and I conducted,[37] Tara Mahdyastha noticed that less than 10% of couples had zero-sum game scores. As I mentioned earlier, that is a definition of betrayal, where operating in one's own best interests is actually the same as operating *against* one's partner's best interests. That qualifies as actual betrayal, rather than merely untrustworthiness.

Tara noticed that a significantly larger percentage of zero-sum game couples in that study ended up not returning to the study for all the waves of data collection. At first we speculated that perhaps these couples had found being in the study so unpleasant that they decided to drop out. However, when Tara investigated further, it turned out that these couples were widowed at a much higher rate than couples who were not zero-sum game couples. The wives were not the ones dying early among the widowed couples—the husbands were.

We identified three groups of couples: pure zero-sum couples, cooperative couples, and mixed zero-sum/cooperative couples. The rate of death over 20 years was a whopping 58.3% for the zero-sum couples, 33.3% for the mixed zero-sum/cooperative couples, and 22.8% for the cooperative couples. These effects were statistically significant.

To isolate the factors that are causing the husbands to die, we performed an analysis called a "logistic regression" with the outcome variable being whether or not the husband died. As expected, husband's age is a major factor in husband dying. However, even accounting for age and health and various psychological factors for both partners, having a zero-sum game conflict conversation increased the husband's odds of dying in that timeframe by over 11 times compared to a cooperative conflict conversation. A mixed zero-sum/cooperative game (neutral slope) increased the husband's odds of dying by 7 times over a cooperative (positive sloped) conflict conversation.

We also expected that couples who engaged in zero-sum conflict discussions would have more health problems than couples who were acting cooperatively and mixed-game couples. The wives who engaged in zero-sum conflict discussions reported more psychological symptoms (using the 90-item Derogatis symptom checklist called the "SCL-90R"[38]) and more physical health symptoms (using the Cornell Medical index[39]) than other wives. There were no significant differences for husbands. However, we did find that husbands in zero-sum game relationships *died more often* than the husbands in more cooperative relationships. That result is consistent with a number of studies that asked men the question: "Does your wife love you?" Feelings of being loved by one's wife were important predictors of significantly lower severity of ulcers, coronary artery blockages, and angina for men.[40]

Coregulation of Partner Fight-or-Flight State Physiologies

As I have noted, psychologist Jim Coan has a theory that the major role that partners in a high-trust relationship can play is to help each other down-regulate their physiologies. Once our limbic fear system is triggered, we are in the fight-or-flight state that signals the activation of our physiological general alarm system. In that state, our frontal cortex has only a weak potential for down-regulating our activated fight-or-flight state. However, here's where trust has its big payoff. In a trusting relationship, even an event as simple as our partner's hand-holding can down-regulate our activated fight-or-flight state. Coan calls this possibility "coregulation."

Three physicians, Thomas Lewis, Fari Amini, and Richard Lannon, proposed a similar theory in *A General Theory of Love*.[41] They called the process "mutually synchronizing exchange limbic regulation." They wrote:

> . . . an individual does not direct all of his own functions. A second person transmits regulatory information that can alter hormone levels, cardio-vascular function, sleep rhythms, immune function, and more—inside the body of the first [person]. The reciprocal process occurs simultaneously: the first person regulates the physiology of the second, even as he himself is regulated. Neither is a functioning whole on his own; each has open loops that only somebody else can complete. Together they create a stable, properly balanced pair of organisms. And the two trade their complimentary data through the open channel their limbic connection provides. (p. 85)

Whereas Lewis, Amini, and Lannon were mostly talking about the coregulation between a parent and an infant, Coan's ideas and experimental paradigm generalize this idea to two adult lovers in a trusting relationship. We have seen that experimental data support such actions of down-regulating the fear system through oxytocin, the hormone of trust.

Joseph LeDoux's research on the fear system in rats demonstrates that there is a critical difference in timing between the cerebral cortex and the fear arm of the limbic system through the amygdala.[42] Simply put, the up-regulation of the fight-or-flight state from the limbic system to the cortex is much faster than the down-regulation of the fight-or-flight state from the cortex to the limbic system. We are adapted by evolution to rapidly activate the fight-or-flight state in the limbic system, but to only slowly become calmed by the cortex. That makes a lot of sense in terms of survival. It *doesn't* make any sense in calming down during a conflict discussion in a relationship. For calming of the fight-or-flight state, Coan would suggest that we need to rely on our partner. What I would add to Coan's idea of coregulation is that it may be effective only in a relationship of high trust, and, according to my data, only when she trusts him.

The theory I am suggesting is that her trust of him operates to downregulate the fight-or-fight states of *both* people by reducing the beta-sympathetic drive to the heart that eventually slows chronic velocity of their blood. *Trust slows the blood,* cooling potentially chronic fight-or-flight states in both partners, and creating the physiological protection that helps a man live longer when he can create a trusting relationship with the woman he loves.

Trust Between Parents and Children

There is one study about the effects of children trusting their parents that is very interesting and deserves mentioning in this chapter. In a study of the Harvard University classes of 1952 and 1954, college students were asked whether their relationship to their mother and father was: (1) very close, (2) warm and friendly, (3) tolerant, or (4) strained and cold.[43] Thirty-five years later medical records were collected on the now middle-aged people. The results were remarkable. Ninety-one percent of participants who did not have a warm relationship with their mothers were diagnosed with a serious medical disease in midlife, compared to only 45% who said they did have a warm relationship with their mothers. Effects for fathers were additive, so that for those people who had a lack of warmth and closeness with both parents, 100% of them were diagnosed with a serious medical disease in midlife, compared to only 47% who rated both mothers and fathers high in warmth and closeness. The study also collected adjectives from the college students describing their parents, and they found that 95% of the students who used few positive words to describe their parents were diagnosed with a serious medical disease in midlife, compared to only 29% who described both parents positively. I mention this study because it is simply one of many studies that suggest to me that the effects of levels of trust in families are likely to have very serious consequences for the entire life course of both parents and their children.

In the following chapters I will outline a blueprint for building this trust in couples, (1) first during small everyday moments when one person expresses a need for emotional connection, (2) during processing negative affect or during processing a regrettable incident that is *in the past*, which has the potential for healing potential attachment injuries, (3) during a conflict discussion (something needs to be decided and the partners disagree), and then finally (4) in intimate conversations, romance, passion, and highly personal sexuality (what I call "intimate trust").

Chapter 5

When It's Time to Bail Out of a Relationship

Memory is a dynamic and ever-changing part of our thinking. This ever-changing memory for the story we tell ourselves about our partner's character and the relationship's history leads to the discovery of the "story-of-us-switch," which is a litmus test of cumulative trust or distrust and a way of knowing with a high degree of certainty when a relationship is dying and will very likely end in dissolution.

We all like having an expiration date on the food we buy—something like, "Do not use after the following date." It would be nice if a neon light would start flashing: "ARE YOU CRAZY? DON'T EAT THIS! THROW THIS STUFF OUT!" Failing that, we'd like to develop a good nose for when milk is about to turn sour or meat is about to go bad.

In a similar way, we psychologists would love to find a switch that goes off when a relationship starts turning sour and is harmful if ingested: "WATCH OUT! THIS RELATIONSHIP IS ABOUT TO SELF-DESTRUCT. IT WILL SOON TURN INTO A NIGHTMARE! DO SOMETHING FAST—FIX IT OR BAIL OUT!"

Many couple therapists are supremely reluctant to have such an "expiration date" or sign of hopelessness for a relationship. We therapists are creatures of hope. We root for love to win out over all obstacles, and we are aware of the tremendous tragedy of a relationship's death. We are aware that when people begin a commitment, they are usually in a state of bliss or joyfulness, full of hope for their future.

On the other hand, we have also seen love that has turned into hate, and hope that has turned into bitterness. We know that sometimes it is best for everyone if these people part. We have helped many people through the tragedy of lost love and into a better place for everyone involved. We have helped divorcing couples do so more amicably and figure out what's best for their children and their future lives as separate individuals.

I have seen many couples in my office in which one person is totally shocked that the partner wants out. She might say, "I want a divorce." He might say, "I really had no idea you were that unhappy," and she will usually say something like, "I have tried to tell you that for the past 9 years." It's not always the man who is clueless. I have seen many couples in which the woman says, "Why didn't you say anything to me about being unhappy? We could have gone for therapy sooner." And the man usually responds with, "What was the point? It would only have led to more arguing, and it would turn out to be all my fault, as usual." These are common statements many couple therapists hear.

The good news is that I have found such an "expiration date" switch when the relationship really stinks. I call it the "story-of-us switch." As we all know, a switch is either on or off—there's not much in-between. It's not very often that one finds such a powerful switch in psychological research.

The switch we discovered comes from our oral history interview, (OHI) in which we interview couples about the history of their relationship and their personal philosophies about love and conflict in their own lives. The interview is actually quite innocuous. We ask people fairly standard questions, some of them just like questions you might ask of a couple you just met at a dinner party. But our questions have been carefully worded based on decades of experience.

We ask partners to tell us how they first met and what their first impressions of each other were. Then we go on to ask them what they recall about dating, how their relationship progressed, what they enjoy doing together, what a good time is for them. We ask them to tell us how their relationship has changed over the years. We also ask, "What led you to decide that, of all the people in the world, this was the person you wanted to marry (or move in with, or commit to)?" "Was it an easy decision?" "Was it a difficult decision?" "Were you ever in love?" "What was that love like for you?" "Tell me about that time in your relationship." We ask about the wedding or commitment ceremony if there was one, or the decision to join their lives together, if there was one, and the honeymoon, their first year together, the transition to becoming parents if they have children or stepchildren together, and what times stand out as the really good times. We ask them to describe and what fun, play, adventure, courtship, sex, romance, and passion are and were for them, and what a really great time was and is like for them.

We also ask them about their hard times. We ask: "Looking back over the years, what moments stand out as the really hard times in your relationship?" "What were they like?" "What happened?" "How did you get through those times?" "Why do you think you stayed together?" "What was successful for weathering difficult times?" "What are your ideas about how people in general ought to get through difficult times?"

We ask them to tell us how their relationship is now different from what it was like at first. They create a kind of graph of their relationship and how it has changed over time. Then we move on to explore their philosophies about relationships, what they think makes them last and be happy. To accomplish this we follow the methods of sociologist Fred Strodtbeck,[1] who in the 1950s traveled the U.S. in a van studying Navaho, Mormon, and Texas Anglo cultures. He found that in all the cultures he studied, couples loved to talk about how people were succeeding or failing at raising good children, and what the differences were between successful and unsuccessful families.

We ask couples to select another couple they know who have a good relationship and yet another couple whose relationship is not so good. We ask them what is different about these two relationships. We say, "We're interested in your ideas about what makes a relationship work." We ask them to compare their own relationship to each of these couples. We also ask them about their parents' relationships and how they are similar and different from their own. We ask again about their happiest and least happy times and how their philosophy about relationships had changed over the years. Then we ask how much they currently know about their partner's major worries, stresses, hopes, dreams, and aspirations (their "love maps" of each other). We ask them how they stay in touch with each other on a daily basis, asking about their routines for staying in and renewing emotional contact.

Couples almost always love the OHI. In this interview they are the experts about their relationship. We are genuinely the ones learning from them, and we genuinely believe that every couple is unique.

Although these questions may seem simple and obvious, it took us many years to develop this interview. It is based on the interviewing methods of Studs Terkel. He was the best interviewer I have ever heard. Terkel had a unique perspective that came from his being a radio man. He was interested in creating great radio programs, so he invented an interviewing style that is very different from anyone else's. He avoided the usual "um-hmms" that most therapists use, because these are extremely annoying to hear on the radio. At the end of people's long monologues, Terkel, smoking his cigar, would respond with great energy and emotion, saying things like, "Wow! That is truly amazing! That's incredible!" Then he'd ask another question and become quiet. He could then splice himself out of the tapes and have a long segment of just the subject talking. Long monologues were what made Terkel's radio programs fascinating to listen to. For example, I absolutely loved his interview of an older woman going through her attic with him. She found dusty old objects and through these treasures she described the memories of her lifetime. I remember her finding a small teddy bear, which she said was given to her by the only man she truly ever loved. Terkel asked her if this man was her husband. She said, no, she loved her husband in a different way, but she was never "in love" with him. She had given her heart only once to a man when she was 16 years old, and her heart broke for the first time when he was killed in a car crash. Terkel wept with her in that attic as she poured out her life story to him. What a great storyteller she was in Terkel's hands.

Our OHI was developed over a period of more than 2 years, using trial-and-error, with my talented student Lowell Krokoff. It began as an interview that lasted many hours and was eventually pared down to about 1 to 2 1/2 hours.

It turned out that there were no quiet people. Our amazingly capable interviewers always found the key that unlocked the many stories people carry inside them and privately tell themselves over and over about their partner and their relationship. Everyone we talked to was a great storyteller. People seem to need to tell their stories. In fact, in one study I did with Robert Levenson, we decided to save time and money, so we decided not to use the OHI. It later turned out that our subjects themselves *insisted* on partaking in an OHI. They were frustrated that we hadn't asked them these important questions about their lives together. They wanted to tell us that story to complete our research study with them. That was as true for happy couples as it was for unhappy couples. They poured out their memories and their stories.

But memory is not a static videotape of history. Modern neuroscience is teaching us that memory is continually being rewritten by current experiences and that it contains a shorthand of experience organized by personal meanings. The stability of our identity endures only because some neural networks continue to endure and evolve, and most of our memories are actually highly malleable. As Lewis, Amini, and Lannon wrote, "memory is not a thing . . . memory is not only mutable, but the nature of the brain's storage mechanism dictates that memories *must* change over time" (p. 103).[2]

We generally have two kinds of memories, explicit and implicit. Whereas explicit memory is entirely conscious, implicit memories may not be. When confronted with repeating kinds of experiences, the brain intuitively extracts rules without knowing why. When confronted with anomalies and cognitive dissonance, the brain rewrites history so that it makes more sense and can be more easily retained. The same process holds for the ever-changing story we tell ourselves about our partner's ever-changing character and the ever-changing story of our relationship's history and meanings.

When I first arrived in Seattle in 1986, I started working with a talented employee in my lab, Kim Buehlman, to develop a set of dimensions for quantitatively describing what people said during the OHI and how they said it. We settled on some basic dimensions that we thought would describe the incredibly rich stories we were hearing. I believe that the Buehlman scoring of the OHI[3] reveals the "final state" of trust or distrust in a relationship. Here are the major dimensions we came up with, along with some transcripts of actual interviews that illustrate these dimensions.

Dimension #1. *The Fondness and Admiration System.* Perhaps the most fundamental aspect of the tales we heard was about love and respect, or their absence. If the couple's story about love and respect was positive, either verbally or nonverbally, the couple expressed positive affect (warmth, humor, affection), emphasized the good times, and offered spontaneous compliments toward the partner. The contrast was the absence of this "fondness and admiration system." Here are some examples of transcripts from couples demonstrating fondness, affection, and admiration.

H: I'll tell my version. I was in the military and got assigned to Baltimore to go to school. And I was down on East Baltimore Street, which is the raunchiest street in town. I was drinking a beer, and all of a sudden somebody kicked my beer right over and I looked up and there sitting behind this bottle was her.

W: And you know that's a fault of his. (*both laughing*) We were dancing and my girlfriend told everyone about me. I was raised in Massachusetts and he was in the military and my best friend worked at the military base, and she said she had met this very charming soldier. And she was going to meet him at this weekly dance. And she called me at work and said, "I don't want to go by myself, you have to go with me." I said no, no, no, but finally she was so nervous she didn't want to go alone—that's why I went.

H: I don't know why I was so sophisticated at the time, but I began to realize that they all come here because of her—that even though she doesn't talk very much, she must be the really interesting one in the group. And so I started to focus in on her.

W: That I was the center.

H: She was the leader of that group.

Here's another couple high on this love and respect dimension:

INTERVIEWER: We're gonna go all the way back to the beginning. Tell me about the first the time you two met and got together.

W: You want to hear it from me because that's my favorite story.

INTERVIEWER: So that's a good place to start. Why don't we start with you?

H: Okay. This is true and in a way is rather unusual. I was . . . Phil worked at a lady's ready-to-wear store. I did not know him at the time. The other person there was the window trimmer, and I went in to buy a garment one time and the garment I wanted was in the window. Later on the saleslady said that the window trimmer asked her to get my phone number. So anyway, to make a long story short, I dated this fellow for a while. His name was Frank. Every time I went anyplace with Frank, no matter where we went all he talked about was this fellow who worked at the store named "PK." So one time Frank and I were at the Press Club having a drink. Phil lived downtown at the time. Anyway, the conversation gets to PK again—he's supposed to be a very intelligent fellow, it was all about PK—and I said, "Well, Frank, I just don't think anyone can be that great. You told me he lives downtown. Why don't you call him up and see if he can join us?" So Frank went to the phone and he said PK couldn't join us, but why didn't we come over to where he lived? He lived in a hotel just a couple of blocks away. So Frank came back and said, "You want to do that?" So I said, "Sure." We went over there. Well, he lived on the third floor, and when we walked down the hall Frank was behind me, and he reached over me to knock on the door. And Philip opened the door and he looked at me and he took my hand and kissed my hand, and I was a dead duck.

Conversely when fondness and admiration are dead, partners will express negative affect toward their partner. They may chose to describe an unfavorable first impression, or they may be cynical, sarcastic, or critical of their partner. Here's an example.

INTERVIEWER: What was the first thing you noticed about Peter? Is there anything that made him stand out? What was your first impression?

W: The wine was watered down.

H: I had a friend with a bottle of wine, that's what she means.

W: Yeah, uh-huh. You know, I was late for the ski bus, I had the wrong date, I was rushing on, I was the last one, I didn't know a soul. And I just wanted to go skiing. So he's with this group of people who were obviously already a group. So I don't really know that I had an impression of him as much as the group. Probably the next evening we all met and sat in one of the people's rooms and partied. We were all supposed to go out for dinner together and he never made it because he and his buddies drank a little too much and I ended up having dinner with one of his friends and we went back to sit in his friend's room. This guy's wife had just left him. So we get back to their room, and on course Pete was there. He had been sent to bed by the Canadian Mounties on his way to the restaurant. And I woke him up and said, "You know, I just don't think you're a very nice person."

Here is another couple:

INTERVIEWER: Anything else you can think of about that time?

H: . . . there was the one time when I really got mad at you on your birthday, and that was . . .

W: Oh yeah, that was ridiculous . . .

H: . . . that was in October of '95. Had to be.

W: Yeah, that was stupid, that was the most ass-i-nine thing.

H: I really got mad.

W: Your behavior was just a total duffus.

H: I went berserk.

W: Yeah.

H: I yelled at her because she was. . . .

W: It was *my* birthday because we'd gone out. . . .

H: I spent like $200 on her in presents.

W: Right, and his friend was sitting in the next room. You know we'd come back from going out to eat and whatever, and his friend was sitting in the other room with me, in the living room talking. And I was having a really heartful conversation and I felt like I couldn't just say, "Well, sorry Harry, you gotta go home now."

H: Meanwhile I was preparing to go to sleep. I was in my pajamas.

W: He was making this big production and I felt like well, yeah, I'd like to get Harry out of here. But I felt I had to be nice to him, polite, generous. And then Bill just had a complete tirade, and my feeling was "just forget him."

H: Yeah, I just didn't understand that. To me it was just she's totally being oblivious to the fact that this is supposed to be time for us.

W: And I wasn't oblivious at all. I just felt like I was being sensitive.

H: It was really a miscommunication. I did kind of go ballistic.

W: Yeah. I was really angry.

H: I don't get mad very often.

W: No, he got really angry with me and I ended up leaving and came back the next day.

H: Next day or the next same night?

W: No, the next day.

H: Oh.

W: I was still living at home at that point.

Dimension #2. "We-ness" Versus "Me-ness." Couples with a high degree of "we-ness" emphasized their ability to communicate well with each other, They also emphasized unity and togetherness, as well as having the same beliefs, the and values, and goals in life. These couples used words like "we," "us," and "our." Conversely, couples with a high degree of "me-ness" used words like "I," "me," and "mine." They described themselves as separate, as in the Beatles song "I Me Mine." Analyzing transcripts of couples during conflict in his laboratory, Robert Levenson has counted the ratio of "we, our, us" words compared to "I, me, mine" words. This index was significantly related to relationship happiness. The more people use the we-ness words, the happier their relationship was. Here's an example.

INTERVIEWER: How satisfied do you feel with the arrangement of who does what in your marriage?

W: Well, I think generally it's pretty satisfactory.

H: We're satisfied, yes.

W: When I change the linens on the bed, because I do have a cleaning lady who sometimes does that, and then sometimes we do it together. I help him and he helps me out.

H: And if there's anything unpleasant about doing the dishes, we have trained two teddy bears to come and stand by and help us.

W: (*laughs*)

In contrast, here is a couple high in me-ness.

> **INTERVIEWER**: How do you come to some resolution?
>
> **W**: He came out with a list of strategic budget items that he thought we would need over the next 5 years. And one of them was replacing his existing fishing boat with a nicer one. We had a new car there on the list. Then a number of other things, brief vacations and stuff.
> And I finally—because he already has a fishing boat, and I've wanted a ski boat for a very long time. But I'm too tight to just go blow $25,000 on a ski boat. It takes a joint decision and then it makes it not quite so stupid. I finally said, "Look, I don't think it's fair that you get a new fishing boat. You've already got one fishing boat, so we need to get the ski boat first and then we'll get the fishing boat next year. Ski boat this year, fishing boat next year." And I kind of just laid it out like that and he said, "Well, we could buy both!" But then I said, "But that's foolish." And that was the end of it. That was pretty much how it happened, right?

She is using words that describe her own experience as quite separate from his.

> **H**: Yeah.
>
> **INTERVIEWER**: So, what's the decision? What are you going to do?
>
> **W**: Well, he's not buying the fishing boat. And I'm terrified to buy a ski boat because it costs a lot of money. So right now, there's just no decision.
>
> **H**: See now here's a case where it causes some tension, you know. Because this is money that *I've* earned, *I've* saved, so it's *mine* really.

He also emphasizes his separateness from her. Some couples go out of their way to say: "Maybe that was a good time for you, but my view is different from yours. I am not you." Note that we are not saying that interdependence is good and independence is bad. Every couple arrives at their own balance of these two aspects of what they need. However, in the OHI, some couples' stories emphasize we-ness and some emphasize me-ness.

Dimension # 3. Do Love Maps Exist? I once saw a cartoon that depicted the thoughts in a couple's brain as two pie charts. The woman's pie chart contained areas with labels like: "How fat am I?" "Do I have anything to wear for that party?" "Kids." "The house." and "The relationship." The area occupied by "The relationship" was 65% of the pie. In the man's pie chart, the areas were labeled: "Work." "Strange nose hair and ear hair growth." "Sports facts." "Foods I like to eat." "Being tired." and "The relationship." "The relationship" was only 2% of the pie. Of course this gender humor is a gross (but not total) exaggeration.

In this love map dimension, couples high on love maps described relationship memories vividly and distinctly, whereas those low on love maps were vague or general about the past, or unable to recall details. High love maps couples were also positive and energetic, versus lacking energy and enthusiasm, in recalling their past. They expressed personal self-disclosures during the interview, versus staying impersonal and guarded. They also expressed personal information about their partner during the interview, versus not mentioning anything about partner's personality or history. Here's an example.

INTERVIEWER: And were there any adjustments you had to make for each other's personality?

W: (*laughs*)

H: (*laughs*) Oh, yeah. (*both burst out laughing at the same time*) We were just married and she decided to make fudge one night. So she makes up this fudge and she's been stirring it with this spoon.

W: (*laughing hysterically*)

H: I go out for a while and come back and tried to have some fudge. I tried to lift the spoon from the pot and the whole pot comes up. She doesn't know how to make fudge. It's as solid as concrete.

W: I grew up with gas cooking and this was an electric.

H: That's another story. She opens up the oven and reaches for a match to try and light an electric oven. I knew we were in trouble.

W: You have to remember I was a young girl who grew up with what were three mothers in the same house. I never had to cook or do any-thing. Even to wash clothes. I never had to do anything. So here was this non-homemaker who had never cooked. And I thought I'd make fudge and we had company that afternoon and when he finally came home and we had to throw the whole pan away because it was like cement. He loved cooking and knew all about it.

H: So she couldn't cook but she learned real fast. And she was a real good sport about my teasing. Always has been.

W: (*laughing*) Oh, yeah, he's quite a teaser. But there were no hyster-ics on my part.

H: And the other thing—right away in this apartment, which as a graduate student I didn't pay much for, the damned bed caved down in the middle.

W: Oh, yes.

H: And you like to cuddle with your wife, you're just married, you like to have a lot of sex, but by God, you like to be able to roll over, which you couldn't, you'd wind up . . .

W: . . . right back in the middle. So there were some fun moments.

H: I remember once incident. (*pats her leg*) This is funny. In terms of sex, we enjoyed it thoroughly, right from the beginning.

W: Oh, yeah, we sure did.

H: But there was a point where she was acting very upset.

W: (*laughs*) Oh yeah, I remember.

H: And she said, "We didn't have sex last night," so sadly.

W: (*laughs harder*) "What's the matter with you?"

H: (*laughs*) I said, "There's a certain limit about how much a guy can do."

BOTH: (*laughing hard*)

Here's an example of a couple with no love map.

INTERVIEWER: So what kinds of things did you do, in those early days, when you were dating?

(*LONG PAUSE*)

H: (*quite, looks at wife*)

W: Not much of anything to do in a college town. We went to the movies, I guess, and . . . (*long pause*)

H: Um-hmm. (*pause*) And the film festival was there.

W: (*pause*) We went out to eat, that's about all. It's a small college town. You know, rent movies. I guess.

H: Went out to eat. (*pause*) Drank a lot of red wine.

W: (*tense laughter*)

INTERVIEWER: You both wine connoisseurs?

H: Not really. We can't afford to be connoisseurs.

INTERVIEWER: But you enjoy some wine?

H: Occasionally. I guess.

Dimension # 4. Chaos or Purpose and Meaning? Couples whose life together is nothing but chaos described unexpected setbacks and a lot of conflict. They argued and fought about recurring issues and felt distant. They also described major, unpleasant life circumstances that kept happening to them that they had to adjust to. They were low in planfulness. Their course in life seemed chaotic and without meaning to them.

INTERVIEWER: How did the two of you meet? And what were your first impressions of one another?

H: We met at a party. She was nice.

W: Yeah, we didn't talk much then.

INTERVIEWER: And then?

H: She moved in with me the next week because there was a fire in her apartment.

INTERVIEWER: Wow, that was fast. How was that decision made?

W: I just had to move somewhere and he said, well, okay, you can stay here for a while.

INTERVIEWER: And your impressions of him?

W: He was okay. Nice, I guess.

INTERVIEWER: Then what happened?

H: Her mom got cancer and we decided to move up there to Wisconsin to take care of her.

INTERVIEWER: That's amazing that you both did that. How long had you been together at that point?

W: About a year.

INTERVIEWER: How did you decided to do that together?

H: I don't remember.

W: It just kind of happened. Like the fire.

H: Yeah, just like that.

Things keep happening to them that they have to adjust to. Here's another couple talking about their separation for a year.

W: I think it was easier for me than it was for you.

H: Yeah. You know, suddenly I'm at a new job, a lot of pressure. New faculty, I'd better be good.

INTERVIEWER: Right.

H: And you don't know many people, a lot of pressure.

INTERVIEWER: Right.

H: And you know, it just happened and I have to adjust to it. She's not around, so in order to sort of not feel so bad about the relationship, her not being there, basically you try to minimize the relationship. Like to where you don't even think about it.

INTERVIEWER: Um-hmm.

H: You have to almost bring yourself to a point of ambivalence about the relationship.

INTERVIEWER: Focus on what's going on right here.

H: Um-hmm.

INTERVIEWER: 'Cause your relationship isn't right there then in a day-to-day way.

W: I got that call and I couldn't turn down that job in Amsterdam. Well, yeah. Your relationship is completely stagnated when you're separated like that. There is no movement forward. There's no change, there's no growth, there's nothing.

INTERVIEWER: How did you make such a hard decision to be apart at the very start of your relationship together?

W: It just sort of happened.

H: And you have to adjust, you know. . . .

W: And then you're in this holding pattern, and you talk once a week, and you do these emails. . . .

H: You start to emphasize, you start thinking about the more negative things.

W: Um-hmm. That's what happened all right.

Conversely, couples whose life together has purpose and meaning tend to glorify the struggle, expressing pride that they have survived difficult, negative times, rather than expressing the futility. They emphasized their commitment, versus questioning whether they really should be with this partner, when they fought, and they were proud of their relationship rather than ashamed of it. They emphasized their common goals, aspirations, and values. Here's an example.

INTERVIEWER: Can you think of a really good marriage you know?

W: We have one.

H: I don't know anyone I'd compare to ours. It may sound arrogant, but. . . .

W: I agree.

INTERVIEWER: That's actually really nice.

W: Yeah. I think it is good. We have respect for each other. We communicate well . . . when we have disagreements, we can sometimes get a little "Wow!" but we can sit down and talk about them, and discuss how I'm feeling about the situation and he's feeling about the situation, and get a feel about, an appreciation about, how as men and women we think so differently. We take the same situation, you know, and he can see it so differently.

H: Like Deborah Tannen said. . . .

W: . . . Yes, Deborah Tannen. I'm sure you read her book *You Just Don't Understand*. We found ourselves in that book real often.

INTERVIEWER: Uh-huh.

H: Oh, yeah. We communicate in the same way, have the same goals. Do these things together. I think another thing I'm conscious of—because it doesn't seem to even exist in our kids' marriages as well as it does in ours—our grandchildren find us fascinating because we laugh a lot together.

W: Uh-huh. Sharing our weird sense of humor.

H: We are more than just tolerating. In a sense enjoying our differences. The fact that we are exactly opposite, separate in each of those Myers-Briggs categories. So it fits in with an ancient Platonic idea that human beings are not separate, they are two halves. And that when they come together they become whole. Because I become more intuitive, more emotional, all those things because of her, because she becomes more rational.

W: Uh-huh. We really are different but we fit together.

H: We are more of a whole and as separate more of a whole because of what we have from the other.

INTERVIEWER: Right. Gaining something that you take with you.

H: Yup. That's it.

W: Yeah.

H: There is a pride in it, because we are complementary to one another.

Dimension #5. Disappointment or Satisfaction? Couples high on the disappointment dimension expressed the view that the relationship wasn't what they thought it would be. They said they were depressed about it, hopeless, disillusioned, and at times bitter. They did not advocate marriage for others and said they thought others should avoid getting married.

INTERVIEWER: What advice would you give to young couples who are thinking about getting married?

H: Wait!

W: (*laughs*) Wait. Just don't do it.

Here's another couple high in disappointment.

H: Things we're going through right now, estate planning—I think I have no right to get involved with, unless she specifically asks me to—her inheritances, or how she structures her will, or those kind of things. That's *her* business. And yet I don't think the opposite is true. I think she thinks very much she has a right to be involved with how I structure my things. Is that reasonably close to true?

W: Yes. See to me, writing wills is this thing you do together. And even though it's *his* will and *her* will, um, you sit down and you talk about taking care of each other, and that's one of those areas where, in my view, there should be this totally open thing, and that's a total together thing. Now we're making out two products, my will and his will, but if he doesn't open up, I'll just go there and knock on the door until it opens. Or just break the door down.

INTERVIEWER: So that's kind of the process then.

W: Yeah, that's the process. Or it ought to be.

H: (*nods*) That's what she thinks. I think different.

W: I'd say that's a pretty accurate description. . . . Our friends were having a disagreement the other night and I said, "Look, this marriage thing . . ."—and this is right before we saw your little article in the paper—I said, "This marriage thing isn't all it's cracked up to be. What it really turns out to be is a big game of control."

When the relationship *isn't* filled with disappointment, it's very obvious. In this case the couple says that their relationship and their partner have met or exceeded their prior expectations. They are satisfied and grateful for what they have in each other. Here's an example.

INTERVIEWER: How'd you make that decision? Out of all the people in the world, how did you decide that this was the person that you really wanted to marry? How'd you guys decide that? And I'm asking each of you individually. How did you decide that?

W: Oh, ask him first.

H: Ask me first. Actually I . . . you know, I can't think of when the decision came, it was just kind of a general feeling, you know.

INTERVIEWER: What was that feeling like?

H: It was . . . she was just fun to be with, you know. I loved being with her.

INTERVIEWER: Mm-hmm. So she's a person that you really love to spend time with, and wanted to be with, yeah. (*Turning to the wife*) How about for you?

W: Well, it was after being, being in a car with the same person for 3 weeks, and that we, I had a great time and I saw parts of the country that I have never even seen before, and that, I mean, it was amazing to me that two people could spend that much time together in that close of a proximity and not fight, and kind of be going in the same direction and have the same goal and have fun and kind of compromise with, um, you know, like how far we wanted to go each day and what we wanted to see and when we wanted to stop and it was just like I had never in my life experienced that.

INTERVIEWER: Uh-huh.

W: And so it was like, "Wow." My mother thought I was crazy. But I knew it was right. And it has been right.

H: (*laughing*) True enough.

W: I called her, my mom, from the road . . . she knew I was going, I mean I had to let her know that.

H: Yeah, she knew that much.

W: I called her from I don't even remember where and she said—and I'm going, "Wow, this is so much fun"—and she said, "I don't know *why* you're doing this, you don't even know this person." (*laughs*) And I mean, this was true, he could have been a murderer or something. I just knew it was easy and right.

Another couple satisfied that their relationship had met their expectations said:

W: Um, yeah, and when I got there, you know, I'm walking down the stairs, and he was there, he was there with his roommate and stuff, and it was good; it was a really great evening. And what was funny was all the funny things that happened that evening—which was basically the consummation of our feelings, I think, towards each other, cause I think that nobody we knew was surprised we got married. They were wondering what took us so long.

H: Yeah, that was funny, too.

W: And they all said that they knew that there was always this thing, this chemistry, between us.

Another couple high on this dimension said:

W: Yep, straightforward, he was not afraid to look at my eyes. He was the kind of person that I just thought, finally I met someone that was direct and we were going to be real good friends.

INTERVIEWER: Did you have first impressions of her?

H: (*looks at wife and smiles while repressing a chuckle*) Um, when we were first introduced, you know, oh, what a sweet smile—and I thought she was kind of cute, and then, when she walked away, and I tell everybody that my first impression was "wow, nice butt!"

INTERVIEWER: That was it?

H: What a nice butt. Real deep.

INTERVIEWER: Yeah.

H: Oh, yeah.

W: It was at that moment that he saw my butt that he fell in love.

H: Just kidding a little here. I guess my first impression was just the big smile and she seemed like a happy person all around, so I guess the attraction was all there.

INTERVIEWER: So, you were interested in her from—

H: Immediately, from immediately.

When to Bail Out: It's Not Rocket Science

The amazing thing about analyzing the statistical data from the Buehlman coding of these oral history interviews[4] was that all of these dimensions essentially fell on one giant dimension. Psychologists talk about the "percent of variation accounted for by one factor" as a way of seeing if they have discovered a switch. On the Buehlman oral-history coding there was strong evidence that there was one factor that operated like a switch. Our figure was that more than 80% of the variation was accounted for by one "story-of-us" factor. We were able to predict divorce or stability over a 4-year period with 94% accuracy with the Buehlman coding.

There has been some gross misunderstanding and poor reasoning in the literature about this prediction.[5] Although it is true that the national divorce rate in the U.S. has been estimated as between 43% and 67%, these estimates are based on projections over 40 years of marriage.[6] The national divorce rate has no logical place in the problem of short-term divorce prediction. In our short-term predictions, only about 2.5% of a sample divorced each year. For example, in our newlywed study, 6 years after the wedding, only 17 out of 130 couples had divorced. That's a 13.1% divorce rate in 6 years. The prediction of divorce in this study is equivalent to drawing 94% of all 17 red balls (representing the couples who eventually divorced) from an urn that also contains 113 white balls (representing the couples who were still together). The probability of correctly selecting 94% of the red balls can easily be computed to be of the order of 10^{-19}, which is .0000000000000000001. That means the prediction is quite hard to do in a short-term longitudinal study. Hence, our ability to predict divorce or stability with the Buehlman Oral History coding is highly unlikely to have occurred by chance alone.

The facts just mean that couples were either one way or the other on the interview: They emphasized their good times together and minimized the bad times, *or* they emphasized their bad times together and minimized the good times. They emphasized their partner's positive traits and minimized the more annoying characteristics, *or* they emphasized their partner's negative traits and minimized the more positive characteristics. There was very little gray area.

Once one knows what do look for, this isn't rocket science. It's pretty obvious when the relationship is going (or has gone) bad.

There's another point I want to make about the oral history interview switch. The positive stories were not from couples who had only positive events in their lives together—not by a long shot. What is important about their story is how they *interpreted* the negative and positive events that happened to them. That's what mattered in making the switch positive or negative. For example, one couple said they had married at age 18 because she was pregnant. Here is their story.

H: Marla, she was 4 months pregnant when we got married.

INTERVIEWER: Uh-huh. So did you think you "had to" get married?

W: No . . . yeah . . . maybe.

H: I think it was more of a respect thing. I don't think it was a "well, you guys have to get married now."

W: No, not at all.

H: I think it was more of me respecting Marla.

W: And I think it was kind of protective, right?

H: Yeah, yeah.

They loved their wedding, even though neither of their families attended.

INTERVIEWER: Mm-hmm. Okay. So tell me about the actual wedding itself, what did you do?

H: It was an awesome wedding.

W: Yeah. we had a beautiful wedding. Yeah.

INTERVIEWER: What did you do?

W: We got married in a—at a gazebo in the—it's called Old Maceda.

H: Old Maceda. There was a boat, all decorated.

W: It's a really old town in the town of Las Crusaz.

H: New Mexico. It's where Billy the Kid and all those guys hung out.

But then that first year, after the baby was born, things got worse. The wife said:

W: I think it was probably a lot harder for Billy because he—he'd been used to kind of being such a free spirit and doing so many things on his own, and kind of, you know, um, that having the responsibility of a family was just a humongous change for him.

H: Yeah. I accepted my responsibilities at home but I don't think I was there a lot. (*looking at wife*)

W: He, he accepted them—he was, you know, he was always . . . he's never had a bad temper, he's never, you know, done anything really, really bad, but he'd come home drunk almost every night.

These were very hard times. But she bore no grudge, no resentment, nor did he. She described their first year as one in which Billy came home drunk most nights because he was out late with his friends. Finally they decided to move to Utah, where they knew no one.

H: I mean, before we moved we were fighting all the time. Everything that would come out of each other's mouth was just a fight.

W: Every day we would fight, and then we, we wouldn't talk, you know. That's the thing.

H: One day she dropped me off at work and told me that we were getting a divorce. (*both laugh*)

INTERVIEWER: Wow!

H: Yeah.

W: It was just a very, very unhappy time for us I think.

H: We really needed to get out of there, away from his friends, and that's what we did. And that changed things a lot.

INTERVIEWER: When you moved to Utah, things really improved at that point.

H: A lot, oh yeah. A lot.

INTERVIEWER: Because you were kind of together?

H: Together—we were *forced* to be together—we couldn't like rely on anybody else.

INTERVIEWER: Mm-hmm.

W: And we had to, you know, kind of rely on each other a lot.

H: Pull each other to make it through.

INTERVIEWER: Mm-hmm.

W: And make friends together.

INTERVIEWER: And you had the baby by that time?

H: Oh, yeah.

W: Oh yeah, yeah. He was a year old? (*looks at husband*)

H: (*nods*) About a year old.

W: He was about 14 months.

H: Fourteen months, yeah.

W: Fourteen months when we moved to Utah.

INTERVIEWER: Mm-hmm.

W: So, um, things gradually started to get better, you know. Just having to be with each other, and having to rely on each other, and get to know each other, you know. And not having outside kind of influence, you know.

INTERVIEWER: Yeah. So tell me about becoming parents. Apart from everything else, what was that like, having your son?

H: It was awesome. It was awesome.

W: I think that that's probably about the only thing that we agreed on in the beginning of our relationship.

INTERVIEWER: Was your feelings about the baby?

W: Yeah.

H: Yeah, how we would do things and what he needed and didn't need.

INTERVIEWER: Mm-hm.

W: Yeah, and I don't think that we ever fought over issues of raising him, or how.

INTERVIEWER: So your values were very similar.

H: Yeah.

W: Yeah, very defined and very similar in the way that we were going to raise him. And despite, you know, his partying and stuff, he was a wonderful father. And so . . . certainly a good experience having the baby.

INTERVIEWER: Mm-hmm. It was a very positive thing.

W: Yeah, mm-hmm. Yeah. (*husband nods*)

W: I think that we just talk about it.

H: Yeah, we just talk about it. Just realizing what's good and not good for us is talking things out.

W: Yeah.

INTERVIEWER: Mm-hmm.

W: One thing that we've really progressed on is being able to tell each other, you know, how we feel about it.

H: Mm-hmm, our communication has gotten, like on a scale of 1 to 10, eight better than it used to be at least.

W: Yeah.

The Dynamic Nature of the "Story of Us" Memories

The positive switch tunes into how partners *currently interpret* their past negative events: Their current story maximizes the positive events and minimizes the negative, maximizes their parents' positive qualities and minimizes negative qualities. Notice that what is so very special about Marla and Billy's story is that they had to rely only on each other—they had to become friends so they could talk about their fights. Their communication about their negative events was the key to their positive oral history switch.

This very malleable "work in progress" story-of-us about our partner and the relationship turns out to become an index of what will eventually happen to the relationship. It is indeed remarkable that by scoring the Buehlman dimensions of the OHI our predictions of the stability or divorce of married couples is 94% accurate.

Unless couples get help to change the fundamental ingredients of trust—those ingredients that make them believe attributions they make about their partner's character and their history together—their story-of-us will, unfortunately, write the future for them. So the best measure of ultimate trust is obtained by asking the couple the OHI questions and coding their responses.

Here trust or distrust gets carved in granite and works its powerful effect on eventual relationship outcomes. People's malleable memories of the past get reworked to fit the present and to determine the future. Trust or distrust in an interaction has now worked its magic or black magic to produce altered thinking about our partner's true character and to recast the history of the relationship. Change now is too little, too late.

The story-of-us switch is very hard to change. A positive switch acts as a strong buffer against momentary irritability and emotional distance. A negative switch means that even if our partner's behavior were to suddenly change dramatically, it is likely to be viewed only as a temporary aberration—the relationship is still seen as hell, and for some unfathomable reason the demon did something nice for a change.

The Next Question: How Did They Get Into This Hell?

Sad as it may seem, it is potentially a great help to have a reliable indicator of when a couple should seriously consider bailing out of a sinking ship. The oral history switch is that indicator. It would also be a great asset to know how couples got to this desperate and horrible place, so that others starting a new relationship, or attempting to repair an ailing relationship, can have a blueprint for how to do so. It turns out that the process for getting to this sorry state of a negative oral history switch is very predictable. It happens through the gradual erosion of trust.

In the next chapter I will present an empirically based theory of how couples either build a negative story-of-us by gradually eroding trust, or build a positive story-of-us by gradually building trust. Unfortunately, the dark and shadowy decline toward the sad and sorry end usually occurs at a glacial pace, and it is often invisible. It would be helpful to have some empirical basis for illuminating that darkness. We need to know how couples naturally either build or erode trust.

Chapter 6

How Couples Build Trust With Attunement

This chapter explains how couples get into the negative story-of-us switch by failing to "attune." It describes how research in my laboratory on "meta-emotion" in parenting and in a couples' relationship led to the discovery of the "attunement skill set." The chapter presents a theory of the skill of attunement and its consequences in three relationship contexts: (1) "sliding-door" moments, (2) negative-affect moments or regrettable incidents, and (3) conflict. The roles of attunement, the Zeigarnik effect, and the story-of-us is explained by this theory. Research shows how attunement builds trust and leads to positive outcomes in relationships. The theory also leads to precise "blueprints" for building trust in each of the three relationship contexts.

How did couples get into the sorry state of the negative story-of-us switch? The simple answer is that they let trust erode. However, we need more from research than that answer. We need to know *how* couples build trust, and how they make it erode.

The Big Trust Question Is "Are You There for Me"?

Colloquially, trust in a relationship is usually expressed as the question: "Are you there for me?" As I mentioned earlier, this question of trust formed the basis for all the 130 newlywed couple conflict discussions I studied in Seattle in my love lab. In their conflicts discussions these couples fought about questions such as: "Can I trust you to choose me over your friends?" "Can I trust you to choose my interests over those of your parents?" "Can I trust you to care more about this relationship than about yourself?" "Can I trust you to be home when you say you will be home?" "Can I trust you to be motivated to earn money and create wealth for our family?"

In these arguments they were asking whether they (1) "truly saw" their partner's real character, which referred to a kind of transparency, and (2) whether their partner was really there for them in the clinch. Most couples colloquially described trust in terms of *two* dimensions.

The first dimension referred to transparency: the partner's keeping promises and doing what he or she says he or she will do. This dimension is the opposite of lying and deceit. Trust for these couples meant that they needed to be able to count on the partner to be a truthful person who is what he or she appears to be within the relationship. However, there was more to trust than just that—no one would be happy, for example, with an evil partner who was nevertheless truthful about his or her evil intentions and evil acts. This means that trust is about more than just truth, honesty, and transparency.

This leads us to the second dimension of trust: *positive moral certainty* about the partner. We must have a confidence and knowledge that our partner is an ethical, *moral* person—a good person, someone who will treat us and others with high moral standards, integrity, honesty, kindness, love, and goodwill. This second dimension of trust is about our partner's intentions, motives, and actions *toward us*. It's about the question: "Just where do I fit into my partner's motivational scheme?" "Do I come first in some important sense, compared to other people or my partner's goal, or do other things take priority over me?"

The question we are asking is whether this colloquial use of the two dimensions of trust is related to our previously defined trust metric. It turns out that they are totally related to each other, empirically.

How Couples Build Trust

Part of the news in this book is that trust is built by couples using the skill of "attunement." In this chapter I am going to start describing this skill as a blueprint for building trust in long-term committed relationships.

To create a constructive blueprint for building trust, it is necessary to discuss the use of the attunement skill in three different relationship contexts. As I have mentioned, the contexts for building trust are like a folding fan. Each area of the fan is about the basic question of trust, "Are you there for me?" These are micro trust tests, where trust has built up over time, or eroded over time. Here are the three major trust-building contexts, or parts of the trust fan: (1) the everyday interactions I call "sliding-door moments," (2) regrettable incidents or past emotional injuries, and (3) conflict interactions.

Sliding-door moments, the first part of the fan, are very small moments in which a need is expressed and the responsiveness of one's partner is a test of trust. In these moments we test whether we can trust that our partner will turn toward our expressed need.

The second part of the fan involves a moment in which at least one person is experiencing negative affect and longs for a voice and connection with the partner. It can be a negative emotion that is about the partner, or it can be just a personal negative emotion that is not about the relationship at all. This second context also includes "regrettable incidents" that are about the relationship, in which we hurt our partner's feelings or have an unfortunate argument.

The third part of the fan involves an actual conflict discussion (Rapoport's debate mode). In this context a couple has decided to discuss an area of impending decision and they expect some disagreement between them.

In the next chapter I will also talk about how the skill of attunement is used by couples for building trust during another important part of the "trust fan": the more intimate romantic, passionate, and sexual moments.

How the Attunement Skill Was Discovered

Here's the story of how the process of attunement in couples was discovered. In 1985 I developed an interview I called the "meta-emotion" interview for parents.[11] In this interview we asked people how they felt about specific feelings in themselves and in their children.

The term "meta" is a reflexive word in psychology that sort of folds back on itself. Here's what I mean. The term "meta-cognition" means how we think about our thinking. The term "meta-communication" refers to how we communicate about communication. By "meta-emotion," I mean how we feel about feelings.

We interviewed people separately. We used that interview to talk to parents about their history of emotion—specific emotions like anger and sadness, but also emotion in general. We asked them how they felt about their own feelings and about their children's feelings, as well as about their general philosophy about emotions, emotional experience, and emotional expression. We asked questions like: "What's been your experience in your life with anger? with sadness?" "Could you tell growing up when your father was angry? What effect did this have on you?" "What has been your own relationship with anger?" "How did your parents show you that they loved you?"

So what's so special about this interview about how people experience emotion? The answer is that people all over the planet experience and display at least seven basic emotions (anger, sadness, disgust, contempt, fear, interest, and happiness) in the same way. Carrol Izard and Paul Ekman established these facts.[2] For example, people have essentially the same spontaneous facial expressions when they feel sad. When people feel sad the inner corners of their eyebrows go up and together, forming a brow that looks like an upside-down V. When people feel angry their brows tend to come down and together, forming a vertical furrow between their eyebrows; their upper lip may also tighten, or their lips may be pressed together. When people are surprised, their entire brow goes up, their mouth may drop open, their upper eyelids raise, and their eyes become wide. When people are afraid, their brow becomes almost totally horizontal, the whites of their eyes may show, and their lips become tightly stretched horizontally. If they feel disgusted, their nose may wrinkle or their upper lip may become raised. If they feel contempt, the left corner of their lip may be pulled to the side by the lateral muscle called the "buccinator" and a dimple may become evident; this may be accompanied by an eye roll.

There is even evidence that people across the planet have the same autonomic physiological responses to each emotion as well, although the "autonomic specificity hypothesis," created by Bob Levenson and Paul Ekman, is still controversial. For example, as part of this specificity Levenson and Ekman discovered that heart rate increases in fear and anger and decreases with disgust. The hands become hot with anger and cold with fear.[3]

Despite the universality of emotional expression and experience, there is huge variation across people in how they say they feel about each of these emotions, about their histories with specific emotions, and about emotional expression and their internal emotional experience. We interviewed people about the history of their experience with the emotions of anger, sadness, fear, affection, pride, and positive states such as play, fun, and adventure. We also asked them about their philosophy about emotion in general. We asked them how they experienced these emotions growing up. We asked them how they and their partner experienced these emotions in their relationship. Our interview is one way of linking individual therapy with couple therapy.

This turned out to be a powerful interview. Let me give you an example. There was one woman who described the deathbed scene of her father. She held his hand and said to him, "Dad, you have never told me you love me. It would mean so much to me if you said it now." Her father said, "If you don't know by now, you never will." And then he died. She left his room furious with him, unable to mourn his death. We asked her what the effect of this experience was on her. She said that she was determined that not a day would pass without her telling her children that she loved them.

I interviewed another woman who said that she and her sisters at a young age made a pact to always convert their sadness into anger because they saw their mom depressed and bullied by their father. They decided that when she was 8 years old. From that time on she said that she was never sad; she was angry instead. How had this decision affected her? She is now a crusader in the community for various social causes, and for their dyslexic son at school. When I then asked, "What do you do when Sam [her 4-year-old son] is sad?" She said, "I go for a run." In that family, Dad was the one who talked to Sam when he was sad.

When we asked, "How did your parents show you that they were proud of you?" many people wept. They said that their parents never came to one of their games, or plays, or recitals. When we asked them, "What are the implications of this for your own family?" people usually had a lot to say about expressing pride in their children.

There was great variability in how people felt about feelings. For example, one man in our study said, "When someone gets angry with me it's like they are relieving themselves in my face." But yet another man said, "Anger is like clearing your throat, natural, just get it out and go on." These two fathers felt very differently when their children became angry with them.

In that study we discovered that there were basically two types of parents in our data: "emotion-coaching" parents and "emotion-dismissing" parents. I am simplifying a bit here, because people can be one way with a specific emotion and another way with another, so the results of the meta-emotion interview are very complex. Some parents were very positive about their children's negative emotions and acted like "emotion coaches." Emotion coaches viewed their own and their children's negative emotion as an opportunity for teaching or intimacy. They noticed lower-intensity negative emotions in their children. Overall they went through five steps during talking about an emotional event. I called these five steps "emotion coaching." I will describe them in a moment.

Other parents were trying to get their children to change what they viewed as their negative emotions to positive emotions. They used many techniques, like distraction, or admonishing their children to "roll with the punches" and change how they felt. They believed that the emotion one had was a choice, and therefore they were impatient with their children's negative emotions. Their attitudes toward negative emotion were called "emotion dismissing," which included being disapproving of the negative emotion.

Here's what emotion dismissing parents were like:

- They didn't notice lower-intensity emotions in themselves or in their children (or in others, either). In one interview we asked two parents about how they reacted to their daughter's sadness. The mom asked the dad, "Has Jessica ever been sad?" He said he didn't think so, except maybe one time when she went to visit her grandmother alone and she was 4 years old. "When she boarded the airplane alone," he said, "she looked a little sad." But all children actually have a wide range of emotions in just a few short hours. A crayon may break, and the child becomes immediately sad and angry. These parents just didn't notice much of Jessica's more subtle emotions.

- They viewed negative affects as if they were toxins. They wanted to protect their child from ever having these negative emotions. They preferred a cheerful child.
- They thought that the longer their child stayed in the negative emotional state, the more toxic its effect was.
- They were impatient with their child's negativity. They might even *punish* a child just for being angry, even if there was no misbehavior.
- They believed in accentuating the positive in life. This is a kind of Norman Vincent Peale, the power-of-positive-thinking philosophy. This is very American view. The idea is: "You can have any emotion you want, and if you choose to have a negative one, it's your own fault." So, they think, pick a positive emotion to have. You will have a much happier life if you do. So they will do things like distract, tickle, or cheer up their child to create that positive emotion.
- They see introspection or looking inside oneself to examine what one feels as a waste of time, or even dangerous.
- They usually have no detailed lexicon or vocabulary for emotions.

Here's an example of an emotion-dismissing attitude. When asked about his daughter's sadness, one father we interviewed said, "When she is sad I tend to her needs. I say, 'What do you need? Do you need to eat something, go outside, watch TV?' I tend to her needs." This child might confuse being sad with being hungry. Here's another example. A father said, "Say my kid has a problem with other kids. Let's say someone took something of his. I say, 'Don't worry about it. He didn't mean it. He will bring it back. Don't dwell on it. Take it lightly. Roll with the punches and get on with life.'" This father's message was: "Get over it. Minimize its importance."

The emotion-coaching philosophy was quite different from the emotion-dismissing philosophy. For example, for the same peer situation, another father we interviewed said, "If a kid were to be mean to him, I'd try to understand what he's feeling and why. Some kid may have hit him or made fun of him. I stop everything then; my heart just goes out to him and I feel like a father here and I empathize."

I interviewed one emotion-coaching couple in my lab. She was a professional cheerleader and he was a quarterback for a professional football team. She told me that the reason she liked her husband was that she once came across a smiley face calendar from her youth when she was unpacking and moving in with her husband. She said that when she was a little girl, if she were cheerful that day, her parents would put a smiley sticker on the calendar. If she got 20 smiley faces a month, she got to buy a toy. She hated that calendar. She said, "What I like about my husband is that I can be in a crabby mood and he still wants to be with me. I don't have to be cheerful."

Following is a summary of what we discovered about emotion-coaching parents:

- They noticed lower-intensity emotions in themselves and in their children. The children didn't have to escalate to get noticed.
- They saw these emotional moments as an opportunity for intimacy or teaching.
- They saw these negative emotions—even sadness, anger, or fear—as a healthy part of normal development.
- They were not impatient with their child's negative affect.
- They communicated understanding of the emotions and didn't get defensive.
- They helped the child verbally label all the emotions he or she was feeling. What does having words do? They are important. With the right words, I think the child processes emotions usually associated with withdrawal (fear, sadness, disgust) very differently. I think it becomes a bilateral frontal-lobe processing. Withdrawal emotions still are experienced, but they are tinged with optimism, control, and a sense that it's possible to cope.

- They empathized with negative emotions, even with negative emotions behind misbehavior. For example, they might say: "I understand your brother made you angry. He makes me mad too sometimes." They do this even if they do not approve of the child's misbehavior. In that way they communicate the value, "All feelings and wishes are acceptable."
- They also communicated their family's values. They set limits if there was misbehavior. In that way they communicated the value, "Although all feelings and wishes are acceptable, not all behavior is acceptable." (We had other parents who did everything else in coaching but this step of setting limits, and their children turned out aggressive.) They were clear and consistent in setting limits to convey their values.
- They problem-solved when there was negative affect without misbehavior. They were not impatient with this step, either. For example, they may have gotten suggestions from the child first.
- They believed that emotional communication is a two-way street. That means that when they were emotional about the child's misbehavior, they let the child know what they were feeling (but not in an insulting manner). They said that was probably the strongest form of discipline, that the child is suddenly disconnected from the parent—less close, more "out."

  Other things were different about these two types of emotion philosophy. In particular, the two groups of parents were very different in the way they taught their children something new. An honors student named Vanessa Kahen-Johnson (now a psychology professor) discovered this. Emotion-dismissing parents taught their child in the following ways:
- They gave lots of information in an excited manner at first.
- They were very involved with the child's mistakes.
- They saw themselves as offering "constructive criticism."
- The child increased the number of mistakes as the parents pointed out errors. This is a common effect during the early stages of skill acquisition.
- As the child made more mistakes, the parents escalated their criticism to insults, using trait labels such as "You are being careless"

or "You are spacey." They sometimes talked to each other about the child in the child's presence, as in: "He is so impulsive. That's his problem."

- As the child made more mistakes, the parents sometimes took over, becoming intrusive.

In a book adult sons wrote about their fathers,[4] a professional writer named Christopher Hallowell said that when he was 6, his dad said, "Son, I'm gonna teach you how to make a box. If you can make a box, you can do anything in the wood shop." Chris's first box was a little shaky, but it had a lid. His dad examined it and said: "Chris this is a wobbly box. If you can't even make a box, you can't do anything in the wood shop." Chris, at age 35, still has that box on his nightstand. He still sees his dad's face in the lid, saying, "Chris, you'll never amount to anything." Small moments can have huge implications for kids, because they tend to believe their parents, even about themselves.

In our lab not all children of emotion-dismissing parents did poorly on the task their parents taught them. Some children with parents dismissing of their negative emotions during learning the task got angry with their parents and did well on the lab task. They did well to spite their parents. So the parents got a good performance out of their kid, but at the expense of trust. In her dissertation, a former graduate student of mine, Eun Young Nahm, compared parenting in Korean-American and Euro-American two-parent families with a 6-year-old child.[5] The Korean-American parents were primarily emotion-dismissing or disapproving, using shame-based tactics to encourage their children during a tower-building task, while the Euro-American parents were primarily emotion-coaching, using praise-based tactics to encourage their children during the tower-building task. The Korean-American children did significantly better on the task than the Euro-American children. However, the levels of depression in the Korean-American children were significantly higher than those of Euro-American children. Higher achievement in this case came at an emotional cost.

Vanessa Kahen-Johnson also discovered that emotion-coaching parents taught their children in a dramatically different way from emotion-dismissing parents.[6]

Emotion-coaching parents:

- Gave little information to the child, but enough for the child to get started.
- Were not involved with the child's mistakes (they ignored them).
- Waited for the child to do something right, and then offered specific praise and added a little bit more information. (The best teaching offers a new tool, just within reach. Then learning feels like remembering.)
- The child attributed the learning to his or her own discovery.
- The child's performance also went up and up.

It's important to point out that when we measured parental warmth, we found that emotion-dismissing parents can be very warm. In our coding we found that warmth was statistically independent of emotion coaching or dismissing. For example, a parent can very warmly say, "What's wrong sweetheart? Put a smile on your face. There, that's daddy's little girl. Isn't that better now?" It is not cruel to be emotion-dismissing. Parents really mean well when they do it.

In fact, I am not saying that emotion dismissing is "bad." It is an action-oriented and problem-solving approach to problems. Both coaching and dismissing attitudes are important in parenting, but we discovered that they need to happen in the right sequence. For example, my daughter Moriah was once afraid of learning mathematics, and she discussed her fears with me. I empathized with the fears and she felt a lot better. However, after all that understanding, she actually did need to learn the math. Problem-solving and an action orientation is absolutely necessary in life and in parenting. However, as Haim Ginott once said, advice is always more effective when *words of understanding precede words of advice*. First a child needs to feel that he or she is not alone. We need to feel understood and supported. Then we are more likely to be able to turn toward action.

It was interesting to me that emotion-dismissing and emotion-coaching people also had different metaphors about negative emotions. Dismissing people saw anger as like an explosion, like losing control, or as aggression. Coaching people saw anger as a natural reaction to a blocked goal. They suggested understanding the frustration, the goal, and what was blocking it. The dismissing people saw sadness as wallowing in self-pity—as inaction and passivity, akin to mental illness—and they had metaphors of death. Coaching people saw sadness as something missing in one's life. They said that they slowed down to discover what was missing. Emotion-dismissing people saw fear as cowardice, and inaction, as being a wimp. Coaching people said that fear was telling you that your world was unsafe. They said that when they felt afraid, they found out how to make their worlds safer. About negative emotion in general, dismissing people said feeling the negativity leads nowhere, that one should roll with the punches, get over it, go on. They viewed examining negative emotions as akin to pouring gasoline on an open fire, very dangerous.

In short, coaching people said that exploring a negative emotion wasn't dangerous or scary. They said that it gave a person direction in life, like a GPS. Dismissing people thought of being positive as a choice, and they viewed dwelling on negative emotions as harmful and pessimistic. They thought it simply invited chaos.

In our initial study, as we followed the 3- to 4-year-old children, there were consequences of these two types of emotion philosophy. We discovered that children who were emotion coached at age 4 turned out to be very different at age 8, and at age 15, compared to the children of emotion-dismissing parents:

- They had higher reading and math scores at age 8, even controlling statistically for IQ differences at age 4.
- This effect was mediated through the attentional system. Coached children had better abilities with focusing attention, sustaining attention, and shifting attention.
- Coached children had greater self-soothing ability even when upset during a parent-child interaction.
- Coached children self-soothed better, delayed gratification better, and had better impulse control.
- Parents didn't have to down-regulate negativity as much.
- Coached children don't whine very much.
- Coached children had fewer behavior problems of all kinds (aggression and depression).

- Coached children had better relations with other children.
- Coached children had fewer infectious illnesses.
- As coached children got into middle childhood and then adolescence, they kept having appropriate "social moxie."
- Emotion-coaching parents also buffered the children in our sample from almost all the negative effects of an ailing marriage, separation, or a divorce (except for their children's sadness). The negative effects that disappeared were: (1) acting out with aggression, (2) falling grades in school, and (3) poor relations with other children.
- As Lynn Katz, Carol Hooven, and I reported in our book *Meta-emotion*, coached children, as they develop, seem to have more emotional intelligence.

The positive effects of teaching parents emotion coaching has been demonstrated in a randomized clinical trial by Sophie Havighurst in Australia,[7] and in a large-scale school-based intervention by Dr. Christina Choi in two Catholic Boystown orphanages in Korea (in Seoul and Busan).[8]

Teaching Emotion Coaching

There are only five steps in emotion coaching and there are now materials that teach this skill to parents.[9] These five steps are not difficult to teach parents. They are:

1. Noticing the negative emotion before it escalates.
2. Seeing it as an opportunity for teaching or intimacy.
3. Validating or empathizing with the emotion.
4. Helping the child give verbal labels to all emotions the child is feeling.
5. Setting limits on misbehavior, or problem-solving if there is no misbehavior. If the parent doesn't do this last step, the kids tend to wind up becoming physically or verbally aggressive toward other children.

It is interesting to note that our research showed that dads made a great deal of difference both for sons and for daughters. Fathers who emotion coached their children were better dads and better husbands. Their children felt closer to them, and moms appreciated them more. During conflict with their wives, emotion-coaching dads were not contemptuous; they were respectful. They knew their wives well and communicated a lot of affection and admiration to them in the oral history interview. They had a positive oral history switch. For the dads we studied, marriage and parenting was made of the same fabric. To read more about this meta-emotion study, see my book with Joan DeClaire, *Raising an Emotionally Intelligent Child*, and my book with Lynn Katz and Carole Hooven, *Meta-emotion*.

Attunement Is Emotion Coaching for Couples

The term "coaching" suggests an asymmetry. Parents coach children, but children don't coach parents. To generalize the concept of emotion coaching, we developed the idea of "attunement." The idea of attunement is based on my former student Dan Yoshimoto's coding of the couples' meta-emotion interview in his dissertation.[10] Dan's interview was an extension of our earlier work on the parental meta-emotion interview. Dan's doctoral thesis extended the meta-emotion interview to couples and developed a new coding system for the new interview.

Each partner was again interviewed separately. The interview was again very rich and a great deal of fun to do. We now think of the interview as a potential bridge between individual therapy and couples' therapy because after doing the interview with both partners, there is an obvious intervention. That intervention is to have them talk to each other about what they each said in their individual interviews. It turned out that a lot of the issues in couples' relationships were at their base about differences between the partners in how they felt about positive emotions (particularly love, affection, and pride) and negative emotions (especially fear, sadness, and anger).

In Dan's interview we asked people about their history and philosophy with five different emotions—anger, sadness, fear, affection, and pride (being proud of one's accomplishment)—and about their philosophy about the experience, exploration, and expression of the emotions in general. Dan's dissertation focused on sadness and anger. We discovered what kind of families and cultures each partner thought they came from as children in terms of the expression and experience of the emotions. Often these childhoods were quite different across partners.

We also scored these interviews for the extent to which people felt that they and their partner could talk fully about their emotions. We wound up dividing people into either dismissing or attuning toward their partner's emotions. Attuning is the opposite of being impatient with, disapproving of, or dismissing of negative emotion.

It's important again to point out that when people are dismissing of their partner's negative emotions, they may still be warm and affectionate in their attitude. They might say: "Oh honey, don't be sad, don't cry, cheer up. Look on the bright side." They are not necessarily being mean. However, it's the case that, as child psychologist Haim Ginott once said,[11] emotions do not vanish by being banished. Dismissing an emotion tends to inadvertently communicate: "I don't want to hear about it when you feel this way." The person doing the dismissing may not mean it that way. The intended message of dismissing is: "Just replace that negative emotion with a positive one." But the person with the emotion hears: "Yuck. Just go away and be unhappy somewhere else! Don't drag everyone down with your negative mood!"

Sometimes emotion-dismissing partners were, in fact, upset with their partner's negative emotions and described their partner as "overly negative" or "overly needy." These people found their partner's negativity a burden because it brought their own mood down, even when their partner's negative emotion wasn't about their relationship. For these people, the meta-emotion mismatch was a serious issue in their relationship.

We discovered that, as with a parental emotion-dismissing attitude, an emotion-dismissing attitude among couples is based on the belief that a person can have *any* emotion that he or she desires—that it is a matter of will. It's like putting on one jacket instead of another jacket. If one holds this belief, it makes sense that if a person feels unhappy, that person should want to put on a happy jacket rather than an unhappy jacket. That's the message someone who is emotion-dismissing is trying to convey.

We also discovered that when people are disapproving of a negative emotion, the disapproval often arises from them taking personal responsibility for making their partner feel good. Unfortunately, one cannot *make* someone feel a particular way. So this added responsibility is doomed.

What's the alternative? If one doesn't take responsibility for one's partner's negative emotion, what do you do with that partner's unhappiness? The answer to this question that our attuning subjects gave is the basis of the attunement skill set. Attunement turns out not to be a very complex social skill. It is the elusive basis for "being there" for one's partner whenever he or she is feeling emotional or has a need. It's essentially about listening nondefensively and emphathetically in order to better understand the partner's emotion.

Scoring the Attunement Interview

We scored the interview for specific aspects of people's awareness of an experience with emotions, and for their ability to respond to each other's emotions. The word "ATTUNE" is an acronym that stands for the following scoring categories:

Awareness of the emotion
Turning toward the emotions
Tolerance of the emotional experience
Understanding the emotion
Nondefensive Listening to the emotion
Empathy toward the emotion

These six dimensions are part of what Dan Yoshimoto's coding system measured. We coded each of these six dimensions for each partner from our videotape of the couples' meta-emotion interview.

Although attunement is not a complex skill, it is difficult to do unless one decides to do it. For emotion-dismissing people, that requires a shift in emotion philosophy from dismissing or disapproving to attunement. It means giving up responsibility for changing someone else's emotion and shifting to genuinely trying to understand one's partner's emotions. Once a person decides to attune, it is possible to get better and better at this skill. If a couple takes turns as speaker and listener, the skill can be broken down as follows:

Awareness. The aware speaker responds to smaller, less escalated displays of negative emotion, without blaming the partner. The aware listener periodically takes the partner's "emotional temperature," usually by asking questions like "How are you doing, honey?" or "What's up with you, baby?" Emotionally aware partners talk about these events as an opportunity for intimacy and closeness, rather than being impatient or annoyed (for example, by asking, "What is it *now*?" or "With you it's always something isn't it?"). In short, aware speakers and listeners are not dismissing or disapproving about the negative emotion.

They also kept in working memory an awareness of what UCLA psychologist Tom Bradbury called the partner's "enduring vulnerabilities" and sensitivities. For example, if the partner was sensitive to being excluded, they said that they remembered this fact, and they softened a discussion of an issue accordingly. If the partner was sensitive to criticism or anger, they reported softening the way they raised an issue, doing what we now call "preemptive repair" (see Chapter 8). In my private practice, I tell clients that no one escapes childhood without some scars, and these scars become triggers that escalate conflict. I suggest that they imagine that each person is wearing a T-shirt with their enduring vulnerabilities written on it. Some of my favorites are: "You don't want to try to improve me with constructive criticism"; "If you want to see defensiveness, just try blaming me"; "Don't scold me"; and "Don't try to control me."

The goal of this part of attunement appears to be soothing to reduce threat in "processing" negativity for both people. We psychologists have learned that a young baby is in one of two modes with respect to incoming stimulation. I call these two modes the "What's this?" response and the "What the hell is this?" response. For example, show a baby a slide of a clown and the baby may orient toward that slide openly, a response Russian psychologist Andre Sokolov called the "orienting reflex." In this mode, the baby's heart rate decreases, the baby stops moving, the baby looks directly at the slide, the baby stops sucking the nipple, and the baby's pupils dilate. This is the "What's this?" response.

Alternatively, the baby might respond as follows: the baby's heart rate increases, the baby starts moving, the baby looks away from the slide, the baby starts sucking the nipple, and the baby's pupils constrict. This is the "What the hell is this?" response. In attunement people try to keep their partner in "What's this?" rather than "What the hell is this?" mode.

Turning Toward. This means that speakers tend to talk about their feelings in terms of their *positive need*, instead of talking about what the speaker does *not* need or want. Positive need is a recipe for success by the listener. It is what would have worked for the speaker if the discussion of a negative emotion or a regrettable incident were replayed. For example, if the speaker were upset by their conversation at dinner, a positive need might be, "I need you to ask me about my day." It's a recipe for success for that speaker. So the rules for attunement were that while the listener has responsibilities, so does the speaker. In turning toward, the speaker cannot begin with blaming or criticism. Instead, it is the responsibility of the speaker to state his or her feelings as neutrally as possible, and then convert any complaint about the partner into a positive need (i.e., something one *does* need, not what one does *not* need). This requires a mental transformation from what is wrong with one's partner to what one's partner can do that would work. It is the speaker's job to discover that recipe. The speaker is really saying, "Here's what I feel, and here's what I need from you." Or, in processing a negative event that has already happened, the speaker is saying, "Here's what I felt, and here's what I needed from you."

How do couples find that positive need? How do they convert "Here's what's wrong with you, and here's what I want you to stop doing" into, "Here's what I feel (or felt) and here's the positive thing I need (or needed) from you"? I think that the answer is that there is a longing or a wish, and therefore a recipe, within every negative emotion. In general, in sadness something is missing. In anger there is a frustrated goal. In disappointment there is a hope, and expectation. In loneliness there is a desire for connection. In a similar way, each negative emotion is a GPS for guiding us toward a longing, a wish, and a hope. The expression of the positive need eliminates the blame and the reproach.

Tolerance. With tolerance, each partner subscribes to the belief that in every negative emotional event there are always two different but equally valid *perceptions* of the event. Although partners may share the same viewpoint, they each believe they can learn from the other's viewpoint. This tolerant viewpoint has to be reciprocal. Although people may not agree with their partner's reporting of the facts, they avoid arguing about the facts and are tolerant of their partner's perceptions. They don't try to change the partner's emotions or talk their partner out of having those emotions. They accept anger as well as sadness. They don't take their partner's negative emotional state personally. The view they seem to have is that (as Ginot suggested) all emotions and wishes are acceptable, although not all behavior is acceptable. Also, the tolerant person subscribed to the belief that emotions have a purpose and logic.

This contrasts with an emotion-dismissing view that everyone can select which emotions to have. Tolerance is a recognition that it makes sense to talk about emotions and that it is productive to fully process emotions with oneself and one's partner. Tolerance does not mean agreement or compliance. Nor does it mean having to adopt the partner's perspective as one's own. Rather, tolerance means that one believes that it is important to inquire about the partner's perspective.

Understanding. These people, while listening, say that they agree that they will seek an understanding of the partner's emotions—their meaning, their history—and whatever events may have escalated the misunderstanding, conflict, or hurt feelings. They are saying, "Talk to me, baby." When they are listening to their partner, they postpone their own agenda in a search for understanding the partner's point of view. "Postpone" is the operative word, instead of ignore. They say that this creates a situation in which both people rest assured that they will each be understood. The only goal is understanding, not giving advice, or correcting and guiding.

I think that this point of view changes the job description in conflict from persuading one's partner that one's point of view is worth understand to trying to find out one's partner's perspective and trying to understanding it. Somewhat counterintuitively, understanding is facilitated by taking *no responsibility* for the partner's feelings, except trying to understand. When one's partner is crying, for example, the response should not be, "Please stop crying," but something like, "Please help me understand what the tears are all about." The goal is understanding, and that is enough. An important part of this understanding is asking, "Is there anything more? Do you have any other feelings and needs about this situation?" I think that a lack of impatience arises from the belief that in every situation people usually have more than one emotion, and they have emotion blends. Emotions line up like dominoes, and people often process only the lead emotion or domino, the primary affect, making it necessary to revisit the situation because they were not done fully processing it.

Nondefensive Listening. To facilitate understanding, attuned people down-regulate their own defensiveness and flooding as they are listening to their partner's negative emotions and perceptions. I think that this is in many ways the most difficult social skill in attunement, probably more important than empathy. These people down-regulate their defensiveness primarily by keeping quiet, pausing a beat before responding, listening a little, and postponing their own agenda while they focus on their partner's pain, getting in touch with their own feelings of love and protection. What's really important, I think, is that they focus also on their partner's *perceptions* of the situation, not on "the facts." They remember that they respect and love their partner. They wait rather than reacting swiftly. They remember to breathe and self-soothe. To the extent possible, they maximize agreement, seek common ground, and try not to take their partner's emotions as a personal attack or something they have to fix.

It isn't easy to down-regulate one's own defensiveness. Therapist Dan Wile suggested that defensive feelings can be turned into self-disclosure, as in: "Right now I am feeling defensive, but I don't want to respond defensively." Down-regulating defensiveness is hard if people are "running on empty" in the relationship. If the emotional bank account is low, they become hypervigilant and overly sensitive to their partner's negative affects. They may even see negativity when it is not there, and they tend to miss some of the positivity their partner is displaying. As noted earlier, in 1980 two researchers, Robinson and Price, did a study in which they put observers in couples' homes just to observe positivity. They also trained the couple to do the same job. When the couple was getting along, the observers and the couple were in synch in terms of their observations, but when the couple was unhappy, the partners missed 50% of the positivity that the observers saw.

Empathy. The final part of the acronym refers to attempting to listen to the partner's negative emotions with compassion and understanding and trying to see the partner's emotions through the partner's eyes. This process reminded me of Mr. Spock's "Vulcan mind meld" in the original *Star Trek*. Spock, who is a Vulcan, can telepathically meld his mind with another person's. He leaves behind his own mind in some ways as he performs the mind meld. He genuinely sees the world through that person's eyes. Empathy, when it works, is like this telepathic seeing of the situation (and feeling it as well) through the eyes of one's partner. Empathic listeners become keenly aware of the distress and pain of their partner. This is a resonant experience of temporarily becoming the partner and experiencing the partner's emotions. They then communicate empathy and validation. A good summary of this validation is being able to communicate something like: "It makes sense to me that you would have these feelings, and needs, because. . . ." Validation is a very important part of the attunement attitude.

That's a general definition of what we code in the attunement interview. Attunement as a general skill set is important in three different social contexts, and it varies with each context.

Context #1. Attunement in Sliding-Door Moments

In the movie *Sliding Doors,* the protagonist, played by Gwyneth Paltrow, decides to go home from work because she is not feeling well. She runs to catch a train in the London tube but just barely misses it. In the next scene, we see her boyfriend, who is about to cheat on her with her best girlfriend. Catching the next train, Paltrow comes home, completely unaware of what her boyfriend has done. Then suddenly we are jerked back in time, back again to the same train platform, only this time Paltrow makes the train and walks in on her cheating boyfriend in the act. Two trajectories thus unfold in the movie, somehow strangely intertwining and meeting at the end.

Here's a sliding-door story that happened to me: I was getting ready for bed, putting a mystery novel I hadn't had time to finish by my bedside. When I went into the bathroom, I saw my wife's face reflected in the bathroom mirror. She was brushing her hair and looked sad. She hadn't seen me yet. In one version of the sliding-door moment I could have slowly backed out of the bathroom, gotten into bed, and picked up my book. In that universe, later my wife would have joined me and I might have turned to her to initiate sex. She, still feeling sad, probably would have pulled away because she wasn't in the mood for sex. But then—like in the movie—I was back to the sliding-door moment, poised at the bathroom entrance. This time, however, I actually did enter the bathroom. I took the brush from my wife's hand and began brushing her hair. That was a different universe. She closed her eyes and leaned back into me, and I said, "What's wrong, baby?" We talked about her sadness, which was about her 92-year-old mother's deteriorating mental alertness with Alzheimer's disease. Later we both got into bed and I did turn to her to initiate sex, and she responded warmly.

Now imagine that we are again back in the first universe. This time when she pulled away I might have become angry. I might have said, "You're being so cold." That could have started a regrettable incident. Thus, in this manner, small moments in a relationship unfold—ordinary moments, with ordinary decisions, but very different trajectories for a relationship over time.

There are many, many such moments in a relationship. At each of them there is a tiny turning point—an opportunity, or a lost opportunity, for connection. Failing to turn toward our partner in any one of these sliding-door moments may not have hugely negative consequences. However, when we add up many such choices to dismiss emotion instead of attuning to it, the result is two different trajectories leading to very different universes.

These frequent sliding-door moments serve as small "trust tests." They are moments of choice, when the partner directly or indirectly asks for something. We call that a "bid for connection"—and the choice is made to turn toward, away, or against that bid. The request for connection can be made directly and verbally or indirectly and nonverbally. In many, many of these moments the trust metric is subjectively evaluated—often without our awareness—and cumulatively, over time, we decide whether we can count on our partner to be truthful and truly "there" for us. This is where our work on trust links to Susan Johnson's emotionally focused couple therapy (EFT). The turning away can have consequences for the security of the partners' attachment to each other and sense of safety with each other.

The request for connection ("being there for me") can be as small as getting the partner's attention for an instant. We may want to show our partner something, comment on something, tell a joke, or in a myriad of ways have our partner see our immediate current need. For example, we may say, "Will you please help me fold the laundry?" or we may just audibly grumble while folding the laundry as our partner walks by. The bid may also ask for more than attention, like asking for the partner's active interest.

What is even more interesting is that these bids for connection in sliding-door moments are actually organized in a hierarchy, kind of like a ladder. The level in the bid hierarchy depends on how much we are asking for in terms of cognitive or emotional effort from our partner. Following are some examples of bids and where they roughly fall in the hierarchy, with the first lowest on the ladder and the last at the top.

1. A bid for attention
2. Simple requests (e.g., "While you're up, get me the butter.")
3. A bid for help, teamwork, or coordination (e.g., help with an errand)
4. A bid for the partner's interest or active excitement
5. Questions or requests for information
6. A bid for conversation
7. A bid for just venting
8. Sharing events of the day
9. Stress reduction
10. Problem solving
11. Humor, laughter
12. Affection
13. Playfulness
14. Adventure
15. Exploration
16. Learning something together
17. Intimate conversation
18. Emotional support
19. Understanding, compassion, empathy
20. Sexual intimacy

For example, "attention" is lower on the list because if you can't even get your partner's attention, you aren't as likely to make a bid for conversation or emotional support. That means that attachment security at an easy level on the ladder leads to more risk taking and vulnerability at a higher level on the ladder. I trust my partner with my vulnerability on a higher level of the ladder if the relationship has passed trust tests at a lower level of the ladder. Couples we see in restaurants who uncomfortably eat an entire meal and never talk to each other are stuck at a low level of connection on the ladder.

My former student Janice Driver coded these bids made in our apartment newlywed study lab in her "bids and turning" coding system.[12] In general, people can *respond* to the bid positively, which we call "turning toward." It doesn't take much. Sometimes even a grunt will do as sufficient turning toward. If partners respond in a large way, which Jani calls "enthusiastic turning toward," that usually has huge possibilities for emotional connection. For example, suppose one partner is watching TV and says "They went to Spain for a honeymoon. Wow!" A minimal turning toward would be "That's nice." Or it can be enthusiastic, as in, "Wow that would be great. Why don't we go there this summer?"

Or a person can totally ignore the bid, as if he or she hasn't heard it or noticed the request, which we call "turning away." Or the partner can respond to the bid in a grumpy, irritable, or aggressive fashion, which we call "turning against."

In our newlywed study Jani found that the couples who had divorced 6 years after the wedding had turned toward their partner (in our love lab) an average of 33%, whereas the couples who were still married 6 years after the wedding had turned toward their partner 86% of the time.[13] That's a big difference.

Jani also discovered that turning toward builds an "emotional bank account" that makes conflict far more likely to be filled with positive emotions, particularly shared humor. Her first discovery was just a correlation, which could have been a chance association. But then we actually did a randomized clinical trial (which was Kim Ryan's dissertation) that showed that changing just the first three levels of the Sound Relationship House (love maps, turning toward, and fondness and admiration) in a one-day workshop increased the amount of positive affect during conflict, particularly shared humor. That study was an important part of verifying the causal model of the Sound Relationship House; it suggested that, in part, turning toward *causes* positive affect during conflict.

Why would this be so interesting? We had previously discovered that what predicted divorce or stability best among our newlyweds was the amount of positive affect during conflict, particularly humor, understanding, and affection. But what good is that piece of information? It's a useless finding because inducing positive affect during conflict is not possible by working on conflict directly, any more than ordering someone to laugh is effective at inducing humor and amusement. However, discovering that turning toward bids is related to positive affect during conflict gave us a clue about how to positively alter the nature of conflict. It therefore gave us our only method for building the very effective repairs of humor and affection during conflict. We can do it without directly working on conflict. We just work on turning toward bids.

Turning Away or Against in Sliding-Door Moments

We noticed on videotapes in the apartment lab that a partner's turning away seemed to make the bidder's body position crumple a bit, which was usually followed by some face-saving activity like straightening the curtains. So it's probably a small hurt, not a big one. Often the person turning away just doesn't think this moment is important; turning away is not necessarily mean-spirited. Yet that small turning away builds the groundwork for a bad habit.

As Susan Johnson noted in training therapists in our clinic, however, there are some bigger moments when a bid means more, and when turning away may in itself lead to a huge loss of trust in the implicit relationship contract that we are in this relationship *for* each other—that it's a contract of mutual nurturance and *being there for each other*. People then often experience great disappointment, anger, and loneliness. Susan Johnson said that the emotional unavailability or unresponsiveness of an "attachment figure"—that is, someone who is supposed to be a source of safety and security, who is supposed to "be there for you"—is a great source of anger and panic in the person who gets a turning away from the partner. Part of Johnson's emotionally focused couple therapy, is, when necessary, spent on understanding, processing, and healing what she calls these "attachment injuries."

The big attachment injuries Johnson is talking about are the moments of turning away that don't just erode trust. They shatter trust. An example is a husband Johnson saw in therapy who earlier had refused to talk about his wife's miscarriage because he didn't find these conversations "positive and constructive," so she was left to deal with her grief and loss alone.

The secret of turning toward bids in sliding-door moments is first noticing the bid, and second responding to the bid. These two steps usually require some *heightened awareness* of how our partner tends to make requests, and an attitude that we wish to meet these needs a large percentage of the time. We are thus communicating: "I hear you, baby. Talk to me. What can I do to meet your need?"

Context #2. Attunement with Regard to Regrettable Incidents

Regrettable incidents are inevitable in all relationships. A simple mathematical proof will suffice to explain this idea. If we were to estimate the percentage of time we are emotionally available when with our partner—ready to listen wholeheartedly—most people would agree that 50% is a generous estimate. That's the probability of tossing an coin and getting heads versus tails. If we then ask, "What is the probability that both partners will be emotionally available at the same time, assuming independence of emotional availability?" that probability is 0.25 (0.5 x 0.5 = 0.25), the probability of tossing two coins and getting *two* heads. Therefore, 75% of the time, even with this generous estimate, the ground is ripe for miscommunications. A more realistic estimate of emotional availability might be 30%, in which case the probability of both people being emotionally available at the same time is 9%, with 91% of the time being ripe ground for miscommunications. Regrettable incidents are par for the course. They don't imply that it's a bad relationship, just that there are two very different minds in any relationship.

After a regrettable incident, in attunement we need first to be able to calm down, and second to have a conversation that *processes* the incident. "Processing" means that a couple can talk about a regrettable incident without getting back into the incident or fight that may have followed it. It's as if they are on a balcony, having observed and being able to talk about a play they saw on stage that involved the two of them. Again, they are saying, "Talk to me, baby. I'm here for you." In my clinical practice I have people take turns doing this. That attitude and the skill of listening with (1) awareness, (2) turning toward, (3) tolerance, (4) nondefensive listening, (5) understanding as a goal, and (6) empathy is the basis for the conversation that can create emotional connection during sliding-door moments.

The late great comedian George Carlin had a section in one of his books called "Here are some things you never see."[14] One of those, he claimed, is the popular bumper sticker S#!T HAPPENS on a Rolls Royce. Only the down-and-out put that sticker on their car, he said. But in all relationships, negative emotions, unfortunate events, and regrettable incidents inevitably happen, whether one is driving down the road in a broken-down Ford or in a Rolls. S#!T HAPPENS to everyone.

What matters for building trust is how one responds to one's partner's negative emotions. What are the most common regrettable incidents or S#!T that happens for couples? Surprisingly, they aren't disputes about particular topics, like sex or money. Reporters often ask me, "What do couples fight about mostly?" I answer, "Absolutely nothing. They fight about nothing." Couples rarely sit down, create an agenda, and argue about specific topics, like the budget. Sometimes they do. Instead, they usually hurt each other's feelings in very ordinary, seemingly meaningless, small moments that seem to arise from about absolutely nothing. S#!T just happens. For example, a couple is watching television and he has the remote control. He is channel surfing when she says, "Leave it on that channel." He says, "Okay, but let me first see what else is on." Generally women want to watch television and men want to see what else is on. She responds by saying, "No! Just leave it. I hate it when you channel surf." He throws down the remote and angrily says, "Fine!" She responds by saying, "I don't like the way you just said 'fine.' That hurt my feelings." He says, "I said 'fine' because you are always going to get your way, so fine, have it your way. I don't want to argue." She says, "I don't even want to watch TV with you anymore." He responds by saying,

"I don't want to talk about it," and leaves the room. Something small has turned into a regrettable incident. They do need to talk about control and influence. If they talk about it using this process of "attuning," they will usually increase their understanding of the event and each other's perception, thereby increasing a sense of trust through connection. If they *dismiss* these negative emotions in this regrettable incident, they typically will still eventually drift together again, but trust will have eroded a small amount.

A Theory of Building Trust When SH#!T Happens

Physicists since Albert Einstein have been searching for what they call the "grand unified theory" (or GUT) that will unify all four of nature's forces: gravitation, electromagnetic force, the weak force of radioactive decay, and the strong force that holds the nucleus of atoms together. They haven't found it yet.

In the area of relationships, things are apparently much simpler than in theoretical physics. I want to propose a GUT theory of trust when S#!T happens in love relationships. Our data show that attunement is the ultimate way to down-regulate flooding and avoid the negative oral history switch. Now we have a theory that can explain why some relationships work and others fail. Here's the theory.

Explaining relationship failure. Negative events in couple relationships are inevitable. The way relationships fail is through something called the "Zeigarnik effect." If a couple's negative events are not fully processed (by attunement), then they are remembered and rehearsed repeatedly, turned over and over in each person's mind. Trust begins to erode. Eventually "cognitive dissonance" arises: One is staying in a relationship, but that relationship is a veritable fountain of negativity. That cognitive dissonance is like a stone in one's shoe. It gets resolved by deciding that one's partner has lasting negative traits that "explain" the continual negativity. Empirically, the most common negative attribution is "my partner is selfish." This fact shows that it is precisely trust that erodes. People stop believing that their partner is thinking about their best interests. The potential for betrayal increases as we start believing that our partner is primarily interested in his or her own gains. During conflict discussions, negativity is more unpleasant, but it is more likely to be reciprocated and escalated. These negative exchanges during conflict become an "absorbing state," easier to enter than to exit. They also build betrayal, because conflict becomes more like a zero-sum game. What is sad is that the absorbing-state quality spreads to non-conflict interactions as well. Gradually, during conflict and non-conflict interactions, people are unable to act with their partner's best interests at heart, and, instead, respond with their own interests at heart. That means that not only has trust eroded, but the potential for betrayal has increased as well. Positive sentiment override becomes replaced by negative sentiment override.

New, continually unprocessed negative events that involve the erosion of trust, as well as increases in the potential for betrayal, add to this picture until eventually a threshold is crossed through the Zeigarnik effect. I believe that this is when the oral history switch flips. A major threshold has then been passed. Then there is an internal retelling of the relationship's history within each partner.

The negative events now trump the positive, and the partner's negative traits now trump his or her positive traits. The cost-benefit analysis of the relationships turns to an imbalance of greater costs instead of greater benefits. Negativity becomes self-generating. People now think, "Even if my partner does something nice for me, it is still a selfish person doing something nice—someone I no longer trust."

Explaining Relationship Success

The way relationships work well is that when negative events are fully processed, there is no Zeigarnik effect. Hence, these events are not very well remembered, nor are they mentally rehearsed. Instead, positive events are remembered and rehearsed. Trust is built because our partner has "been there" for us. We believe that our partner acts with our best interests in mind. Our partner, through processing *our* negative emotions, has demonstrated that he or she has our best interests at heart and is "there for us." We remember these positive moments because thinking about them is intrinsically rewarding. Our needs matter to our partner. We then go on to forget the specific information about our hurts, and we minimize the negative in the relationship. There is no cognitive dissonance. One is staying in a relationship, and that relationship appears to be a veritable fountain of positivity. We decide that our partner has mostly lasting positive traits that "explain" why we are staying with this person who generally makes us happy, whom we can trust, whom we feel safe with, and whose negativity is somewhat hard to remember. The most common positive attribution is "my partner is so loving and generous." Now, if our partner is thoughtless, irritable, emotionally distant, or unkind, our explanation is that he or she must be "stressed," because we trust this person. Negativity does not become an absorbing state because when we try repairing the negativity, our partner tends to accept our repair attempt. In fact, we see our partner being gentle with us and doing "preemptive" repair to soften any discussion of a disagreement. We are able to laugh together even when we discuss a disagreement. There is a lot of affection between us.

New, continually processed negative events are recalled, but only dimly. The oral history switch stays positive. There is even a retelling of the relationship's history emphasizing the positive. The positive events trump the negative; the partner's positive traits trump his or her negative traits. The cost-benefit analysis of the relationship stays with much greater benefits than costs. Now positivity becomes self-generating. Even if the partner does something nasty, he or she is seen as a wonderful and trustworthy person who is temporarily stressed or in a bad mood. The event is minimized. If it lasts too long, the partners will attune again.

A Flowchart for Building Trust in Context #2

The diagram pictured in Figure 6.1 shows the two possible tracks for a relationship. As mentioned, negative events, or regrettable incidents, are inevitable. In the right hand track, the emotional event is dismissed or disapproved of. There is no emotion processing. No connection. Flooding occurs, or it continues and distrust builds. The Zeigarnik effect leads this event to be remembered and rehearsed. Negativity during conflict and non-conflict interactions becomes an absorbing state. Cognitive dissonance leads to a negative oral history switch. The negative event is "explained" through the lasting negative traits of the partner and the fleeting, situationally based positive traits of the partner.

In the left hand track, the flooding is down-regulated and attunement occurs. Conflict is not an absorbing state, and it is easily exited through repair and positive affect like shared humor and affection. There is no

Zeigarnik effect and mostly positive events are recalled and "explained" through the lasting positive traits of the partner and the fleeting, situationally based negative traits of the partner.

Let's look at the Five phases a little more closely. The diagram in Figure 6.1 sums them up.

Phase 1. S#IT HAPPENS As I discussed, negative emotions and regrettable incidents are inevitable in all relationships. However, the response to these moments is critical. That leads to Phase 2.

Phase 2. Attune or Dismiss/Disapprove. After a regrettable incident happens, there is a sliding-door choice point, one of two paths: or attuning to the partner's negative feelings or feelings about the regrettable incident, or dismissing or disapproving of them. Escalation and alienation occur when we listen defensively to the hurt caused during the regrettable incident. The escalation and alienation take place instead of the attunement conversation the couple needs to have. With attunement trust is built.

Conversely, with dismissing, trust is eroded. Our partner is not there for us. Dismissing is also more likely to occur when there is a power asymmetry. The dismisser has more power than the person whose emotion is being dismissed. Power asymmetry is therefore a setting condition

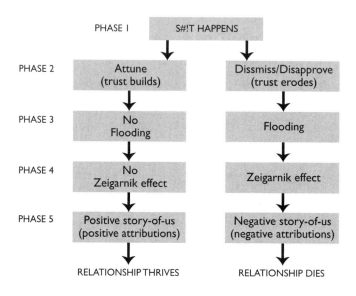

Figure 6.1   The Five Phases of Regrettable Incidents

for dismissing. The dismisser is more removed, like the withdrawer is in the demand-withdraw pattern.

An analogy to attunement is tuning two musical instruments to each other, which requires grounding in a reference note. The choir may need to hear an A-tone. Similarly, in relationships, we need to become grounded in our partner's point of view when our partner needs to talk about a negative emotion or when there's been a regrettable incident. It's easy for a choir to drift out of tune; it's natural. There is a need for the choir to tune up periodically, and that is the way it is in relationships, too. What happens when one partner doesn't attune? Trust is eroded. The dismisser usually withdraws more, and becomes the distancer. The pursue-distance dynamic is created, and Phase 3 happens—we become flooded. This creates asymmetry in power, with the pursuer suddenly becoming less powerful. (In the final chapter of this book I will talk about how these power asymmetries can be defined and measured mathematically.)

Phase 3. No Flooding or Flooding. During the expression of negative emotions or during a regrettable incident and the dismissing afterwards, most of us will become flooded, or overwhelmed by negative affect. Being flooded often is the cumulative effect of repeatedly getting into a physiological fight-or-flight state. When we're feeling flooded we would rather be anywhere on the planet than in this room talking to our partner. Flooding predicts that our shields will go up, because we feel overwhelmed and either want to flee or immediately vanquish our partner's negativity. But it turns out that the more flooded we are, the more we initiate nasty interchanges, and the more we summarize ourselves instead of taking in new information.

Overall, in a regrettable incident following a negative sliding-door moment, flooding is the biggest block to reconnecting and repair. As noted earlier, our data also show that men become flooded far more easily than women do, and they have much more trouble self-soothing. In general, when we become flooded we cannot process information very well, and we have dramatically reduced access to our ability to be empathic, compassionate, creative, or laugh at ourselves. All these wonderful capabilities seem to evaporate when we become flooded. When we are flooded not only has trust already eroded a bit, but also the untrustworthiness metric has increased. We start seeing our partner not as our irritating friend but as our adversary, and *we start acting out of our own self-interest.* We are in great danger of seeing the regrettable incident as a power struggle and a zero-sum game. We are inviting the dynamics of betrayal.

When we're flooded we are not a bad person, nor do we suddenly develop a psychopathology, nor are we necessarily in a bad relationship. We are simply flooded. We can't compassionately listen to our partner, even if we wanted to. Our recent data suggest that there are three parts to flooding. The first part is the shock of feeling attacked, blamed, and abandoned. The second part is awareness that we can't calm down. The third part is emotional shutdown. When we are flooded we become like a city under siege. Conflict then starts becoming an absorbing state.

Understanding the concept of flooding itself provides some relief to partners who have trouble listening to their partner. It suggests that when people are flooded they can't listen, even though they might wish to. It's not anyone's fault that they can't listen when flooded; it's a natural fight-or-flight response, though operating a bit out of context. The concept of flooding also suggests the importance of attuning to oneself when one is flooded, and the overwhelming importance of knowing what we are feeling and of self-soothing rather than fighting or fleeing. When flooded, we can't recall why we ever liked our partner, and we can't be very creative.

Phase 4. No Zeigarnik Effect or Zeigarnik Effect. In 1922, a petite 21-year-old newlywed Jewish woman named Bluma Zeigarnik sat in a café in Vienna and watched as professional waiters listened carefully to huge orders from large gatherings without writing anything down.[15] Then she watched as the waiters flawlessly filled their orders. Always the astute observer, Zeigarnik later interviewed these waiters. As they moved rapidly from table to kitchen to table, she found that they remembered everything the customers asked for. However, when she interviewed the waiters after they had filled the orders, they had forgotten everything. In other words, when the orders remained unfilled, they remembered them, but after the orders were completely processed, the orders were forgotten. This was later coined the "Zeigarnik effect." It is defined as follows: We have better recall for events that we have not completely processed. Zeigarnik found that, on average, there is 90% better recall for "unfinished events" than for events we have somehow completed.

The famous social psychologist Morton Deutch, reviewing Kurt

Lewin's social psychological field theory in the *Handbook of Social Psychology* in 1968, discussed what he called the "Zeigarnik quotient," which is the ratio of unfinished tasks that are recalled divided by completed tasks that are recalled.[16] Zeigarnik predicted that this ratio would be greater than 1.0. Deutch reviewed research that found that the Zeigarnik quotient averaged 1.9.

Some writers have even claimed that the Zeigarnik effect forms the basis for night dreams, as we often dream about uncompleted daily events. Others, like psychiatrist Daniel Siegel, have claimed that the Zeigarnik effect could explain why traumatic events linger in the body, ready to be activated again with the right trigger.[18] Yet if equally traumatic events later become completed autobiographical stories with words attached to the traumatic bodily sensations, the traumas lose their lethality. In other words, they have been fully "processed." We are done with them, so they occupy a less potent memory space.

The Zeigarnik effect may not merely be limited to memory for facts, but also govern how negative emotional events are stored in memory. Berkeley researcher Mary Main developed an interview called the "Adult Attachment Interview." In this interview, Main scored how people told the story of their childhoods, and whether or not these childhoods were painful and traumatic. She was less interested in the content of the stories than in *how the stories were told*. People who were able to tell coherent stories about their traumatic childhood were observed to be very different kinds of parents than people who had the same amount of childhood trauma but were somehow not done with it. They were anxious, preoccupied, dismissing, or simply incoherent in their account of these childhood events. When studying the babies of these two types of parents, Mary Main discovered an amazing effect. The people who were somehow done with the trauma, who could tell a coherent story about it, who were not disorganized and flooded with emotion while telling the story, had infants who were securely attached. On the other hand, the people who were not done with the trauma, who could not tell a coherent story about it, who were disorganized and flooded with emotion while telling the story, had infants who were insecurely attached. The security of infant attachment had been established as one of the central buffers conferred by healthy parenting on children, a buffer that saw them well throughout life. Securely attached children did better in school, did better in social relationships, and generally fared better throughout life than insecurely attached children.

The Mary Main findings—and the Zeigarnik effect—became the basis for Daniel Siegel and Mary Hartzell's program for improving parenting (see their book *Parenting from the Inside Out*) Other writers such as Ian A. James proposed that the Zeigarnik effect was the basis of all emotional disorders. He suggested that the maintenance of intrusions and "perseverations" reflect the presence of unresolved issues, which he called mental "pop ups." James suggested that the Zeigarnik effect may have important implications in a wide range of psychiatric disorders such as post-traumatic stress disorder, unresolved grief, obsessive-compulsive disorders, and general anxiety disorders. James suggested there is a strong "completion tendency" in these disorders.

Recently Carol Tavris and Eliot Aronson published a book titled *Mistakes Were Made (But Not by Me)*.[18] The title is a quote taken from Henry Kissinger, who, when asked what it was like to serve in the Nixon administration, said that mistakes were made, but not by him. Tavris and Aronson's book is about self-justification, or how people complete memories for which there is a discord—some mismatch between memory and experience. The *Wall Street Journal* said in its review of the book that the volume was entertaining and amusing, until one realized that it was about one's own tendency toward self-justification, at which point it suddenly became horrifying. The book was an excursion into the phenomenon called "cognitive dissonance," first discovered by social psychologist Leon Festinger. Festinger had written a book titled *When Prophesy Fails*, which was about his observation of a cult who believed strongly that the world would be destroyed on a specific date. Festinger was present when the moment came and went. He wanted to know what the cult members would do when their prophesy failed—how would they resolve the "cognitive dissonance" created by their obviously false belief. Here's what happened. The cult leader waited a long time until she was sure that the prophesy had actually failed. Then she announced to the group that it was *their* faith that had miraculously saved the world from annihilation. Festinger reported that the cult's belief became even stronger and more steadfast. They had found a way to resolve their cognitive dissonance.

The potential role of the Zeigarnik effect is colossal. If we engage in attuned processing of a negative emotional event or regrettable incident with our partner, we will only foggily remember it. The details will become hazy, and the event, insignificant. On the other hand, if we dismiss and avoid processing a negative emotional event, it will not disappear. It will fester, ready to be triggered again.

This is why attuning to a negative regrettable incident is so incredibly important. Like the Vienesse waiters in Zeigarnik's café, if partners avoid processing the incident with attunement, the event and its negative emotion will lie inside of each partner like an improvised explosive device (IED), ready to explode if inadvertently stepped on.

We have two indices in our lab that tap into the extent of the Zeigarnik effect. The first index is the average value of the video-recall rating dial. The reasoning is that, if negative things are unfinished, the ratings will be lower than if negative things are finished. The second index is all about the attributions people eventually start making about their partner's lasting personality traits. As I mentioned, the most common research finding across labs is that the first negative attribution people start making when the relationship becomes less happy is "my partner is selfish," a direct reflection of a decrease in the trust metric. They then start to see their partner's momentary emotional distance and irritability as a sign of a lasting negative trait. On the other hand, in happier relationships people make lasting positive trait attributions, like "my partner is sweet," and tend to write off their partner's momentary emotional distance and irritability as a temporary attribution, like "my partner is stressed."

Phase 5. The Ever-Changing "Story of Us." When the Zeigarnik effect takes hold, unresolved negative emotions capture people's consciousness. Over time, as the relationship passes a critical threshold of dismissed negative emotion, we will enter negative sentiment override. In negative sentiment override, our cost-benefit analysis of staying in the relationship begins to change, tilting more to the cost side than to the benefit side. Our thoughts naturally drift more toward leaving the relationship rather than staying in it.

How does this happen? The final phase in a relationship's slow death transforms the innermost story that we tell ourselves about our relationship's history and our partner's underlying character. The lesson is this:

Negative emotions do not vanish by being banished. When they are not fully processed, they linger, and the Zeigarnik effect takes over. Our thoughts dwell on these emotional injuries. The injuries become a stone in our shoe that we cannot remove. We turn these events over and over in our mind, studying every facet, trying to make sense out of what happened. We are faced with a cognitive dissonance, an internal mismatch. On the one hand, we think, "I am staying in this relationship," but on the other hand, we think, "I am having all these negative emotions and repeated regrettable incidents that I can't seem to get out of my mind." Something is really wrong.

We eventually resolve this intensely uncomfortable cognitive dissonance by telling ourselves a negative story-of-us. Unfortunately, this process also includes mentally attributing negative, lasting traits to our partner, such as selfishness. Now conflict is becoming an absorbing state, a zero-sum game. In this new story-of-us, we drift slowly toward scanning the past for clues of selfishness and other negative traits. We maximize the importance of past negative events and minimize the importance of past positive events. We tell ourselves that our fights were truly meaningless, as they ultimately failed to improve our relationship.

We now wear a perceptual filter that tells us everything is getting worse. Once we switch to making these negative attributions about our partner, it's very hard for us to alter them. For example, if our partner is suddenly and surprisingly nice to us, we still think it's our selfish partner doing something nice, so the effect of our partner's niceness is trivialized.

If switched to a negative story-of-us, the relationship will almost certainly follow a sad, predictable trajectory. But if switched to a positive story-of-us, the relationship will most likely take a very different trajectory, toward positive sentiment override, a buffer against momentary negativity or emotional distance.

Clearly, the skills of attunement can make all the difference between a relationship's strength versus its demise.

Context #3. Attunement During Conflict

The third context in which attunement is needed is conflict. Recall the finding that trust is eroded is when conflict becomes an absorbing state.

If partners are unable to repair their interaction during the conflict, if the conflict escalates or they withdraw, if the conflict becomes an absorbing state, if they are unable to avoid flooding or DPA, and if the four horsemen emerge during the conflict, then trust will be seriously eroded. If this pattern of conflict becomes characteristic of how partners handle all conflicts, trust will eventually disappear, and the couple will enter what we call the "distance and isolation cascade."[19]

In the distance and isolation cascade, partners will gradually start to avoid talking about that issue, start believing that there is no point in trying to talk to their partner, eventually avoid each other entirely, begin living their lives in parallel, and become increasingly unhappy and lonely. Conflict avoidance becomes the norm.

The Blueprint of Attunement in the Three Contexts

I now will discuss the blueprints necessary for attunement in each of the three relational contexts.

Blueprint #1. Attunement During Sliding-Door Moments

One of the most common causes of shattered trust in these three contexts is a mismatch in partners' meta-emotion. Sometimes these differences in meta-emotion can become perpetual sources of conflict. Let me give you an example of a couple I saw in therapy, Bill and Diane.

In his individual interview, Bill said that whenever his wife came into a room he tensed up, and he scanned her body to see if there was any evidence of a dark mood. He was always on edge, afraid that a big negative incident might be on his hands at any moment. He wanted me to determine if there was something mentally wrong with his wife.

Diane came in to her individual interview and said that whenever she walked into a room, Bill became like the Batmobile, with shields coming up immediately, making him invulnerable, like a knight in armor with two slits for his eyes. There was no way she could get close to him. She claimed he never listened to her. "You are never there for me when I need you," she said. He claimed that he listened to her all the time.

As I observed them together it was clear that his attitude toward her bids and negative emotions was impatience, a kind of "What is it now?"

attitude. He also didn't make very many discriminations between one negative emotion and another; things were equally bad if she was sad, angry, afraid, or anxious, or even if she just had mixed feelings about something. Anything less than cheerfulness and optimism worried him enormously. She described him as constantly irritable.

As Bill tried to listen to her, he said that he saw himself as responsible for changing her negative state to an optimistic one. He was also impatient with her because he was so focused on his work; he claimed that his time was in short supply, and he was always in a hurry. Yet he saw his role as her husband to make her happy, so when she was unhappy he would suggest a way that *he* would solve a problem like hers and make himself feel good in spite of how the world was treating him, so he snapped quickly into advice mode. He became angry with her "yes, buts" in response to what he saw as his excellent advice. His sense of responsibility for changing her negative moods was the root of his Batmobile behavior.

Bill was full of what he saw as sage advice, but this advice was dismissing, like "When the world deals you a bad hand, you just play the hand you are dealt." The advice did nothing to help his wife feel listened to. On the contrary, it made her feel that he thought she was stupid to be distressed at all, so she felt humiliated for having been so emotional.

What is the solution to this couple's dilemma? Part of the solution was for Bill to learn that if Diane made a bid for emotional connection, he made enough of a contribution by just listening to her and being understanding, and by turning toward the expressed need in the bid. To facilitate that end, Bill needed to believe that there would be a good outcome if he just listened without giving Diane advice. That took some work. The blueprint for this context requires two things: (1) building awareness of how one's partner makes bids for emotional connection, and (2) the attitude that one ought to turn toward bids whenever that is possible.

Blueprint #2. Attuning During Regrettable Incidents

The second context for building trust through attunement is processing past regrettable incidents, or emotional injuries. For this we learn to use the "aftermath procedure." As William Faulkner wrote in *Requiem for a Nun,* "The past is not dead. It is not even past." Emotional injuries live in current issues when they are unaddressed. The Zeigarnik effect is operating to make sure that the dissonance is resolved.

We have used the the "Gottman Recovery Kit" to process a fight or regrettable incident (see www.gottman.com for a copy). Couples are guided in a full reprocessing of the past events. By "processing" we mean that the couple has enough emotional distance on the situation that they can talk about the incident without getting back into it, preferably with neutral or positive affect. That means they are not flooded as they talk about the event.

Specifically, they will not argue about "the facts" of the situation, but rather subscribe to two beliefs: (1) perception is everything, and (2) there are always two valid points of view in every situation. An outline of the six steps in this aftermath method follows:

1. *Feelings.* Each partner describes how he or she felt, without any explanation of why he or she felt that way. They can select from a list of 45 possible feelings provided by the form, or add their own. There is no debating here, just a neutral listing of how each person felt *during* the incident.

2. *Subjective realities.* They take turns as each person describes his or her *subjective reality* during the incident—what happened—without blaming the partner, making the partner defensive (no attacks), or using "you" statements (except to describe the scene as neutrally as possible). They can talk about what they might have needed from the other person in that situation, selecting from a list of 29 possible needs, or adding their own. The other person then *validates* the partner's reality by saying something like: "It makes sense to me how you saw this and what your perceptions were. I get it."

3. *Accepting responsibility.* Each person then shares what might have set him or her up to become hurt, respond defensively, withdraw, or otherwise escalate the quarrel. They can select from a list of 22 sample items, or add their own items. Then they summarize overall what their contribution was to the fight or regrettable incident. This moves the couple into what therapist Dan Wile calls "The Admitting Mode."

4. *My triggers.* They share what triggers escalated them, consulting a list of 27 possible triggers or adding their own. They describe these as their "enduring vulnerabilities."

5. *Why these triggers?* If it is possible, they also take turns sharing a story that explains what experiences early in life have created these triggers and resulted in what Tom Bradbury calls "enduring vulnerabilities." These are vulnerabilities each person wants the partner to remember so the partner can be more sensitive to these old wounds.

6. *Constructive plans.* Each person talks about (1) what the partner can do to make this better the next time this kind of situation arises, and (2) what he or she can do to make it better next time.

The Gottman Recovery Kit makes these six steps easier by following Dan Wile's three modes of conflict (Figure 6.3).

The message here is: You have to go through admitting mode to get to collaborative mode, or there is no taking responsibility for the miscommunication. Anything less is dismissive. Dan Wile has anticipated my research results through his astute clinical intuition and articulate writing.

Let's revisit Bill and Diane. There was a problem that Bill expressed about his being able to talk issues over with Diane. Whenever he was angry with her, or hurt, or embarrassed by her, or disappointed, he

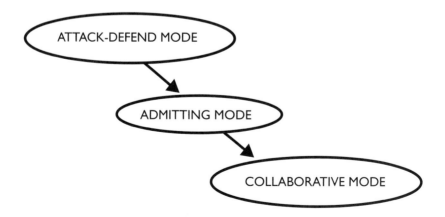

Figure 6.3   **The Three Modes of Conflict**

would try to tell her what he felt. His goal was to raise an issue, solve the problem, and be done with it. He was trying to be constructive, to improve her and the relationship, but he claimed that she would almost always become upset with the *way* he had expressed himself. Then, he claimed, the conversation would become all about her reaction to him, and about how he had said things wrong. He said that they would rarely get back to the original problem that he had raised. He was right. I saw that very thing happen in my office. She felt criticized, rapidly became flooded, and counter-attacked. She would become very emotional, usually crying, and then he would begin comforting her about the hurt he had caused. He'd wind up sort of apologizing, and then they'd drop the subject entirely.

There was a hidden problem for her as well. For her, the way he raised a problem was very much like the way her father had raised a problem with her personality, like a disappointed, corrective mentor. She would immediately respond with shame, and then *her* shields would be up. She was instantly flooded. Both of them became triggered.

For him, the way she raised an issue was to state the problem but then to blame him for insensitivity to her, which was very much like the way his mother had controlled him when he was growing up. He called it the "ultimate guilt trip." He was especially sensitive to the question, "What is wrong with you?"—which seems like a question but is really not. Very few people ever answer that question by saying; "Oh, I'm glad you asked. Let me take a look at myself and see what part of me is defective at the moment." So they each triggered their old enduring vulnerabilities.

The problem they each had was not that they became emotional, disappointed, hurt, angry, sad, or upset. The problem was they just couldn't talk about it. They then fell prey to the Zeigarnik effect.

Because this couple hadn't fully talked things over, both of them turned the negative incident over and over in their minds, examining every facet of it, until, finally, their only explanation was that something was horribly wrong with their partner. He thought she must have mental problems because she was always so negative. She rejected any and all solutions he proposed. Despite his good intentions, he always wound up being the bad guy. She thought that he was just like her father, critical and never satisfied with her. She decided that he simply didn't love her.

He needed someone else, she thought, a more perfect woman, like her father had needed a more perfect daughter. Their oral history switch was flipped into the negative position.

Many self-help books suggest communication "rules" so that negative things can be avoided and people can say things in a more "constructive" manner. There is nothing inherently wrong with this kind of advice. In fact, we also suggest rules for the start of conversations, like Thomas Gordon's suggestion to begin with an "I" statement, like "I'm really upset," rather than a "you" statement, like "You don't care about me."[20] Clearly "I" statements might result in a less defensive response than a "you" statement. However, the problem with communication rules is that when people are flooded, they say things in their characteristically negative ways, so they are likely to become critical and more likely to use negative "you" statements. As Dan Wile says, in the heat of battle you can't remember what an "I" statement is, and you don't give a damn either. So the ultimate solution is *not* to avoid having negative emotions or being perfect in the way you say things. You can try, but these regrettable events are unavoidable.

Instead, our research suggests that the ultimate goal is being able to fully *process* these inevitable negative events with each other. That's what I mean by "attunement" in context #2. Once the negative event is fully processed, it isn't remembered very well. Dan Wile said that a lot of conflict is about the conversation the couple never had but needed to have.[21] Instead of having the conversation they needed to have, they had the fight. The conversation they still need to have becomes evident when they attune.

Blueprint #3. Attunement During Conflict

Attunement also becomes a blueprint for making conflict discussions more constructive. Based on Rapoport's theories, this is called the "Gottman-Rapoport blueprint."

The Weekly "State of the Union" Meeting
Most couples are willing to spend an hour a week talking about their relationship. I suggest that emotional attunement can take place (at a minimum) in that weekly "state of the union" meeting. That means that

at least an hour a week is devoted to the relationship and the process-ing of negative emotions. Couples can count on this as a time to attune. Later, after the skill of attunement is mastered, they can process negative emotions more quickly and efficiently as they occur.

If the couple is willing, they take turns as speaker and listener. They get two clipboards, yellow pads, and pens for jotting down their ideas when they become a speaker, and for taking notes when they become a listener. It's not a very high-tech solution, but the process of taking notes also helps people stay out of the flooded state.

I suggest that at the start of the state of the union meeting, before beginning processing a negative event, each person talks about what is going right in the relationship, followed by giving at least five apprecia-tions for positive things their partner has done that week. The meeting then continues by each partner talking about an issue in the relationship. If there is an issue they can use attunement to fully process the issue.

What is the skill of attunement during conflict? The answer is given, in part, in Anatol Rapoport's book *Games, Fights, and Debates*. In that book Rapoport talks about increasing the likelihood that people will choose cooperation over self-interest in a debate. His suggestion is that we need to reduce threat—that people need to feel safe to cooperate and give up their self-interest.

Another very important principle in Rapoport's theory is that to make conflict safe, we first need to *postpone persuasion* until each person can state the partner's position to the partner's satisfaction.

Rapoport's idea is not very complex, but it is sufficient to create attun-ement and increase cooperation. I have built on Rapoport's suggestion and adapted it for couples. My changes simply involve an understanding of flooding. I agree with Rapoport that it is important to reduce threat. However, I believe that to accomplish this attunement, it is also neces-sary to constrain the speaker. Our research reveals that once the speaker starts harshly, almost every listener will become defensive, and attun-ement will go out the window.

So my blueprint is that although the listener does need to attune, not all the attunement responsibility is on the listener. No one can listen nondefensively to a perceived attack. The speaker cannot begin express-ing negative affect with blaming or criticism. There appears to be no such thing as "constructive criticism." Instead, the speaker must state his or her feelings as *neutrally* as possible, and then convert any complaint about his or her partner into a *positive need*. A positive need is a recipe for one's partner to be successful.

The reason, again, for down-regulating the speaker is that even in happy relationships, in the relatively rare times when people begin the conflict with an attack, the sequences of interaction are not very different than they are in an unhappy relationship. We found that although it happened less often for happy couples, the consequence of an attack was usually defensiveness, the same as it would be in an unhappy relationship. So the speaker has to take responsibility for softened startup (starting gently).

Converting a complaint into a positive need requires a mental transformation from what is wrong with one's partner to what one's partner can do that would work. It may be helpful here to review my belief that within every negative feeling there is a longing, a wish, and, because of that, there is a recipe for success. It is the speaker's job to discover that recipe. The speaker is really saying "Here's what I feel, and here's what I need from you." Or, in processing a negative event that has already happened, the speaker is saying, "Here's what I felt, and here's what I needed from you."

The ultimate goal of attunement is to reduce threat for both people and avoid flooding, so that nondefensiveness, understanding, and empathy can occur. Making that work requires postponing persuasion and problem solving, and down-regulating defensiveness. It means staying in "What's this?" mode and staying out of "What the hell is this?" mode until each person can state and validate the partner's position to the partner's satisfaction.

It is important to find the positive need. The speaker starts with "Here's what's wrong with you, and here's what I want you to stop doing" and converts it to "Here's what I feel (or felt) and here's the positive thing I need (or needed) from you."

The idea is that each negative emotion is a GPS for guiding us toward a longing, a wish, and a hope. As mentioned earlier, each negative contains within it a recipe that will work. As noted, it's the speaker's job (not the listener's) to identify that recipe. The positive need eliminates the blame. It eliminates the reproach.

Attunement need not always be reciprocal. However, attunement during conflict *does* needs to be reciprocal. One can postpone one's own agenda and be an attuned listener, but for only so long. In my practice, when using attunement during conflict, I have people take turns as speaker and listener. The speaker will eventually become the attuned listener. I give each partner a pen and a notepad. The speaker is required to express a feeling and then convert it into a positive need. The listener is required to attune, take notes, and be able to repeat the speaker's position to the speaker's satisfaction. That requires not only summarizing what the speaker has said, but also validating the speaker's feelings and need. That means, specifically, being able to complete a sentence like the following, "It makes sense to me that you would have these feelings and needs, because. . . ." It is not required that the listener agree with the speaker, just that the listener can see how the speaker's point of view makes sense from a particular perspective and set of perceptions. Usually, to accomplish this feat, the listener needs to focus not on the speaker's facts, but on the speaker's pain, distress, and anguish, and to get in touch with his or her feelings of love and protectiveness.

To sum up, the attunement-during-conflict blueprint for the speaker is:

- No blaming, no "you" statements
- Talk about how you feel in a specific situation, use "I" statements
- Express a positive need

The attunement-during-conflict blueprint for the listener is:

- Awareness of partner's enduring vulnerabilities
- Turning toward partner by postponing own agenda
- Tolerance by believing there are always two valid realities
- Making understanding the partner the goal of listening
- Nondefensive listening, not responding right away, getting in touch with the partner's pain
- Empathy—summarizing the partner's view and validating by completing a sentence like "I can totally understand why you have these feelings and needs, because. . . ."

The Potential Ease of Attunement

All the couples I see in my practice learn the skill of emotional attunement in the three contexts I have outlined. I tell them that attunement is not a difficult skill set to acquire. I also tell them that this is basically *the* skill set they will need to create a relationship that really works for them. At first attunement will seem awkward and inefficient. It certainly is *not natural*. What is "natural" for many people is avoiding talking about negative emotions, or dismissing them, and assuming that just the passage of time will heal all emotional wounds. What is natural is avoiding conflict, but then paying a huge price for that avoidance. Attunement seems unnatural and inefficient, but it is actually potentially more efficient. Like in the acquisition of any skill, the beginning seems strange and awkward. When my teenage daughter was learning how to drive a car, she said, "If they didn't want people to get mixed up they would put the brake and the accelerator pedals much farther apart instead of right next to each other." We forget that it took us a long time before driving was automatic. The same is true for attunement.

What Attunement During Conflict Looks Like

David and Barbara came into therapy very close to deciding to get a divorce. Concern about the negative effects of divorce on their two young children is what made them decide to try again. They had been to three couple therapists with very mixed results. Their relationship was riddled with unresolved conflict and negative incidents. She recalled the details of every one of their endless arguments. He was very disappointed in marriage and hated the fact that nothing he did was adequate.

They learned attunement and used it often and effectively. One day they told me that they overheard one of their children saying to the other, "Let's leave mom and dad alone. They're attuning."

Here is an example of one of their attunement conflict conversations in my office. They were using the Gottman-Rapoport attunement-in-conflict blueprint. Not every state of the union attunement goes this easily, so some sessions are longer than this one. I will fill in their conversation with thoughts that I think they were each having. She was the first speaker.

BARBARA: I appreciate you giving me time to myself last weekend. I really needed it. I also appreciate your taking me out to dinner for a date night.

DAVID: Good, that's great. You're welcome.

She thinks	He thinks
It's hard to start with appreciations. I want to get right to my complaint about him.	This is much better.

BARBARA: Just a little more about that. Weekends are a real challenge, with swim lessons, religious school, errands, and so many things I have to do for the family.

DAVID: Well, I appreciate your making breakfast for us every Saturday and letting me sleep in a little.

BARBARA: You're welcome. I love us all eating together Saturday morning. Is it okay to raise an issue?

DAVID: Sure.

BARBARA: I still feel like I get very little time to myself, so it was great to have that last week. But here's what I also feel and need. The house is upside down, and when you announced to me that you have that project to build a fence and a gate for the dog, that just made me crazy. It made me feel lonely, all alone, each of us in our separate worlds. Because what I really need is for us to have a plan we make together for cleaning up the house on the weekend, especially if we're having company.

DAVID: Okay, so what you're saying is that this time alone, a break from errands, is terrific and you appreciate it, but you want us to also make a plan for cleaning up the house on the weekends, because it's upside down, messy with two little kids intent on destroying any order we might create. Well, I get that. It makes a lot of sense to me, because you are doing that cleaning during the week on your own, mostly.

She thinks	He thinks
He did it. Great. He mostly heard me.	I did it, I think. Let's see if it's enough for her.

BARBARA: Yes that's it, but maybe one thing you missed was the doing it together part. I don't want to feel so alone, like we are in our separate worlds.

She thinks	He thinks
Okay, let's see if he gets defensive.	Oh, no, I got it wrong. Calm down, boy.

DAVID: Okay, I'm feeling a little defensive, so I have to breathe. (*pause*) Okay, so what I missed was the togetherness part of it, that weekends also need to be a time when we have a plan that involves us doing things for the family together. That deals with the lonely feeling you have, right?

BARBARA: Right, that's it.

DAVID: Well, I get that. That makes sense to me. I can see why if we have our own projects for the house, and I'm also exercising, and you get alone time, and we separately take the kids to their weekend events, we might not even see each other all weekend, except for the date. Right. Okay.

BARBARA: Okay, I feel heard. Your turn.

She thinks	He thinks
I did feel heard, and he didn't get defensive. Maybe this is working.	All right. Now I get to talk. This is where it all breaks down, I'd bet. Let's see—appreciations. . . .

DAVID: What I also appreciated this week was you taking a real interest in my leadership at work. Your making that dinner for my work team at our house was great. It was really delicious, and also I appreciated that you socialized with the guys and they got to know you, and really liked you, by the way. That makes my work life so much more personal. So I really appreciated those two things a lot.

BARBARA: That is very nice to hear. Thank you. So now what about the negative stuff?

She thinks	He thinks
Now he's going to criticize me.	This is where the rubber meets the road.

DAVID: Okay, so here's what I need. Two things—it's to sleep in Sunday morning, too, with you taking the kids so Sammy doesn't jump on me at 6 A.M. and say, "Papa get up! It's morning!" And my feeling about that is just I am so tired by then because these work weeks have been so grueling. And second, what I need is about 2 hours to hop on my bike and ride it hard, maybe with a few of the people in the bike club. The feeling there is all about freedom, feeling free, almost like a kid again myself.

BARBARA: Okay, two things. Sleep in Sunday morning, until when?

DAVID: Say 9:00, is that okay?

BARBARA: That'd be okay. I could make them breakfast, get them started doing things they like until you get up. Could that wakeup be 8:30 instead of 9? Would that still do it for you?

She thinks	He thinks
I have to change some of what he's asking for. Look out.	Stay calm. Listen to her. That's not too bad; I still get to sleep in.

DAVID: Yeah, that'd still be great.

BARBARA: Okay, let me summarize and validate the first need. So you're really wiped out right now from the stresses of the new work team and getting this new project started, and you need to sleep in Sunday morning. I get that; I can understand how that makes sense. And since I am getting some alone time I am really okay with it. Then the second one, the bike ride. I get that one also. I'm okay with it, and I understand the feeling of freedom. But I'm having a problem again with us living our lives in parallel on the weekend, so I'm thinking, "Does he want to be with the bike club to get away from me?" I'm having a problem with that.

She thinks	He thinks
I have to stick to my guns.	This could be breaking down.

DAVID: What do you need here?

BARBARA: Thanks for asking me. Maybe some reassurance, I don't know.

DAVID: What if your mom could come over for a few hours on Sunday and we got your bike out, fixed it up a bit, and you rode with us?

BARBARA: I'm afraid that I can't keep up with you.

She thinks	He thinks
I still have to stick to my guns.	Try to be positive.

DAVID: You can ride with the people who are just getting started with the bike club. We wait for them, circle back, we have coffee sometimes.

BARBARA: Maybe that would work. I don't think I'd always join your bike club, but if I felt welcomed then that'd be fine. Would you still feel free?

DAVID: Yeah, I probably would. Sure.

BARBARA: Okay, then that makes it easier for me to validate that need to work out and be free. Those two things, sleeping in and the bike ride, I can understand the needs and I get it. It makes sense to me that you'd want that.

DAVID: Great. Are we done?

BARBARA: We're done.

She thinks	He thinks
I can't believe how much easier that was.	Amazing. That actually worked!

That's all there is to the process. It's unnatural and it's hard work. Perhaps it looks easy, but couples have to do a lot of work knowing what they feel, knowing what positive need they have, and being constructive. A lot of gain is made in just knowing that they have emotional access to each other for at least an hour a week. Now let's take a look at what happens with a couple who has not gone through this process, and who quite naturally fails to attune.

What the Failure to Attune Looks Like

The couple I am about to describe was very unhappily married. They were not a therapy case. They were part of a research project in which there was no intervention. In that research project we learned a lot about attunement from the couples who did attune and also from those who did not attune.

Fred and Angel were in the bottom 1% in marital satisfaction. This couple was very low in both husband and wife attunement for sadness (husband in bottom 30th percentile, wife in bottom 19th percentile) and in husband and wife attunement for anger (husband in bottom 28th percentile, wife in bottom 21st percentile).

Meta-Emotion Interview With Fred

In this excerpt from the husband's meta-emotion interview, Fred says that he cannot talk to his wife when he is sad. He feels that she will confront him (call him out) when he is sad, so he chooses not to share his sadness with her. He also mentions not being appreciated, encouraged, or respected by his wife.

INTERVIEWER: What sorts of things make you sad?

FRED: I don't feel that I get the respect I need or deserve from my wife. The thing that makes me the saddest is when I feel I'm getting shortchanged. I'm not able, you know, to continue to grow, go back to school. My wife, she's quitting her job. She's going back to school and the burden falls on me. To cover all the bills. All the money, you know. I do side contracting like family counseling, so I'm trying to do all these things to keep the money flowing. And she doesn't want to even see that as viable. You know, by that I mean that she doesn't encourage me, "Hey, you know, you're doing a great job." Family counseling, I make great money at it. She's, "Oh, no, you're going to be out late tonight talking to this family. When you going to be home?" Those types of things, they make me sad or angry. I suppose a little bit of both. Where I just want to just be away.

INTERVIEWER: In general, what are your thoughts and feelings about being sad? How do you feel about your sadness? How does your wife respond to you when you're sad? Respond to your sadness?

FRED: Oh, yeah, well, she calls me out, challenges me. "Oh, there you go being moody again. Blah, blah, blah . . . yak, yak, yak." (*laughs*) She doesn't really acknowledge it. Therefore I choose not to share it when I'm sad. I keep it to myself.

So what Fred has told the interviewer is that when he is sad, he just keeps it to himself, rather than run the risk of being challenged by his wife for being sad. Whether it is true or not, that is his perception. When he was interviewed about his anger, he said that anger was a real problem for him. When asked if he could talk to his wife when he felt angry, he said that he could not, because all he got in return was her anger, and they invariably would get into an escalated fight. So he suppressed all his negative emotions. He also said that he was not very successful at the suppression, and they would have major "blowups."

Meta-Emotion Interview With Angel

Let's listen to part of the meta-emotion interview with the wife. She talks about Fred always taking her sadness personally. She says that he feels as if he's done something wrong when she is sad; he feels blamed and does not know what to do.

INTERVIEWER: What sorts of things make you sad?

ANGEL: With me crying is a way for me to express my sadness. It makes me feel a lot better. And it's something I usually like to do on my own. I don't like to share it with someone and start bawling. (*laughs*) But I'm the kind of person where if I feel sad, I can get in the shower and I'll just bawl my head off. (*laughs*) I feel much better.

INTERVIEWER: Would your husband know if you were sad, would he pick up on it?

ANGEL: Yeah, he would pick up on it. Not necessarily know what to do about it.

INTERVIEWER: So, how does he respond to you? What would I see and hear when he responded to your sadness?

ANGEL: I would say really, probably, he would be really busy. He would make himself busy and he would retreat more. Because again I think for him, if I'm sad he thinks of it as "Oh gosh." And a lot of times he doesn't *know* what to do. And so he deals with it in a way that he feels he can deal with it. Rarely would he be loving and affectionate. I don't think he would do that. Even though if I said to him, "Oh, give me a hug," or "I need affection," he would, no problem. But he doesn't figure that out on his own. Like he would think to do that.

INTERVIEWER: How do you feel about this response?

ANGEL: (*angry facial expression*) I would certainly like for him to be more affectionate. And loving and understanding. And not internalize it. I would certainly like for that to be different. I think I've communicated that to him. But for him that takes a lot of effort. Thinking "Oh, okay, because she said it's not my fault. It's not like something I've done wrong, or she's not trying to tell me that I need to be doing something different." That kind of thing. And there's times when I'm depressed and he says, "Why are you depressed?" And I don't know *why* I'm depressed.

So, Angel also says that she cannot talk to Fred when she's sad without Fred feeling blamed. She wishes that Fred could simply be affectionate and loving when she is sad and not become defensive, but she believes it's a lost cause. Her perceptions about anger were different from Fred's. Rather than being afraid of escalation, Angel expressed the view that getting angry with Fred was the only way she was able to get his attention. It wasn't a positive experience, but, she said, at least she was getting the issues out on the table. The result was that she respected herself more than if she had kept quiet about her anger.

What About Flooding for Fred and Angel?

No surprises here. Fred was in the top 90th percentile of all people in the study in being flooded. He was definitely flooded. Conversely, Angel was not very flooded at all (bottom 30th percentile). That's the most common pattern in our data.

Fred and Angel's Oral History Interview

On the oral history interview, for the positive oral history codes both Fred and Angel were in the bottom half of all people in the sample. For negative oral history codes, Fred was in the top 1%, and Angel was in the top 7%. So they really were in the negative oral history switch. This brief excerpt from the interview is characterized by them not being very positive or expansive about their relationship or their first impressions of each other. The interviewer is working hard to elicit much of anything from them.

> **INTERVIEWER**: I want to start at the beginning with you guys and ask how you met, how you got together. (*She pokes him.*)

> **FRED**: Well, we met through one of my best friends. Probably my best friend. On the platonic level, though. She was going out with somebody. How old were you then?

> **ANGEL**: 18.

> **FRED**: I was a senior in college. She was a young little freshman. And I was in the lunchroom. I didn't have any coins. She was loaded down with coins. She loaned me some coins.

> **ANGEL**: Because his friend was a good friend of mine.

> **FRED**: Yeah.

> **ANGEL**: I thought, okay, I'll feed you guys today, and then they owed me a dinner. They of course lived off campus and I lived in a dorm.

> **INTERVIEWER**: Do you remember anything about her standing out?

> **FRED**: She walked around all stuck up and stuff. (*imitates a swagger*)

> **ANGEL**: He's lying.

> **FRED**: She was kind of stuck on herself. I always tell her about that.

She thinks	He thinks
Why is he bringing up my faults?	I remember how unpleasant that was.

> **INTERVIEWER**: Do you remember anything about him standing out?

ANGEL: He was with his friend and there was these two big guys. Getting into this little car, two big enormous guys getting into this little car. That was pretty much all.

FRED: (*chuckles*)

ANGEL: I didn't pay a lot of attention, especially to the seniors. He seemed like a nice guy, I guess. I really didn't give it any more thought. I thought, he's doing good, so okay.

FRED: Later we dated and got engaged.

ANGEL: We were on, we were off.

FRED: We broke up the engagement.

She thinks	He thinks
I wish he were more positive.	I should have seen it coming even back then. I was an idiot.

ANGEL: Exactly, broke up the engagement. Broke up and decided no, we need to see other people and we never stopped seeing each other.

FRED: But also we saw other people.

ANGEL: But also saw other people. We were just too young and not ready. For the . . .

FRED: Rigors of . . .

ANGEL: (*laughs*) . . . the rigors of . . . marriage.

She thinks	He thinks
I will admit it hasn't been much fun.	Things are really unpleasant now.

So, the oral history switch is negative for this couple. We expect that their conflict discussion will be characterized by escalation and negativity, what we call the "summarizing yourself syndrome," which is characteristic of flooding. People keep repeating themselves, falsely thinking, "This time my partner will finally get it and suddenly feel close to me."

The Nasty-Nasty Cell of the Conflict Discussion was an Absorbing State

The observational coding of Fred and Angel's conflict discussion was highly negative (he was in the top 4% and she was in the top 14%) and not very positive (he was in the bottom 2% and she in the bottom 9%).

FRED: Okay, chores . . . what else is there to say that we didn't already say?

ANGEL: (*laughs*) You turned the bills over to me and you appreciated that. You have never told me.

FRED: (*defensive*) A lot of things maybe you haven't told me.

ANGEL: I'm just saying that goes to appreciation.

FRED: We're talking about chores.

She thinks	He thinks
Why can't he just appreciate me?	I have to eat crow to appreciate her.

ANGEL: You've never once said thank you. . . .

FRED: No, I did bills before that also, and you never said anything to me about it.

ANGEL: You didn't do the job very well.

FRED: (*laughing, shaking his head*)

She thinks	He thinks
Why can't he just admit he screwed it up?	I did just fine, but she doesn't realize how much easier she has it now that I am working two jobs.

ANGEL: If paid on time, which you never did on a regular basis.

FRED: That's not true.

ANGEL: (*eye roll*) Oh, that's so true!

FRED: And the other thing is the money just wasn't there when I did it. Now I am working an extra job.

ANGEL: There is the same money now as then. We did not win a lottery.

FRED: No, but our expenses have grown, with more kids. And there's more money now.

She thinks	He thinks
Why is he so stubborn?	I can't get any encouragement.

ANGEL: Okay, so you do not appreciate my doing bills, right? (*derisive laugh*)

FRED: Well, yeah, sure.

ANGEL: Does that mean you do appreciate it?

FRED: Yes, I do, but what about my working so hard—do you appreciate that?

ANGEL: We are talking about household chores like the bills, so stick with that topic.

FRED: Right. Have it your way, you always do, you always will.

She thinks	He thinks
I have to fight him every step of the way.	She is so bossy, I can never win unless I just give in.

ANGEL: What makes me mad (*laughs to soften her complaint*) about you is last night after I had gotten home from work and had gotten the kids fed and straightened up the apartment, you came home and changed your clothes and the clothes you wore to work were all over the dining room chair. (*laughs harder*)

FRED: (*smiling*) I usually clean it up eventually.

ANGEL: Okay, so you do. But I do more chores than you, right? Will you admit that? Will you go to some appreciation for that?

FRED: (*looking away, stonewalling*)

ANGEL: I want you to do more, cook, take the kids on the weekends sometimes.

FRED: I do. I do all that.

ANGEL: I'm not saying that you don't. Just you do things, but I do more. Isn't that right?

FRED: I know you do.

ANGEL: And every day don't I make dinner? Don't I clean up? Don't I do those bills?

FRED: (*nodding*) Enough, just stop.

She thinks	He thinks
Okay, let him talk now or he'll shut down.	I wish I could leave. I am repeating myself, but I need to.

ANGEL: So, what is your thing here?

FRED: I cook. I clean up weekends, when I don't work two jobs. I try to get up and make breakfast, I try to let you sleep in.

ANGEL: True, you do.

FRED: So say that.

ANGEL: I was asking, "What do you want me to do differently?"

FRED: I want you to stop just trying to compete with me, I just get tired of everything being "Well I do this, I do that, I do this" and I just constantly feel like I'm always having to defend my position. I understand. I know what you do. I try to do what I can do, but by the time I come home it's late, so I leave some stuff somewhere some of the time, but on weekends I do a lot, what I can. . . .

ANGEL: But just admit I do more.

FRED: See there you go again, competing with me.

She thinks	He thinks
How do we get into these negative places? I am repeating myself. But I need to.	She just doesn't get that "competing" point of mine.

ANGEL: I have something to say. . . .

FRED: I thought it was *my* turn, so just hold on, hold on. I'm not finished.

ANGEL: What I am trying to say . . .

FRED: See and this is what I'm talking about. . . .

ANGEL: Right, I know, because I do not . . .

FRED: You cut in. . . .

ANGEL: I have to say something now. . . .

FRED: No. Because when you cut in . . .

ANGEL: I have something to say here. . . .

FRED: Hold on! Shut up!

She thinks	He thinks
If he'd just let me say one thing . . .	Now I'm really angry.

ANGEL: (*smiling*) See, that's what I'm saying. You are just like this all the time.

FRED: Because I'm trying to finish my thoughts.

ANGEL: I know, but what I'm saying . . .

FRED: . . . and you cut in . . .

ANGEL: Okay. But I've got a thing to add.

FRED: Just let me talk. See, I'm on a thought process.

ANGEL: Go ahead.

FRED: So let me finish my thoughts.

ANGEL: You're going off on a tangent now.

FRED: No, I am not. You know that's not the case. I can clean up too, and I do, and sometimes you don't clean up too, you are not the perfect housewife. You know that's not the case.

She thinks	He thinks
He's not going to give an inch.	She's painting a false picture and I can't let her get away with that.

ANGEL: I didn't say that it was.

FRED: Yes, you did!

ANGEL: I just clean up and you don't.

FRED: Yes, I do. I pick up just as you do. You pick up . . .

ANGEL: You pick up when you feel like it. I do it all the time.

FRED: Just like the other night when you went to the meeting. Did you come back to a clean kitchen?

ANGEL: I did.

FRED: Okay. So shut up.

ANGEL: Who made dinner for you before I left?

FRED: See, you're competing with me again.

She thinks	He thinks
He will never appreciate all that I do.	I give up.

ANGEL: No.

FRED: I'm just stating the fact.

ANGEL: Are you done? Can I speak again?

FRED: No. Those are the things that make me resentful.

ANGEL: Okay. Tell me when I can talk.

FRED: Go ahead, I'm done talking.

ANGEL: 'Cause it's easy to say "I appreciate that," but you. . . .

FRED: I don't show appreciation.

ANGEL: Okay. Now the same would be true of you. You're saying of me that I don't appreciate what you do, although you do far less than I do. Far, far less.

FRED: (*silent*)

ANGEL: You do your little things (*laughs*), your things you do (*laughs*), you clean the bathroom. Occasionally. You do the yardwork. You take out the garbage (*laughing harder*). (*pause*)

FRED: (*stonewalling*)

The failure to attune was clear in both of them coming close to stating what they needed, but not being able to ask for what they needed in a way that didn't fault the other person. The result was increasing amounts of defensiveness and no understanding, validation, or empathy. They came very close to stating feelings and positive needs, but they were far from attunement. Instead, defensiveness and attack characterized their interaction. In the end Fred was clearly flooded and stonewalling. Angel felt like she hadn't gotten through to him at all. They had been stating their positions *at one another*; they were broadcasting, but neither of them was picking up the other's signal.

If Fred and Angel Had Only Attuned

How would it have looked if they had attuned? It might have gone something like this:

ANGEL: (*laughs*) You turned the bills over to me, and during the interview you said you appreciated that. You have never told me that before.

FRED: You're right, I haven't told you.

ANGEL: I'm just saying I need your appreciation.

FRED: Well actually, I really do appreciate the great job you are doing with the bills.

She thinks	He thinks
Wow! There's the appreciation I've needed, and it even seems genuine.	She is doing a good job. But there's more money now that I have two jobs.

ANGEL: Thank you. . . .

FRED: Okay, but what I need here is for you to appreciate that I have made a real contribution by having that second job. There's a lot more money available right now, and I am knocking myself out.

ANGEL: You do the job very well. I do appreciate how hard you're working now, and that you come home wiped out a lot of days. I know your feet are killing you.

FRED: That's right, my poor feet. Anyway that's good to hear that you appreciate our financial situation is changed now.

ANGEL: We are a great team.

She thinks	He thinks
Okay, he needs appreciation just like I do.	That's the encouragement from her I needed. But there's more. . . .

FRED: We are a great team. But you're still mad about something.

ANGEL: That is so true. I'm mad that I do so much more housework than you. I know you're working a lot harder now, but I need you to do more on weekends. I know you do a lot, but maybe just pick up after yourself and the kids a little more, even during the week.

FRED: Okay, I can understand that. That makes sense to me. You're tired, too.

ANGEL: I am. Like last night after I had gotten home from work and had gotten the kids fed and straightened up the apartment, you came home and changed your clothes and the clothes you wore to work were all over the dining room chair. (*laughs harder*)

FRED: (*smiling*) Now, I think that I do, I usually do clean it up eventually, but you're right, last night I just didn't. And you did it for me. I knew you were mad. But I was too tired to care.

ANGEL: Okay, you're right, I was mad. So could you please just put your stuff in the bedroom? And I think I need some appreciation for the work I do all week, picking up after you and the kids.

FRED: Okay, I do appreciate what you do. And, sure, I can put my stuff in the bedroom when I come home. I understand that you do a lot, and you're saying that a little bit of my help would go a long way.

ANGEL: Yes, that's it. That'd be great. Thank you.

FRED: Okay, is it my turn? Okay. You will admit that I do a lot. I do straighten, I do get breakfast on the weekends and I do let you sleep in. I need some appreciation for all that I *do* do.

ANGEL: I hear that, baby. I do appreciate the sleeping in and the breakfasts, especially the sleeping in. So, thank you for all that.

FRED: You're welcome. I know you do a lot and I'm grateful.

ANGEL: That's good to hear. I think we're done.

FRED: I am so done talking about all this. Yahoo!

It could have gone that way. But it didn't.

An Attuned Discussion of a Happy Couple

The following example of George and Judy shows how happy couples practice attunement.

Meta-Emotion Interview With George

INTERVIEWER: What sorts of things make you sad?

GEORGE: I feel sad about how hard we are both working now that the baby has arrived. We used to have much more fun. And romance. So it makes me sad that we don't get to hear great jazz anymore, or have those romantic getaways I lived for.

INTERVIEWER: In general, what are your thoughts and feelings about being sad? How do you feel about your sadness? How does your wife respond to you when you're sad? Respond to your sadness?

GEORGE: She's usually great. The thing about Judy is that she's usually sad about the same stuff I'm sad about. Maybe I'm sadder about not having much sex anymore. I don't think she misses that a lot right now. Her libido is way down. Also, I was sad that I missed the baby's taking her first steps. I was gone at a conference that week, but Judy couldn't empathize with that sadness because she had the baby and work all alone that week, so she was stressed out when I came back home, so I didn't get a lot of understanding for missing the baby's first steps. She was mad at me instead. We miss each other's feelings sometimes now, which we didn't used to before the baby as much. So we're fighting more. I'm sad about that. That and the reduced sex. (*laughs*)

What do we see here? George feels appreciated by Judy, and his sadness is generally understood by her. They are struggling because there is a loss of connection between them at times, but he seems aware of what the issues are and they are talking about them. As we will see, this emotional connection between them is a "setting condition" for regrettable incidents getting processed and attuned to. Because of attunement, fights have the possibility of repair. George is not suppressing his negative emotions from Judy. There are still regrettable incidents, like their lack of connection when he returned from his weeklong business trip.

Meta-Emotion Interview With Judy

Let's listen to part of the meta-emotion interview with Judy. She talks about George's generally responding to her sadness and anger and being there for her. She says that he feels bad that she isn't more interested in sex now, but she feels hugely unattractive since she had the baby, and that when he wants to have sex she feels she has done something wrong and does not know what to do.

INTERVIEWER: What sorts of things make you sad?

JUDY: With me it's not wanting sex anymore, but George wanting sex constantly. I can't believe how much work a baby is, and I resent working now, which came as a big surprise to me. I used to love my career, but now I just want to be with Carla. So at work sometimes I find myself crying for no reason. I want to share it with George. (laughs) So I do, but then George will bring up his own sadness, and it's unfortunately sadness with *me*! So that makes me sadder. (laughs) Still, talking about all of that makes me feel much better.

INTERVIEWER: Would your husband know if you were sad? Would he pick up on it?

JUDY: Yeah, absolutely, he's pretty sharp. He will hold me and be very sweet. But then he'll go from stroking my hair to stroking my ass.

INTERVIEWER: So that causes problems then.

JUDY: Sometimes I like it.

INTERVIEWER: How does he respond to you? What would I see and hear when he responded to your sadness?

JUDY: You'd see a pretty savvy guy. George is so different from my father, who would say something like: "Stop whining. I hate when you whine. Just grow up and get on with life. Roll with the punches!" So I would stuff my sadness with my dad, but I don't do that with George. He will listen to me and not judge me for being sad, or angry. I just have trouble hearing about his being so horny.

INTERVIEWER: How do you feel about George's overall response?

JUDY: It's good. I just wish at times that he'd just hear me for longer before talking about his own needs. But he has needs too. Maybe he's too impatient with my own frustrations being a new mother. But I feel guilty saying that. So we're talking, but he does actually need more sex. I'm just not there.

Judy also says that she can talk to George when she's sad. She is struggling with the differences they feel about sexuality, but they are working on this issue.

What About Flooding for George and Judy?

No surprises here. Neither George nor Judy were flooded during their conflict discussion.

Regrettable Incidents Don't Escalate Because There Is Attunement.

One of the regrettable incidents this couple discussed was George's coming home from his weeklong trip and the argument they had. In the following discussion George and Judy discussed the incident.

The observational coding of this couple's conflict discussion was highly positive and not very negative. Their conflict was not an absorbing state, meaning: (1) it was easier to exit than to enter, and (2) most repairs—for exiting the nasty-nasty state—worked.

GEORGE: Okay, so when I got home you were in no mood to listen to me. There you were with Carla, brushing her hair, and I felt like a third wheel. Or fifth wheel, whatever. *I was pissed.* Coming home and getting ignored!

JUDY: (*laughs*) I know, and I just hate it when you come home angry. You were so sad you'd missed her walking. When she left she was a crawler, scooting around, and now she had become a young lady, a toddler. I wanted you to come home and just take over.

GEORGE: I wanted to take over, but after a warm welcome. I had that pictured in my mind.

JUDY: The reality didn't fit the picture?

GEORGE: Not at all.

JUDY: My reality was that I wanted relief. Yours was that you'd missed a milestone in Carla's development.

GEORGE: Yeah, she's now in a whole new chapter in that book we're reading. I was still in the baby chapter. She's now in the toddler chapter.

JUDY: For me, I had it up to here with you being gone all week. I mean, life is tough when you're here, but it's an absolute nightmare when you're gone.

GEORGE: But we have a nanny. You have lots of help when I'm gone.

JUDY: A nanny whose kids had the flu this week and she herself was running a fever, so I couldn't very well have her around the baby, could I? And getting people to cover for me when I had to be at work was hell. Then you come home and want my attention? What?

GEORGE: Like having a second baby.

JUDY: Exactly.

She thinks	He thinks
He's getting this, finally.	How do I get her to see what I was going through?

JUDY: On the phone you never once asked about the stresses I was having.

GEORGE: Well, you never asked about how my presentation went, either. (*defensive*) It went fine, thank you!

JUDY: I knew you'd do fine. But I wasn't doing fine, was I?

GEORGE: But you've cut down on work and I have done exactly the opposite.

JUDY: With you gone, you just have no idea what a nightmare it can be. And I am all alone! No adult conversation.

GEORGE: Good point. I remember the time you went to visit your dad when he was sick. That was 2 days and I just about died from all the added stress.

JUDY: I needed you to ask about my stresses.

GEORGE: No, that's true. I was so busy at the conference that I had very little time to even make the phone calls. I was building my career.

JUDY: I get that. But you could have asked.

GEORGE: That's true. I'm *really* sorry.

She thinks	He thinks
I need him to admit that I do so much and when he's gone having fun at the conference, I am in agony back home.	I didn't want to even go to the conference, but the contacts were important for both of us. I could use a little appreciation here.

JUDY: I know you were sad because that moment of her walking was really amazing.

GEORGE: Right. Hearing about it on the phone was not the same as being there.

JUDY: That's for sure. It was one of the only good parts of the week, though.

GEORGE: I had quite a lot of success at the conference, and I need you to appreciate that it was good that I went.

JUDY: That's a good point. I know you needed to go to that presentation. I'm really glad you went. But all I could think about was the nightmare I had on my hands, and I thought, here's you going out for great dinners and grownup company. All I ate was Lean Cuisine meals. I only got to shower once all week.

GEORGE: That truly sucks, and you're right, some of those dinners were really great. I just wished you'd been there.

JUDY: Me too. Which was the best?

She thinks	He thinks
He's getting it.	I finally got some encouragement. Feels good.

GEORGE: There was a French meal you'd have loved. With an amazing chocolate dessert.

JUDY: Sounds great to me.

GEORGE: I wish we could do an overnight at that B&B on Bainbridge Island.

JUDY: That was such a romantic place. But I don't feel comfortable leaving the baby yet.

GEORGE: Even for one night?

JUDY: Maybe that'd be okay.

GEORGE: Well, you know my main complaint.

JUDY: I sure do. I think we should plan for an overnight there. Just be patient with me.

GEORGE: I can do that. You really mean it?

JUDY: Sure, why not? She loves being with Mary. Go ahead and see what vacancies they have for the weekend after next.

GEORGE: Right. Right. Good, that's good.

She thinks	He thinks
That will be nice. It'll deal with my guilt too.	This is going to be great.

Their attunement worked. It wasn't totally smooth, but it eventually was successful.

Rapoport's "Assumption of Similarity"

One thing that can help attunement is another brilliant point that Anatol Rapoport made. The point was that during conflict people will see their partner ("opponent") as dissimilar to them, and tend to see themselves as having all the positive history, traits, and qualities. They may also see their partner as having several negative traits as well. This is related to social psychologist Fritz Heider's idea that all humans tend to make the "fundamental attribution error": "I'm okay; you're defective."[22] Such is human nature. We all think we are the central character of the Great Play of Life. Everyone else is a minor player. We each think we are being watched very sympathetically by novelist Kurt Vonnegut's Great Eye in the Sky.[23] As a result, most humans are very forgiving toward their own mistakes and less forgiving of the mistakes of others. People also tend to see themselves as having very few negative traits, little negative history with their partner, and few negative qualities. But people may see their partner/adversary as having most of these negative qualities and few positive qualities. Hence, Rapoport suggested two things. First, when we identify a negative quality in our partner (or adversary), we try to see that very quality in ourselves. That is a truly amazing suggestion. Second, he suggested that when we identify a positive quality in ourselves, we try to see that very quality in our partner (or adversary). Another truly amazing suggestion. To facilitate these suggestions we may try thinking, "The two of us want the same things" or "He is a great father" or "She was very nice to me when I was last sick" or "It's true that I think she is being selfish right now, but so am I right now; maybe we both need to be a little selfish for this to be a great relationship."

Building Trust and Trustworthiness With the Gottman Institute's "Art and Science of Love" Workshop

Our institute's 2-day "Art and Science of Love" workshop, which my wife and I do four times a year in Seattle, was evaluated in my laboratory in a randomized clinical trial with 47 couples. The workshop was designed to teach the skills of the Sound Relationship House. (See www. gottman.com for a description of this workshop, which is now available on DVDs with an accompanying manual.) This was a "proximal change experiment," meaning that we only evaluated changes immediately following the workshop. This experiment is clearly only a beginning in attempting to increase trust and trustworthiness experimentally.

In this study, couples were randomly assigned to one of four conditions: (1) a 1-day workshop focusing only on building friendship and intimacy (N=11 couples), (2) a 1-day workshop focusing only on making conflict constructive (N=14 couples), (3) a 2-day workshop combining the first two workshops (N=10 couples), (4) a bibliotherapy control group in which couples were given Gottman and Silver's *The Seven Principles for Making Marriage Work* (N=13 couples).

Controlling for whether either partner or the couple ever received therapy, the wife's trust metric increased significantly only in the 1-day workshop focusing only on building friendship and intimacy, compared to the other groups. There was no effect in the wife's trustworthiness metric. The husband's trust metric increased significantly only in the 1-day workshop focusing only on making conflict constructive, compared to the other groups. The 1-day conflict intervention also significantly increased the husband's trustworthiness metric. This study is only a beginning, but it does suggest that the variables of the Sound Relationship House are effective in increasing trust and trustworthiness. A limitation of this study is that we did not test whether the changes held after a longer follow-up.

It is interesting that the conflict intervention was effective for husbands, whereas friendship-and-intimacy intervention was effective for wives. We have observed that the major issue men complain about is conflict, whereas the major problem women complain about is intimacy.

Chapter 7

How Couples Build Intimate Trust

In this chapter the attunement blueprints for building trust are extended to include building emotional intimacy and personal sexual intimacy. Personal sex is contrasted with impersonal sex, which is "pornography."

In this chapter I want to talk about applying attunement to build "intimate" trust. Marriages and other love relationships are special because they are uniquely and reciprocally intimate. They are supposed to be affectionate, trusting, enduring, loyal, loving, and also sexual, erotic, passionate, and romantic.

This wasn't always the case. In fact, in the Middle Ages, marriage was not at all about romance; it was about property.[1] Stability was the goal, not passion. Passion and love were known to be fickle, so how could they be the basis of stable marriage? Punch-and-Judy puppet shows at fairs in the Middle Ages parodied everything from the local farmer to the king. They also parodied the husband who was in love with his wife. No kidding! The word "uxorious" was coined for this fool of the Middle Ages, the fool husband who was "in love" with his wife. Uxorious sounds like a disease, or a white-collar crime, doesn't it? So this idea that marriages and other lasting relationships should be loyal and stable as well as romantic, lustfully sexual, and passionate is really a new idea.

Some writers have argued that these are in fact two distinct forms of love—that "loving" a person in a lasting relationship is antithetical to being "in love" with that person. Helen Fisher, for example, has claimed that these are two separate chemical systems: "in love" being about the neurotransmitter dopamine (the chemical of the reward centers of the brain), and the "loving" system being all about oxytocin and vasopressin, the hormones of bonding and trust. Some have claimed that the "in love" state has nothing to do with trust, but instead with the madness of an obsessive and manic state. Some psychologists, like University of Hawaii psychologist Elaine Hatfield,[2] have even given a separate name for the "in love" state, calling it "limmerance." Perhaps it is, in fact, true that love and limmerance are different. But at this time we cannot conclude that trust isn't a part of being in limmerance.

Lewis, Amini, and Lannon certainly agreed with the hypothesis that these two states are distinct. They wrote:

> *Loving* is limbically distinct from *in love*. Loving is mutuality; loving is synchronous attunement and modulation. As such, adult love depends critically upon *knowing* the other. *In love* demands only the brief acquaintance necessary to establish an emotional genre but does not demand that the book of the beloved's soul be perused from preface to epilogue. *Loving* derives from intimacy, the prolonged and detailed surveillance of a foreign soul. (p. 207)[3]

But are they right? Isn't it possible to have romance, passion, and loyal love and trust in a lasting relationship? I say it can be, and it can be one state rather than two states, and I call that state "intimate trust." I could be wrong, but I personally certainly feel love for my wife, and I also feel "in love" with her.

It may surprise you that there seems to be a confusion even among therapists about how to become intimate and how to nurture intimate trust. Some therapists have claimed that intimacy is created by establishing boundaries between partners. In her book *Mating in Captivity*, Esther Perel actually claimed that the secret to long-term sexual intimacy is emotional distance.[4]

As strange as that idea may seem, she is actually following in the footsteps of a famous psychiatrist, Murray Bowen,[5] and the sex therapist David Schnarch.[6] All three of these writers have claimed that the greatest danger to intimate trust and to great sex is too much connection, which they describe with insulting terms such as "fusion," "merging," "enmeshment," and "symbiosis." Too much togetherness, they argue, kills erotic attraction.

Instead, these writers claim that intimacy is established by a process they call "individuation." The term was initially invented by Murray Bowen, who defined an individuation scale from 1 to 100.[7] People low on the scale were those unable to control their emotions with reason, whereas people high on the scale were able to control their emotions with reason. The definition of individuation has recently been extended to also mean that individuated people in a relationship are those who have very separate identities from each other and are very clear with each other about their own self-interests. They are considered developmentally more mature by people who use the term in that way. Reframed in that way, individuation doesn't sound like such a bad idea.

However, these ideas are somewhat at odds with what I am proposing. Although not all followers of Bowen think this way, unfortunately, the Bowen definition of individuation is often an emotion-dismissing philosophy. That philosophy creates a Bowen-type scale in which "reason" is at one end and "emotion" is at the other end of a continuum. The establishing boundaries part of that individuation definition emphasizes separateness and self-interest, which is antithetical to the interdependent, cooperative methods I have been proposing for building trust.

Of course, there are always two separate minds in a relationship. That is the basis for attraction and also the basis for regrettable incidents. But what is needed to build intimate trust is cooperation, not self-interest.

The Perel hypothesis is that boundaries between people and emotional distance create great sex and intimacy. The alternative hypothesis, which I favor, is that emotional attunement creates intimate trust and makes intimacy personal.

Romance, Passion, and Personal Sex

Many people on our planet clearly enjoy, and perhaps even prefer, what I would call "impersonal sex" to what I am calling "personal sex." Impersonal sex is not necessarily about the particular person we are paired with, but about some more detached impersonal aspect of sexuality—a fantasy, or a sexy body part, or a photograph or video of a stranger or of strangers in the act of being seductive or being overtly sexual. Impersonal sex may also be about erotic correspondence with a total stranger.

If many people didn't prefer impersonal sex, then prostitution, pornography, and all the sex fetishes, such as kink and S&M, wouldn't be as popular as they are. There are an astounding estimated 500 million pornography websites on the Internet. As a scientist, I do not judge people for preferring impersonal over personal sex. It is what it is. But what is it?

Neil Jacobson and I spent 9 years studying extremely violent men and their wives, and at the end of our research we decided to do exit interviews of all 61 women who were in these very violent relationships. The men were perpetrators and the women were victims. We did a sequence analysis and found that in these relationships absolutely nothing the woman did set off the abuse, and nothing they did terminated the violent sequence. We now call this "characterological" domestic violence. It isn't an argument that goes out of control, where both people have a responsibility for the violence.

Many of these relationships had dissolved in the 9-year period of our study. As we interviewed these abused women, Neil and I were astounded by one consistent story about half of these women told us. They said that the best sex they had ever had in their lives occurred right after a violent beating they took from their husbands. The very thought of having sex with someone who had just hit you was totally out of the realm of our experience. Is that the combined result of dopamine and oxytocin?

Paul Gebhard had told our seminar in the Kinsey Institute that the range of what people find erotic is enormous. Yet I wasn't prepared for what these interviews told us about the relationship between sex and violence for these women. So, given that experience, I am not surprised that Esther Perel and her clients might find that no affection or cuddling and greater emotional distance and erotic sex in long-term relationships works to some degree. Perel advises clients not to cuddle, not to mix affection with eroticism, and she cautions against the dreaded image of the flannel nightgown. Once a woman dons the dreaded flannel nightgown, she claims, their sex life is over forever. Her point is that familiarity kills great sex. So it seems reasonable to her that making one's partner more of a stranger might increase the erotic value of the partner for some couples. Maybe she's right, to some degree.

A recent article in *Discover* magazine speculated about the future possibility of robots being used as sex surrogates.[8] Hardware and software have already been created for making these robots quite lifelike. Their skin and outer coverings can be made to resemble that of humans; some are also capable of making human facial expressions. Animations have already succeeded in recreating the range of human emotional expressions. We also know that computer programs (like the program "Eliza"[9]) have been created to simulate the language of an accepting therapist. So theoretically these robots can be designed to appear understanding and accepting, even loving. They can be programmed to remember what someone has said and create sentences like: "I remember when you were last sad like you are today. It was when you were talking about your best friend's drowning. So this new loss is a big moment for you. I'm so sorry for your loss." I imagine that this will someday be a growth industry, and its effects won't be all bad.

If these robots can be made to cook and clean, they may even suffice as "Stepford partners" for many people in our population who would rather not be bothered with (or may lack the social skills for) establishing a real relationship with a real person. Not everyone should be in a relationship with a real person. There is no question that it does take a lot of work to make an intimate personal relationship work well. That entails some cost.

Perhaps these robots might eliminate or significantly change the professions of prostitution. A horrifying example of a professor who exclusively uses a group of blowup dolls for sex was described in Chris Hedges's *The Empire of Illusion*.[10] This man dresses up his sex-surrogate dolls, adds makeup, and has both sex and extended conversations with them. Of course, robots are an extreme of impersonal sex.

However, I want to talk about the opposite possibility. I want to talk about very personal sex in a committed, trusting relationship. The great psychiatrist Viktor Frankl actually defined "pornography" as impersonal sex.[11] After all, pornographic sex is sex that's not really about that particular other person, nor does it come from knowing and cherishing a specific person. I think Frankl's definition is interesting. I also agree with Perel that people can have distant and impersonal sex repeatedly with the same partner, and that that sex might even be highly erotic and satisfying. However, unlike Perel, I am primarily interested in personal romance, personal passion, and very personal and intimate sex.

What do I mean by these vague terms? Defining "romance" and "passion" scientifically isn't easy, but let me try. I define "romance" as the state that follows an agreement made with one's partner to nurture acts and thoughts that cherish qualities of each partner as special, unique, and irreplaceable. I define "passion" as nurturing communications of strong—and at times almost obsessive—interest in, curiosity about, desire for, and attraction to one's partner. My definitions are designed to make these aspects of intimacy very personal, something that people in a trusting relationship find themselves doing naturally. They are building intimate trust.

Just like the definition of trust that I offered in my trust metric, these definitions involve our partner's thinking positively about us, even when we're not together, and perhaps even nurturing a fantasy kind of halo about our partner. Trust is all about believing that our partner has our interests in mind by behaving that way, even in disagreements.

Intimate trust takes that one step further. It nurtures the reality or the fantasy that our partner is unique, special, and to be cherished. Paul Newman was so handsome and attractive that people often asked him why he had never had an affair. He once replied, "Why should I eat hamburger outside the home when I can get steak at home?" Nurturing these ideas is what made his marriage to Joanne Woodward so happy. They celebrated their golden anniversary in 2008. Lore has it that their marriage remained romantic, passionate, and trusting throughout their lives. David Letterman once asked Paul Newman if he was going to do a particular role in a Broadway play. He said that Joanne Woodward wanted him to, so he probably would do it. Letterman asked him if he did everything she asked. Newman answered, "Pretty much," and then added, "I don't know what that woman puts in my food."

Our research with couples having their first baby revealed that for couples whose sex life was going well 3 years after the baby arrived (compared to those for whom it wasn't going well), intimate trust, affection, intimate conversations that created emotional connection, and good sex were all part of the same continuum. These couples were not separating affection, cuddling, and sexuality from intimate emotional connection. They even had sex when the flannel nightgown was on. These couples also reported that they often had intimate conversations, and that being able to have these intimate conversations was intricately related to their friendship, their romance, their passion, and having good sex even after having a baby. So these data suggest that one can have both.

Our admittedly meager research data are not unique. A friend of mine, the late sex therapist Bernie Zilbergeld, conducted an unpublished study with 100 couples.[12] All of them were 45 years old or older. Half of the couples were selected because they said that they had a good sex life and half were selected because they said that they had a bad sex life. Zilbergeld was interested in which techniques couples used to create a satisfying sex life, and how they dealt with the problems of aging. His overwhelming finding wasn't at all about sex techniques. What distinguished the two groups of couples were only two things. Couples who said that they had a good sex life more often than couples whose sex life was poor consistently mentioned: (1) maintaining a close, connected, and trusting friendship, and (2) making sex a priority in their lives.

These findings run contrary to Esther Perel's idea that lasting good sex in a committed relationship comes from emotional distance and from avoiding affection, cuddling, and the dreaded flannel nightgown. In Perel's own words, "eroticism requires separateness." Maybe for some people it does. For many others, research suggests that this is not the case.

In fact, in our three studies of partners becoming parents, it is unfortunately separateness in a relationship that comes easily, not intimate connection. No one has to work at separateness after a baby arrives. It comes just from two people leading very busy and separate lives. The usual story is that she gets very involved with the baby and he goes to work harder and for more hours a day. The issue when a baby arrives is not how to be more separate, but how to continue connecting on a deep emotional level, instead of having lives together turn into an infinite to-do list where partners never talk, never play, never get to be listened to, never get to dream together, and never get to have any more adventures together. Separateness is a real enemy that divides people after a baby arrives, not a good friend that makes our partner always new and perpetually erotic.

I think that Perel's thinking may be that because many people find that sex with their partner becomes dull and strangers seem more exciting, the secret to good sex in a lasting relationship must be to turn the partner into a stranger. If there is emotional distance and the partner is a stranger, then the partner seems exciting and "hot." There were indeed couples in our studies of the transition to parenthood who played games such as pretending to be strangers, making up new identities, and going to a bar and picking each other up. Their fantasies spiced up their sex life. However, these were the playful and fun activities of two people who knew and trusted each other to a great degree. Sharing individual and mutual sexual fantasies requires intimate trust, not emotional distance.

In sum, our data suggest quite the opposite of Perel's recommendation that for lasting romance we need to "remove the protective layer of affection." That certainly was not true for the couples in our sample who just had their first baby. Romance, passion, and good sex were part of one equation for creating and establishing intimate trust. Building the friendship in a relationship, as Zilbergeld's study showed, was essential for a satisfying sex and romantic life, not antithetical to it.

Our data also suggest that building intimacy occurs with *conversations* that bring people closer. These intimate conversations are especially important for women. The overwhelming majority of our couples agreed with the statement that "generally most women want sex when they already feel emotionally close, but for men sex is a way of becoming emotionally close." The art of having intimate emotional conversations is foreign to many families. For many people having these conversations is a mystery, or requires a great deal of alcohol.

The Art of Intimate Conversation

At a party I recently attended I was talking with a man and a woman about how we all had fared on Orcas Island during the previous winter's snowstorm. The man was telling a story about how his truck went into a ditch near his house and he couldn't get it out, how he couldn't get any traction. He said, "I went inside the house to get something to help improve traction." At this point the woman said, "Well, my family and I were in a head-on collision on Highway 5." When she paused briefly the man added, "So I got an old quilt from the house, and I put it under the rear wheels, and by gum it worked!" I exclaimed, "My god, you were in a head-on collision? What happened?" It turned out to be a very slow collision, and everyone in the other car and in her family was okay.

This story is one example of what I have observed during countless parties and casual conversations I have overheard. Unfortunately, these kinds of conversations are also common in the lives of the couples we see in treatment. People generally don't listen very well to each other. Furthermore, they rarely ask each other questions, or follow a line of thought and feelings with connected conversation. The famous Swiss child psychologist Jean Piaget called this kind of interaction "collective monologue."[13] However, he used it to characterize the conversations of preschoolers, not adults. Yet collective monologue seems to pass for a great deal of conversation even among adults.

Partners who have a high degree of trust share their worlds with each other and create a strong emotional connection, which is the basis for intimate trust and personal sex. They practice the art of intimate conversation and view moments of emotion or high stress in themselves or their partner as an opportunity for intimacy and greater understanding of each other's inner worlds.

How is this emotional connection in intimate conversations created? There are four things I observe as characteristic of an intimate conversation: (1) being able to identify in words what one is feeling, (2) asking one's partner open-ended questions, (3) using statements that follow up on the answers to these questions by probing for a deeper understanding of one's partner's thoughts and feelings, and (4) using statements of compassion and empathy to express understanding of one's partner's thoughts and feelings. That seems to be all it takes to make an intimate conversation feel good to couples.

In one therapy case I had, I taught these four skills to the husband, who was an engineer who claimed that he simply did not know what to do to be close with his wife and daughters. He said that they were very frustrated with him. He said that he hated interacting with people at work at the many necessary banquets and retreats where he would have to make what he called "small talk" with people. He considered his aversion to small talk to be a part of his personality that he liked. I took him at his word that he did not know what to do, and asked him how he would feel about learning this skill. He said he would be willing to try it.

He worked hard at acquiring the four skills. Although he decided not to use these skills a great deal, he agreed they did help build better relationships with his wife and daughters. In one session he also reported with amusement that he had used the skills with a fellow employee he was seated next to at a banquet, someone he usually avoided because he thought she talked too much. However, he applied his skills, asking her questions, talking about his own feelings, following up on her statements and making probe statements and questions, and empathizing. He said that she later said that she never knew what a "very nice person" he was and that he was "easy to talk to." He marveled at these conclusions because they just didn't fit his image of himself as a curmudgeon.

Eugene Gendlin, in his book *Focusing*, elaborated a detailed program for therapists to teach people how to put their feelings into words.[14] Gendlin found that "focusing moments" in psychotherapy were the moments of the most rapid change, and, once he discovered that fact, he developed a method for teaching clients the skill of focusing, and for teaching therapists to use focusing in therapy. In focusing, a client is taught how to keep checking the words with his or her body to see if the words are right for the feelings, if a feeling of a kind of physical "resolution" occurs.

For example, Gendlin talked to one woman about her job, asking her how she felt about it. She initially said that she felt sad, but when Gendlin asked her to check in with her body to see if "sad" was the right word, she then said it wasn't. He had her close her eyes and use her imagination, and the image that came to mind was her standing on a railroad platform and the train leaving without her. That's how she felt, she said—that she was getting left behind. She said that she kept helping other people with their projects and they got the credit and the raises and promotions, not her. Those turned out to be the right words and images for her feeling about her job, which was very different from "sad." When the words and images are right, Gendlin claimed, there is a significant relaxation in the body that one can learn to become sensitive to. Knowing what one feels through focusing is the first part of being able to talk intimately to one's partner.

The basis of sexual intimacy in my research is first building emotional connection. One way that connection is built is through attunement in sliding-door moments, in processing negative affect or regrettable incidents, and in conflict. However, another way is having intimate conversations.

The Sex-Therapy Industry

Masters and Johnson's important research about the physiology of the human sexual response was based on studying people while they were masturbating.[15] For example, women used a transparent dildo that contained a camera that could observe and measure physiological responses. To qualify for Master and Johnson's study, the women had to be able to have orgasms regularly through sexual intercourse.

Masters and Johnson scientifically defined the human sexual response. They divided this response into distinct phases that included: (1) foreplay, whose function and goal was erection in the male and lubrication in the female, (2) excitement, whose function and goal was greater arousal, (3) intromission, where the penis went into the vagina, and (4) a final phase whose goal was orgasm. I will call this the "standard model" of sex.

Masters and Johnson destroyed the Freudian myth of the vaginal orgasm as the hallmark of the mature female. Orgasm through stimulation of the clitoris suddenly became scientifically acceptable. Some people claim that Masters and Johnson discovered the clitoris, but many women dispute that claim. Masters and Johnson's research was able to specify the goals of each phase and thereby establish standards of competence and "sexual dysfunctions." They also created tools for treating these sexual dysfunctions, and in so doing, they created an industry of professional sex therapists. One of the major dysfunctions they identified was performance anxiety, and they suggested creative techniques like nondemand pleasuring for dealing with this performance anxiety.

However, performance anxiety was actually an unexpected corollary of their identification of the phases of sex. To see this point, consider the game of chess. In chess there is a beginning game, a middle game, and an end game. Although the goal of the game is always checkmate, in general-strategy terms the goal of the beginning game is control of the center of the chessboard. The goal of the middle game is the favorable exchange of pieces, which have different point values. The goal of the end game is checkmate. By identifying these phases of a chess game, it became possible to write books of strategy for establishing competence in each phase of the game. Masters and Johnson succeeded in making sex like a game of chess. Because competence ("function") and incompetence ("sexual dysfunction") could now be defined at each stage of the human sexual response, performance anxiety was a necessary consequence of the standard model.

Inadequate time for foreplay, inadequate turgidity of the penis for intromission (the sexual dysfunction is erectile "failure"), premature ejaculation, inadequate libido, and inadequate lubrication of the vagina were some of the sexual dysfunctions they identified. Drug companies went to work to create medications to heal each sexual dysfunction. Viagra and Cialis were created for male erectile failure, and other medications like Zoloft were found to delay ejaculation. There were medical "cures" for these new "illnesses."

Shere Hite's work on the human sexual response used a different research strategy.[16] She asked her subjects open-ended questions and had thousands of them write their extensive replies to her questions. She discovered that 70% of her women subjects would not have qualified for the Masters and Johnson study because they did not regularly experience an orgasm through intercourse. Many of her women were able to have an orgasm through masturbation, although many of these women (back in 1975) felt uncomfortable with the practice. Subsequent research has corroborated her finding that most women have an orgasm through masturbation in about 10 minutes, not very different from males. Of further interest is that most females do not need to simulate the conditions of romance or extended foreplay when they masturbate.

Hite's major discovery, in my opinion, was that most of her heterosexual women said that what truly impeded their ability to have satisfying sex was their partner's adherence to *the standard model* of sex. The heterosexual women in Hite's study said that their real problem was that men didn't consider every kind of intimate touch as "sex," but only as the royal road to orgasm. They claimed that because of the men's adherence to the standard model, sex became problematic and emotionally distancing. Many of Hite's women said that they faked orgasm so that they wouldn't hurt their partner's feelings. They said that they wished they could just talk to their partner about what they wanted. The absence of emotional communication and trust was impeding the sex lives of many of the women in Hite's study.

In my opinion, the implications of Hite's report are revolutionary. If everything partners do with each other physically is defined as "sex," the standard model bites the dust. That means if a couple is kissing and fondling each other and he has an orgasm, there is nothing wrong with that. It's not actually a "dysfunction." For the woman it may raise the question "now what about me?" but there is no "dysfunction" without the standard model, except possibly for conditions that create pain. Even if the male's penis became soft after his orgasm, his hands and tongue remain workable for loving his partner and meeting her needs.

However, he needs to know *what she likes and needs at that moment*, and the basis for knowing is in being able to openly talk about sex. Hite's report made sexual functioning all about the open emotional communication about what both partners want and need sexually at any particular moment. It linked good sex to verbal and nonverbal communication about sex. In one fell swoop, Hite eliminated performance anxiety and most of the sexual dysfunctions.

In any bookstore there are usually two separate sections on couple relationships, one about "sex" itself and the other about communication. The communication books focus mostly on conflict and rarely mention sex, or they have very brief sections about sex. The sex books rarely mention communication or conflict, but discuss having fun and joy, and give advice about where and how to caress, suck, or lick. There is a need to bring these two sections of the bookstore together.

It may be surprising to discover that books about sex do not sell very well. I was very surprised when my literary agent, Katinka Matson, told me that. The only book about sex that has ever sold well is Shere Hite's book on female sexuality, which has sold an amazing 48 million copies since its publication in 1975. I believe the reason Hite's book has sold so well is that it speaks so truthfully to women, who wish that they could honestly talk to their men about sex. They couldn't do that very well in 1975, and I think they can't do it very well even today.

Talking About Sex

There is considerable evidence that talking about sex is related to overall happiness in couples' relationships. Both the frequency and the quality of talking about sex are strongly correlated with a couple's happiness, particularly for women.[17] In one study, 50% of the women who said that they discussed their sexual feelings with their husbands were also very satisfied with the relationship, compared to 9% who did not discuss their sexual feelings with their husbands. These are simple questions about preferences and dislikes, questions that make sex very personal.

The Wisdom of the Male Porcupine

When Masters and Johnson's books came out in the early 1970s, I was an assistant professor at Indiana University, home of the famous Kinsey Institute. Having been raised in the 1950s, I and many other young couple therapists were uncomfortable talking to couples about their sex lives. So I and many of my students took a seminar offered by Paul Gebhard, the head of the Kinsey Institute.

To desensitize us, Paul showed us films that the Institute had available of every animal on the planet having sex. We saw mice having sex, elephants having sex, giraffes having sex, zebras having sex, and so on. But what impressed me the most was the film showing two porcupines having sex. I will never forget that film. The male porcupine has a special problem to solve, because if he tries to mount the female when her quills are up, he will seriously injure himself. So this male porcupine sat down in front of the female and put his paws on either side of her face and began gently stroking her face. She closed her eyes and permitted him to caress her face. After a while the male went around behind her and checked on her quills. He came back after this inspection and continued patiently stroking her face. After a long time, he mounted a very relaxed and willing female.

That male porcupine really made an impression on me.

The Power of Touch

We are, unfortunately, a very low-touch culture. Psychologist Sydney Jourard studied how many times people touched one another when they were out to dinner in several cities.[18] In Paris the average number of times people touched one another in an hour was 115 times. In Mexico City the number was 185 times in an hour. In London the average was zero. In Gainesville, Florida, the average was 2.

Words are not enough for establishing intimate trust. University of Miami psychologist Tiffany Field developed a set of "touch institutes" to study the power of touch.[19] She developed an interest in touch after she gave birth to a premature baby. She noticed that these babies were in incubators and that parents were prevented by hospital staff from touching the premature newborn babies. Field thus created incubators that made it possible for parents to affectionately touch and deeply massage their newborn babies. The intervention was powerful. The parents felt more connected to their newborn, and the babies who were massaged by parents gained 47% of their body weight in just 10 days! These babies were able to leave the hospital and go home with their parents much sooner than babies who weren't touched.

Massage and other forms of touch aren't just powerful for babies. Field also discovered that just 15 minutes a day of massage by a husband of a woman who was suffering from postpartum depression was as powerful as antidepressant medication. Furthermore, whereas about 50% of people stop taking antidepressant medication after a year against medical advice, people did not stop massage. It literally kept partners in touch after the baby arrived and built emotional connection. Field's recommendations became a central part of our "Bringing Baby Home" workshop for maintaining intimacy and reducing conflict among parents who had just had a baby (see our website www.bbhonline.org, and the book I wrote with my wife, Dr. Julie Schwartz Gottman, called *And Baby Makes Three*).

As we now know, affection, massage, cuddling, and other forms of intimate touch are also events that stimulate the secretion of oxytocin in both men and women. Recall that oxytocin is the hormone of trust and bonding, and it is the very hormone that is secreted during orgasm. The more powerful the orgasm, the more oxytocin is secreted. That's why having sex too early may create bonding with people who may not be trustworthy.

The Penis and Clitoris Are Not Complicated

The heart is an extremely complex organ. Its pumping action is very sophisticated. It wasn't until William Harvey's lifetime of research in the 16th and 17th centuries that hundreds of years of wrongheaded ideas by Galen about the anatomy and physiology of the heart and lungs were reversed.[20] It took Harvey his entire lifetime to understand how the heart pumps. He published only one short book explaining all his results, and he never would have gotten tenure today for this groundbreaking research. How the heart is innervated and regulated by the brain are still active areas of research today. The heart is indeed a very complicated organ.

Each kidney is also an amazingly complex network of a million nephrons that purify the blood.[21] The kidneys are indeed very complicated organs. The brain is also amazingly intricate and complex. We are only beginning to understand how the brain works. Every year, thousands of papers are presented at national neuroscience meetings.

But the penis and the clitoris are really quite simple. It's true they are wonderful, but they are not very complicated. Go to any large bookstore and you will find a section of books on sex. Usually they suggest various ways of rubbing, caressing, sucking, and licking the penis and the clitoris. Sometimes they suggest exploring using ice, feathers, and food like whipped cream.[22] These are all very good ideas, and they create stimulation, excitement, engorgement and erection of the penis and clitoris, and lubrication of the vagina as couples prepare for sensual play or intercourse. Nowadays these books even include photographs or erotic sketches.

But this advice is really quite simple. Sex itself is really quite simple.

What makes sex complicated is that it requires talking, touching, and knowing one's partner romantically, and establishing the emotional connection that makes both people want to be excited, or carefree, or playful, or open, or vulnerable, or erotic, or use fantasies with each other. All that requires trust. Trust becomes easier if we are able to talk to each other about sex.

Talking About Sex With One's Partner

Shere Hite's reports on sexuality in men and women strongly point to the importance of being able to talk intimately about sex and lovemaking with one's partner to enhance communication about intimate, personal sex. Having these conversations is very difficult for American couples from an African, Anglo-Saxon, or East European cultural background. For decades I have been making videotapes of couples talking about their sex life, and most couples with these cultural backgrounds have a great deal of trouble being clear and specific about what they find erotic and what they need and don't want in the bedroom. Most of the time it's impossible to tell what they are talking about. For example, here's an excerpt of one of these conversations:

HIM: So we're going to talk about this?

HER: I guess so. So do you think it's gotten better?

HIM: Well, sure, it's gotten better, but still a long way to go.

HER: You don't like it?

HIM: Sure I like it, but there's a lot we can still do.

HER: Well at least we're not like Paul and Diane.

HIM: I never said we were. I don't know how he puts up with her.

HER: He's no picnic either, I can tell you that.

HIM: I know that, I don't know how they put up with each other.

HER: So we're okay?

HIM: Sure we're okay. But we could be better, right?

HER: I have been trying.

HIM: I know you have, and I appreciate that.

HER: Good.

They could have been talking about almost anything. It's hard to tell that sex is the topic because they are so uncomfortable with being that personal with each other. There is an enormous fear of rejection, which comes from a lack of trust and openness with each other. That may not be as true of heterosexual couples who are Latino. These cultures support direct and frank nondefensive conversations with one's partner about sex, romance, and passion. I discovered these facts in a national survey I designed for the *Readers Digest*. I also discovered that the same was true of gay and lesbian committed couples in a 12-year study that Robert Levenson and I did in the San Francisco Bay area.[23] Latino and same-sex couples didn't make assumptions about eroticism. They considered it their responsibility as a lover to know what their partner found erotic and what their partner didn't like.

To facilitate the process of intimate conversation about sex, romance, and passion for American couples who may feel uncomfortable with these intimate topics, it is important for a man to ask his woman or his man, and for a woman to ask her man or her woman, basic questions about sexual preferences, and then to also remember the answers. That means making a love map of one's partner's sexual preferences.

Chapter 8

The Importance of Repairing Negativity During Conflict

Effective repair is probably the single most important process that a long-term relationship needs to survive and stay mutually satisfying. In this chapter I report the results of a very detailed analysis of how couples effectively repair negativity during conflict itself. The concept of preemptive repair is proposed, and repair at the 11th hour is also discussed. Later in this book I will talk about how the failure to repair during conflict is intimately connected to the dynamics of betrayal.

Trust is also built by repairing negativity when it arises, particularly during a conflict discussion. Tronick and Gianino studied the interaction of infants and mothers at the baby age of 3 months; they proposed a model they called the "mutual regulation model."[1] Contrary to Brazelton's original beautiful sketch of the mother-infant relationship as sensitively rhythmically connected,[2] Tronick discovered that mothers and their 3-month-old infants were actually miscoordinated a whopping 70% of the time. Tronick also later discovered that the mothers who noticed this miscoordination and repaired the interaction had infants who were securely attached at one year of age. In his invention of the "still face" paradigm, Tronick also discovered that some babies also sometimes repair the interaction.[3]

As Nancy Dreyfus noted, the concept of repair also makes sense in understanding couples' relationships.[4] Nancy had created a very clever flipbook of statements people could make when they were stuck in a conflict discussion that had some chance of repairing the conflict and exiting the absorbing nasty-nasty states. She called her flipbook *Talk to Me Like I Am Someone You Love*, which is a great title because it suggests that when people are in the absorbing state, they can't recall that they even like this person and hence don't know what to say to make things better.

Nancy's visit to my lab 14 years ago started me on the study of natural repair attempts that couples made during conflict in my own lab. That work also allowed us to examine the hypothesis that what makes repair work isn't just the repair attempt itself but also the way the receiver interprets the attempt. In a fair proportion of miscommunications we tend to have, we might have hurt feelings, frustration, or loneliness. Hence, as Nancy noted, in a very good adult relationship there will also be a high need for repair.

Because of these facts about interaction, expecting communication and harmony to be "par for the course" is unreasonable. In fact, we can expect miscommunication to be the most likely even in attempts at communication. Some of these events will create hurt, misunderstandings, fights, and regrettable incidents. A great task for couples is minimizing miscommunication and developing a way of dealing with these inevitable miscommunications.

In this chapter I examine with some precision how couples actually go about this process of repair, how effective some repairs are, and what factors control the effectiveness of repair during conflict discussions in our lab.

The Driver-Tabares Repair Coding System

In our laboratory, Janice Driver and Amber Tabares developed a detailed observational coding system for describing the repairs newlyweds make during conflict discussions just a few months after their wedding. Their categories for repair attempts, outlined in Figure 8.1, are wonderfully specific.

Figure 8.1   **Categories of Repair Attempts During Conflict Discussions Among Newlywed Couples**

Agreement: a 180 degree turnaround by a partner	Repair question: asking a question to get to partner's feelings
Affection: compliments, caring	Softening: "I" or "we" statements, without blame
Compromise: finding a middle ground	Request for direction: trying to gain information
Defining the conflict, summarizing both points of view	Taking responsibility for own part of conflict
Guarding: a warning to back off	Self-disclosure: revealing personal thoughts as reasons for negative behavior
Humor	Topic change: ending topic or changing subject
Making promises to change	Understanding, positive mind reading, empathy, showing they are grasping what other is saying
Monitoring discussion: keeping it on track, addressing negativity in interaction	"We're okay": complimenting the relationship or teamwork
"Tooting our own horn": complimenting the relationship or viewing it as superior	Damaged repairs: repairs that start off well, but then contains a "yes but" ending that damages the intended repair. They need editing.

Their painstaking research had the precision and detail necessary for answering many questions about repair—its nature, timing, and effectiveness.

They summarized the occurrence of repairs and their acceptance by the partner in five 3-minute time blocks of the conflict discussion. They categorized repair attempts into either a *cognitive* or an *affective* approach to repair. The cognitive repairs appealed to logic and rationality: They included compromise, defining the conflict, making promises to change, monitoring the discussion and keeping it on track, questions, and requests for direction. The affective repairs were attempts at creating emotional closeness: They included agreement, self-disclosure, taking responsibility, understanding and empathy, and "we're okay." We also assessed the affective climate in the first 3 minutes of the conflict using the SPAFF coding system as an index of affect.

Topic change as a repair may seem surprising, because clinicians are often trained to think of a topic change as a diversion from the main conflict issue, and therefore perhaps dysfunctional. However, they have often noticed that a naturally occurring topic change can actually reduce physiological arousal and therefore be soothing and highly functional. They also noticed that some couples started what seemed like it might become an effective repair, but then damaged the repair by tagging on a criticism or other hostile or blaming comment. For example, a partner might appear to start taking responsibility, as in, "I have been pretty grumpy lately," but then add, "but I think it's mostly because you're ignoring me." These repairs seemed to require a good editor. We predicted that these repairs would increase negative affect.

What Determines the Effectiveness of Repair?

To address the question of what factors in the relationship might influence the success of a repair attempt, my Sound Relationship House theory was used in this study. That theory predicted that the quality of the couple's friendship, assessed from the Buehlman coding of the oral history interview (love maps, fondness, and admiration), and turning toward bids in the apartment laboratory, should determine whether the repair attempt was accepted or rejected—that is, how repair attempts were *received* during the conflict interaction. To assess the validity of these predictions, we coded the couple's behavior during the oral history interview and the couple's interaction during a 10-minute dinnertime segment in the apartment laboratory.

What did we discover? First, I will examine the shape of affect over time for the entire conflict discussion. Second, I will present microanalytic analyses of repair effectiveness. Third, I will present our analyses of whether the quality of the newlywed couple's friendship is significantly related to the effectiveness of repair.

The Shape of Affect Over Time During Conflict

The figures speak for themselves. In general, negative affect increased significantly over time during the conflict discussion (linear trend), with a significant drop in the husband's negative affect toward the end of the discussion (quadratic trend), but no such drop in the wife's negative affect toward the end of the discussion. However, this overall trend did not hold for all couples. Hence, based on the overall trend, there is a pressing need to investigate whether repair processes were effective in down-regulating this general trend.

These data show that because negative affect tends to build during a conflict discussion, there is therefore a need for being able to repair negativity during conflict. As I will discuss later, repair is an important part of building trust and commitment in the relationship.

The Repair Analyses

Our repair analyses were guided by the following seven questions:

1. *Cognitively-based Repairs.* First, is there any evidence that cognitively-oriented repair attempts that appealed to logic and problem solving are significantly correlated with overall increased positivity and reduced negativity?

2. *Emotionally-based Repairs.* Next we ask, is there is any evidence that the emotionally-oriented repair attempts focused on creating closeness are significantly correlated with overall increased positivity and reduced negativity?

3. *Damaged Repairs and Topic Change.* Is there any evidence that damaged repair attempts and topic change are significantly correlated with overall increased positivity and reduced negativity?

4. *The 11th Hour.* We will then ask examine the question, is there is any evidence that repair attempts might be significantly correlated with positivity or negativity if they are delivered at the "11th hour," that is, if they were delivered in the last 3 minutes of the conflict discussion?

5. *Pre-emptive Repairs.* On the other hand, is there any evidence that that "pre-emptive repair," which is a repair attempt made in the first 3 minutes of the conflict conversation, is significantly correlated with overall increased positivity and reduced negativity? In many ways these first 3 minutes set the tone of the entire conflict discussion. Janice Driver and Amber Tabares developed the hypothesis that happily married newlyweds were not waiting for negativity to develop very much before making attempts to improve the entire climate of the discussion. This hypothesis was consistent with our math modeling of newlywed interaction that found that the "threshold" for repair was far less negative for couples who remained stable 6 years after the wedding compared to couples who were divorced 6 years after the wedding.

6. Next we will examine the response to the repair attempt. This asks the question of whether we can fully hope to understand the processes of repair simply by examining the nature of the repair *attempt,* or if we need to also look at the *recipient* of the repair attempt?

7. Was the beginning affective climate in the first 3 minutes predictive of the overall positivity and negativity in the entire interaction? In some ways this question is not about repair, it's about whether the way people begin the emotional climate of the interaction is something that repairs need to work against. We can only guess at the answer to this question, but the answers may tell us something about the strength of the couple's history in determining how much work a repair has to do to turn things around.

Of course, all these analyses are correlational, not causal. We are making our best inferences about possible causal connections from correlational data. We need proximal change experiments to truly test which types of repair processes are effective. But we can still do the best we can to use correlational data to try to *disconfirm* some hypotheses about repair, and tell us if we are on the right track. That's good enough for now.

1. Repair Attempts Focused on Appealing to Logic
Increases in positive affect.

- *Wife Compromise.* Only the wife's compromise was significantly related to increases in the husband's positive affect.
- No other cognitively-based repair attempt was significantly related to increased positive affect.

Decreases in negative affect.

The following repair attempts were significantly related to reductions in negative affect.

- *Questions.* Only the husband's repair questions were significantly related to reductions in his own negativity.
- *Request for direction.* The husband's and the wife's requests for direction were significantly related to decreases in her positivity and increases in her negativity.
- *All other cognitively-based repair attempts.* All other cognitively-based repair attempts were non-significantly related to decreases in either partner's negativity or increases in either partner's positivity.

2. Repair Attempts Focused on Creating Emotional Closeness
Increases in positive affect.

- *Husband Affection.* The husband's affection as a repair attempt was significantly related to increases in the wife's positivity.
- *Husband Agreement.* The husband's agreement (180-degree turn around) was significantly related to his and his wife's increases in positivity.
- *Husband Humor.* The husband's humor was significantly related to greater husband and wife positivity.
- *Wife Affection.* The wife's affection was significantly related to increases in her positivity.
- *Wife Agreement.* The wife's agreement was significantly related to increases in his and her positivity.
- *Wife Humor.* The wife's humor was significantly related to increases in his and her positivity.
- *Husband Self-disclosure, Empathy, Reassurance, and Understanding.* The husband's self-disclosure was significantly related to increases

in wife positivity. The husband's understanding (empathy) was significantly related to increases in his own positivity.

- *Wife "We're Okay."* The wife's "we're okay" repair attempt was significantly related to both his and her positivity.
- *Husband Taking Responsibility.* The husband's taking responsibility for even a part of the problem was significantly related to increases in wife positivity.
- *Wife Taking Responsibility.* The wife taking responsibility for even a part of the problem was significantly related to increase in both husband and wife positivity.

Decreases in negative affect.

- *Husband Humor.* The husband's humor was significantly related to less husband negativity.
- *Wife Humor.* The wife's humor was significantly related to decreases in his and her negativity.
- *Husband Understanding.* The husband's understanding (empathy) was significantly related to decreases in his own negativity.

3. Damaged Repair and Topic Change
Increases in positive affect.

- *Husband's Damaged Repair Attempt: Doing Harm with a Repair.* The husband's damaged repair was significantly related to reductions in his own and his wife's positivity.
- *Husband's Change of Topic.* The husband's stop-repair (change of topic) was significantly related to increases in his own positivity.
- *Wife's Change of Topic.* The husband's stop-repair (change of topic) was significantly related to increases in both his and her own positivity.

Decreases in negative affect.

- *The damaged repair attempt: Doing harm with a repair.* The husband's damaged repair was significantly related to increases in his negativity.

- *Husband's Change of Topic.* The husband's stop-repair (change of topic) was significantly related to decreases in his own negativity.

4. Was there any evidence that any repair attempts might be effective at the 11th hour?

Was there any evidence that a repair attempt might be effective at the 11th hour? Actually, not much.

Repair Attempts Focused on Appealing to Logic

Increases in Positivity

- *Wife Defining the Conflict.* In the cognitive repair attempt category, at the 11th hour only the wife's defining the conflict was related significantly to increases in her own positivity.

Decreases in Negativity

- No cognitively-based repair attempts at the 11th hour were significantly related to decreases in negativity.

Repair Attempts Focused on Creating Emotional Closeness

Increases in Positivity

- *Wife Affection.* The wife's affection at the 11th hour was significantly related to increases in her own positivity, and her understanding was related to increases in his positivity.
- *Wife Understanding.* The wife's understanding at the 11th hour was significantly related to the husband's positivity.
- *Wife "We're Okay."* The wife's "we're okay" repair attempt at the 11th hour was significantly related to increases in husband positivity.

5. Was there any evidence of preemptive repair?

We wondered if there was any evidence for the hypothesis that preemptive repair might be an effective device for increased positivity and decreased negativity.

Repair Attempts Focused on Appealing to Logic

Increases in Positivity

- *Husband Asking for Direction in the first 3 minutes.* This cognitive repair attempt was related significantly to increases in his own positivity.
- *Husband's self-disclosure.* The husband's self disclosure was significantly related to increases in both partner's positivity.
- *Wife Asking for Direction in the first 3 minutes.* This cognitive repair attempt was related significantly to increases in her and his positivity.
- *Wife Affection.* The wife's affection was significantly related to increases in the husbands positivity.
- *Wife Humor.* The wife's humor was significantly related to increases in the husbands positivity.
- *Wife Taking Responsibility.* The wife's taking responsibility was significantly related to increases in both partners' positivity.

Decreases in Negativity

- *Wife Affection.* The wife's affection was significantly related to decreases in the husbands negativity.

Repair Attempts Focused on Creating Emotional Closeness

Increases in Positivity

- *Wife Affection.* The wife's affection at the 11th hour was significantly related to increases in her own positivity, and her understanding was related to increases in his positivity.
- *Wife Understanding.* The wife's understanding at the 11th hour was significantly related to the husband's positivity.
- *Wife "We're Okay."* The wife's "we're okay" repair attempt at the 11th hour was significantly related to increases in husband positivity.

6. Was the response to the repair attempt important?

To answer this question, we asked whether the *partner's response* to the repair attempt, rather than the nature of the repair attempt itself, predicted positivity or negativity. To address this question we examined Jani and Amber's coding of the acceptance or rejection of the repair attempt by the partner. The answer was a resounding yes. The strength of the answer suggests the hypothesis that we cannot just examine the nature of the repair *attempt,* but we must look to the partner to fully understand how repair processes work.

- Both partners' acceptance of repair attempts was significantly related to both his and her positivity.
- Both partners' acceptance of his wife's repair attempts was significantly related to decreases in both partners' negative affect.

Furthermore, judging only by the statistical significance of correlations (clearly not causal), there is support for the hypothesis that the acceptance of repairs by one's partner is even more effective in the first three minutes than it is in minutes 4 to 12. Furthermore, the acceptance of repairs by one's partner appears to be ineffective in the last three minutes.

7. Was the beginning overall affective climate important?

A critical question remains unanswered by these analyses. Forgetting about repairing the interaction, to what extent is the way the conversation simply starts off affectively in the first 3 minutes predictive of how it will end? Our previous math modeling of newlywed interaction (see Chapter 11) showed that the amount of negativity each partner brings to the interaction before being influenced (called the "uninfluenced steady state") and each partner's emotional inertia (tendency to stay emotional) were the best predictors of the future of couple relationships, and this held for heterosexual as well as gay and lesbian relationships. Could we predict the entire contour of the conversation just by examining the affect of each person in the first 3 minutes of the conflict discussion?

The overall pattern of which repairs are effective led us to ask the question of whether the effective preemptive repairs are effective because they are tapping an overall initial positivity of affect, of if they are effective because they are tapping a neutral affective climate, or both. As we have seen, both positive and neutral affect are quite functional during conflict, and neutral is even weighted slightly positive (+0.1) in our time-series weighting of the SPAFF codes. But we do wish to distinguish between positive and neutral starts, because it is probably easier to be neutral when starting a conflict discussion than to be positive. Fortunately, we have those data for the first 3 minutes of the conflict discussion with our SPAFF coding.

When we compute the overall positive or neutral starting affective climate, we find that the correlations are quite large between starting neutrally and the overall positivity being low. Beginning with positive affect, though, leads to a different pattern of high overall positivity in the conflict discussion. Although preemptive repair was useful, staring with a mix of neutral and positive affect strongly determined the outcome of the conflict discussion.

Testing the Sound Relationship House Theory: Is the Quality of the Couple's Friendship Related to the Effectiveness of Repair?

Our Sound Relationship House theory predicted that the quality of the couple's friendship, assessed from the Buehlman coding of the oral history interview (we-ness), and turning toward bids (attentive or enthusiastic turning toward) should correlate significantly with the way repairs are received in the conflict interaction. Were those predictions supported by the repair data? We computed acceptance of repair attempts in the first 3 minutes, and overall. The husband's attentive turning toward his wife's bids during the apartment lab dinnertime was significantly correlated with both husband and wife acceptance of repair in the first 3 minutes of the conflict and the overall acceptance of repair by the wife. The wife's attentive turning toward her husband's bids during the apartment lab dinnertime was marginally correlated with her overall acceptance of repair. The husband's enthusiastic turning toward his wife's bids during the apartment lab dinnertime was unrelated to either husband or wife acceptance of repair in the first 3 minutes of the conflict or the overall acceptance of repair by the both partners. However, the wife's enthusiastic turning toward her husband's bids during the apartment lab dinnertime was significantly related to the wife's acceptance of repair in the first 3 minutes of the conflict and both partners' overall acceptance of repair.

The husband's and the wife's we-ness in the oral history interview were significantly related to the wife accepting repair in the first 3 minutes of the conflict discussion. Hence many of the predictions of the Sound Relationship House theory were supported by the newlywed data.

I usually don't like to burden my readers with statistical tables, but the one in Figure 8.2 is so interesting it's worth talking about. When we compute the overall positive or neutral starting affective climate, we find that the correlations are quite large between starting neutrally and the overall negativity being low. (The correlation runs from −1.0 to +1.0; a hefty correlation is usually one that exceeds 0.5; a large one exceeds .7) These correlations are in the upper left of the table and appear in bold. Beginning with positive affect, though, leads to a different pattern of high overall positivity in the conflict discussion. These correlations are italicized.

Figure 8.2 The importance of neutral and positive affect in the first 3 minutes of the conflict discussion.

	H Negative Overall	W Negative Overall	H Positive Overall	W Positive Overall
H neutral—first 3 minutes	**−.66*****	**−.38***	.01	.25*
W neutral—first 3 minutes	**−.55*****	**−.66*****	.27*	.25*
H positive—first 3 minutes	−.36**	−.27*	*.74****	*.37***
W positive—first 3 minutes	−.34**	−.24a	.26*	*.57****

a p < .10; * p < .05; ** p < .01; *** p < .001

This table tells us that, although preemptive repair is useful, a starting mix of neutrality and positivity also helps determine the outcomes of the conflict discussion. It is likely that the history of the couple's past shapes every conflict discussion's beginning. This is reminiscent of William Faulkner's comment in *Requiem for a Nun:* "The past is not dead. In fact, it's not even past."

Discussion of Repair

Clearly most newlywed couples in this study increased their negativity over time during the conflict discussion. Again, with the important caveat that we are talking about correlational and not causal data, let's see what we can conclude as hypotheses from these correlations. There is therefore a huge need to explore repair processes that might be effective in reducing negativity for the newlywed married couples in this study. The results on repair suggest some very specific ways that couples can and do create a climate of agreement and do *preemptive* repair. When we compare cognitively based repairs that appeal to logic and rational problem solving, we must generally conclude that these repair attempts are quite ineffective. However, repair attempts that are based on increasing emotional closeness (taking responsibility, agreement, affection, humor, self-disclosure, understanding and empathy, and "we're okay") were highly effective.

These methods also are connected to creating a positive affective climate at the start of the conflict interaction, by starting neutrally or positively, by doing preemptive repair (particularly by the wife's taking responsibility and by being affectionate), and by her accepting her partner's repair attempts.

The data also suggest that even when the conflict becomes more heightened and negative in minutes 4 to 12, there are still things that couples can do to turn around the conflict's negativity and even make the affect during conflict more positive. The major ways of accomplishing that feat are the husband and wife's taking responsibility for even a part of the problem, their demonstrated affection toward each other, their agreement, and humor, self-disclosure, empathy, reassurance, and understanding. Additionally, both partners' stop-repair (change of topic), and the wife's compromise repair, were surprisingly effective. It's a bit like taking a mini-break from conflict.

The importance of the wife's initial repair attempts is of some interest. We know that wives introduce 80% of the issues for the couple to discuss in heterosexual relationships.[5] These results imply that women who soften their startup have husbands who can down-regulate their negativity. These may be specific instructions on *how* women can soften their startup dramatically by taking responsibility. At the 11th hour only the wife's affection, understanding, and "we're okay" repair were effective, but they were not *very* effective.

These results on repair suggest that the power in turning around a negative conflict and making it constructive from the outset lies in creating emotional connection. These results are entirely consistent with Wile's clinical descriptions of the power of moving from an "attack-defend" mode to "admitting" mode by taking responsibility for a part of the issue, and to "collaborative" mode by changing an adversarial conflict into one based on self-disclosure, compassion, and understanding. The mechanism through which these emotional-connection repairs work may be by reducing physiological arousal during conflict. There is some evidence that this may be the case. For example, Levenson has established that humor during couples' conflict interactions is effective in reducing physiological arousal (personal communication, 2010). Repairs that induce neutral or positive affect, or increase the couple's sense of cohesiveness, may reduce the threat in the conflict interaction. Subsequent research will need to explore the precise mechanism through which repair may do its good work.

These results on repair may also suggest that there exists a true and unfortunate ceiling in the extent to which it is possible for an unhappy couple to turn around an interaction that has started harshly. These findings are consistent with the findings that Levenson and I reported with our cumulative point-graph plots that only 4% of couples were able to turn around a conversation that had started negatively.[6] One might conclude that the data on repair are somewhat grim for unhappily married couples, who tend to start the conflict discussion harshly with a great deal of negative affect. The results explain why our efforts as clinicians sometimes seem like trying to stop the runaway freight train of negativity by standing on the tracks, raising our hands, and yelling, "Please stop!" The negativity of conflict has simply taken over the unhappy relationship, even for newlyweds, and repair has very little chance of success—unless, as Dan Wile has noted, both people *quickly accept responsibility* for the problem and move into "admitting mode" within the first 3 minutes of the conflict, and use positive and neutral affect at the very start of the conflict.[7] Once again, Wile has arrived at the same conclusion through practice-based evidence that has taken us a decade to discover through evidence-based research.

The repair results explain our ability to predict divorce 6 years after the wedding for newlyweds from the first 3 minutes of their conflict discussion.[8] Beginning neutrally and positively, as well as taking responsibility for the problem, is hard for unhappily married couples to do. Instead, the data in this study suggest that they tend to start in "attack mode" and amplify attack and defensiveness as the interaction unfolds, finding it increasingly difficult to repair. Conflict then becomes an absorbing state, difficult to exit once entered, because successful repair is the way out.

That grim absorbing state exists unless the quality of the couple's friendship is high—the emotional bank account has been built by attentive or enthusiastic turning toward and nurturing a sense of we-ness in the relationship. The central role of the wife in repair is highlighted in these data. This isn't to say that husbands don't play a major role, just that more wife repair codes were, in general, more effective. The attainment of the collaborative mode during conflict is not an easy thing to do, even for newlywed couples.

There is, however, some indication of how we might help couples accomplish the feat of collaborative conflict management. There is some light in this dark tunnel of the significant trend of generally increasing negative affect during conflict. The data suggest that the basis for accomplishing the feat of having conflict become more collaborative happily lies, in part, *outside* the conflict context. It may be strongly rooted in how couples establish and maintain their friendship and intimacy. They create a sense of we-ness in the way they tell their narrative about the history of their relationship and their partner's personality traits, as assessed by the Buehlman coding of our oral history interview. Furthermore, these couples enhance their friendship by turning toward their partner's bids for emotional connection, even while they are eating dinner, well outside the conflict context. We suggest that these results propose the hypothesis that it may be effective to build friendship outside the conflict context—when negative affect and physiological arousal are not as likely—as a base for effective repair during conflict, when negative affect runs high. How does friendship in a marriage accomplish this feat? Perhaps the secret to attaining the collaborative mode during conflict can be understood as having a conflict with one's situationally, temporarily annoying friend, rather than with one's ubiquitously and permanently hostile adversary.

The Role of Building Trust and Increasing Trustworthiness (Reducing the Potential for Betrayal) in Newlyweds

Just exactly what are we clinicians facing when it comes to helping couples for whom negativity has become an absorbing state and repair has little prospect of turning around their negative conflicts? Even for newlyweds, where intervention is primarily prevention, what is the battle we face as clinicians?

The answer has to do with helping couples build trust and reduce the potential for betrayal. That appears to be much of the task of new relationships. When one examines the content of most of the conflict discussions of the newlyweds in our longitudinal study, the underlying issues of trust and the potential for betrayal become clear. At the very start of marriages these couples seem to be asking each other, and demanding of each other, that they establish trust at the various tasks an intimate relationship must accomplish in building a life together. There are still many unanswered questions for these new young couples, and that's mostly what their conflict discussions are about. That's often the subtext, even if the main issue isn't ostensibly about trust and betrayal.

I have selected two conversations from our 130 Seattle newlywed couples' transcripts to illustrate these issues couples face in establishing trust and minimizing betrayal. They were selected because they are representative of most of the rest, not exceptional. The first conversation is about jealousy, which is about establishing trust in the fundamental issue of sexual fidelity. The second conversation is more complex. It is about whether the husband is truly part of a "we," or still part of his friends' circle. She is asking: "Will he abandon me when I need him?" and "Who comes first, me or his friends?" Particularly when she is emotionally upset, she is asking him: "Will he be there for me? Will he not leave, not abandon me? Will he not only not leave, but also listen to me empathetically? And furthermore, will he believe that my feelings are important, and that attunement is what I need and deserve from him?" In this case she is directly confronting his emotion-dismissing philosophy that militates against their potential attunement, which is the mechanism for building trust. He attributes his emotion-dismissing attitudes to being a guy.

These two couples are doing very well with their trust issues because for them conflict hasn't yet become an absorbing state, but it still isn't easy. In these new relationships, trust and betrayal are always issues that form the subtext of the conflict conversation. My comments are in italics.

Conversation #1: Sexual Fidelity. Newlywed Couple #31

W: Oh, the green light's on. (*laughs*)

H: Oh, boy. Well. All right. So . . .

W: Jealousy. That's the issue.

(*both laugh*)

W: I raised that one.

H: Yeah. Ah, so, you're jealous?

It seems that it is apparently her issue, not his.

W: Well, you know I am.

H: Yeah? Well—

W: I've gotten a lot better about it.

H: Yeah. I, I mean, I suppose if you said some of the things to me that I said to you, I'd probably feel pretty lousy.

This is a good move. He is accepting responsibility for a part of the problem. Good repair move.

W: When we first started dating, *you* were constantly jealous of Matt, and then of Wayne, and—

H: Constantly jealous. (*laughs*) No I wasn't, was I?

W: You could barely stand to have Matt in the same apartment. And at the time, you decided it was all because he was after me, but now that you know he's not, you just (*laughs*) don't like him anymore. Simply that, not jealous.

H: (*laughs*) True, I don't like him! I thought I saw you—well, I still think he is interested in you. Well, when I . . .

So he agrees that it's not just her issue.

W: See, now logically—

H: I do think he's waiting around for me to get tired of you or something. That's what I think. . . .

W: Great.

H: . . . I honestly think. . . . I mean look, the guy's a jerk.

W: (*laughs*)

H: But he's still your friend. (*laughs*)

W: But see, is that—is that logical, or is that emotional?

Clearly this distinction is an issue for them. Can they discuss the issue at all if it isn't rational?

H: Well, it's logical. When *I* feel it, it's always logical. (*both laugh*)

The hidden joke suggests that he has expressed the thought that she isn't that rational.

W: Of course!

She agrees that it is a joke, not really true.

H: Ahh—

W: 'Cause logically, I know that you're not gonna—every time I, I'm at work and you have a day off—you're not gonna call up somebody, call up Mandy or somebody, and go run off, frolicking through the trees with them, but—

H: Hmm. No, I'm not. But maybe I am.

He is teasing her, ignoring her insecurity.

W: (*laughs*) You're not—(*laughs*) you're teasing, right?

H: (*laughing*) Oh, am I?

He seems to be enjoying her squirming.

W: But emotionally, I'm kind of like, how do I know you won't lose interest in me?

There is the heart of her insecurity—will he leave me for someone else?

H: You think, "What if he was"—yeah, I get it.

W: And I feel—I feel stupid then for even thinking that.

H: That's why I cleaned up the apartment. So you know I was there all day. Doing stuff. I was busy.

Change of topic—reduces physiological arousal.

W: What a reason to clean up. That's just like, "Oh no!"

H: I guess I like reassurance. 'Cause when you're jealous of me, that means you care. You know?

Now he has returned to the heart of the issue.

W: Yeah, I get that. But I find that hard, too.

It has now emerged that her jealousy shows him that she cares about him.

H: Well, you find it hard to believe that I'd be jealous, and that's why I think you never tease me. That's why you don't try to make me jealous.

W: (*sigh*) I guess . . .

H: Just, jus—

W: I feel horrible.

H: Well, okay.

W: I'd feel horrible trying to make you jealous, but you tease me—

She hates his teasing.

H: I mean, it's not that I try to make you jealous.

He is getting it.

W: (*laughs*) It's just so darn easy?

(*both laugh*)

H: Okay.

He does try to make her jealous by his teasing.

W: But (*sighs*) I don't get nearly so upset about those as I used to. (*sighs*)

H: Well, where did you rate it on your paper? From 0 to 100, where did you put it?

W: 50.

H: Wow! Really?

W: What'd you write down?

H: 20.

They rated the severity of the problem on a 0 to 100 scale with 0 representing not at all severe, and a 100 representing extremely severe.

W: Just 'cause it's something that's been consistently bothering me.

H: Teasing you?

W: It really bugs me, and you've gotten a lot funnier about your teasing now, 'cause you know, you're like, "uh-uh-uh," when you do it, so it's really obvious when you're teasing now.

H: Does it still hurt?

W: I don't know. It's logically, like you said, logically I feel really stupid—like even all this ah, ah, every single person you work with is a woman.

H: All of 'em.

W: Just like when I, I've been waiting in the car for like, 15 minutes, and, and I'm finally like, "God!" and you were waiting out front, and see, that was my mistake, so it was my fault. And then I see you standing with this blonde, and you're saying, "Oh, see you later Betty," and she scooted off down the street, like she wouldn't even look at me!

H: Well, she didn't know who you were. She was leaving anyway.

A bad response, dismissing her feelings and defending the coworker.

W: Yeah, but couldn't she just say, "Hi," you know?

H: Yeah, it was kind of weird the way she left abruptly like that.

That's some support of her feelings.

W: It . . . yeah. And it was your reaction. I mean, *my* coworkers, when they see you, they say hello, not suspicious like she left.

H: She might be a bit paranoid, but—

W: (*laughs*)

H: She might, she might be worried that she's making you jealous, and she wouldn't want to do that.

He is still defending the wrong person here.

W: Well, it doesn't seem like that was the greatest way to show the fact that she isn't trying to make me jealous.

H: Well, no.

W: I don't know.

H: She's much younger than we are, not too smooth.

Good move, which we call "we against others."

W: Who is she anyway?

H: She's my manager.

W: Carey?

H: Uh-huh.

W: (*both laugh*) The one that lives with Hunter? (*both laugh*)

W: I felt really stupid for thinking that, and—

H: Well, you did kind of suddenly appear, and sort of jump on me.

Blaming his wife again. Bad move.

W: I was mad that I had to wait so long. (*laughs*)

H: I told you to meet me out front!

Even worse.

W: Yeah, see, I didn't even hear that. Maybe I was still asleep this morning. It's not like I, I sit up late at night and worry about it. She is a real babe—I can't believe she's your boss.

H: She is a babe, and she is my boss.

No reassurance there.

W: I'm not used to you being away from home a lot.

H: See, I see. I might feel that way, you working with a bunch of men, I mean. If you came home, told me about some guy.

He's offering some empathy, finally.

W: (*laughs*) You're secure because I just work with goofballs and women, don't I?

H: See it all, it all goes back to my old girlfriend Cat, 'cause she would come home and tell me . . .

W: "Oh I had so much fun today. Flirted with three guys today!"

H: Yeah, that's a good imitation. It, it'd just be that's exactly what she'd say. I'd be like, "grrr."

W: You'd want to say, "Shut up!"

(*both laugh*)

H: "Shut up" would have been good. I don't know. So I try to avoid when I talk about my boss Carey and stuff. I try to avoid saying anything good about her.

This self-disclosure and talking about a former girlfriend, mutual enemy, is good.

W: You're like, "Boy is she beautiful, don't you agree?"

H: I'd never say that to tease you. With Cat, I just kind of stayed in that relationship too long.

W: If I met Cat or something, it won't be such a big deal, but, I would say "he doesn't talk about you very specifically, but he does feel betrayed by you, hmmmm!" (*both laugh*)

The wife offers some solidarity. Good move.

H: Oh, god! That'd be funny. Really? Oh. Well, but—

W: I don't think about her anymore. Or Carey either. It's not like I sit there—

H: Hmm. Maybe if you asked more questions.

W: Gritting my teeth on it. Well, but if I—

H: 'Course I know it's—I don't know, you don't want to be probing me.

W: Yeah—yes, see—interrogating you.

They are circling around the topic of expressing a need for reassurance.

H: "What'd you do for lunch?" "Oh, I had lunch with Carey today, actually. She is so beautiful."

W: Oh, and did you have lunch with her, huh? (*giggles*)

H: Yeah, I did, actually. She just happened to have her lunch at the same time. And we sat there talking during lunch. Does it bother you?

W: Not really, unless you, like, sat and plotted it all morning.

H: No, it just happened.

He is trying to reassure her.

W: When did you get your break?

H: But then she's the manager, so she picks when people get their break.

W: So she arranged it specially?

H: No, I don't think she did. No, 'cause Patty was supposed to go on break, and then she decided she didn't want to.

W: Well, maybe I shouldn't have put that down as an area of disagreement.

She is now somewhat reassured.

H: What was that other—what would have been our other discussion?

W: One of 'em was about (*laughs*) respon—the one word I'm trying to avoid.

H: Responsibilities, oh yeah.

W: . . . responsibilities. (*laughs*) Give, give me a candy bar (*laughs*) make me happy! (*both laugh*) . . . which was really dumb. So my grades weren't so good. I feel like you expect me to suddenly wake up one morning and have totally different habits.

A self-disclosure. Good repair.

H: No.

W: That's what I feel like sometimes. . . .

H: Well, I didn't mean this whole session—it's turning into a (*laughs*) "pick on Jill" session. It seems like. Am I doing anything wrong?

W: I don't feel like it is picking on me. You're twiddling your toes a lot. (*laughs*)

H: They can't see that on camera.

W: Oh.

(*both laugh*)

H: I don't know.

W: (*sighs*) Yep. Is it just the general purpose where the apartment's been such a, a holy mess since we've moved into it?

Her guilt about not cleaning enough.

H: Well, it seems to stay nicer when the coat closet gets used.

W: (*giggles*)

H: 'Course, I'm guilty of it too.

Good move. This is the taking-responsibility repair.

W: I feel like ever since we moved into the apartment, you've suddenly got on this appearances kick again. I don't know, like we have to keep it neat and tidy all the time, and—

H: Well, it's small. I mean, I—

W: It's not that small.

H: I don't know. I feel a lot more crowded when it's, it's cluttered.

W: Yeah, it does seem kind of—even when it's clean, it seems kind of cluttered. I don't if it's—I think a part of it's that big rug, personally, but—

H: Really? Oh.

W: It makes the whole room seem a lot smaller. 'Cause it brings your eye to the center of that really dark rug color. And it could be the fact that—I don't know. But it has seemed really dirty and messy in there, but it seems like I clean up—well, like my days off, I clean up a lot, and—it doesn't really seem to make a dent in it . . .

H: Really—

W: . . . and I don't know why that is.

H: Really? Oh.

W: Yeah.

H: Hmm.

W: 'Cause it seems like if I can get, like, all they laundry done, and the bed made and blah, blah, blah—seems like we're always doing laundry, too.

H: Um-hmm.

W: (*giggles*) Like every day, and it, it just is kind of weird. But it just seems like there's only been like 2 days where everything's clean.

H: That's because we tend to just drop our clothes on the floor, and—

W: (*giggles*) Well, yeah.

H: Leave our plates where we finished eating—I don't know.

W: Does that really bother you a lot? We need a maid, that's what we need. (*laughs*)

H: Yeah, I know. (*laughs*) Well, we'll have one. We wouldn't have to worry about it anymore when we're filthy rich. But—

W: Yeah.

H: Well 'til then. . . . Yeah, then I guess it does bother me.

W: I, I, it's just a matter of being more conscious of it.

H: Well—

W: . . . 'cause a lot of times, I'll walk past a pile of dirty dishes. "Oh, I should pick those up," (*laughs*) and I don't. And I'm sure there's times when you do the same thing.

H: Never. Not me, never.

W: (*giggles*) "No, no, no, never, not me, no." I would really like to— ah, since I've got a 4-day weekend coming up, I will try and really organize that stuff in the office.

This is about trust as well. The questions is: "Are we a team in cleaning up?"

H: Okay.

W: 'Cause it's—it's a mess, and we need to do something about the cat box, too, as far as the apartment. (*laughs*) Maybe we're getting a little off our subject of jealousy.

This couple has made a lot of progress talking about the jealousy issue. They are facing their feelings and exploring their needs, and getting some insight about why this is an issue for each of them. They are attuning and building trust.

Conversation #2: Are We a "We"? Newlywed Couple #73

They are discussing a regrettable incident in which he chose to be with his friends rather than help her fix a toilet she was very upset about.

Again this is an issue of trust, "Can I trust you to be there for me when I'm upset and need you? Do I come before your friends?"

W: A problem more than anything, I would just wish that you wouldn't, ah, be so negative, to me. When you communicate to me, everything is in a negative light. That's what makes me defensive, and I know you don't like it when I get defensive.

H: Yeah, I know. That's a very circular argument, too, because . . .

W: Um-hmm.

H: . . . of course I would say, "well, I wouldn't be negative if you wouldn't be negative," you know. Then you just get this whole spiraling effect.

It may look like he is just being accusing, but he is also doing something else. He is saying he feels defensive rather than being defensive. This is constructive.

W: Um-hmm.

H: We—but we've talked about this before.

W: Um-hmm.

H: We both, you know, have tried to work on it. And, you know, there've been some improvements.

W: Um-hmm.

H: In general. So—

W: Well, do you think it has to do with criticism?

H: Criticism?

W: Um-hmm. . . . Us just both being so critical?

Taking responsibility again, which you will remember is effective, if done early.

H: Um, yeah, it's those darn Type-A behavioral traits (*chuckles*), I guess, I don't know.

W: So, how could we approach it so that we're not that way?

H: Just have to practice, and make a conscious effort not to.

W: I think maybe one thing that would be really good would be, okay, 'cause we both have faults and we both make mistakes, and we both end up, in a, a disagreement or being critical or whatever, maybe they should have driving on there, as an area of disagreement. (*chuckles*)

H: (*chuckles*) Yeah.

W: Ah, just the fact that, okay, I know that I'm a pain in the butt when you're driving. And if you could just, you know, like, instead of—say the first person does something negative, and then the second? The response wouldn't necessarily be negative. And so you could say, "Come on now, you're, you shouldn't—you know, you shouldn't be like that. Let's not do this." But neither of us do that. Both of us just, like, dig in and go for the guilt.

H: Well, it's hard, though, if somebody gives, presents to you in a negative light, or puts you in a defense posture. I mean, it's really hard. You have to make a conscious thing to say, okay, you're gonna counter with a positive statement, and not, you know, throw some more dirt back, you know. It's hard to do. I mean, it's really hard to do.

W: Well, what other solution could we—

H: Well, that's the solution. And it's you know, it's not easy. And no one ever said it was. So—

W: So, do you think we can do it?

H: Well, yeah. You just have to—I don't know, like . . . I remember when we had the old buzz word, "profiglian-thing"?

W: Um-hmm.

H: You know, that was my solution, was, okay, when you say something negative, instead of saying something negative back, say this silly word, "profiglian."

W: Um-hmm.

H: No, it was "profigliano."

W: Um-hmm. We haven't done that in a long time.

H: And that was our—that's what got us through Europe, you know. We'd go negative and one of us would say "profigliano."

They are discussing how to repair the interaction when it becomes too nega-tive. This is good. They are having a great meta-level discussion.

W: Um-hmm.

H: And what was yours? Was it "schwartz"?

W: (*chuckles*) I can't remember. Maybe.

H: Something. So anyway, that was my solution, was to use the funny word when somebody said something negative, so that way, it's a neutralizing statement. "Profigliano."

W: It doesn't solve the problem, though.

H: But it's a neutralizing statement, so then the other person is conscious of the fact that they just made a negative statement, without you saying something negative to them.

"Profigliano" puts the other person on notice that they've said something they might regret if they thought about it. Then they could think about it, and then they can approach the situation having thought about it instead of just speaking without thinking.

W: Um-hmm. Well, it's kind of like—

H: But I mean, you, then you couldn't remember the word, so— (*laughs*)

W: (*chuckles*) Um-hmm. Ah, well, it's kind of like—with your best friend, you want to help them become a better person and always show them in a good limelight, you would overlook all the bad things about them. But it's like we see each other way too closely to do that. It's, like, so easy to find fault because we're together all the time.

It was her turn to say something wise and wonderful.

H: Definitely. I mean, you don't even have to think about it.

W: Yeah, but then you think about it.

H: Yeah, I mean it's—it's a very human quality, but it's something that, you know, you want to try to conquer. I mean . . .

W: Um-hmm.

H: . . . bring more good in—

W: That's what I'd like to do.

H: Yeah. A conscious infusion of good.

W: So how can we start? We'll use "profligiano." I'll remember the word . . . if you'll help me.

H: Yeah, we can try that for a while. But that was, like, that was even before we got married.

W: Um-hmm.

H: That was just sort of the way I used to try to deal with the situation. 'Cause you were kind of unhappy and, and, being kind of a drag, and I know I was—you know—I had to just figure out some way to neutralize myself because. . . .

W: When did it start?

Changing the topic as a repair.

H: Well, it was like when we drove across the United States.

W: You're right.

H: You—

W: Car criticism.

H: Well, I mean, you had the burned-hand problem and all that, you know. And I—I was in a very—I mean, I was trying to take exams, take you to the therapist, and I was just in a really stressed-out situation. And—I mean, I was snappy. I know I was snappy. . . .

He is taking responsibility.

W: Um-hmm.

H: . . . and, and I was just trying to figure a way to make myself think before I snapped or said anything, because you were like, you know, always—you couldn't do anything, so every time I came home, I had to wait on you hand and foot, and it just got very taxing for me, 'cause I was trying to study and take exams—

W: It seemed like that was kind of the beginning of our down period.

H: Yeah. So that's why I invented the profigliano thing to try to say, okay, just say, "profigliano," instead of saying, "I can't take this anymore!" So that was my way of dealing with it. Then we kind of forgot about it.

W: Not really. I never forgot about it.

H: Yeah, you did.

W: Maybe profigliano, that exact word, but not really—not really when it started and why it started and—like, I don't think all that ever healed completely for me. You know.

H: Probably. I don't know. I kind of forgot about it—moved on, but—I know it was a tough time for you.

Empathy.

W: With my job and everything.

H: Yeah, it was. I mean, generally, though, you're in a generally better mood overall than you have been in a long time.

Tooting their horn

W: Um-hmm.

H: Now that you've got a job that you like, and, life is just sweller. I mean—

W: Sweller? That a word?

H: Yeah. You don't get stressed out as much.

W: Um-hmm.

H: But the other thing that it—that I wanted to talk about, it's—is just the way you deal with stress, in a stressful situation?

He is introducing an important topic: the way she handles her emotions when she is stressed.

W: Um-hmm.

H: And I think it—this is something, I mean, just that I notice—that, I mean, you and I handle stress in a completely different way.

W: How so?

H: I mean, if I see a stressful situation, the first thing I try to do is just figure a way to make it less stressful, and just come to terms with it. And you, like, panic, and—and just start being irrational and thinking out loud, and stuff like that. And—from my perspective—and I, if you could come up with some way of, when you have a stressful situation, of dealing with stress, it would probably—because then, when you're stressed, you bring that to me . . . all emotional.

This is getting at the difference between them in meta-emotion, although he is in danger of casting the problem as her fault. He is saying he is dismissing and she isn't. Can they attune? This is the issue they will now address.

W: Um-hmm.

H: . . . and then I—if I don't act exactly the way you want when you're stressed, and if I act laid back, like, "Okay, it'll work out, just don't worry about it," then you attribute me to your stress, I'm now the source of it, and then I get brought into this, and, see, I'm not really a party to it. It's all you.

W: Give me an example.

H: Well, it's like, ah, that one Sunday that I was playing Frisbee with my friends and the toilet backed up.

W: Yeah, but that situation didn't stress me out as much as the fact that. . . .

H: Well—

W: . . . your total disregard for me, in that situation.

This has given her the opportunity to bring up her issue if whether she can trust him to be a "we" and to care about her stresses, to choose her over frisbee with his friends.

H: Um-hmm. What?

W: And it didn't stress me—

H: Well, to me I saw it more as a stress of the little incident that set all this off.

W: No. No, no. I was more upset about the fact that you just took off, and you just never said to me, "This is gonna be your responsibility today." You just kinda said, well, you know, you just left it up in the air, and I assumed you were coming over there. And then you didn't, and I thought that was just really mean of you.

She felt abandoned by him.

H: Hmm. Yeah, but I mean I guess from—

W: It didn't stress me—the situation, that toilet thing—that didn't stress me out that much.

What stressed her out was that he left when she was in need of him. Can she trust him to be there for her?

H: Hmm. I was again the source of the stress, ultimately, in your mind it was me. But you were all upset about that and didn't seem to be too—

W: No. I mean, what am I gonna say, in front of somebody? "You're being a jerk, you need to get to work"?

H: Yeah, well, I mean, I felt, you know, if I would have been running back and forth there, then nobody would have been able to get anything done, and you and I would've just spent the whole day zipping back and forth trying to make each of us *partially* happy, and neither one of us would have been truly happy, and my friends wouldn't have been happy at all, because you and I would've been playing cat and mouse.

Whose happiness comes first? His friends' happiness, his, or hers?

W: Not really.

H: So, my attitude was, well, if somebody better—somebody better be wholly happy. . . .

He chose his own payoffs over hers. That's betrayal, and a zero-sum game.

W: You could be happy and I could be wholly unhappy.

Or what she is not saying is, "if you'd change we could be cooperative, maximizing both our payoffs."

H: Exactly . . . and the friends are happy, and somebody's gonna have to suffer. It was kind of like that. . . .

He is not getting it.

W: So, it was kind of like you just made the decision that I would be the one to suffer.

She states the issue of trust forcefully.

H: Yeah, in that particular instance, you were the, you were the one that was absent from the decision-making process, and—

He finally agrees, he chose his self-interests over hers.

W: Not really. I was there, and I was a phone call away in the beginning.

H: Yeah. Well anyway, and you just missed out.

W: But that was your fault.

H: So I avoided all the stress and emotion around the toilet, which was going to wind up being that I was the cause of the stress, so I avoided that. That's my whole point.

He is "explaining" that since he avoided the stress, his was a good choice for him, not understanding that he is building betrayal.

W: You brought that upon yourself.

H: See, I didn't feel, really feel any guilt in that situation, because I thought it was just—the way things like that sometimes happen. And, you know.

W: Well, it's because you made it happen. It just didn't "happen" like that.

She is making him face the fact that he chose this course of action.

H: Hmm. Well, I guess you weren't there to see it all develop, but I mean, we were standing around waiting for about 20 minutes—

W: Well, you just—you become a victim of circumstance, though, and you just say that's okay.

H: Well—

W: I mean, you just accepted it. You made it happen, and you accepted it, and you can't say that "it just happened." I mean, by you accepting it, you become party to it. You left me with the toilet all alone because otherwise you'd have to deal with this hysterical woman who blames you for all her stress, right?

She is finally acknowledging her feelings about being dismissed emotionally by him.

H: Well, yeah, but that wasn't the sole instigator.

Defensive. Not good.

W: So it was somebody else's fault that it happened that way?

Good confrontation. Gentle.

H: Well, we stood around and waited for you for like, a half an hour, we're staying out in the street, waiting, waiting, waiting, you know, and the sun was getting brighter and brighter. Pat comes by, and Pat's riding his bike around in circles in the middle of the street, and we're standing there whistling—

He is inarticulate, fishing for an excuse.

W: Yeah, but that wasn't the main circumstance that had to do with it. The circumstance that had to do with it is when *I* showed up, you could have come and helped me with the toilet, and I could have stayed. But instead you didn't even talk . . .

H: Yeah, but we only had a—

W: . . . to me. You didn't even look at me. You didn't even acknowledge, like "hey," you know. You didn't even "ask" me if, I could, you know, if you could stay. You just assumed, well, you know, "tough luck, you take care of it, I'm gonna stay and have fun."

He is not getting off the hook so easily. She needs to trust that he will be there for her when she needs him.

H: Huh.

W: So you didn't even give me any, I mean, what would it have taken for you to say, "hold on a minute, guys," and to come over, and just to give me . . .

H: Guys ain't girls.

The gender excuse for dismissing negative emotions.

W: . . . a little bit of regard, to say, "Hey, you know, would it be okay?" It's like you didn't even care. I mean, I looked for you for 20 minutes, and then I found you, and nobody even said a friggin' word. So—

H: Yeah, we were kind of intent, we were involved in our game.

Friends come first.

W: Well, so what? How much would it have taken? I mean, don't you think—don't you think that would have been nice?

H: Yeah, well, I apologize, but we were intense into our game.

Good move, good repair, accepting responsibility at last.

W: But wouldn't—I mean, just stop for a minute and tell me, like, if you would have thought that would have been the nice thing to do?

H: Yeah, but I just didn't even think about it at the time, you know. I was just intently concentrating on this particular game, and I wasn't even going—

W: Well, I think that was really selfish.

The first symptom and the heart of the lack of trust is the attribution of selfishness.

H: Thinking in a broad sense, yeah. And, and I mean the teams had an even number of players, and if I, if I would have left, the whole game would've collapsed. That would also have been selfish. So it's between two selfishes. Pick one.

He isn't part of a "we" yet. His loyalty to his friends is equal in his mind to his loyalty to her.

W: Yeah, but I would have stayed.

There's the difference between them, made raw.

H: But you weren't—I mean, it wasn't the same.

W: So?

H: The teams are evenly divided, as they are, with me on one side.

W: So? But they—I mean, other people that were there said to me, "come on and play."

H: Yeah. But I mean, I, I was just into my competitive nature mode, and . . .

W: Well, maybe you should've—

H: I was . . . intensely involved in the competition and wasn't really paying attention to, ah, anything other than what I was concentrating on.

Exactly her point.

W: Pretty egocentric.

H: Yeah, very. Very felt like I was in high school on the football field again, you know. Just kind of lock in and do what you have to do.

Good taking responsibility.

W: Do you like it when I'm like that on the ski slopes?

H: What?

W: Do you like it when I'm like that on the ski slopes?

H: No. No, I admit it. I mean, it's not, it's not—it's an individual thing. It's not, it's not a very cooperative mode, but, you know, it happens to all of us, so—but now we know the circumstances that we're in, and it's probably gonna happen again.

He is talking about the heart of trust: cooperation instead of the zero-sum game.

W: Well, if it happens again and you would accept those circumstances, I'd be really upset.

An ultimatum that he needs to change for her to trust him.

H: So, you know, next time I should at least know that I'd better not do that or I'd better "think" of you.

He is starting to get it.

W: Or maybe you just stop for a minute and talk to me.

H: Yeah. That would have been good.

W: And, you know, ask me if it would be okay, so it's, you know, it was kind of an agreement in the beginning that, you know, it was gonna be a split endeavor, and then it ended up being dumped on me, with nothing ever being said, no apology ever being made, kind of like, "well, that's your fault," I mean, "well, that's just, you know, tough—I was busy playing." . . . I mean, now you wonder why I don't even want to go over there, because it's like, I'm not gonna get stuck over there and have you just take off.

She needs to keep going over this point again. Like sewing on a button to make it secure takes many passes of the thread through the holes, she needs to know she can trust him to be there for her when she is upset. This will not be their last conversation on this point.

H: Profigliano, profigliano. It's like, you make up all these excuses all weekend. Half of 'em may . . .

W: So?

H: . . . never come true. I'm like, "Yeah, right, boy, this looks—sounds to me like reciprocity."

W: I'm not gonna get stuck with that. Oh the light's on. We're done.

H: Yeah. (*whispers*) Oh, that's good.

As you can see trust is tested, established, or eroded in small moments of ordinary conversation discussing regrettable incidents. I am aware that these dialogues are quite extensive and elaborated. It takes a lot of concentration to follow along and develop a sensitivity for these tests of trust and betrayal that arise moment-to-moment during conflicts. This couple has also had a good conversation about trust in terms of his being there for her and their becoming a "we" instead of two "me"s. But they have a long way to go on this issue. The last two-thirds of their conversation was tricky. She was trying to make a point and partly did, but it was also an argument that had a nontrusting element. A therapist could have been helpful to them at this stage of their development of trust.

Both couples were discussing what they need to do to be able to trust each other in the many aspects of building a life together where trust needs to be established and betrayal minimized. This was typical of the conversations of most of the newlywed couples. The clinician can help these couples by realizing and helping the couple to realize that their fundamental issues are about trust and betrayal. The clinician can also recall that applying attunement is the mechanism for building trust.

Example of a Couple Where Trust Has Been Shattered and Has Not Healed

Contrast these conversations with a couple whose trust was shattered by a recent extramarital affair on the husband's part. Although they sought consultation of some sort from their minister, many of the issues the affair raised have not been healed. Both partners are in their mid-forties.

W: (*whispers*) Doug?

H: Okay, start it. (*inhales*) Yeah, uh, I guess, uh, the subject is jealousy. Uh . . . maybe sex. I don't know.

W: No, it's jealousy.

H: Mainly jealousy.

W: Yeah.

H: Okay. Um . . . I feel, that . . . you're gonna trust me as long as . . . and not be jealous as long as I am real, real careful about . . . what I do. But, let's say, for instance, uh . . . (*smacks lips*) uh, you saw . . . a woman in my car with me. What would happen? What would be your first reaction, and what would you do?

He is either probing the issue or he is teasing her.

W: Why? Is there a woman in your car?

Her upset voice tone shows that she doesn't find his teasing at all funny.

H: (*laughs softly*) Uh, these are hypotheticals.

She is reassured.

W: Well, if I saw Joanne Fisher in your car . . .

H: (*chuckles*) It'd be business. She's in real estate, right?

W: . . . I would, I would—yes, I would believe that it was business.

Now it seems as if she is referring to some trust having been built back after the affair. She is congratulating both of them. This is the repair of "tooting their own horn."

H: Oh, wonderful. You'd give—in other words, you would give me the benefit of the doubt.

W: I'd—uh, yes I would.

H: But you, you would ask me about it, of course, and I, and I would appreciate the fact that you asked me.

W: Oh, you'd probably tell me.

H: But you wouldn't jump to a conclusion?

W: No. Because I trust you.

Again, she refers to an accomplishment of having recreated some trust.

H: Yeah. See, I called her yesterday.

W: Oh. You did?

H: Yeah.

W: Why?

He's on thin ice here.

H: (*inhales*) Because they're having a meeting tonight, uh, regarding the . . . uh, city council passage of a common driveway ordinance. And some builders are gonna be there. And I can't be there because I've gotta go to my class tonight.

W: (*tension*) What class do you have tonight?

H: History of Architecture.

W: (*exhaling*) Oh.

She is reassured.

H: And . . .

W: (*faint chuckle*)

H: . . . she needed—uh, and, and I'd gotten a copy of the new ordinance and read it. And that—and I put it up in the mailing tube this morning. And then you moved it, and I . . .

W: Oh.

H: . . . moved it back. And I notice now it's gone, so she must have picked it up. (*swallows*) Uh, I—I wouldn't do business with her, anyway.

He actively reassures her. Good repair.

W: Really? You feel that way about her?

H: Yeah.

W: Okay, good. So, I—there's no reason I will be seeing a woman in your car.

She is asking for more reassurance and a "we're okay" repair.

H: No. But, but, for instance . . .

W: . . . you driving around with her in your car.

H: . . . I mean, I'm just—I'm just saying, uh . . . I think jealousy results from lack of trust. Almost a hundred percent. That's where it comes from.

W: Uh-huh. And a fear . . .

H: If you trusted—

W: . . . a real—

H: Well, a fear. Yeah.

W: A fear of losing something very precious.

H: Right. But I've, I've . . . explained to you . . .

W: I know.

H: . . . that, uh, my family is the number one important—uh, number one thing in my life, and that (*inhales*) there's no need to fear.

Another reassurance, good.

W: I know it.

The repair seems to have been effective.

H: I made that decision, conscious decision, 3 years ago, and that's not gonna change. I guaranteed you that, right?

W: (*inhales*) And you know, I'm convinced of it? And so it's dissipated the jealousy. But because my feelings . . .

She states her appreciation of his declaration of commitment. But she is going to refer back to the affair and her suspicions having been true once.

H: Okay, maybe it's—

W: . . . of jealousy have been well-founded before.

She refers back to the trauma of the betrayal, his affair with Jenny.

H: Uh, see, there's where I disagree. There's where I disagree. Uhh . . . you know, I, I resent the fact, that, in the case of Jenny, that I can never see her again. For the rest of . . .

W: Oh, really?

H: . . . my life.

He is stating the fact that his commitment comes at a great price to him. He's on very thin ice here. He wants to see his former affair partner.

W: Do you *want* to see her again?

H: Yeah.

W: You do?

H: Yeah. And I resent the fact that you don't trust me enough. (*inhales*) That, that she couldn't—you know, uh, after all, I dated her before I even met you, a year before I even met you. (*inhales*) I kind of resent the fact that you don't trust me enough, uh, for her to come over and, uh, meet you and . . .

Now he has created a very serious breach of the trust they had created. He apparently felt confident enough to be able to push the limits of what he is allowed to do, given his recommitment to their relationship.

W: (*exhales*)

H: . . . meet our kids.

W: (*smacks lips*) I'm really upset now.

She needs his empathy. This is a bid.

H: It's like . . . look, it's like a—if I hadn't seen—

No empathy from him.

W: What would be gained by it?

H: If I hadn't seen Don Phillips . . . or, or, or, uh, one of my old, uh boyfriends. I just want to stay in touch.

W: No, there's a big difference between an old boyfriend and old girlfriend.

Her heart rate is very high right now. She is flooded.

H: There is, uh, there is a . . .

W: Huge difference.

H: . . . difference. But that shouldn't mean that I, I can never have contact with somebody from the past?

W: Why would you want to?

H: Just to talk over old times.

He has become careless about her feelings.

W: You said on Sunday that there was no reason, it was over . . .

H: (*faintly*) No.

W: . . . it was resolved, and done, and finished.

H: I, I said that, because I know . . .

W: (*exhales deeply*)

H: . . . how jealous you are, and that that's the only way that's gonna work.

The jealousy is now her fault. He is in danger of undoing whatever trust he and she have built after the affair.

W: (*smack lips*) So, now I'm supposed to trust you after you just now tell me this?

H: (*chuckles, swallows*) If you trusted me, it wouldn't be a problem.

He may be cruelly playing with her.

W: (*smacks lips*) I don't see . . .

H: It—

W: . . . anything to be gained by your seeing her. Have you made contact since Sunday?

H: No. No, I haven't.

He has probably gone too far.

W: I think we need counseling.

H: Well, uh, that's a possibility.

W: Yeah, we definitely need counseling.

Yes, he's definitely made a mess of it now.

H: It's something that we do need to work out.

W: Uh-huh. Because—

H: I mean, it's not a—it's not a big, it's not a big issue for me. But it is, it is a resentment that I have.

He is trying to minimize the issue, but it may be a repair that's too late.

W: (*smacks lips*) Well, okay. We need to.

H: That you're so jealous that I can't, uh, visit with an old friend.

W: An old ex-girlfriend.

H: It, it's the fact that I can never have contact again?

W: But why would you want to?

H: (*inhales and exhales deeply*) Why not?

W: What would be gained by it?

The only way he can rescue this is to apologize, backtrack, and empathize.

H: It's just like saying, uh, anybody that we knew back at, at Iowa State. When we were going to school there.

W: No, this is a, a person that you obviously still carry a torch for.

H: (*exhales*) The question of carrying a torch—I'm telling you, Judy, I already told you that my family is the most important thing. So obviously I cannot . . .

He thinks logically that his recommitment should allow him enormous freedoms. He has really blown it.

W: (*inhales*) I see no . . .

H: . . . establish—

W: . . . reason for me to become, uh, a friend of hers. I don't see any reason for me to befriend her.

H: Listen, it's not a question of becoming her friend. She moved over to the peninsula so that, uh, it—it's just like, uh, the Johnsons. We don't see them that much because of the bridges, and we're all busy with . . . whatever.

W: (*smacks lips*) We have a lot in common with the Johnsons. What do we have in common with her?

H: But we still—but we still don't see them.

W: What do I have in common with her?

H: Well, you don't know because you never met her.

W: Well, I don't see any reason to.

H: (*inhales*) Well—

W: She's a big threat to me.

Now she is again trying to express her true feelings and get him to empathize with her. That takes courage to suddenly become that vulnerable.

H: A big threat? Because you think that I'm really not committed like I say I'm committed. Totally committed.

He's back to his commitment statement being all his wife should need to be comfortable with him seeing an old flame.

W: (*inhales*) If you were really committed like you say you are, you would not do this. You would not—you would realize where I'm coming from.

H: (*chuckles softly*) You know, probably, if you said it didn't matter to you, then it'd be less important to me.

His humor is not shared by his wife. Furthermore, he is suggesting that her reaction is causing him to dig in his heels on this issue.

W: Well, I'd be dishonest if I said it didn't matter. It does . . .

H: Okay.

W: . . . matter to me.

H: Well, then you're still very jealous. And, and you still don't trust me.

He is continuing to blame her now.

W: I am, that you want to see her. It wasn't because I don't trust you.

H: (*faint chuckle*)

Again humor that is not shared, so it won't be an effective repair.

W: If (*inhales*) if you can say, on Sunday—

H: Okay. Okay, that's what it—you said that you trusted me, and now you're saying you don't.

W: (*inhales*) I thought you said on Sunday, Dan, that it was over . . . finally over.

H: It—

W: Was resolved. That it was finished. (*inhales*)

H: It is, because I know how jealous you are.

W: You lied to me.

Now she has become escalated. For her now his deception never really ended. She is on the attack. Nothing is working well for her.

H: (*chuckling*) I didn't lie to you.

Failed humor again.

W: You did, because I said . . .

H: Hey.

W: . . . "Then there's no reason to ever see her again?" You said, "Right." That was, what? Sunday? No, that was Monday.

H: (*faintly*) Uh.

W: We talked about it again Monday. (*inhales*) Now, on Wednesday, you want to see her again.

His repair attempts from now on will be futile. He has shattered her trust again.

H: Like I said, it's not a pressing need. But it, it—I resent the fact that I can't. Whenever you tell somebody "you can never do that"—

It's her fault again. He is blameless.

W: (*inhales*) Do you know why I, I don't think it's a good idea?

H: Because you don't trust me, that's (*chuckle*) why. That's it. If you trusted me, it wouldn't . . .

W: Because I think you're weak.

Contempt, the most corrosive of the four horsemen.

H: . . . matter. (*chuckling*) Oh, you think I'm weak. (*chuckles*)

Failed humor.

W: (*chuckle*) I think the flesh is weak. The flesh is weak.

She is trying to minimize her attack on his character.

H: (*inhales*)

W: And I don't see . . .

H: Yeah.

W: . . . any purpose, that it would help our marriage. It would not be good for the marriage.

A rationally based repair, which tends to be ineffective.

H: It would be good from the standpoint that if you—that would be proof that you trusted me, and that would help the marriage.

W: (*faint sniff*) No, I don't go for that. That line of reasoning, no.

She continues the rational approach.

H: Hey, you know, if you don't, if you don't trust your kid, let's say with David or something, if you don't trust him, and you tell you don't trust him, he's more likely to do something wrong that you don't want him to do than if you trust him.

He's saying that if he cheats on her, it's her fault.

W: (*inhales*) I trust David. But I'm saying . . .

H: And show him you've got confidence.

W: . . . you should run away from temptation. You don't seek it. You run away. You resist temptation. I'd say that to David too.

H: Yeah, but now we're not dealing with, uh . . . with an adolescent. We're dealing with an adult. Me.

W: Yes. And it goes for all of us human beings. You resist temptation. You don't go running into its arms. (*inhales*) You resist it.

H: Okay. It's not like . . . with Fred, where he was living with us. I'm not, I'm not suggesting that she live with us. I'm suggesting that (*inhales*) uh, that it would be possible to have a conversation with her.

W: Why?

H: Because. It's just like anybody that's part of—that, that was part of your life. (*inhales*)

W: She wasn't part of my life.

H: Hey—hey, I—

W: She's not part of our life.

H: She's part of Iowa State. You went to Iowa State. You may have— you have more . . . in common with her . . .

He thinks that because they went to the same school, his wife might like her.

W: She's not part of my life.

H: . . . things in common with her than you know.

W: We need counseling. Maybe this lab, maybe Sally, can help us, refer us.

H: (*chuckle*) Well. (*pause*) But you don't understand my logic. Evidently.

W: (*inhales and exhales deeply*)

H: That, hey, it's easy not to be—it's easy not to . . .

W: (*smacks lips*) I understand it.

H: . . . be jealous, and it's easy to say you trust me when there's no threat.

W: (*inhales*) But, Dan? If I wanted you to trust me, I wouldn't set up situations that were threatening to you. To say—

She has hit the nail on the head.

H: What could be threatening?

W: To challenge—

H: What could be threatening, uh, about her coming to our house?

W: Well, we can—I, uh, I don't want her to . . .

H: And meeting our kids?

W: . . . come to our house, and I don't want her to meet my kids.

H: Why?

W: Our kids. (*inhales*)

H: Why?

W: I don't want her to. I don't want her to become a part of our lives.

H: Because you don't trust me.

W: (*smacks lips*) I don't want—I have no desire whatsoever (*inhales*) to bring her into my life. (*inhales*) And I don't want my children befriending her. There's no purpose in the world for it.

H: Hmm.

W: (*inhales*) Unless you're doing like you did a couple years ago, (*inhales*) where you can kind of gradually get the kids to like her, and then kind of . . .

H: (*chuckle*)

W: . . . work into a . . .

H: Oh, geez.

W: . . . "bye-bye Judy."

H: No.

W: "The kids like her better than you."

H: No.

W: "Here's your *new* mother."

H: No way. No way.

W: You tried that once.

H: I know. And, and that's when I made the decision that it was impossible.

W: And I'm supposed to trust you. But you've done it once.

H: It was impossible. I know. That's when I learned it was impossible.

W: Yeah, well, see. Trust. Yeah, it's something that you build upon. (*exhales*) You need a job. You need to be working. You're sitting around too much.

The conversation is escalating into different issues now.

H: (*chuckles*) I am working.

Failed humor again.

W: Now you want it more than ever. Sex . . .

H: "Sitting around." Judy, you know what I did today? I went down . . .

W: What did you do?

H: . . . and saw Tom . . . about that project that's, uh, going in by the police station. That's work.

In Chapter 10 I will talk about how to help couples like this one heal from betrayal.

Chapter 9

The Dynamics of Betrayal

How is it that when we trust the untrustworthy we are inviting betrayal? In the "trust game" of life we see revealed the life-and-death consequences of trusting the right person or making errors of trust, trusting the wrong person, or failing to trust people at all. This chapter details the dynamics of betrayal by integrating the legacy of the late Caryl Rusbult into my thinking about trust, trustworthiness, and betrayal. Betrayal is born in the small, unfavorable comparisons of our partner with real or imagined other relationships, in "trashing" versus "cherishing" our partner and the relationship, and in "resentment" versus "gratefulness." The atom of distrust is distinguished from the atom of betrayal by discussing sliding-door moments when we turn away or against. The chapter describes how most affairs happen, 12 ways to betray one's partner other than a deceptive affair, and how a woman's power with negative affect may be her safety from betrayal.

Figure 9.1 shows the usual way to diagram what has been called the "trust game."[1] I have changed the table so the entries represent the kinds of choices about trust and betrayal that people actually face in deciding whether or not have a committed relationship with someone. I have also changed the entries in the cells of the trust game table so that they represent the potential payoffs and costs for each option in terms of *their* effect on people's longevity. In some cases I have solid empirical sources for making up the entries of this table. In other cases I am guessing based upon more meager information. What I want to suggest in this version of the trust game matrix is that these are the most important choices we will ever make in our lives, because they will affect how long we live.

Figure 9.1   The Trust Game

	B is Trustworthy	B is Untrustworthy
Person A trusts person B and enters into a committed relationship with B	Large documented gains in health, recovery from illness, increasing personal wealth, happiness, well-being, longevity, and raising secure, strong children. Payoff = +15 years of life.[2] Payoff = +15 years of life; these are the same people as high-trust people.[5]	Large cost of betrayal— relationship ends or continues as a low-trust relationship. High beta-SNS activation and high blood pressure. So far we only know that the negative payoff = between −4 and −8 years of life.[3]
Person A doesn't trust person B and decides on no committed relationship with B	Large cost of lifelong loneliness, including alpha-SNS activation and high blood pressure. Payoff = −10 years of life.[4]	Savvy = ability to detect this treachery, and instead commit to a trustworthy person.

These entries in the matrix of the trust game are the bottom line of *the most important social choices we will make in our lives*. The data suggest that we ought to enter into relationships with people who are trustworthy.

As I already mentioned, the classic epidemiological study, by Lisa Berkman and Len Syme of the University of California at Berkeley, of 9,000 people in Alameda county showed that close friendships and staying married granted people about a decade of life.[6] As I previously reviewed, later work by Lois Verbrugge showed that the effect is greater if both partners in a marriage are happy with each other.[7] In the Alameda County study, Berkman and Syme found that the survival probability of people who were married and had confidants (read: a trusting relationship) after 6 years was approximately 0.8, whereas those without a relationship and confidants was 0.5. Even an unhappy marriage gave benefits, especially to men. This gives a remaining life expectancy difference of 15 years of life for adults 30 years of age. If my numbers are right, they suggest that the risk of betrayal is not as bad as the risk of life long loneliness, which comes from not trusting people who are trustworthy.

Physician Dean Ornish's book *Love and Survival* summarized the spate of studies linking a stable trusting love relationship with health, rapid recovery from illness, longevity, and survival from cardiovascular disease, cancer, surgery, and other illnesses.[8] He wrote: "Love and intimacy are at the root of what makes us sick, and what makes us well, what causes sadness and what brings happiness, what makes us suffer and what leads to healing. If a new drug had the same impact, virtually every doctor in the country would be recommending it for their patients" (p. 3).

Linda Waite's book *The Case for Marriage* similarly documents the benefits of a stable, trusting love relationship.[9] Steve Nock's book *Marriage in Men's Lives* documents how dramatically marriage changes men, including the creation of wealth.[10] Hence, the cell that talks about the benefits of a trusting relationship is well established by more than half a century of social epidemiological research.

The cell in my table that assesses the costs of a relationship betrayal comes from the research of Friedman, who followed a Stanford longitudinal sample. The original sample came from the work of Louis Terman,[11] one of the inventors of the IQ test. Terman studied many generations of gifted children and gathered a great deal of information about the children and their families. Later, Friedman and colleagues examined the data to see what they had to say about the longevity of these children.[12] It turned out that the best predictor of earlier death was whether the children's parents had divorced. These children lived an average of 4 years less. They were also more likely to divorce when they grew up, and if they divorced as well as their parents having divorced, they lived an average of 8 years less.

Research shows that loneliness in people doesn't get better over time by itself. I think we can argue that lonely people, in part, are people who do not trust the trustworthy. Lonely people are more rejecting and judgmental of strangers, and somewhat more paranoid, more likely to expect rejection and unfair treatment. When thinking of an interactive event, parts of their brain characteristic of fear light up in a functional MRI scan. Although the data here are somewhat weaker, there is evidence that lonely people live a decade less than people live a decade less than people who are not lonely.

The cell I was initially the least confident about was what the gain was for people who can accurately spot untrustworthiness in others. However, the research of Toshio Yamagishi demonstrates that these are the very same people who are also trusting in relationships.[13] High trusters, as measured by Julien Rottter's Interpersonal Trust Scale, turned out to have higher social intelligence than low trusters. Research by Geller showed that high trusters were trustful when there was no reason to be suspicious (the default position), but they were not trustful when there was reason for suspicion.[14] High trusters are not more gullible than low trusters; quite the contrary is true. In Yamagishi's research high trusters were accurately able to judge who would defect or cooperate on a Prisoner's Dilemma game, in which people could either cooperate or betray their opponent. In fact, Yamagishi showed that "generalized distrust is not a gainful strategy for anyone who is reasonably skilled at detecting signs of untrustworthiness in risky but potentially lucrative social interactions" (p. 125). High trusters were also more educated than low trusters.

We know little about *how* these high-trusting people also know, in general, how to discern people who are untrustworthy. We do not know how this inherent astuteness occurs. However, we can make some informed guesses.

Experimental Version of the Trust Game

Two researchers, Elinor Ostrom and James Walker, summarized the results of an experimental version of the trust game.[15] In this version of the trust game there are two individuals. Here's how the game works: Individuals 1 and 2 both have 10 dollars. In the first move, Individual 1 can keep this money or send all or part of it to an anonymous Individual 2. Individual 1 knows that any money sent to Individual 2 will later triple in value. But then Individual 2 has the same choices. He or she can either keep all of this money, or send some or all of it back to Individual 1, knowing that this money sent back will also triple in value for Individual 1. The choice to send the money back is partly altruistic, and partly self-interested, if the game were to continue for another round.

This exchange of money can either be a one-shot event, or it can be repeated with the same two people. In one such one-shot study, researchers found that 30 of 32 subjects in the role of Individual 1 sent money to Individual 2 ($5.36 on average). Of the 30 subjects in the role of Individual 2, 18 returned more than $1 ($4.66 on average), and 11 sent the original amount allocated by Individual 1. On average, trusting people left the game with more money than untrusting people.[16]

In a cross-national version of this study, it was found that cultures with a greater orientation toward group outcomes versus individual outcomes gave significantly more.[17] They also took home greater wealth. Subsequent research has found that in more than one round of the game, trust becomes substantially reduced, although this effect is not well understood.

Scientists have also studied patients with borderline personality disorder.[18] These patients have usually had a checkered history with close relationships, and it is hard for them to trust others. They tend to cycle between idealizing and vilifying a person. Borderline patients acting as Individual 1 transferred significantly less money to Individual 2 across five shots of the game, compared to depressed patients or controls. In another version of the game, Individual 1 gave money not to another person but to a high-risk lottery. In this version of the game there were no differences between groups. Therefore, the lack of trust of the borderline patients only emerged when a real person was involved as Individual 2, not some generalized other.

Assessing Trustworthiness in Others

If my numbers are right, it's smart to take the risk of trusting people, and it is also smart to know whom not to trust. How can we develop that skill of high trusters? Most of us wish we could reduce the risks of trusting someone who is untrustworthy, or what I called in the table being "savvy." Perhaps that savvy can also come, in part, from analyzing what betrayal is all about.

I suggest five criteria for evaluating the trustworthiness of others: (1) honesty, (2) transparency, (3) accountability, (4) ethics, and (5) alliance.

Honesty. The criterion of honesty means that as far as you can tell, this person practices no deceptions, leads no life apart from you, and does not lie to you.

Transparency. Transparency means that his or her life is an open book to you, and he or she has no secrets from you. You know this person; he or she does not remain hidden from you. You can tell anyone the main characters in his or her life, you know his or her friends, relatives, and family, his or her main stresses in life, ambitions and goals in life, and life dreams. When you request information from this person, he or she is totally forthcoming.

Accountability. Accountability means that this person does what he or she says and promises, and you can get proof of it—meaning the details of any significant transactions this person has with others, financially or otherwise. If that person remains vague or unreachable about accountability, he or she is not to be trusted.

Ethics. Ethics means that this person has good ethical standards that you agree with, and that you are confident that you have witnessed this person having consistent standards of just and fair conduct with others.

Alliance. Alliance means that this person has been totally on your side, perhaps even against others. Truly on your side means that you have evidence that this person does not operate out of self-interest, or form coalitions against you, but has your true interests at heart. I have another suggestion about alliance, based on my experience. If someone says "just trust me" in response to a specific inquiry of yours, that person may be automatically untrustworthy. I always think of Woody Allen in the film *A Midsummer Night's Sex Comedy,* when he's about to go outside for a late-night tryst with another woman, and he says to his wife, with his sincerest expression, "Just trust me." Be suspicious.

We also need to be able to read situations if we are to develop the savvy of knowing whom to trust and when to bail out of a relationship filled with the potential for betrayal. So, I ask, what is the atom of betrayal—the smallest unit we can detect?

The Legacy of Caryl Rusbult

I once heard an academic at a meeting say that theories are like toothbrushes— everyone wants one, but no one wants to use someone else's. But that isn't true for me. I am happy to employ and celebrate other people's thinking if it makes sense or has empirical validation, or both. As my friend Daniel Siegel once said, there is a need for practice-based evidence, and also a need for evidence-based practice. Clinical experience and intuition, as well as empirical research, can help us understand very complex phenomena.

In particular, in this chapter and the next I want to celebrate the amazing legacy of the late Caryl Rusbult and use it in building a theory of how people either create loyalty or create betrayal, and how we might be able to help couples heal from betrayal.

The "Unfavorable CL-ALT" Is the Engine of Betrayal

Thibaut and Kelley suggested that in every relationship behavior exchange (think of a particular cell of a game-theory matrix) people have a "comparison level" in which they evaluate the payoffs they *do* receive against the payoffs they *might* receive in alternative relationships—imagined or real. Thibaut and Kelley suggested that if people evaluate what they do receive in the relationship more highly than what they think they *might* receive elsewhere (especially in the *best* alternative), then they are likely to stay committed to the relationship. This level of comparison is called "the comparison level for alternatives" (CL-ALT). The hypothesis is that if one's payoffs are greater than CL-ALT, then the individuals will stay committed. Otherwise, that person will not remain committed.

Thibaut and Kelley never suggested a way to actually measure CL-ALT, but Rusbult's brilliant theory of commitment *was* able to successfully measure it. Unfortunately, Rusbult died prematurely in 2010 at the age of 51. What a huge loss to our field. In a series of studies over three decades of research on her "investment model of commitment," Rusbult showed that "commitment" to a relationship is a gradual process of a person's making favorable CL-ALT comparisons, increasingly becoming dependent on the relationship, relying on that relationship to get his or her central needs met, denigrating alternative relationships, investing more and more in the relationship, thinking "pro-relationship" thoughts, and realizing that losing the relationship would be catastrophic.

The opposite process of becoming "uncommitted" is a gradual process of CL-ALTs unfavorable to a relationship, a person's increasingly becoming less dependent on the relationship, not relying only on that relationship to get his or her central needs met, idealizing alternative relationships, investing less and less in the relationship, and thinking that losing the relationship might be a relief.

What starts the process of commitment or the process of uncommitment are CL-ALTs either favorable or unfavorable to the relationship, respectively. Additionally, it makes sense to suggest that the unfavorable CL-ALT is the engine of betrayal. It also makes sense to suggest that the favorable CL-ALT is the engine of loyalty. The CL-ALT comparisons made either provide the comfort that "this is the right relationship for me," or the anxiety that "uh-oh, this may be the wrong relationship for me." Things build from the starting point, rapidly creating divergent accelerating trajectories. What is this hypothesis? Simply stated, it is that: *The missing ingredient in understanding betrayal is the CL-ALT.*

What is the evidence supporting this hypothesis?

Rusbult showed that the process of either building commitment and loyalty or avoiding commitment and creating betrayal works with dating relationships, and the process of unfavorable CL-ALTs and low commitment actually *predicts* sexual infidelity. Although other studies have been done on infidelity, they were post-hoc recollection studies rather than predictive studies. Hence, Rusbult's *prediction* of infidelity with her investment model is a major accomplishment in understanding the dynamics of betrayal.[19]

"Cherishing" Versus "Trashing," and "Gratefulness" Versus "Resentment"

Rusbult's model describes how people come to value their partner's personality and the relationship, which leads them to be less reactive to their partner's destructive conflict and to respond instead with a constructive behavior, making aggression, passivity, or withdrawal less likely in the face of conflict. They also denigrate alternatives to the relationship.

In my experience, people committed to their relationship think of the relationship and their partner even when they are *not* together, engaging in a process I call "cherishing" the partner. What I mean by "cherishing" is that people think fondly of their partner even when they are apart, and have a habit of mind that dwells on being *grateful* for the partner's positive qualities.

Cherishing the partner creates a large fence around other possible liaisons, leading people to denigrate alternatives to the relationship and avoid being tempted to cross boundaries that would upset the partner if the partner were present. In effect, the partner *is present* in one's mind even when not physically present. This process of cherishing is an active one. It includes magnifying feelings of *gratitude* for the positive qualities of the partner and the relationship. Rusbult has shown that commitment leads people to make sacrifices for the relationship and to denigrate alternatives. The word "sacrifice" is the origin of the word "sacred," so Rusbult's investment model could also be described as "creating the relationship as sacred."

Cherishing and expressing gratitude is part of that process of sacrificing for the relationship. In the Jewish Friday-night Sabbath ritual, a husband traditionally sings a song to his wife called the "Eyshet Chayil," or "Woman of Valor," which pronounces formally how much he cherishes her. It is taken from Proverbs 30.[20] There is also evidence among Christians that married couples who consider their relationship to be somehow "sacred" are more constructive during conflict and have relationships more resistant to divorce. With cherishing and gratitude, a wide fence is placed between oneself and the potential for other entanglements. Situations that could lead to interactions with another person that would make one's partner uncomfortable are avoided. Secrets are avoided.

Conversely, according to Rusbult's findings, when people compare their relationship unfavorably to alternative relationships, when they think that some needs could be better met elsewhere, they invest less in their relationship and they become less dependent over time on the relationship to meet their needs. In that case neither commitment nor dependency fully develop. I suggest then that people could be described as engaging in a process of "trashing" the partner and the relationship. Part of trashing the partner is magnifying resentment about the partner's and the relationship's negative qualities. Trashing denigrates the partner. People who trash the partner do not denigrate but instead *idealize* alternative relationships, and they avoid putting boundaries between themselves and other possible partners, even if that would be upsetting to their partner were the partner present. Over time, trashing can lead people to either playfully or aggressively seek other entanglements, which is a cognitive process consistent with Rusbult's ability to predict infidelity. With trashing and resentment, no fence is placed between oneself and the potential for other entanglements. Situations that could lead to interactions with another person that would make one's partner uncomfortable are encouraged. Secrets are created.

There may also be a direct dyadic impact on one's partner even of unstated unfavorable CL-ALTs, because they tend to give one permission to cross small boundaries. For example, if one sees one's partner engaging in interactions with others that appear like flirting with alternative relationships—even simple acts such as looking too long or too longingly at an attractive potential partner—that could be enough to stimulate one's own unfavorable CL-ALTs. In this way unfavorable CL-ALTs may prove contagious.

Rusbult has shown that this internal process of holding on to attractive alternatives and thus avoiding dependency and commitment is also related to insecure attachment classifications. Thus, it may be the case that previous insecurity in one partner could lead to suspicion about the other's commitment, even when that suspicion is not warranted. Furthermore, assurances about commitment that are not felt may breed deception in the relationship, because these assurances will be violated by behavior that demonstrates unfavorable CL-ALT comparisons. These unfavorable CL-ALT comparisons become especially salient when a partner turns away from bids for emotional connection in sliding-door moments.

The Atom of Distrust and the Atom of Betrayal

Rusbult's model of commitment is especially relevant to psychotherapist and researcher Susan Johnson's ideas in her emotion-focused couple therapy (EFT). Johnson is a great pioneer in our field. She has shown us how to focus on emotion in couple therapy, a profound and sharp contrast to cognitive-behavioral marital therapy. Sometimes, when it is called for, her therapy helps couples deal with what she calls "attachment injuries." These are moments when one partner intensely needs the other for comfort and the other isn't emotionally available or responsive to the need. When the need was very intense, these were the moments when what might be called very "core bids for connection" were left hanging in the air, alone and limp. I suggest that this is the atom in which distrust is born as core trust is eroded.

Thus, the "atom of betrayal" may involve moments of turning away or against, but these moments also necessarily include an unfavorable CL-ALT comparison. That suggestion successfully integrates Rusbult's model with Johnson's model, and with my own work with Jani Driver on bids and turning. I suggest that in these moments turning away or against is accompanied by thoughts by one partner that another relationship—real or imagined—would have to be better than this one, and thoughts by the other partner that in an alternative real or imagined relationship turning toward would have replaced one's real partner's turning away or against. For example, the person turning away might think that another relationship might be less demanding, and the real or imagined alternative partner might be less "needy" or less negative. The partner left hanging with a rejected bid might think that in another real or imagined relationship that same bid for connection would have been turned toward.

An example may prove useful. One couple I saw in therapy had been to five other therapists before they saw me. After six sessions with me they surprisingly announced that this would be their last session. I said that was too bad, but because they were still paying for this session, I asked them if I could talk to them about why my therapy wasn't working for them. They agreed.

They had two small children. As we talked I realized that the husband had not made the transformation that many fathers go through from "me-ness" to "we-ness." He still bargained mightily with his wife for time alone so that he could go snowboarding with his friends for at least 2 days a week during the winter. He felt that he *deserved* this time alone, even though his wife was handling a disproportionate share of the childcare. He argued that because he brought in a disproportionate share of their money, his time with his friends snowboarding was only a fair exchange. His wife hated this arrangement.

In this last session he said that one evening during the previous week he and his wife went to a party. He got engrossed in an enjoyable conversation with a woman he had just met at the party. His wife asked him to leave, because she was exhausted. He left reluctantly, thinking he would rather be in a relationship with that woman, who was so much more fun than his tired, irritable wife. Later that night he expressed his frustration about not having much fun anymore, and he said that he found this woman more attractive than his wife had been this evening, and a fight ensued. During the fight his wife also thought that she would be happier with another man who was more understanding of how tired she was, being a mother to two young children and still working to contribute to the family income. He thought that the fight confirmed his suspicions that he might be happier with the more positive new woman he'd just met at the party.

Both partners turned away from each other, with the accompanying unfavorable CL-ALT that other relationships would be more satisfying than this one. I thanked them and told them I now understood why couple therapy was ineffective with them. I said that therapy was ineffective because in their minds they weren't really fully committed to each other. They were conditionally committed. Every negative interaction started thoughts of leaving the relationship because every turning away was justified in their minds by an unfavorable CL-ALT comparison. I told them that commitment was like what Alice did in Wonderland: She followed the white rabbit down the hole without hesitation. She didn't peer down the rabbit hole suspended between action and doubt. She jumped in with both feet, falling into the wonders and horrors of Wonderland. It was her journey, totally. Commitment, I said, meant deciding that this family was your journey, that you were in it for better or for worse, making sacrifices for the good of the group, deciding that this was where you'd get your needs met.

Rusbult might have said that this couple was in the process of *uncommitting* to each other. In terms of my data with Levenson, they were low in we-ness, already far down the distance and isolation cascade toward divorce, already beginning to lead parallel lives (see my book *What Predicts Divorce?*). Their commitment to each other had become conditional and marginal, because they were often engaging in unfavorable CL-ALT comparisons to justify their turning away or against. A few months later I called them up and asked if they were already separated. They said that their last session had stunned them and they were now talking a great deal about how to become more committed to their family. I was pleased that they had been able to use this information.

Trust and Attachment Theory

Susan Johnson's EFT is based on attachment theory. The attachment system between a mother and infant was first described by British psychiatrist John Bowlby during the Second World War. Bowlby noticed that as 700,000 children were evacuated from London during the Nazi Blitz attacks on London, many of these children suffered terribly from separation from their mothers, even though they were placed in very good homes.[21] Later, primatologist Harry Harlow studied this attachment system experimentally with baby monkeys.[22] Harlow's classic research destroyed the psychoanalytic tenet that the baby's attachment to the mother is centered around getting milk from the mother's nipple. Harlow's baby rhesus monkeys always preferred a surrogate model of a soft terrycloth mother to a surrogate model of a wire mother who gave milk but provided no contact comfort. Attachment turned out to be the basis through which babies learned to master their own fear, connected effectively with their parents, explored the word, and built confidence in their abilities with other people. In studying the behavioral elements of secure attachment, researchers identified the twin skills of emotional availability and responsiveness.

Attachment researchers have now generalized Bowlby's theory of attachment to adult relationships.[23] Susan Johnson suggested that to feel safe with our life partner and lover, both partners need to attach securely to each other. In my language, feeling safe in a relationship means "being there" for each other during important moments that qualify as turning toward in sliding-door moments in which a bid has been made.

I conclude from this work on attachment and attachment injury that the atom of eroding trust is the unavailability or the unresponsiveness (or turning against) of a partner when the other is in need of understanding, comfort, or love—that is, not "being there" for our partner when he or she needs us.

Betrayal Is Not Just Losing Trust

I suggest that if turning away or against is combined with an unfavorable CL-ALT comparison by either partner, it will become an atom of betrayal. Combining this idea with our work on trust, I suggest that: *The atom of betrayal is an event of turning away from a bid in a sliding-door moment by being emotionally unavailable and unresponsive, combined with an unfavorable CL-ALT comparison.*

Betrayals thrive in the environmental soil of low trust, but I am suggesting that low trust is not sufficient for building the betrayal metric; for that to happen, it has to also be accompanied by an unfavorable CL-ALT comparison. The favorable CL-ALT comparison is about accepting the partner's enduring but annoying personality traits and deciding to cherish the partner in spite of these traits. Favorable CL-ALT comparisons are the basis of cherishing one's partner, which builds trust and commitment rather than betrayal. Therefore, I would conclude that: *Turning away, not "being there" for each other, is the atom of distrust, the erosion of the trust metric.* However, *if that turning away is also accompanied by an unfavorable CL-ALT comparison, that moment doesn't erode the trust metric, it rather builds the betrayal metric.*

As I will discuss later, the surprising ingredient that turns the atom of betrayal into a further significant increase in the betrayal metric is *conflict avoidance*. The turning away with an unfavorable CL-ALT comparison is usually enough to create a regrettable incident. If that incident is subsequently dismissed, there may be subsequent flooding, and then the incident is unlikely to ever get processed. The result, via the Zeigarnik effect, is an even more significant increase in the betrayal metric as unfavorable CL-ALTs continue.

How Some Affairs Happen— Combining Low Trust with Betrayal

The late psychologist Shirley Glass dedicated her life to helping people understand how affairs happen and how they can be healed.[24] She wrote that the way affairs often happen is that people slowly give themselves permission to cross small or large boundaries. For example, if there's a new baby in a person's life, it is probably the case that he or she doesn't get as much romance, intimacy, or even compliments and appreciations from one's partner. Suppose something as innocent as having a nice talk with a member of the opposite sex at work happens. One may think to oneself, "My partner and I haven't talked like that for a long time." That is a turning away moment that is accompanied by an unfavorable CL-ALT comparison.

One may even think: "I really should talk to my partner about that. I should say, 'You know, I had a real nice talk with someone at work and I am worried because we haven't talked that good in a long time.'" But a conflict avoider may also think: "Well, nothing much happened. If I bring that up at home it will only lead to a big argument, so I will just keep quiet about it. Nothing happened anyway." And so for the goal of avoiding conflict, for the sake of peace and quiet, a secret has blossomed. I think Rusbult would add that within that secret there also lurks an unfavorable CL-ALT comparison that erodes the process of dependency, commitment, denigrating the alternative relationship, and sacrifice.

Once we do that avoidance of potential conflict, the conflict avoider has a secret, so what has also blossomed is the practice of deception by omission. In Glass's terminology, there is now a "wall" that's been created between one and one's partner. If a person gets unhappy in the relationship and talks to someone else about it rather than to the partner, that other person has a window into the relationship. What has now happened is that walls and windows have been reversed. The architecture of the Sound Relationship House has become scrambled by this secret. In a close relationship there are walls keeping it safe from people outside, and the two people have a window in which they both look out at the world together. Together they create a trusting relationship. But that trust is less likely to last in the face of conflict avoidance. There's comfort in the peace and quiet that comes from avoiding conflict, but it comes at a price of increased emotional distance. That emotional distance can increase loneliness within the relationship and leave us even more vulnerable to reversing walls and windows.

Most people apparently think that no harm is done by this innocent secret if the partner does not know about it. However, our analysis using Rusbult's model suggests that the emotional distance created by the secret also cripples one's own ability to fully love one's partner, because it reverses the process of commitment. We have gone elsewhere for comfort and support, and the secret is weaving a tangled web that will compromise *our own trust*, not our partner's trust in our relationship. In Glass's terminology, the weight-bearing walls have now become paper-thin windows, which will no longer stand.

This process can happen very slowly, where people keep innocently crossing boundaries with another person and keep this information from the partner, ostensibly to "protect" the partner by avoiding unnecessary conflict. But what is really changing during this period of attrition is the person who is keeping the secrets. That person's ability to love the partner will become compromised, because the Rusbult process of commitment has come to a halt and the gears have begun moving into reverse. It is in this way that people may slowly give themselves permission to cross boundaries, talking about intimate things, confiding, looking directly into another person's eyes, touching briefly, then touching less briefly, lingering, kissing, starting to become a "we" with the other person, and so on. One may have slowly woven a web of deceit around oneself merely by avoiding sharing conflict-inducing information.

People may then begin lying to their partner about what is really happening emotionally or sexually with someone else. The affair has begun from the very first secret. That secret changes people and constrains their ability to love the partner. The real effects of the small betrayals are that the person with the secrets begins changing by building a wall between himself or herself and the partner, and starting to create a new bond with the stranger. A wall has been inadvertently built and there is hiding behind that wall as "the affair" unfolds. Although it is in the service of avoiding conflict, not talking about small incidents and also not turning away from them, letting them unfold by crossing boundaries, is the root cause of many affairs.

Glass's analysis shows how naturally affairs can evolve. People do not have to be monsters to have an affair. In her book *Not Just Friends*, Glass took affairs out of the pulpit and into the social psychology laboratory, where they can be studied and understood, as Rusbult did in predicting affairs in new relationships.

Therefore, it is consistent with Glass's analysis for me to suggest that the atom of betrayal (a turning away that is accompanied by an unfavorable CL-ALT comparison) is heightened and moved along by conflict avoidance.

What Determines Unfavorable CL-ALTs?

It would be useful to better understand CL-ALTs that are either favorable or unfavorable to the partner and the relationship. In a study recently conducted in my laboratory with 46 lower-income married and unmarried couples in Seattle, we computed our observational, physiological, rating-dial, and game-theory variables during conflict discussions and also were able to correlate them with Rusbult's measure of CL-ALT for both partners.

First of all, what was the validity of the CL-ALT ratings? Our results were that unfavorable levels of CL-ALT for the relationship by the male were significantly and highly related to his ratings of the probability that his partner might have an extra-relationship affair in the future.[25] The correlation was not significant between the female's CL-ALT and her ratings of the probability that he might have an extra-relationship affair in the future. Unfavorable male CL-ALTs were significantly associated with cohabiting and significantly negatively associated with being married. Therefore the male's CL-ALT established its validity in this study.

However, what was related to CL-ALT that might help us understand it? With respect to my mathematical model (see Chapter 11), less favorable male CL-ALT ratings were significantly associated with: (1) more negative female uninfluenced start values (meaning that even before his influence, she begins the conversation with greater negative effect), (2) more female emotional inertia (meaning that her prior emotional state is influencing her a great deal, which places a limit on how much she can accept his influence) (3) less female power with negative affect (which means that she can get as negative and as escalated as she wants to, but it won't change his behavior at all), (4) a higher female negative repair threshold (meaning she waits until the interactions get very negative before attempting a repair), and (5) a higher positive female damping threshold (meaning that he has to become *very* positive before his positivity has any effect on her), and less effectiveness of her damping (meaning that her eventual response to his escalated positive affect has no effect on *him*).

Therefore less favorable CL-ALT ratings by the male was associated with more female negative startup and less emotion regulation by the female during conflict. The female's more negative start values and her lower power with negative affect during conflict were also significantly associated with less favorable male CL-ALT ratings. This is consistent with my previous analyses about the importance of female power in heterosexual relationships.

Less favorable male CL-ALT ratings were also significantly related to his domineering behavior during conflict, although paradoxically his domineering was significantly related to *her* more favorable CL-ALT ratings. More favorable male CL-ALT ratings were significantly related to his high validation—that is, his understanding and empathy of her during conflict.

Also, the cardiovascular-based sympathetic nervous system measure that the female was physiologically aroused during the baseline before the conflict discussion began[26] was significantly related to less favorable male CL-ALT ratings. She is more physiologically aroused during conflict when she is with a male who makes unfavorable CL-ALT judgments.

More positive female and male rating-dial measures (payoffs) were related significantly to more favorable male CL-ALT ratings. That kind of consistency is gratifying to a researcher. Also, for her CL-ALT ratings, the more frequently she was neutral when he was nasty, the more favorable were her CL-ALT ratings. That is what Rusbult would call "accommodations"—namely a positive response to a partner's destructive comment— are more likely when *she* makes favorable CL-ALT judgments.

Therefore, in this study there was empirical validation for my earlier theorizing about CL-ALT and the dynamics of betrayal, particularly for understanding the male's unfavorable or favorable CL-ALTs. The determinants of unfavorable male CL-ALTs appear to be very negative and dysregulated conflict, particularly by the female.

Are Men More Prone to Negative CL-ALTs Than Women?

Harvard professor Robert Weiss's classic book, *Staying the Course,* qualitatively analyzed the relationships of 100 successful men.[27] He reported that these couples had about two serious arguments a year. Furthermore, he reported that, after an argument, women generally said that even though it was an unpleasant experience, it was constructive because issues became raised and were now out on the table. In contrast, most of the men had serious thoughts of leaving the relationship after the same argument. Paired with the finding that men are significantly more flooded than women, it may be the case that high levels of negativity in conflict drive men, through flooding, toward more unfavorable levels of CL-ALT. There were, however, no significant differences between men and women in CL-ALT in my lower-income couples' pilot study, as measured by Rusbult's measure.

Research on sexual initiations in married and cohabiting heterosexual relationships shows that men initiate sex more than women;[28] the rate was 75% to 25% in the first year of marriage and in later years 60% to 40%. In our own research of couples 3 years after the first baby arrived, men said on average that they would like to have sex with their wives about three times a week; women said on average that they would like to have sex with their husbands once every two weeks, which is a ratio of six to one. Another study dramatically showed men's greater receptiveness to casual sex.[29] A male or a female confederate of average attractiveness approached strangers of the opposite sex and asked them if they would like to (1) go out with them tonight, (2) come to their apartment, or (3) go to bed with them. The overwhelming majority of men said that they would be willing to have sex, whereas none of the women approached said they would. Women have far more requirements for sex than men do. That finding has been replicated.[30] One study reported that "men are more apt to see sex as a bodily function like eating, whereas women tend to see it in more emotionally laden terms, like the communion of two souls" (p. 150).[31] The great comedian Billy Crystal once said that women need a reason to make love, but men just need a place.

Books have been written on men's reluctance to become committed to a relationship.[33] In an interesting keynote address titled "What Is It with Men and Commitment, Anyway?" psychologist Scott Stanley suggested the hypothesis that whereas emotional attachment may be adequate for commitment for women, it is inadequate for men's commitment.[34] He suggested that for men, commitment also requires a belief that she will become his marriage partner, will be his partner for life, and will be his "soul mate," meaning that she will accept him as he is without trying to change him. Attachment for men, Stanley suggested, is adequate for cohabitation, but not for commitment. Men claimed that they could get many of the benefits of marriage by cohabiting, without the risks (e.g., financial loss, or children arriving before they wanted them). It is still an open question, but the evidence seems to be pointing to the validity of the hypothesis that men may make CL-ALT comparisons less favorable to the relationship than women do.

A Dozen Ways to Betray Your Partner

A committed romantic relationship is a contract of mutual trust, mutual respect, mutual protection, and mutual nurturance. Sexual betrayal is only one way of betraying your partner. Here are a dozen other ways to betray your partner.

- *Betrayals by violations of commitment.* In this case commitment (even for one partner) is actually a conditional commitment. One or both people seem as if they are waiting for someone better to come along; they have not really decided that this relationship is their journey in life. They may stare at other men or women, flirt, or suggest in various ways that they are still available. They have reservations about being fully committed to their partner. That means their commitment is sometimes diminished by arguing, or by emotional distance (or even by being out of town) by their partner's illness, and by their partner's demands. Their commitment is challenged by issues that come up between them, by bad times, by extreme stress, by sickness, by financial insecurity, and so on. People occasionally leave or threaten to leave when times are bad between them. According to the Blumstein and Schwartz "American Couples" study, that attitude was characteristic of American cohabiting couples in the early 1980s.
- *Betrayals of emotional, or romantic, or sexual exclusivity.* Contrary to the agreement, partners do not turn away from other relationships, from flirtations (or even sexual partnerships or secret emotional attachments), or from other kinds of secret liaisons (for example, financial) that may present themselves. They do not discuss these attractions or liaisons within the relationship before boundaries are crossed. Although they may have agreed to always discuss these opportunities, they play with flirtations and with other emotional liaisons. They may give themselves permission inadvertently and secretly to cross some boundaries.
- *Betrayals by secrets, lies, and deceptions.* Although partners have agreed to the principle of being honest and open and to not keeping secrets from each other, in fact they do keep secrets and lie to their partner. These lies may begin by lies of omission. These betrayals are part of a pattern of lies, omissions, deceptions, violations of confidence, broken promises, and inconsistencies.
- *Coalitions with others against the partner.* One partner forms coalitions with another person, friend, or relative that exclude or hurt the partner. An example of this could be talking negatively about one's partner with a friend or sibling.

- *Betrayals by disinterest.* They stop expressing interest in their partner. They may stop showing an active interest in their partner's thoughts, feelings, or inner life.
- *Betrayals by unfairness and lack of care.* Although they agree in principle that finances, resources, and the division of labor in the relationship will be mutually fair and equitable for both people, in practice this agreement is violated. It may not ever get discussed, but both people are aware of it. There are defaults in taking care of each other (for example, abandonment when one person is sick or otherwise in need) and abandonment of emotional comfort and understanding. This is one aspect of "being there" for each other.
- *Betrayals of affection.* Although partners have agreed to treat each other with affection, one or both become unaffectionate, unresponsive, or cold to the other.
- *Betrayals by lack of sexual interest.* They demonstrate a lack of attraction, interest, and physical intimacy toward the partner.
- *Betrayals by abuse.* They betray each other by emotional or physical abuse. Emotional abuse consists of: (1) social isolation, (2) sexual coercion, (3) extreme jealousy, (4) public humiliation, belittling, or degradation, (5) threats of violence or other acts that induce fear, (6) damage or threats of damage to property, pets, or children. Physical abuse is any unwanted touch.
- *Betrayals by disrespect.* Privately partners do not cherish each other, compliment each other, or express pride in each other's accomplishments. On the contrary, they express disrespect, mockery, ridicule, sarcasm, or other means of asserting superiority or denigrating the partner.
- *Betrayals by not meeting each other's needs.* A relationship is about legitimating dependency upon each other. Partners violate the principle that they should try to meet each other's essential needs cooperatively and honestly. This involves agreeing to emotional presence, openness, emotional availability, and responsiveness to the partner. They do not agree, or act as if they do not agree, that the relationship will entail sacrifice at times, putting one's partner's needs or the family's needs ahead of one's own.
- *Betrayals by breaking sacred promises and vows.* Partners make prom-

ises that they do not keep. Eventually they may make promises that they never *intend* to keep.

Is A Woman's Power With Negative Affect Her Safety from Betrayal?

There is an asymmetry in the potential for sexual betrayal that has been duly noted by sociobiologists.[35] Research has consistently found that men have more affairs and think about sex more often than women. Although these gender gaps have been closing as women have entered the workforce and can meet men more interesting than the mailman, we reported that even three years after the first baby arrives men say that they want sex an average of 3 times a week, while their wives want it an average of once every 2 weeks. Hence, there may be more challenge for women in trusting their men with infidelity, than for men in trusting their women. Since negative affect is a major mechanism for repair, it may be more important for a woman to be able to influence her man with negative affect than vice versa.

Indeed, I recently discovered that there is a strong relationship between how powerful a woman actually is with her own negative affect during conflict in influencing her husband and her sense of safety in the relationship as assessed by the betrayal metric (see Chapter 11). To feel safe in the relationship, meaning that there is a low potential for betrayal, she needs to actually be powerful in influence during conflict with her negative affect. That means that even during a conflict discussion, he is responsive and "there for her" when she is upset. That way if her suspicions are voiced, she has an effect on a partner who is turning away or against from her and doing more unfavorable CL-ALT comparisons when turning away or against. The system can repair itself better than if she has no power expressing her negative affects.

In this way I have demonstrated that a woman's power in the relationship with negative affect and her sense of safety are intricately related. I also found that to the extent that she was powerful with negative affect, she felt that: (1) her husband was not looking out for his own interests in a conflict, (2) the conflict was cooperative and not a zero-sum game where his gain was her loss (measured as the correlation between rating dial slopes), (3) the marriage had less gender stereotypy (as assessed by the Buehlman Oral History Interview coding), and (4) in the Amber Tabares thesis, using the Betrayal Detector, he was more positive, particularly with the Negative Adjectives Checklist, and there was also more positive than negative affect with the Negative Adjective Checklist exercise. Therefore, a woman's power with negative affect is an important index of how safe she feels in the relationship.

Chapter 10

Healing From Betrayal

This chapter discusses the following questions: How can we heal from a betrayal? When is it foolish to forgive a betrayer? What maximizes the probability of forgiveness? What strategies facilitate forgiveness being effective? The chapter also introduces our "betrayal detector." It explains the mathematics of forgiveness and what relationship processes maximize forgiveness. A theory is presented in two flowcharts for the cascade toward betrayal and distrust and for the cascade toward loyalty and trust. The chapter discusses individual traits that may determine turning away with social comparisons unfavorable to one's partner and the relationship, whether conflict erodes trust or low trust creates conflict, when wounds are not healed by time, and the betrayals of pornography "addiction" and sexual "addiction."

When Is It Foolish to Forgive? Our "Untrustworthiness"

It would be great of we could have a litmus test of whether or not to trust again after a betrayal. Then a clinician could administer the test to a couple and be able to say: "It looks good. I think you will probably succeed at rebuilding trust in this relationship, and here's why I think so." Or, alternatively, the clinician would be able to say, "No, I don't think the conditions are right for rebuilding trust at this point, and here's why I think so." That test could be called "the untrustworthiness detector."

We may have created such a test. It turned out that our trust and betrayal metrics significantly correlated with the measures of an important dissertation done in our lab by my former graduate student Amber Tabares.[1] These results make it possible for us to create a "untrustworthiness detector." Here's the story of that dissertation.

Amber's thesis was based on a study in my lab with 94 married couples. The couples had two conflict discussions, separated by one of four interventions. The interventions occurred between the two conflict discussions. One intervention group was called the "Praise Group." They selected three traits characteristic of their partner from a list of 60 positive traits; these were traits such as "kind," "generous," "sexy," and "handsome." Then they were asked to explain why they chose each of the three traits and to describe an example of a time that their partner exhibited each trait. Another group was called the "Complain Group." This group selected three "areas of concern," which were potential negative traits characteristic of their partner, from a list of 60 negative traits; these were traits such as "stingy," "stubborn," "mean," and "selfish." Then they were asked to explain why they selected each negative trait and describe an example of a time that their partner exhibited each negative trait they selected.

There were two control groups who read magazines during the 20-minute break. For the control groups, following the first 15-minute conflict discussion (D1), the facilitator came into the room and told couples they could read magazines while research staff prepared equipment for the second discussion (D2). Couples were told they could speak to each other if they needed to but they were asked to not discuss their areas of disagreement during that time. Couples were monitored from a control room and interrupted if they began talking about a conflictual issue. In the first control group the couples did the video recall rating dial immediately after the first conflict discussion. For the second control group, the video recall was delayed until after the second conflict discussion.

Spouses in the non-control groups were randomly assigned to start the second discussion, in each intervention, telling the partner which adjectives he or she selected, along with examples. The starting spouse (the speaker) was given 10 minutes to tell the partner (the listener) which adjectives he or she selected and to give examples. The speaker was assigned to lead during the 10 minutes, but couples were told that they could make the 10 minutes a discussion between the two of them, as long as they kept the focus of the adjectives on the listener. After the 10 minutes was up, a green light came on in the room to notify the couple to switch turns as the speaker and listener and repeat the proce-dure for 10 minutes.

Amber coded how people actually did the two interventions. They were coded with her Praise and Complain Coding System (PPC).[2] The PPC coders were blind to couples' marital-satisfaction scores.

For all groups, following the 20-minute break, the facilitator reen-tered the room and reminded couples of the remaining issues that were selected for the second conflict discussion. The facilitator then left the room and the couple began their second videotaped conflict discussion.

Here's what Amber discovered. Contrary to our expectations, there was no difference in affect from the first conflict discussion to the second conflict discussion among any of the four groups. The strange thing that happened was that many of the couples in the Praise intervention followed the instructions, but many others turned the Praise condition into criti-cism. They said things like: "I had a lot of trouble coming up with three positive traits you have. Instead, I picked three traits I wish you had." Similarly, many of the couples in the Complain intervention followed the instructions, but many others turned the Complain condition into a positive experience. They said things like: "I had a lot of trouble coming up with three negative traits you have. You really don't have any negative traits." Then the partner might say, "I know I'm not perfect. Please tell me your concerns. I want to hear them." Then the partner would talk about the concerns, but very gently, minimizing their importance.

When Amber examined her coding of *how* couples acted during either intervention, there was a significant interaction effect. Couples who created their own negativity in either intervention demonstrated low positivity and high negativity in their post-intervention conflict.

Also, couples who created their own positivity in either condition demonstrated less negativity and more positivity in their post-intervention conflict. Pre-intervention affect during conflict, and marital satisfaction significantly predicted how couples would act any of the interventions. The other thing that predicted how people would act in either condition was the wife's untrustworthiness metric. If wives were high on the potential-for-untrustworthiness metric, they became very negative in either condition. If they were low on the untrustworthiness metric, they became very positive in either condition.

Therefore, noticing how people acted in both of these conditions turned out to be a test of whether the relationship still had a high trust metric or had a untrustworthiness metric. Here's what Amber's thesis suggests to look for in speaker and listener to assess a high potential for untrustworthiness during these exercises. These dimensions formed the basis of Amber's coding of how the interventions were done in her thesis.

Listener with a high potential for untrustworthiness. In this case the listener did not maintain eye contact, did not use positive humor, didn't laugh, did not give the usual listener backchannels (uh-huh, hmm, ah, head nods), had low energy, was inattentive, and was not affectionate.

Listener with a low potential for untrustworthiness. In this case the listener maintained eye contact, used positive humor, laughed, gave the usual listener backchannels, had high energy, was attentive, was animated, and was affectionate.

Speaker with a high potential for untrustworthiness. In this case the speaker used negative teasing, derisive humor, sarcasm, or mocked the partner. The speaker may have mimicked the partner's way of talking and found it funny, even though partner was not amused. The speaker may have been verbally negative, insulting, may have used "you always" or "you never" when describing the partner's negative traits (which is criticism), or described a negative trait as a reason why their relationship has problems. When trying to be nice, the speaker appeared false, vague, or forced. The speaker may have had a lot of trouble coming up with specific examples of the partner's positive traits, but had little trouble coming up with examples of negative traits.

Speaker with a low potential for untrustworthiness. In this case the speaker was verbally positive, was affectionate, and softened negativity by minimizing complaints. When being nice the speaker appeared genuine, easily giving very specific about examples of positive traits but having lots of trouble coming up with examples of negative traits. The speaker was generally affectionate and validating.

Summary on the Untrustworthiness Detector

What I am recommending is a hypothesis—a test for continued untrustworthiness. As a test we observe the betrayer's behavior when both partners take turns talking about the other's most positive qualities, and while they each talk about traits of the partner that are greater "areas of concern." What I like about this test is that it is not obvious that it measures the potential for untrustworthiness. We examine how the betrayer acts during these two exercises using Amber Tabares's dimensions as a guide. Assuming that partners "pass" this test, and they want to stay together and heal from the untrustworthiness, the remaining part of this chapter talks about how that healing might be facilitated.

Clearly this test is only a guide. It needs to be accompanied with genuine remorse for the untrustworthiness and a willingness to stay together and work on forgiveness by the betrayed partner. What do we know about untrustworthiness, its dynamics, and processes that may help a couple recover from a untrustworthiness? Game theorists have done a lot of thinking about this question, in the context of maximizing "cooperation" rather than "defection" in two-person games.

The Mathematics of Forgiveness

It may be surprising that game theory has anything to say about healing from untrustworthiness. Bear with me for a while. Rapoport started this work, but fortunately it has continued after his death in 2007.

The most famous mathematical game about trust and untrustworthiness is the non-zero-sum Prisoner's Dilemma game. As explained earlier, in the Prisoner's Dilemma game two prisoners are arrested by the police; they are suspected of a crime, but the police do not have enough evidence for a conviction, so they try to extract a confession. They separate the two prisoners. If prisoner A confesses and his accomplice does not confess, prisoner A turn's state's evidence and he gets a shorter sentence, while his accomplice, Prisoner B, gets the book thrown at him. If neither confesses they both get a smaller sentence. If they should happen to both confess, they get a different, but perhaps somewhat severe sentence. See Figure 9.2 for one example of what the payoff matrix might look like for the Prisoner's Dilemma type of game.

Figure 9.2   **Prisoner's Dilemma Matrix**

	B Cooperates: Does Not Confess	B Betrays: Confesses
A Cooperates: Does Not Confess	Both get a 1-year sentence (payoff: −1)	A gets 10 years (−10), B gets no sentence (0)
A Betrays: Confesses	A gets no sentence (0), B gets 10 years (−10)	Both get 8 years (−8)

Examining this matrix, we can see that double-betrayal cell, in which they both get 8 years (−8, −8), is the Nash equilibrium. That means that neither prisoner can do better than that by changing his strategy alone. If A moves up a row, and changes strategy his strategy to cooperation, he gets 10 years. If B moves left a column, changing his strategy to cooperation, he also gets 10 years. Yet the Nash equilibrium seems like a most unsatisfying outcome.

The von Neumann-Morgenstern equilibrium is the double-cooperation cell (−1, −1), as for both players it is the "best of the worst," or minimax equilibrium point. However, in actual one-time play of Prisoner's Dilemma, players hardly ever choose the von Neumann-Morgenstern equilibrium. Research has shown that people tend to consistently pick betrayal as the best alternative. That is a very disappointing result about human nature. So the major research question in Prisoner's Dilemma has been: How do we maximize cooperation so that the best mutual outcome (−1, −1) will be chosen?

The most interesting aspect of Prisoner's Dilemma for our purposes in this chapter about healing from betrayal is when the game is played over and over again. In a real relationship one can think of this non-zero-sum game as being repeated many times—we continually have the choice of cooperating or betraying our partner, increasing the trust metric or increasing the betrayal metric. Research by Robert Axelrod with repeated Prisoner's Dilemma has been the most revealing. His form of the Prisoner's Dilemma game is shown in Figure 9.3.

Figure 9.3   Robert Axelrod's Repeated Prisoner's Dilemma Matrix

	B Cooperates: Does Not Confess	B Betrays: Confesses
A Cooperates: Does Not Confess	Both get a reward (+3)	A gets no reward (0) "sucker's payoff," B gets a reward (+5) "temptation reward"
A Betrays: Confesses	A gets a reward (+5) "temptation reward," B gets no reward (0) "sucker's payoff"	Both get punished (+1)

Axelrod used sophisticated computer simulation comparing strategies for playing the Prisoner Dilemma game repeatedly, and found that Anatol Rapoport's "tit-for-tat" strategy was the most effective of 14 strategies at eliciting cooperation in a round-robin tournament. As explained earlier, in this strategy a player begins by cooperating on the first move and then does whatever the other player does on his preceding move. Hence, tit-for-tat is a strategy based upon reciprocity.

Subsequent research by Axelrod examined five other strategies for eliciting maximum cooperation in the repeated Prisoner's Dilemma game. They were:

- *Don't rock the boat*: Continue to cooperate after three mutual cooperations.
- *Be capable of being provoked*: Betray when the partner betrays out of the blue.
- *Accept apology*: Continue to cooperate after cooperation has been restored.
- *Forgive*: Cooperate once again, but only when mutual cooperation has been restored.
- *Accept betrayal addiction*: Betray, but only after three mutual betrayals.

These strategies may be relevant for thinking about helping couples to heal from betrayal and to establish the greatest likelihood for subsequent cooperation. These five strategies, or "rules," were compared by Axelrod to the successful Rapoport tit-for-tat strategy. Most of the rules did as well as the tit-for-tat strategy, but no better. Only in a minority of 11 of 40 simulations that Axelrod conducted did these rules actually do better than the tit-for-tat strategy. So there was some suggestion, albeit weak evidence, that these rules could increase the potential for cooperation.

However, here's the brilliant part of Axelrod's research strategy. Axelrod then went on to compare these strategies when there was "noise" in the system. What he called "noise" was allowing for the possibility of people making "mistakes." He suggested that any person may do something untrustworthy once in a while. This may be akin to what I have called a "regrettable incident." Axelrod was asking the question of whether there could be a strategy for repeated Prisoner's Dilemma play that would maximize cooperation in the face of these "errors," or noise in the trust/betrayal system.

Remember this discussion of strategies in the face of noise is still in the context of the Prisoner's Dilemma game. Axelrod was aware of the idea that too much forgiveness could potentially lead to exploitation in Prisoner's Dilemma. So he designed two new strategies, or "rules." One of his two new strategies for dealing with noise, or mistakes, was called *generosity*, in which a partner stays cooperative, but only 10% of the time when he or she might have ordinarily chosen to no longer cooperate. His second new strategy was more complex. It was called *contrition*. Contrition had three possibilities: (1) being "contrite" about one's *own* mistake, (2) being "content" or okay with the uncooperative person by calling it a "mistake," or (3) being provoked" by the mistake. In the contrition strategy, there is the possibility of repair.[3]

In a complex computer simulation of many "generations" of repeated Prisoner's Dilemma play with noise, with four additional strategies, initially the generosity strategy was most effective in eliciting cooperation, but eventually the contrition strategy was by far most effective in eliciting cooperation in the face of mistakes.[4] Contrition was "less effective at correcting one's own error but not the error of other players . . . on the other hand contrition is very effective as the environment becomes dominated by rules that are successful in the noisy environment. . . . In the presence of noise, reciprocity still works, provided that it is accompanied either by generosity (some chance of cooperating when one would otherwise defect) [read: betray], or contrition (cooperating after the other player defects [read: betrays] in response to one's own defection [read: betrayal])." (p. 37)

Hence, Axelrod came up with some useful modifications to Rapoport's tit-for-tat for maximizing cooperation, in the face of noise in the two-person trust/betrayal system. If we put all these strategies together, they are:

- *Rapoport's tit-for-tat:* Start with cooperation, but thereafter do what the partner does, cooperating if the partner cooperates, and not cooperating of the partner does not cooperate.
- *Don't rock the boat:* Continue to cooperate after mutual cooperations.
- *Be capable of being provoked:* Don't cooperate when the partner betrays out of the blue.
- *Accept apology:* Continue to cooperate after cooperation has been restored.
- *Forgive:* Cooperate, but only when mutual cooperation has been restored.
- *Accept betrayal addiction:* Stop cooperating, but only after three mutual betrayals.
- *Generosity:* Allow for "mistakes" at least 10% of the time, continuing to cooperate.
- *Contrition:* Restore trust by cooperating after one's own betrayal.

So these are eight rules that have been shown to maximize cooperation in the repeated Prisoner's dilemma play, with noise. They even do better than Rapoport's tit-for-tat strategy in the face of mistakes, but not by much.

The Use of Norms and Meta-Norms

As intriguing as the repeated Prisoner's Dilemma game is, it is only a game, or a model for actual interaction. Rapoport's interest in it was in applications to international conflict. Attempting to generalize beyond the Prisoner's Dilemma game, Axelrod suggested that societies establish norms by punishing betrayal as well as rewarding cooperation. He suggested that this punishment would be heavily costly for the betrayer, but also somewhat costly to the enforcer as well. "Meta-norms" meant the "willingness to punish not only those who violate norms, but also anyone who fails to punish the violators" (p. 41).[5]

Recently I had the opportunity to work with the Michigan State Legislature and their partners. Forty percent of these legislators were women. In a closed, confidential session, I heard legislators and their partners talk about how their staff often naturally would work at cross-purposes to their spouses. In more subtle ways the legislators' staff also often had goals in opposition to the legislator's family. The spouse might want the legislator to spend more time at home, with the spouse, or with the children, whereas the staff wanted the legislator to spend more time campaigning or raising money.

Sometimes the staff actually procured women for male legislators' illicit sexual liaisons. This was also the case when John F. Kennedy was president of the United States.[6] Experienced legislators told stories of how they dealt with these conflicts by having their partners involved in hiring their staff, insuring that norms and meta-norms of loyalty replaced conflicting norms that could involve family betrayal.

Norms and meta-norms are ways of socially enforcing cooperation even in the face of potential betrayal. These ideas work not only for a group or a society but also for a couple who is healing from betrayal. Other people, friends, family members, children, kin, work colleagues, and perhaps even therapists often join the couple in helping them to heal from betrayal by establishing informal norms and meta-norms.

Like Anatol Rapoport, Robert Axelrod was interested in minimizing the tensions of the Cold War. He knew that cooperation between these nations had been repeatedly hurt by brinksmanship, so that *international verification* (for example, evidence of nuclear disarmament by inspection) was necessary, a situation of more perfect information rather than a situation of secrecy and deception.

Hence, part of meta-norms is another consideration in healing from betrayal—namely, that additional betrayal has to become extremely costly. For example, in empirical work on trust in social networks, such as the network of Orthodox Jewish diamond merchants, research by Vincent Buskens concluded that "actors who are untrustworthy must be expelled or punished severely enough for other actors to see that untrustworthy behavior is only worthwhile in the short term" (p. 21).[7] The diamond merchants, as described earlier, are amazing in having created a very high-trust network. Based on a handshake, they may exchange jewels valued at millions of dollars. But there is an enormous cost for betrayal in this culture—namely, complete ostracism from this vital community. This suggests we add ninth rule for maximizing cooperation and minimizing betrayal:

- *High cost for subsequent betrayal:* There needs to be an understanding that subsequent untrustworthiness will have severe costs or negative consequences.

Why Healing From Betrayal Isn't Easy: Wounds Are Not Healed by Time

In his thought-provoking book *Wounds Not Healed by Time*, Solomon Schimmel critically examines forgiveness.[8] The major religions of the world—Judaism, Christianity, Islam, and Buddhism—all call for forgiveness for wounds received by others. The concept of forgiveness has also recently become a popular part of the psychotherapy literature. Schimmel raises many questions about forgiveness. He asks whether forgiveness is always more moral or just than not forgiving. When is requiring forgiveness merely blaming the victim? When is remorse or repentance a precondition for forgiveness, and what does "repentance" entail? Schimmel explores these questions in many contexts, from ordinary personal relationships to huge crimes like the Holocaust and to post-apartheid South Africa.

Fortunately Schimmel raises questions and discusses issues without drawing a final conclusion. In perfect Talmudic and Socratic fashion, he strips away the veil of assumptions we probably hold about transgressions, sin, evil, and atonement. He leaves conclusions to the reader. For example, he examines the case of a person who has been the victim of incest, and asks whether it is in the best psychological interests of the victim to ever forgive the abuser. He also asks who has the right to forgive an injury. In a Minnesota church, a minister asked his congregation to take a few moments and forgive Timothy McVeigh, the perpetrator who bombed the Oklahoma City Federal building, killing scores of innocent people and children in a daycare center. Schimmel reacts to this event by saying that only the victims have the right to forgive McVeigh, not the Minnesota congregation.

Shirley Glass's analysis of betrayal in extramarital affairs also looked at the post-traumatic stress disorder (PTSD) that is created in the betrayed person. A contract has been broken in an affair. In heterosexual relationships that subscribe to monogamy and sexual exclusivity, and to the norm of no secrets or betrayals, the affair causes the spouse to question everything—even who this person really is, and what the real marriage contract is. The whole world of the betrayed partner has come crashing down. The betrayed partner goes over the many times they had together where a hidden condition of lying and deception existed. All the symptoms of PTSD are present in the betrayed partner, including disturbed sleep, flashbacks, depression, obsessional intrusive thoughts, emotional numbing, insecurity, self-doubt, and generalized anxiety. How can the relationship be saved, how can these people heal from the betrayal, how can they ever trust each other again, and how can they cooperate again and rebuild the trust metric?

These questions Schimmel raises go considerably beyond the mathematics of cooperation using the repeated Prisoner's Dilemma game. However, some of the Axelrod rules for creating new cooperation may nonetheless prove useful.

When Should We Not Forgive? And Reasons to Be Hopeful

There are times when it is more damaging to forgive than to move on: when the injury has been so deep, the deception and betrayal so grave, the evil perpetrated so serious, that forgiving would be damaging psychologically to the person who was betrayed. This is true at times when people heal from violent crimes, incest, or other forms of abuse. Some wounds can never be understood and can never be reconciled.

Fortunately, recent research shows that the prognosis is good of healing from betrayal when, and only when, both people are determined to make this journey. Both Donald Baucom at the University of North Carolina and Andy Christensen at UCLA have conducted research showing although couples dealing with a known affair start lower in relationship satisfaction than other distressed couples, following structured therapy they wind up in the same place.[9] The road back to trust isn't an easy one, but there is indeed reason to be hopeful, and I couldn't have said that 5 years ago, before the work of Shirley Glass, Donald Baucom, and Andy Christensen.

I suggest that healing from betrayal first requires us to understand the science of how couples create either betrayal and distrust or loyalty and trust. In the following section, I offer a theory.

A Theory of the Cascade Toward Betrayal and Distrust

How can one summarize what we know about the dynamics of betrayal and distrust? Can we describe this as an orderly process? If so, can we use that knowledge to keep betrayal from happening? It turns out that there is a natural cascade of processes that reliably lead to betrayal. Once the ball gets rolling in this direction, even very nice people who tried very hard to have a great relationship can wind up with a dissolved relationship on their hands. Understanding the processes of betrayal takes the horns and tails off people who eventually betray their partner. They are not devils, but ordinary, well-meaning people caught in a cascade of events of which they are mostly unaware.

How do couples make betrayal and distrust happen? Does it simply happen by neglect? The answer is yes, in part, but it's a far more active process than that. It is true that one can purchase the best car available, and after 10 years of neglect that car would probably be a miserable wreck. But in relationships the cascade toward betrayal involves more than just neglect.

Let's summarize what we know about the dynamics of creating a relationship characterized by no trust and high betrayal using the flowchart shown in Figure 9.4 to summarize what we now think is true. This is clearly a work in progress, although we do know quite a bit about these processes.

The distrust and betrayal flowchart begins with turning away or against a bid for emotional connection. The left-hand limb of the flow-chart shows the *trust-erosion consequences* of a cascade that begins by simply turning away coupled with emotion dismissing. I have already talked a lot about this limb in Chapter 6.

As we have seen, in such a regrettable incident the trust metric erodes as a consequence of turning away and dismissing or disapproving of the negative emotions. This could be the basis of a Susan Johnson concept of an attachment injury.

As I have noted, flooding is the usual result of turning away and dismissing (and is sometimes accompanied by diffuse physiological arousal), with a consequent increase in the untrustworthiness metric. Two metrics therefore change: We trust our partner less and also deem our partner as less trustworthy. These two metrics are not equivalent because of the way they are each measured by my use of game theory.

If this regrettable event is not repaired, and if it keeps happening, that leads to rumination and the Zeigarnik effect sets in. Next comes a very critical step, which is about conflict. Over many such incidents of turning away and emotion dismissing, or several very powerful regret-table incidents that are not healed, the Zeigarnik effect and continued low trust lead to negative affect exchanges during conflict becoming an *absorbing state* in which repair is ineffective. That state is enough to trig-ger the right-hand limb in which unfavorable CL-ALTs begin to shape consciousness about the partner and the relationship. It is one way (but only one way) that the right-hand limb of the flowchart can be turned on. My concept of the absorbing state turns out to be very similar to Rusbult's concept of "low accommodation." What she meant by "accom-modation" was that when a person acts *destructively* (which she called "neglect" or "exit"), the partner responds but acts *constructively* (which she called "voice" or "loyalty"). Low accommodation was related to unfa-vorable CL-ALTs in Rusbult's data, which in her research was based on self-report data alone.

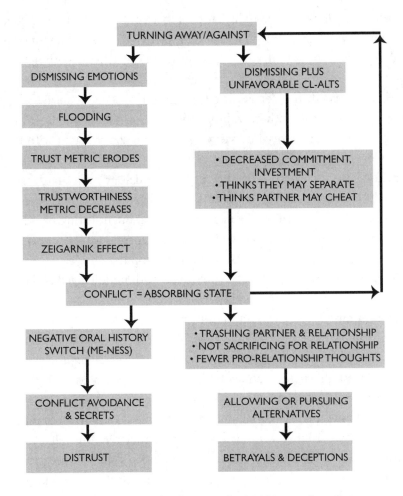

Figure 9.4   **Flowchart for how couples build betrayal or distrust**

Low commitment thus leads to negative processes during conflict, which Rusbult called "exit" or "neglect" (destructiveness either active or passive), as opposed to "voice" or "loyalty" (active or passive constructiveness). In Rusbult's scheme, conflict was also described as a low-accommodation state, by which she meant a state of reciprocated destructive negativity. This is very much like the absorbing state of negativity during conflict. I am pleased that her self-report measures are now supported by our observational measures.

Now let's look at the right-hand limb of the flowchart. Our data combined with Caryl Rusbult's measure of CL-ALT in our low-income couples' decision-making study suggests that destructive absorbing-state conflict is related to increased unfavorable CL-ALTs.

As I discussed, the Zeigarnik effect and conflict being an absorbing state then implies that there will be a negative switch for the Buehlman coding of the oral history interview. That finding is consistent with Rusbult's data that shows that unfavorable CL-ALTs imply low "we-ness," measured in her research by the use of "we-us-our" adjectives in her thought-listing paradigm, compared to high "me-ness," measured in her research by "I-me-mine" adjectives in her thought-listing paradigm. Her finding is also consistent with Robert Levenson's actual counting of we-ness words using a linguistically based computer analysis of conflict transcripts during the oral history interview with middle-aged and older couples in our longitudinal study. Her finding is also consistent with a similar finding by Stanley and Markman.

The right-hand limb of my flowchart illustrates the *building of betrayal*, a cascade that begins by a turning away *coupled with an unfavorable CL-ALT*. In Rusbult's model, unfavorable CL-ALTs are related to decreased commitment, which involves a trio of: (1) decreased satisfaction, (2) decreased investment in the relationship, and (3) decreased mutual "dependency" on the relationship. "Dependency" in Rusbult's model means decreased confidence that the relationship will meet the person's needs. This effect is dyadic because low investment and commitment by one partner negatively affect the investment and commitment of the other partner.

Rusbult has shown that low commitment leads people to further denigrate the relationship and idealize alternatives to the relationship, whereas high commitment leads people to denigrate alternatives to the relationship.

In our study of decision-making in lower-income couples, low commitment was significantly correlated with beliefs that the couple would separate in the future and beliefs that the partner would cheat (sexual betrayal) in the future. I suggest that this state of low commitment, when coupled with conflict becoming an absorbing state (repair fails, conflict escalates, with physiological arousal), leads the person to *trash* rather than *cherish* the partner and the relationship, not sacrifice for the relationship, and not have a cognitive system that Rusbult described as "pro-relationship." Stanley, Rhoades, and Markman also described a similar process.[10] The low commitment leads people to fail to put boundaries around other people and themselves, and to flirt with or actively pursue alternative relationships, a process that leads to betrayal (and potentially deception). Stanley and Markman also described a similar process they called low "constraint."

Hypotheses: Distrust Can "Turn On" the Betrayal Limb

I also hypothesize that the two limbs of the flowchart are connected. First, the distrust limb is hypothesized to connect to unfavorable CL-ALTs following the increase of the untrustworthiness metric. Once one has deemed one's partner untrustworthy, the unfavorable comparison to other relationships is enhanced. That link was supported empirically by our decision-making study.

A second link is between conflict and increased unfavorable CL-ALTs by the male partner with lower video-recall rating dial scores of both partners, increased sympathetic nervous system activation of both partners, and by higher male domineering (which increases his unfavorable CL-ALTs and decreases her unfavorable CL-ALTs). Also if the male is higher in high-validation (understanding and empathy, this decreases his unfavorable CL-ALTs. Furthermore, female high-domination and female anger increased female unfavorable CL-ALTs). These link, were supported by our decision-making study.

A final more speculative link between the betrayal limb and the distrust limb, supported by Rusbult's data, is a link between thinking a partner will cheat and lower we-ness—a dimension of our Buehlman oral history coding. In our decision-making study we measured the perceived chances that the couple would separate in the future and the chances that the partner would cheat in the future, and they were significantly related to unfavorable CL-ALTs by the male and lower commitment by both partners.

In this flowchart there is also a hypothesized link from betrayal to distrust. Betrayal, once confirmed, certainly leads to distrust, but I am also suggesting that the façade of deception surrounding an unrevealed betrayal must necessarily also compromise trust, because betrayal compromises one's ability to fully love one's partner. Even an unrevealed betrayal can have this effect because it changes the person doing the secret betrayal.

A Theory of the Cascade Toward Loyalty and Trust

Let's now consider the positive alternative. The importance of the positive flowchart is that it represents a cascade of positivity. Once the positive ball gets rolling, the relationship will naturally invoke processes that build loyalty, gratitude, and cherishing. The trust and loyalty flowchart (Figure 9.5) begins with turning toward a bid for emotional connection.

The left-hand limb of the flowchart shows the *trust-building consequences* of a cascade that begins by simply turning toward coupled with emotional attunement. As we have seen, the trust metric builds as a consequence of turning toward and attuning to the partner's emotions. Calm and no flooding is the usual result, with a decrease in the untrustworthiness metric. The absence of the Zeigarnik effect and the presence high trust leads to effective repair during the negative-affect exchanges during conflict, so conflict is not an absorbing state because repair is effective.

Our data with Rusbult's measure of CL-ALT also suggest that this effective repair during conflict and low physiological arousal of the partner increases favorable CL-ALTs. The effective repair state is very similar to Rusbult's concept of accommodation (when a person responds constructively to the partner's destructive acts, or "exit" and "neglect". Accommodation is related to favorable CL-ALTs in Rusbult's data. Accommodation would seem logically to be related to conflict not being an absorbing state and repair being effective, although Rusbult did not measure accommodation with observational methods.

The absence of a Zeigarnik effect and conflict not being an absorbing state implies that there will be a positive switch for the Buehlman coding of the oral history interview, part of which is consistent with Rusbult's data showing commitment is related to high we-ness (we-us-our) adjectives in her thought-listing paradigm, compared to high me-ness (I-me-mine) adjectives. The finding is consistent with a finding by Stanley, Rhoades, and Markman.[11]

The right-hand limb of the flowchart shows the *building of loyalty*, which is a cascade that begins by simply turning toward coupled with favorable CL-ALTs. In Rusbult's model, these favorable CL-ALTs are related to increased commitment, which involves a trio of increased satisfaction, increased investment in the relationship, and increased mutual dependency (confidence that the relationship will meet both people's needs). This effect tends to be dyadic because high investment

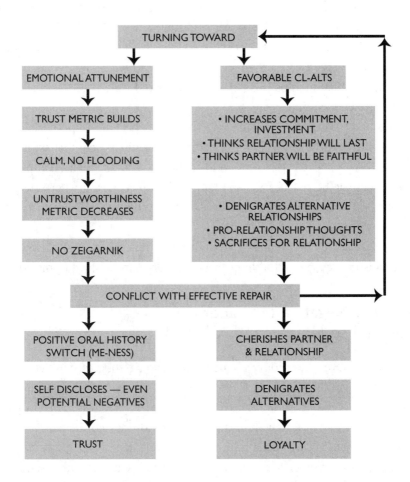

Figure 9.5 **Flowchart for how couples build loyalty and trust**

and commitment by one partner positively affect the investment and commitment of the other partner (contagion). There is an active process of being grateful for the partner's positive traits as well as minimizing the partner's negative traits. The high commitment leads people to denigrate relationship alternatives. High commitment also leads to positive processes during conflict, which Rusbult called "voice" or "loyalty" (actively or passively being constructive during conflict). In Rusbult's scheme, conflict is also described as a high-accomodation state, by which she meant a state of unreciprocated negativity.

I propose that this leads the person to *cherish* rather than *trash* the partner and the relationship, sacrifice for the relationship, feel and express *gratitude*, and have a cognitive system that Rusbult described as "pro-relationship." Stanley and Markman have described a similar process. The commitment process leads people to put active boundaries around other people and themselves and not flirt with or actively pursue alternative relationships, a process that leads to loyalty and transparency rather than deception.

The two limbs of the loyalty and trust flowchart are hypothesized to be linked in three ways. First, effective repair during conflict is linked to more positive CL-ALTs. Second, a belief that the relationship will last and that the partner will be faithful is linked to a greater sense of we-ness. Third, a downward change in the untrustworthiness metric is linked to more positive CL-ALTs.

In this flowchart there is a hypothesized link from trust to loyalty, which is the reverse of the hypothesized link from betrayal to distrust.

How Is Negative Interaction Related to Unfavorable CL-ALTs?

So far we have talked only about the absorbing state of conflict relating to unfavorable CL-ALTs. However, in our couples' decision-making study using the Rusbult measures of CL-ALT, we also had couples engage in a task that usually is a lot of fun and does not usually induce conflict. That task was called the "paper tower" task.

Couples were given a box of materials like newspapers, twine, scissors, scotch tape, poster board, crayons, colored cellophane, and other decorative materials, and they were asked to construct a freestanding paper tower in 20 minutes. The tower would be judged on height, strength, and beauty. This is a wonderful example of how couples can work together as a team and have fun, or how they fail to become a team and instead have an awful time. We coded their behavior using our Specific Affect Coding System. It turned out that the female's whining during this task and the male's defensiveness were both significantly related to his greater tendency to engage in CL-ALTs unfavorable to the relationship. Both partners' lack of any emotions during this task, which is probably a measure of the lack of fun and enthusiasm, were significantly related to her greater tendency to engage in CL-ALTs unfavorable to the relationship. From these data it appears that we can amend the flowcharts so that negative interaction during a potentially fun experience is also related to CL-ALTs unfavorable to the relationship. Of course, we don't yet really know the direction of causation in this correlation.

What Determines the Decision to Turn Away?

The models I presented about creating betrayal versus loyalty start with the decision to turn away and to dismiss negative emotions in sliding-door moments. But what determines this decision? Research shows that the decision to turn toward versus away is mediated, to some extent, by individual variables. There is an effect of low self-esteem in the decision to choose the goals of self-interest and protection rather than connectedness.

Eight experiments manipulating risk and the strength of these two goals of self-interest and protection rather than connectedness found that for people high in self-esteem, risk directs them toward the connectedness goal and toward depending on their relationship.[12] For people low in self-esteem, risk triggers them toward self-protection as a goal, avoiding depending on their relationship. In another study, when they manipulated feeling inferior to one's partner (for example, feeling less attractive than one's partner), low-self-esteem (but not high-self-esteem) newlyweds used another strategy—they tried to increase their partner's dependence on them.

It is also quite likely that the low-self-esteem variable may be related to a person's attachment history. There is extensive empirical evidence for this contention,[13] although the two constructs of low self-esteem and insecure attachment history may not be identical. For example, research studying children has found that self-esteem acted as a variable helping to explain the relationship between attachment security and others' appraisal of the child's social competence.[14] Clinically this means that to understand the decision to turn away and dismiss versus to turn toward and attune, it may be productive to explore each individual's attachment history and also the individual's self-esteem, as well as the strategies they use to increase their partner's dependency when they feel insecure or inferior to the partner on some dimension. That somewhat complex picture of individual variables is what we have to deal with at the current time.

Does Conflict Erode Trust or Does Low Trust Create Conflict?

In the flowcharts I presented, I suggested that the *nature of the conflict* determined whether unfavorable or favorable CL-ALTs would be enhanced. A creative study examined the question of whether conflict deteriorates trust or low trust creates conflict in 174 five-person new work teams.[15] Although they did not discriminate the nature of the conflict (that is, whether conflict was an absorbing state versus effective repair), in statistical modeling they concluded that low trust created conflict, rather than conflict itself creating low trust. This result is very interesting. Perhaps in more established relationships there may be a bi-directional relationship between trust and conflict. One study did actually find evidence that the length of a work relationship moderates trust and the kind of information used as a basis for trust.[16]

How Can We Maximize the Probability of Forgiveness?

In her penetrating analysis of the film *The War of the Roses*, Caryl Rusbult wrote:

> The unfolding narrative reveals the troubled marriage of Barbara and Oliver Rose: Oliver belittles Barbara's career; Barbara neglects Oliver during a

frightening health crisis; each humiliates the other, delivering impossible-to-forget attacks on the other's tastes and habits. During their marital Armageddon, Barbara and Oliver become entangled in a chandelier suspended above a hallway. The mechanism suspending the chandelier gives way and—embraced in the arms of the chandelier—the two crash to the unyielding terrazzo floor 30 feet below. With his dying breath, Oliver reaches out to touch Barbara's shoulder, offering amends and seeking forgiveness . . . (perhaps, one imagines, to reciprocate Oliver's act) . . . Barbara's hand slowly rises to meet Oliver's and with her dying breath, Barbara flings Oliver's hand away from her. (p. 251).[17]

In the context of this tragic failure of a relationship, Rusbult's chapter suggests mechanisms for maximizing forgiveness.

Until recently forgiveness remained in the world of theology. However, scientists have begun trying to understand how betrayal and forgiveness occur, how they are perceived, and how forgiveness can be encouraged.

In that chapter Rusbult distinguished between forgiveness as *intra*personal (inside oneself) versus *inter*personal (toward another person). The usual use of the term "forgiveness" entwines both parts. However, it may make some sense to separate them. She wrote: ". . . intrapersonal forgiveness without interpersonal forgiveness seems a bit hollow (the perpetrator's reaction might be 'thank you very much for forgiving me; now why won't you forgive me?')" (p. 257). Rusbult's analysis chooses the interpersonal rather than the intrapersonal definition of forgiveness, choosing instead to "define forgiveness as the victim's resumption of pre-betrayal behavioral tendencies—that is, as the tendency to forego vengeance and other destructive patterns of interaction, instead behaving toward the perpetrator in a positive and constructive manner" (p. 258).

Of course, the betrayal is a violation of the norms of the pre-betrayal relationship. Rusbult described how effortful renegotiation and reconciliation can rewrite the broader contract of a relationship, transforming gut-level preferences to retaliate following a betrayal into effortful processes to alter gut-level motivations to instead continue the relationship. In that case the betrayal can be thought of as a wake-up call rather than the end of the relationship. It turns out that the processes of commitment promote the pro-relationship motivation and behavior that make this renegotiation more likely.

Rusbult's analysis of maximizing forgiveness can be integrated into my theory of building loyalty and trust in the following practical proposal for renegotiation and reconciliation in the new relationship contract following the betrayal.

A Proposal for Healing From Betrayal and Distrust

In most cases the couple is actually creating a new relationship. What needs to be accomplished?

First, the relationship has to pass the untrustworthiness detector, and the betrayed partner has to decide to rebuild a new relationship. There may be a lot of ambivalence and mixed feelings on the part of both partners. These emotions need to be processed and a decision needs to be made to begin rebuilding the relationship. This cannot happen as long as the other relationship is ongoing. A new relationship between partners needs to be built. That new relationship has to one in which the processes of betrayal are replaced by the processes of loyalty, and the processes of distrust are replaced by the processes of trust. There are three phases of that work.

Phase I. Partners Express Remorse, Establish Transparency, and Create Understanding, Acceptance, and the Beginnings of Forgiveness.

1. *The betrayer listens to repeated expressions of the hurt partner's feelings without defensiveness.* There is a great need for the betrayer to listen and just take in the feelings of the hurt partner without defending him- or herself. This will be very difficult for the betrayer to do without the disastrous error of blaming the hurt partner for any setting conditions that have contributed to the betrayal. But this nondefensiveness is critical. It follows, then, that one of the most egregious errors a therapist can make is to allow the betrayer to shift blame onto the partner for the affair, in order to make the therapy "balanced." Betrayal is not a balanced process. One partner has deeply wounded the other. Therefore, the feelings of the betrayed must be listened to nondefen-

sively and with no excuses offered by the betrayer. The therapist must guide the questions so that they avoid whatever details of the affair (for example explicit details about sex) may create ruminations on the part of the betrayed partner and thus reactivate that person's trauma. Also, the therapist should consider limiting the question-asking to the consulting office.

2. The betrayer expresses genuine remorse. There needs to be genuine remorse for the betrayal, along with guided questions and answers that create honesty and transparency about the betrayal. This begins to reverse the post-traumatic stress reaction that the betrayal has caused.

3. The couple creates transparency, verification, and the "don't rock the boat" rule. Part of what happens with a disclosed betrayal is that the hurt person feels like he or she no longer knows the partner. Transparency is about understanding that information about the partner can be relied upon, so that a trustworthy love map can be rebuilt.

The couple now follows Axelrod's "don't rock the boat" rule. Neither person wishes to destroy this fragile state of rebuilding trust, so they do not rock the boat, which means that they continue to cooperate reciprocally, reassure, and avoid frightening the hurt partner. The hurt person cooperates, too, but only if there is mutual cooperation. This begins with a fragile belief in the process of healing, which requires total honesty, transparency, and respect. This stage is very painful. With an affair, for example, the hurt partner asks and the other partner answers questions about the betrayal so they can both understand what caused it. But the therapist makes sure that the questions and answers are not going to stimulate obsessive ruminations by the hurt partner (for example asking about the details of sex with the affair partner). What builds trust on an ongoing basis in this phase is being transparent with one's partner. Each person agrees to the principle that there will be no more secrets and that promises will be kept. Some people we have seen in couple therapy are uncomfortable with this principle, but without it, trust stays a perpetual issue in the relationship—it never goes away and never gets laid to rest. But honesty does not mean saying painful and hurtful things to one's partner. Tact and gentleness are still important in building trust. Mutual respect and trust also go hand in hand. Only honesty will heal the deceptions and begin to reestablish trust, and help deal with the PTSD of the hurt partner. Furthermore, the "strategies" previously available to the person who perpetrated the betrayal will naturally become constricted, so that trust can be rebuilt, in part, by some *checking and verifying* that the cooperation is real. Like international verification of nuclear disarmament, the strategies of both players become restricted so that checking for betrayals becomes easier in an atmosphere of greater honesty and transparency.

4. The couple creates understanding by individualizing the "processes of betrayal." This understanding needs to involve a historical review of how processes of betrayal and distrust occurred in *this relationship*. The couple identifies the negative patterns that are unique to the couple's history. This understanding is essential for being able to reverse betrayal and distrust processes. This is where Axelrod's principle of "establishing generosity and more contrition" fits in. There is a need for the couple to understand what the "setting conditions" were for the betrayal in order to begin using Axelrod's generosity and contrition. Contrition, as I have already discussed is, in fact, here recognized as a necessary, but not sufficient, condition for generosity. *Real behavior change* must now accompany remorse in order for the generosity of the hurt partner to follow.

5. The couple processes their major emotional wounds. The couple needs to learn the skills of emotional processing and to apply them on a regular basis. With the understanding that comes from knowing what factors trigger conflict avoidance, turning away, and escalated conflict and anger—in other words, each other's enduring vulnerabilities—the couple can understand and *accept* the conditions that have led to betrayal processes. They also both need to understand the meaning of the betrayer's having decided to come back to the partner. Why was that decision made, and what does it mean?

6. The couple establishes Rapoport's process for maximizing cooperation, "tit-for-tat." Once the couple decides to try to heal from a betrayal, they have also decided to maximize cooperation and try to understand the dynamics of the betrayal. They are, in effect, starting with Rapoport's tit-for-tat, which is the beginning stage of very fragile cooperation, but they can withdraw that cooperation if there is any renewed evidence of potential betrayal by the partner. Tit-for-tat has proven superior to any other strategy for maximizing cooperation in the face of potential deceit or defection in repeated Prisoner's Dilemma play (with no noise). Applied to couples, this is a strange version of the Golden Rule. In Phase 1 they start out by being minimally trusting and cooperative.

7. *The hurt partner (1) accepts apology, and (2) begins to forgive.* For these two Axelrod rules, the hurt partner now needs to keep seeing genuine remorse, but we add *steps toward behavior change*. The hurt partner may start *accepting apology* and to continue to cooperate even after cooperation has initially been restored, and *to begin to forgive—* that is, to continue to cooperate, but only once mutual cooperation has been truly restored. By "forgiveness" in this context I mean only an enhanced willingness to cooperate, even in the face of uncertainty and possible "mistakes." This is Axelrod's technical term of "noise," in this system. Emotionally, forgiveness is no small thing. It means risking being vulnerable again with one's partner, even in the face of fear and the hypervigilance that usually accompanies the PTSD effects of having been betrayed. In Phase 1 of our therapy we spend a lot of time on this rule of accepting apology and forgiving the betrayal.

Phase 2. The Couple Reverses Betrayal Processes That Have Been Active in This Relationship

1. *The couple learns constructive conflict and self-disclosure, versus conflict avoidance or escalation.* The couple needs to understand how the betrayal processes have led to both conflict avoidance and conflict having become an absorbing state. The couple needs to replace their methods of dealing with conflict with the Gottman-Rapoport blueprint for making conflict constructive. This involves reversing the staying-hidden part of the avoidance of conflict. The couple learns to *disclose and express their needs, even when it is most difficult.* They have to stop being invisible by denying what they really need from their partner, and to begin the processes of self-disclosure. This means understanding their own feelings and disclosing their needs even when this may lead to conflict, which will be made easier by using the Gottman-Rapoport blueprint. Some people will need help just knowing what they feel. The couple can ritualize this self-disclosure in the hour-long "state of the union" weekly meeting.

2. The couple agrees to the principle of mutually meeting needs. They now both agree that a relationship is partly about meeting each other's needs.

3. The couple agrees to turn toward bids in sliding-door moments. They need to understand the alternative of turning toward bids in sliding-door moments, without creating comparisons or unfavorable CL-ALTs. They also need to understand and learn the processes involved in turning toward—including how each partner characteristically expresses needs—and to also "take in" the positive turning toward. They also need to ritualize asking each other about current thoughts and feelings, or "check in emotionally."

4. The couple creates the lasting behavior change of cherishing versus trashing—they thus reverse the habit of mind of making unfavorable CL-ALTS. The betrayer needs to express genuine and firm intention to change his or her behavior and *patterns of thinking* to pro-relationship thinking and behavior. Both people need to understand, and the betrayer needs to reverse the processes that have led to the betrayal, starting with the initial process of turning away or against and following that event with an unfavorable CL-ALT. The process of cherishing the partner needs to become established as an essential part of their lives.

5. The couple establishes norms and meta-norms that are set up in order to "create the sacred" in the relationship. Part of cherishing each other involves creating the "sacred" in the relationship. As noted earlier, the word "sacred" has its roots in ancient practices of religious sacrifice. In many ways, the creation of new ground rules for the new relationship requires personal sacrifice. What I mean by "creating the sacred" is mutually agreeing to enhance romance. This means making the commitment to cherish one's partner as unique and irreplaceable, and letting important people in on the norms and meta-norms of the new relationship, so that the norms and meta-norms can become firmly established. Both Rusbult and Stanley and Markman found that a willingness to sacrifice for the relationship was essential to commitment.[18] What can be helpful is building a *culture of appreciation and respect*. This actually does mean creating a new relationship—that is, a relationship with new ground rules. The norms can be reified by making them known to the community of people who are involved with the couple.

Phase 3. The Couple Begins Building Trust and Intimate Trust

1. *The couple learns the skills of intimate conversation.* They learn the skills of expressing emotions, probing, following up, exploration, and empathy. They regularly agree to have these conversations, beginning with a stress-reducing conversation upon reunion at the end of each day, and moving on to building the shared-meaning system (rituals of connection, shared goals, and dreams). Materials for the stress-reducing conversation can be found in the *Art and Science of Love* materials, DVD, and manual on the gottman.com website.

2. *The couple increases investment and mutual dependency in the relationship.* They need to understand how the habit of mind of creating unfavorable CL-ALTs led to decreased investment in the relationship and decreased commitment. Then they need to make a plan for increasing investment, sacrifice, and pro-relationship thinking in the relationship.

3. *They set up a high cost for subsequent betrayals.* To be effective, these meta-norms may need to include openly discussing the high cost for subsequent betrayals. That is, there needs to be an understanding that subsequent untrustworthiness will have severe costs or negative consequences for the relationship. In the therapeutic work with couples, this "high cost" for subsequent betrayals is what Salvador Minuchin called a "sense of responsibility" for the partner's welfare (personal communication, 2009). It comes from a moral sense of justice, deep empathy, and not wanting to be part of the brotherhood or sisterhood of those who have deeply hurt their partner. I am far more comfortable with this concept than the concept of "punishment." However, making the cost of subsequent betrayal high remains an incentive to prevent future betrayal. There is a mathematical basis for this idea of the high cost of subsequent betrayal. Hauert applied it to the evolutionary organization of human societies. He showed that in a world of loners, cooperation can evolve and provide an evolutionary advantage, but in order to deal with the rise of "free riders," those who enjoy the fruits of cooperation without contributing, a new type of citizen, the punisher, is needed (see Nicholas Christakis and James Fowler's book *Connected*, p. 220).

4. The couple creates personal sex and intimate trust. This process begins with knowledge about each other's personal preferences in sex, love, and romance as part of building emotional connection and knowledge of each other. This may require reversing processes of impersonal sex (i.e., pornography). For many couples, reestablishing intimacy and personal sex may be the phase of building trust and loyalty.

This entire process is by no means simple. In fact, I have often thought that if people could see these steps involved in healing from betrayal, they might decide not to start the betrayal cascade at all. The fact that they do suggests that the betrayal process is not entirely rational. Information alone does not help. As Robin Williams once joked, "God gave men a penis and a brain, but only enough blood to run one at a time." That may be as true for the clitoris as it is for the penis.

The process of healing from betrayal is highly emotional, it is fragile and tender, it involves a great deal of pain and courage, and it requires building enormous commitment on the part of both partners. I am not claiming that this is all that it takes to heal from betrayal, but this process attempts to change and get at the root causes of the betrayal.

There may be an initial period of ambivalence before an affair partner is discarded, or before the hurt partner agrees to try to rebuild trust again. It may help the ambivalent partner to know that only an estimated 11% of affairs lead to an actual relationship between the betrayer and the affair partners.[19] Also, anger and hurt cannot have deteriorated into *bitterness*, which has an inconsolable quality. There needs to be an adequate amount of love and rededication in the couple. In addition, there needs to be an understanding of the betrayal itself and a healing and rewriting of the relationship's contract. Methods for reassurance need to be created, as well as mechanisms for checking the strength of cooperation. In contrast, cooperation will eventually stop if there is a series of subsequent mistakes or smaller betrayals.

Once the forces leading to betrayal are understood and reversed in the relationship, trust must be rebuilt by: (1) replacing conflict avoidance by constructive conflict management, (2) creating trust through attunement, and (3) building intimate trust through personal sex.

The Vaughan Study

Peggy Vaughan conducted a landmark survey of over 1,000 people whose spouses had affairs.[20] Her study shows how confidential communication from people on the Internet can be used to advance science in areas that are very hard to study. The survey shows that people who have healed from affairs and preserved their relationship did so by talking about the affair and following principles very much like the ones I have outlined. I was privileged to be able to help Peggy design her survey.

The result is an important book called *Help for Therapists (and their Clients) in dealing with affairs*. It is available for free and can be downloaded from Vaughan's website at www.dearpeggy.com/shop/bookstore. php. There is very specific advice in the responses to this survey and very good information about affairs and how people have successfully worked through them. I love this book.

A case history for working with a couple after an affair is presented in detail in my wife Dr. Julie Schwartz Gottman's chapter in the book she edited titled *The Marriage Clinic: A Casebook*.[21]

Pornography Addiction and Sexual Addiction

There has been a lot of writing recently in the media about pornography and sexual addiction. The technical use of the term "addiction" requires the twin criteria of *tolerance* and *withdrawal*. Hence, the use of pornography or high sexual activity need not be an addiction. Yet it is clear that the use of pornography is increasing. Rather than pornography being used as erotic stimulation for a couple's sex life, in a significant number of cases, the use of pornography at times can become a source of betrayal in a couple's relationship.

The Internet has stimulated this rise in porn use. There are more than 400 million pages of porn on the Internet. Pornography is an industry that generates more than 97 billion dollars a year worldwide, with a 70% increase in sales from 2003 to 2007. Porn has also changed its form and escalated over time, continually pushing the limits of what is depicted with increasing degradation and violence toward women. Also, moving from mere pictures or videos, the porn industry has added voyeuristic sites, chat rooms, phone sex, and opportunities to actually hook up with professional sex workers or amateurs in one's neighborhood. The users of pornography naively expect that their Internet use is anonymous, but nothing could be further from the truth. Porn users leave a potentially public electronic paper trail as indelible as a personal diary, open for all to view.

And what do they typically see? Social psychologist Dolf Zillman's book *Pornography* concludes that pornographic scripts involve people who have just met, are in no way attached or committed to each other, and who will part shortly, never to meet again.[22] Pornography is all about impersonal, unromantic, unemotional, casual sex. Pornography literally sexually objectifies people.

Furthermore, even if the habitual and compulsive use of pornography does not become an addiction, it can affect the inner life of the user and can have serious consequences for an ongoing relationship. Often a porn user expects sex in the bedroom to become more like the porn that is watched—namely, impersonal and ritualistic. The porn user expects the partner to act out fetishistic fantasies that the user has habitually orgasmed to during pornographic viewing. Furthermore, most of the fantasies depicted in pornography involve the degradation and humiliation of women, or the control of women purely to satisfy men, or the use of power and control over women, including violence and assault.[23] This can have traumatic consequences for the compliant partner, or it may alienate the noncompliant and often disgusted partner or lead to increased levels of interpersonal conflict in the relationship.

Even if it doesn't have traumatic consequences, porn use may lead to a gradual decline in real sex with the partner or sex with real people in general. Dr. Jennifer Schneider, an expert on sexual addiction, reported that among 70% of couples in which there was a cybersex addiction, one or both partners lost interest in relational sex.[24]

Habitual pornography use promotes unfavorable CL-ALT comparisons and supports denigrating rather than cherishing the partner. Furthermore, because all orgasms result in the secretion of oxytocin, orgasms during pornographic activity lead to bonding with images that are not of the partner, images that are often detached and idealized female or male images. Two thirds of the American Academy of Matrimonial Lawyers reported that compulsive pornography use had played a significant role in well over 50% of the divorce cases. Studies show that men are twice as likely as women to report feeling attracted to visual erotica. Thus, not surprisingly, most regular porn users are male (75 to 85%), and youth under the age of 18 have become one of the largest groups of regular porn users.[25]

The "Porn Trap"

In their book *The Porn Trap*, Wendy and Larry Maltz wrote that porn delivers an instant sexual turn on, a "get right to it" genital stimulation with a multitude of surprising images available with just the repeated clicking of a mouse (without all the time-consuming preliminaries like conversation or touching).[26] They claimed that these activities induce a drug-like euphoria that involves "feel good" chemicals and neurochemical cascades such as adrenaline, endorphins, dopamine, and serotonin. They claimed that these chemicals associated with arousal lead to cravings and preoccupation with the pornographic images, and deprivation when they are missing. The excitement produced is like that of playing a slot machine in a casino in which the player keeps winning. The player is involved in the hunt for the ideal erotic partner, the ideal image. Some images are highly disappointing but some are very exciting and surprising, so the hunt continues, resulting in the porn user being on a variable ratio schedule of reinforcement, which is highly resistant to extinction.

Porn use usually also involves dishonesty and deception. Rather than facilitating eroticism in the relationship, it winds up creating an object that competes with the intimate partner in erotic value. The Maltzes wrote that porn is the hunt "for someone unreal who can meet every sexual desire whenever and wherever—without asking for anything in return" (p. 43). Another male writer suggested that "for many people porn is a substitute for an intimate relationship, shutting off feelings of needing closeness and emotional intimacy."[27] Pornography use avoids the possible rejection that may happen in a real encounter with a potential partner in more typical courtship settings such as singles' bars. Pornography use does not quench feelings of loneliness and the need for real social connection; in fact, its use may make these encounter less successful because it does not build the skills of real interaction with a real person. Hence, porn use by unpaired people may lead them to greater social isolation. Porn may therefore increase the incidence of unfavorable CL-ALTs with one's real partner.

The escalation of erotic fantasy that is characteristic of the programming of some porn websites may lead the porn user to risky and dangerous behavior. For example, it is estimated that 20 to 25% of Internet porn sites contain child pornography. Such behaviors may include unprotected sex, illegal behavior such as public exposure of the user's genitals, or aggressive predatory behavior such as molestation or rape.

For the individual, the Maltzes suggest four steps for dealing with a pornography addiction: (1) Acknowledge how porn use causes you problems, (2) identify what matters most to you, (3) face your fears, and (4) take responsibility for your own recovery. They also suggest six basic action steps: (1) Tell someone else about your porn problem, (2) get involved in a treatment program, (3) create a porn-free environment, (4) establish 24-hour support and accountability, (5) take care of your physical and emotional health, and (6) start healing your sexuality. For couples, the Maltzes suggest two steps, the first being forgiveness and the second being the building of what I have called personal sex.

Out of the Shadows

Patrick Carnes's book[28] *Out of the Shadows* is probably the most influential work on understanding and treating sexual addiction. Carnes treated the golfer Tiger Woods. He focuses on the sexual addict's belief system, which he characterizes as having impaired thinking. Impaired thinking involves *rationalization* and *denial*. Sincere delusion involves believing one's own lies. In Carnes's view, the sexual-addiction cycle involves: (1) Preoccupation—addicts become hostages to their own preoccupation; every encounter and thought passes through the sexually obsessive filter. (2) Ritualization—the creation of routines that foster the addiction. (3) Compulsive sexual behavior—involvement with the final sexual act, and an inability to stop or control this behavior. (4) Despair—feeling powerless and hopeless to be able to change. Sexual obsession is part of all parts of the cycle.

Carnes delineates three levels of addiction. Level 1 contains normal use of pornography, masturbation, and the use of prostitutes. Level 1 can also involve: masturbation that, for the addict, becomes a degrading compulsive event; compulsive relationships; multiple relationships that end before becoming truly emotionally intimate; cruising for sex; hustling in bars, streets, and parties in a search for sexual excitement; the use of porn, strip shows; and anonymous casual sex. Level 1 addicts rationalize that they are not very different from most people. Level 2 extends to behaviors that are victimizing to others and for which legal sanctions are enforced, such as voyeurism and exhibitionism. Exhibitionists often expose themselves when driving and report car accidents because they are totally entranced by their victim. The voyeur may go to strip clubs or subscribe to minicam websites where cameras are installed where young women live and the voyeur maybe sexually underdeveloped and has eroticized a part of courtship that excludes intimacy. In combination, these last two factors may lead to indecent calls and taking liberties, such as touching others with their knowledge but without their consent. Level 3 addiction has grave consequences for the victims and grave legal consequences for the addicts (examples are incest, molestation, child molestation, violence, or rape). However, as Carnes wrote, "suggesting levels does not mean that addicts cannot destroy their lives with Level 1 behavior" (p. 37).

Carnes suggested that the sexual addict finally settles on a specific "arousal template." That template becomes the object of the addict's obsessions and compulsions. Carnes identifies a treatment program.

He believes that the sexual addiction has replaced all meaningful relationship in the addict's life. The secret life has become more important than everything the addict once valued—family, friends, work, ethics, religion, community. The addict's belief system needs to change—the impaired thinking, compulsive behavior, and unmanageability. I am not advocating this program, but it may be of interest to know that Carnes uses a 12-step model for recovery from sexual addiction. He argues that a set of core beliefs need to be replaced: (1) I am basically a bad, unworthy person, (2) no one would love me as I am, (3) my needs are never going to be met of I am to depend on others, and (4) sex is my most important need. Four attitudes are changed in Carnes's therapy, which spell the acronym SAFE. The S stands for the sexual addiction being *secret*. The A stands for the sexual addiction being *abusive*. The F stands for the sexual addiction being a way to avoid painful *feelings* and shift one's mood away from the pain. The E stands for the sexual addiction being *empty* of a committed relationship.

Chapter 11

The Mathematics of Relationships: Power Imbalance, Trust, and Betrayal

Can trust exist when there is an asymmetry in power in a relationship? Or is asymmetry in power a sufficient setting condition for distrust and betrayal? We are living through a nearly worldwide revolution in women's rights and economic, social, and political power. What are the implications of relationships that fail to create a fair balance of power? When is that imbalance catastrophic? How should power be conceptualized and measured? This chapter tackles these problems using a field of math invented by Henri Poincaré in the 19th century called "nonlinear dynamics" and recently called "chaos theory." The chapter is written for the non-mathematician, and it is designed to illustrate the usefulness of mathematical thinking about systems of social relationships and processes of self- and partner influence.

Many scholars who write about trust have contended that trust cannot develop in a relationship of power asymmetry. For example, Hardin wrote: "There are inherent problems in trusting another who has great power over one's prospects . . . moreover, in the context of great differences in personal power, distrust is malignant" (p. 101).[1] Hardin also wrote: "Large power differences undercut motivations of trustworthiness to act on behalf of another" (p. 152). Is this conclusion generally true? How are we to precisely define and measure "differences in personal power"?

There have been many approaches to the conceptualization and measurement of "power" in relationships and social interaction. Calfred Broderick's classic book *Understanding Family Process* summarized research on power in families as follows:

> Literally hundreds of studies have been done on family power, who wields it and at whose expense. The matter has turned out to be complicated and elusive. As a result, the scholarly literature on family power is voluminous, complex, and often contradictory. . . . The great majority if these studies are based on questionnaires that ask the respondent to report on who wins the most contested decisions in his or her family. (p. 164)[2]

These questionnaire methods are subject to many criticisms. Particularly important for this book is the problem that people's reports of their own actual behavior, particularly in such a sensitive area as power, may not be reliable indices of actual power.

In research based on *observing* family power, Broderick noted that the assumption of stable patterns of power and domination in families may be faulty. "An enormous body of research based on this premise has failed to yield a coherent body of results. This systematic failure suggests a systematic flaw in the logic of the approach adopted by most investigators" (p. 165). For example, in observing families in naturalistic settings, psychologist Sam Vuchinich studied families during dinner with a recorder.[3] He identified 200 examples of conflict and found that two thirds of them resulted in standoffs in which neither child nor parent yielded to the other's opinion. Of the remaining third, the most frequent response was withdrawal. The least common responses were submission and compromise.

Examining studies of men and women in interaction, Elizabeth Aries's book *Men and Women in Interaction* concluded that "although research shows that men are more likely than women to emerge as leaders in initially leaderless groups, it also shows that gender is not a good predictor of dominance and leadership when groups meet for extended periods of time, when participants know each other well, and when the tasks draw on skills and expertise more commonly acquired by women" (p. 75).[4] The lack of gender differences in talk time and leadership was particularly true of married partners.[5]

In our analysis of power we wished to be able to describe power *within one interaction*. We also wanted to determine whether power varied with affect.

The Mathematics of Power (for the non-mathematician)

My own thinking differs from prior conceptualizations about power in two ways: (1) as with trust, trustworthiness, and betrayal, we are measuring the concept of power *within one interaction*; and (2) we are examining power as potentially differing as a function of the amount of positive or negative emotion within that interaction. Power thus becomes each partner's power as a continuous function of the amount of positive or negative affect. Asymmetries in power are easily measured by subtracting one person's power function from their partner's power function.

First I need to say, "Don't freak out." It's important for you to not panic because I will be using the word "mathematics" to precisely describe power in relationships.

I have been building a mathematical model of relationships with mathematical biologist James Murray for the past 15 years. But so far I have been afraid to talk to clinicians and other professionals about it, partly because so many people in the social sciences seem to have a math phobia.

As I mentioned earlier in this book, part of my "coming out" as a mathematician was made possible by the television show *Numb3rs*, in which two brothers team up to solve crimes. One brother is an FBI agent and the other is a math professor. The great thing about the show is that all the math is right—almost none of it is made up. So the show emboldened me to talk to you about how James Murray and I applied math to the study of couples. In our 2002 book *The Mathematics of Marriage*, we actually applied math to the study of both gay and lesbian relationships as well as heterosexual married couples.[6] So the approach is quite general.

Why We Need the Math to Understand "Power Imbalances" in Relationships

We need the math so that we can define "power" in relationships precisely. Without the precision that mathematics provides, we would never have been able to discover why male dominance is detrimental to trust and love in close relationships.

Results on Male Dominance

One of the major motivations for creating the math model was a desire to take a precise look at the implications of asymmetry in power between partners in any couple relationships. As you will see, we have two equations, one for one partner (for example, the husband) and another for the other partner (for example, the wife). These two equations also hold for the gay and lesbian couples we studied. The desire to give a precise definition to power was the motivation for interlocking the two equations. So I want to tell you the story of what happened once we used the precise math model. What did we find to be the correlates of an imbalance in power?

We computed two numbers: the husband having more power than wife with positive affect, and the husband having more power than the wife with negative affect (we did the same kind of computation for gay and lesbian couples). Therefore, in heterosexual couples we are examining the correlates of male dominance in power over his wife across the domain of affect. In same-sex relationship we are examining power asymmetry between partners. I will define the terms used in this chapter.

Here is a sampler of our findings on power, just to keep your interest in this chapter. Think of it as an advertisement for reading about the math. *When he had more power than she did with negative affect, there was:*

- Significantly more gender stereotypy in the marriage (measured with our Buehlman Oral History Coding).
- She had significantly more emotional inertia.
- He was significantly less effective at repair.
- She was less positive when there was a negative stable influenced steady state.
- But she was significantly more effective at repair.
- Therefore, aside from her increased effectiveness at repair, overall

his greater power with negative affect seems to be a highly negative thing for one sample of couples.

When he had more power than she did with positive affect, there were:

- Significantly more influenced negative-negative steady states.
- He was significantly more effective at damping down positive affect.
- He had significantly more emotional inertia.
- He had a significantly less positive influenced steady state.
- His maximum score was significantly less positive, and she was significantly less effective at damping down positive affect.
- Hence, overall it appears that his greater power with positive affect also seems to be a highly negative thing for this sample of couples.

Just from that sample of results, which I don't expect you to understand at this point in the chapter, you can see that there were quite a few findings about power asymmetry using our mathematics.

My only point with this advertisement is that we need the mathematics to understand how power and affect work in relationships to build trust and to avoid betrayal.

A Bit of History

Starting in the 1960s, an area called "general systems theory" was a revolution in our understanding of how to help couples and families. It was the first focus on *interaction* in a complete *system* of people rather than just an examination of surveys, or personality variables in one person, or individual psychopathology to study individuals or families. Let's now take a brief look at the history of general systems theory in studying families to see that the roots for doing this math go back to over 50 years ago.

The General Systems Theory of von Bertalanffy

General systems thinking led therapists to see more than one person at a time in treatment for the first time. Amazingly, this was initially considered unethical because it was seen as a violation of confidentiality.

Therapists were actually afraid of losing their licenses and saw couples secretly at first. General systems thinking also created a revolution against a passive therapist. The passive therapist was standard in the early years of psychoanalytic treatment (that has now changed).

With general systems theory, therapists suddenly became active. They also began seeing whole interacting system (like a whole family) right in front of them. They no longer had to rely on one person's account of his or her life's events. They could immediately hear from the other side. They could also see interactive events unfold right in front of their eyes.

Everything in systems therapy became about action, and that action often changed right in front of the therapist's eyes in one therapy session. The changes this wrought on therapy were very dramatic. The therapists' personalities also emerged. They became more of an open book. All this happened in the 1950s and 1960s. I recall that being a very exciting time to become a family therapist.

The changes general systems theory brought to psychotherapy were practical as well as conceptual. Mathematics was initially part of this revolution in therapy, although it remained a silent part. The application of mathematics to the study of relationships was actually kicked off during this revolution by von Bertalanffy, the father of general systems theory himself.[7]

Von Bertalanffy's book *General System Theory* was an attempt to view biological and other complex organizational units across a wide variety of sciences in terms of the interaction of these units. The work was an attempt to provide a holistic approach to complex systems. This revolutionary work fit a general zeitgeist of the 1960s, which was all about change—social change, social justice, civil rights, economic inequality, ending poverty, community organizing, and political change. Von Bertalanffy's work also fit conceptually with Norbert Wiener's work on cybernetics,[8] which introduced the idea of feedback and control in systems. It also fit with the work of Shannon and Weaver, who introduced the idea that messages contain "information," which could actually be quantified;[9] with von Neumann and Morgenstern's game theory, and with concepts of "homeostasis," derived from the physiologist Walter Cannon.[10] "Feedback" and "information" in messages provided the basis for this new approach to the study of complex interacting systems. So there was a confluence of "systems thinking" during this period, and a lot of the ideas came directly from mathematicians.

In psychology and in therapy, von Bertalanffy's book started it all. It influenced famous thinkers like Gregory Bateson,[11] Don Jackson,[12] Paul Watzlawick,[13] Virginia Satir,[14] Salvador Minuchin,[15] and others to start talking about families as "systems." Therefore, a whole new approach to therapy with interacting family systems was spawned by these ideas. I was in graduate school at the University of Wisconsin at the time and I found these writings very exciting.

But let's get to the silent math behind this revolution. The mathematics von Bertalanffy put into his book on general system theory was unfortunately lost on most of the people in the social sciences who were otherwise inspired by his work. So my lab's applying math is, therefore, just a return to von Bertalanffy's original thinking, and my hope is that by the end of this chapter you will not only *not* be freaked out by the math, but also will find the ideas in the math really useful. No kidding. Bear with me.

Von Bertalanffy had a dream. His dream was that the interaction of complex systems with many "units" could be characterized by a set of values that changed over time. He used the symbols Q_1, Q_2, Q_3, and so on, to describe the components of these "systems." Think of each "Q variable" as an index of a particular aspect or unit in the system. For example, Q_1 could be the mother's behavior, Q_2 could be the father's behavior, and Q_3 could be the behavior of one of the children. A former graduate student of mine, Alyson Shapiro, actually studied mother-father-baby interaction using two cameras in a paradigm called the "Lausanne Triadic Play,"[16] in which mom, dad, and baby play together as a triad and all the dyadic configurations. Alyson actually coded all three people as they played with one another.[17] So the Qs became very real in Alyson's thesis.

Or maybe the Qs could even be variables that measure some relevant characteristics of how *one* person changed over time. For instance, Q_1 could be the number of a husband's angry facial expressions per unit time, and Q_2 could be the number of times he interrupted his wife. The math doesn't care where the Qs come from.

It's important to think of the Qs as varying over time, like the Dow Jones Industrial Average. Actually, initially the Qs were supposed to be *quantitative* variables like the Dow Jones, but in his book the Qs were variables that von Bertalanffy never specified. But I'm sure that he imagined that somebody, someday, would specify what these variables were. And so I am going to do just that.

Von Bertalanffy thought that the system could be best described by a set of equations called "ordinary differential equations." (Again, please don't freak out! Keep reading.) A "differential equation" just expresses *how* something changes over time. That's all it is. The left-hand side of the equation (to the left of the equal sign), is the *rate of change* in some variable that changes over time. Mathematicians call it a "derivative." Here's how mathematicians would write this all down:

Equation #1. Rate of Change in Q_1 (like the dad) over time = some function of all the Qs (call it f_1)
Equation #2. Rate of Change in Q_2 (like the mom) over time = some other function of all the Qs (call it f_2)
Equation #3. Rate of Change in Q_3 (like the baby) over time = some other function of all the Qs (call it f_3). And so on for every Q_4, Q_5, et cetera.

The terms on the left of the equal signs are time "derivatives"—that is, the rates of change of the quantitative sets of values Q_1, Q_2, Q_3, and so on.

The left-hand side of the equations, the derivative, is the basis for *a language of change* that mathematicians call "calculus." Isaac Newton and Gottfried Wilhelm Leibnitz invented calculus in the 17th Century and it was used to create the new quantitative science of physics that Isaac Newton single-handedly invented.[18] Calculus rocketed science forward because the language of math made things like gravity precise and tractable.

The terms on the *right-hand side* of the equal sign are the "functions" (f_1, f_2, etc.). They depend on all the Qs. A "function" is just a real number that gets assigned to every combination of the numbers the Qs take on. These "functions" can be plotted in a graph. von Bertalanffy thought that these functions, the fs, would generally be nonlinear (not a straight line). But von Bertalanffy was terrified of nonlinear functions and he even presented a table in which these nonlinear equations were classified by him as "impossible." He secretly liked the linear form of **f** better. He was referring to the very popular mathematical method of approximating nonlinear functions with a linear approximation, which a lot of mathematicians use to this day.

However, although he was a very smart person, von Bertalanffy was basically wrong about the equations. It is not the case that these nonlinear systems are "impossible" at all; von Bertalanffy was just unaware of the extensive mathematical work that begin in the latter part of the 19th century. This was work that the very famous French mathematician Henri Poincaré did on nonlinear differential equations, chaos, and fractal theory—work that was only to become known to the general public in the 1980s with the publication of Gleick's book *Chaos*.[19]

In fact, in science in the past 30 years, the modeling of complex systems with a set of nonlinear difference or differential equations has become a very productive enterprise across a wide set of fields and phenomena, and across a wide range of sciences, including the biological sciences. It has given birth to a whole new field of applied mathematics called "mathematical biology."

My friend James Murray (who helped develop our math model for relationships) was in some ways the father of that field of mathematical biology. Nowadays, every applied math department in the world has a group of mathematical biologists, so Murray has been a very influen-tial man.

Murray is a very open-minded guy, full of humor and charm. He is probably the only one in the world who would have agreed to try to create math models for couple relationships. It was my great luck that he was a professor of applied mathematics at the University of Washington, where I was also teaching in the psychology department. I just happened to receive his book *Mathematical Biology*[20] from a book club I belonged to at the time. I was trying to learn about nonlinear math in order to apply it to my own data, but I couldn't figure out how to do it on my own. I must have bought 50 math books on the topic, but it wasn't until I read Murray's book that I understood how that might be accomplished.

I loved Murray's book, and it listed him as a professor at Oxford, so I sent him a letter, which was forwarded to the University of Washington in Seattle, and one day James called me up. All I had to do was walk down to the Faculty Club and meet the best person in the world to help me build a mathematical model to explain the results Bob Levenson and I were getting.

What evolved into the "couples' math project" became the talk of Murray's applied math department because professors and students alike could simply not believe that anyone would be stupid enough to try to create a math model for anything as flimsy and vague as marriage. But as they were laughing at us, they were also intrigued. And they were really happy that their initial reaction was wrong. After 4 years we finally succeeded in creating a math model for marriage and also for gay and lesbian relationships that has been widely published and publicized in the media.

That work is summarized in our 2002 book *The Mathematics of Marriage*. The math of marriage model is also now a chapter in Murray's second edition of his book *Mathematical Biology*. We are still working on improving this math model. Once we got math I started understanding how important von Bertalanffy's ideas really were in building theory on the "dynamics" of couples' interaction over time.

What "Dynamics" Really Means

We were really applying a relatively old approach in math to the new problem of modeling social interaction. We wound up using the mathematics of nonlinear difference and differential equations. These equations expressed, in mathematical form, a proposed *mechanism* of change over time as a couple interacts. That's a new idea in using math in psychology, because in the social sciences we usually use statistics at the *end* of our research projects to analyze the data. We rarely use math to *conceptualize* mechanisms at the beginning of the research project.

The equations we developed therefore do not represent the usual statistical approach to modeling that we are familiar with in psychology and the other social sciences.

We needed two equations, one for each partner. As we started studying babies and their playful interactions with both parents, we had three equations, one for each person. The equations are designed to suggest a *precise mechanism* of how interaction changes over time, or unfolds. As I've mentioned, this method has been employed with great success in the physical and the biological sciences.

A Four-Year Glitch

It is important to realize that this is a quantitative approach that requires the modeler to be able to write down, in mathematical form, *on the basis of some theory,* the causes of change in the dependent variables. So, of course when Murray and his students first sat down with me, they asked me what the theory was in this field. They wanted to get right to the business of writing down those functions, the **f**s. I told them that I didn't have a clue. My field didn't have a theory.

Yikes! It seemed at that point that our project was dead in the water. The math group needed—demanded—some way to write down what the **f**s were supposed to be. They turned to *me* for those answers and my jaw dropped very stupidly.

Let me give you an example of what they were looking for. In the classic biology problem of a predator pursuing a prey, mathematicians write down the equation that the rate of change in the population is some function of the current population. The equations are designed to write down the precise form of how the rate of change in the population changes over time. They call it the "logistic" function, and it makes good theoretical sense in terms of the predator-prey biology. Biologists know from observation that as the predators eat the prey, they become well-fed and contented animals, and so the predators reproduce and multiply until there eventually are too many of these predators, and they wind up eating too many prey, so the prey population diminishes too much. Then some of the predators start starving, and dying out, which then gives the prey population a breather and helps it increase its population because there are fewer predators to worry about. Then, because food is again abundant, the predator population increases again. Hence, there is a rising and falling of predator population and prey populations, kind of like waves that interlace. It's a multiple-cylic system. There is an inherent stability in the predator-prey system.[21] The populations change over time, but the whole *process* is regulated, or else everyone would die out. If the process is unregulated and the predators eat too many prey, the prey won't reproduce fast enough to sustain the predators, so every population in the system eventually dies out. That rarely happens in nature.

Nature was regulated until we homo sapiens arrived on the planet a few hundred thousand years ago. So biologists have learned to write the predator-prey equation using an **f** called the "logistic function."

Great ideas came from this predator-prey modeling. Here's one of them, called the "carrying capacity" of the ecology.[22] I loved that idea because I thought every couple probably also has a "carrying capacity" for negative affect. Some couples can withstand more than others; the ones who can't take much negative affect tend to be conflict avoiders. Also, perhaps when some couples exceed their carrying capacity for negativity, they become abusive, or even violent. That idea works well for what we now call "situational" domestic violence, where arguments have gone out of control and there is no clear perpetrator or victim in the violent actions; they are more symmetrical and they don't deny responsibility for the physical aggression.

I could see from these examples of mathematical biology that applied math might allow us to come up with some interesting ideas that could help me understand relationships.

As I mentioned, the ideal mathematical technique for describing change is the differential equation, because these are the equations of change over time. In the past these equations usually used linear terms or linear approximations of nonlinear terms, and they often gave good results. In fact, most of the statistics psychology uses are based on linear models. In the area of differential equations, linear equations simply assume that rates of change follow generalized straight-line functions of the variables rather than curved-line functions.

Unfortunately, I learned that linear models are generally unstable, so they would be useless for describing complex systems like families, where we think things are highly stable most of the time and there may be some homeostatic mechanism that regulates the family system. But these family systems also can be unstable when there is some catastrophe like a betrayal, or violence, or divorce, when trust is suddenly shattered.

As I sat in on Murray's math course, I learned that in recent years it had become clear that most living systems are complex and must be described by *nonlinear* terms. What was amazing to everyone was that by employing nonlinear terms in the equations, some very complex processes could be represented with very few parameters. That's the upside of the story. Scientists like models that use very few parameters because they are easier to understand and easier to estimate. Scientists that use the flattering term "parsimonious" to refer to systems that have few parameters and can describe a complex process. Sometimes they even use words like "elegant" and "beautiful" to describe systems that describe complex systems with very few parameters.

A great example in physics was James Clerk Maxwell's revolutionary set of equations in the 19th century that represented electricity, magnetism, and all electromagnetic energy, even light, with only four short, very lovely equations.[23] Yes, mathematicians think that some equations are beautiful, the way some people admire the "Mona Lisa." These beautiful Maxwell equations unified what until then had been seen as very disparate fields of electricity, magnetism, and light. Albert Einstein couldn't have developed his theory of relativity without these equations.[24] When he was a young man they weren't even teaching Maxwell's equations in his graduate school. They were too new. Einstein had to learn them on his own. And they had this "funny" constant representing the speed of light. That got Einstein thinking they weren't consistent with Newton's equations, and he was right about that inconsistency.

The downside about nonlinearity is that, unlike many linear equations, nonlinear equations are generally not solvable in closed functional mathematical form. That frustrates many mathematicians because they don't feel that the equation is solved if they have to estimate the parameters numerically or graphically. For this reason the methods used to understand nonlinear equations have been also called "qualitative," as visual methods and graphics are often relied on.

Yet for this reason numerical and graphical methods, such as "phase space plots," have been developed. In phase space each partner would have one axis; for example, the husband might have the horizontal x-axis, and the wife might have the vertical y-axis. All their interaction data would then be plotted in this two-dimensional "phase space." If we also had data over time of a baby's interaction with the parents, we would have a third axis in "phase space" just for the baby. These very visual approaches to nonlinear mathematical modeling can be very appealing because they can engage the intuition of a scientist or a clinician working in a field that really has no mathematically stated theory.

If the scientist has an intuitive familiarity with the data of the field, the nonlinear graphical approach can suggest a way of *building* theory using mathematics in an initially qualitative manner.

This may seem very abstract, but let me make it concrete. I'm working with a psychotherapy researcher named Paul Peluso. Paul is using the equations of the math model to study psychotherapy of one therapist with one client.[25] He and his group are using a program called MAT-LAB.[26] They are creating their own equations, in which the *shape* of the mutual influences between client and therapist are very different from the ones Murray and I tested with couples. Paul has developed a program in which they can vary the influence functions to see which functions would be a best fit to a particular therapist-client pair. Paul and his group are trying to make the therapist-client relationship very concrete, measurable, and mathematical, which would be a first for the field of psychotherapy.

Back to the world of couples, and my glitch. I had to come up with the **f**s. Ignorance was certainly the state of things when James Murray and I started doing this modeling. There was no theory, so we needed to use the math to build a mathematically tractable theory. Thankfully, the use of these graphical solutions to nonlinear differential equations makes it possible to talk about "qualitative" mathematical modeling. In qualitative mathematical modeling, we search for solutions that have similarly shaped phase space plots. So the Murray group needed to teach me their methods so that I could start to use the graphical approach and give them a reasonable starting point for the **f**s. Once I saw that graphical approach and understood what they needed, I started getting ideas for the **f**s.

It took us 4 years, meeting once a week, to get to that point. I will now describe these methods of the Murray group's mathematical modeling in detail. I realized that, in just about all the research in couples' interaction, negative affect was a better predictor of relationships than positive affect. So that "triumph" of negative affect over positive affect could be a starting point for writing down the **f**s. We called it the "bilinear model," because we would get two straight lines for the influence functions—one line for negative affect, which would have a steeper slope (greater influence), and one line for positive affect, which would have a less steep slope. That's not much theory, but it was enough to get started. We could now write down the **f**s.

Steady States

Once we were able to write down the theoretical equations of a couple's interaction, the first mathematical question we could then ask became: "What values is the system drawn toward?" We couldn't answer that question without the math. To answer the question, mathematicians define what they call a "steady state." That's a state for which the derivatives (the rates of change on the left side of the von Bertalanffy equations) are zero. This means that we are looking for lines in husband-wife phase space where the system is *at a steady state and does not change*. Once we have the **f**s, we can solve the equations for these no-change curves in two-dimensional phase space (or no-change surfaces in three-dimensional phase space).

Mathematicians call these curves the "null clines" of the equations. They are the lines where each **f** in the equations stays constant and unchanging—that is, where the derivatives are zero. We get one null-cline line for each partner. The amazing thing is that in phase space, the points where these two null-cline lines intersect are called the "steady states" of the equations. They are called "steady" states because they are the points of intersection where neither partner changes.

The Stability of Steady States

Steady states can be either stable or unstable. What does "stability" mean for a couple system? Mathematicians have a precise answer. In general systems theory it was a vague notion called "homeostasis," taken from Walter Cannon's physiology. For example, 98.6°F is normal temperature in the human body, so it's a homeostatic stable point. The body, in some sense, defends that state, and regulates physiology so that temperature is maintained.

In the math this somewhat vague notion is given a very precise meaning. It means that if you perturb the system slightly from a steady state, it will return to that steady state. It is as if the steady state is an *attractor* that pulls the system back to the steady state. This is like a rubber band snapping back once pulled and released, or a magnetic field operating on iron.

If the steady state is *unstable*, on the other hand, it will move away from that steady state if you perturb the system slightly.

One way to think of stable and unstable steady states is to imagine a ball at rest at the bottom of a U-shaped hill (a stable steady state) and a ball at rest at the top of an inverted U-shaped hill (an unstable steady state). A slight perturbation of the ball at the bottom of the U-shaped hill will cause the ball to roll around for a while, but it will eventually come to rest again at the bottom of the U. That's a stable steady state. However, a slight perturbation of the ball at the top of the inverted U-shaped hill will cause it to keep rolling down the hill. It was only temporarily or unstably at rest, with a lot of potential energy for action and movement away from its unstable resting place. Once perturbed it does not return to the steady state. It is as if it is repelling stability, like similar poles of a magnet repel each other.

An example of steady states comes from research on body weight. In that field steady states are called "set points." It has been noted that the body defends a particular weight as a set point, adjusting metabolism to maintain the body's weight in homeostatic fashion. It is also interesting that the existence of a stable state (homeostasis) does not, by itself, imply that the system is regulated in a *functional* manner. For example, in 2010 a man who weighed 1,000 pounds died in his early thirties. The unfortunate man had to be lifted out of his apartment with a crane. Clearly this 1,000 pound set point was dysfunctional for this man's health, despite the fact that his body defended this set point. In a family, the existence of homeostasis *does* imply that system is regulated; it *doesn't* imply that the set point is healthy. The early general systems theorists were well aware of this idea. Just because a system is regulated doesn't mean it's functional. In our modeling of couples, we defined two possible set points for any couple, a positive set point and a negative set point.

The Model We Created

The next step in math modeling was to describe the behavior of the model near each steady state, and the behavior of the model as the parameters of the model varied. We want to know what the model tells us *qualitatively* about how the system is supposed to act near a steady state. Then, if the model isn't acting the way we think it ought to (given the phenomena we are trying to model), we would alter the model by changing the theoretical function "**f**."

This process gives us a method for empirically building theory over time. We begin by identifying the phenomenon or phenomena we wish to model. This is given to us by our insights and intuitions about the science. Then we write the equations for building the model. The model is a theory, or a simplified representation of the system that generated the data. As I have noted, this is a difficult task, one that requires some knowledge about what we are trying to model, as well as of the mathematics. Then we find the steady states of the model—those points where the derivatives (rates of change) are zero. Then we determine if these steady states are stable or unstable. Then we study the qualitative behavior of the model near the steady states. Then we study how the model behaves as we vary the parameters of the model. Finally, we return to the science. We ask whether this model is doing the job we want, and, if not, we modify the model. So the math gives us a way to build theory and to keep making that theory better and better.

The Equations

First, what's our data for the modeling? As explained earlier, in modeling couples' interaction we write down two equations, one for the husband and one for the wife. We start with defining what our data are. We needed to measure what we thought was important in creating the Qs of von Bertalanffy. So, what are our dependent variables? They were already worked out before I met with the Murray group. When Robert Levenson and I started our research we actually had three kinds of dependent variables, three candidates for the Qs. One candidate was our dependent variable of the positive minus negative points at each turn of speech.

In our early work we used a coding system called "RCISS."[27] A second kind of variable was the video-recall rating dial for each partner. A third kind of variable was the physiology. We measured heart rate, blood velocity to the ear and the finger of the person's nondominant hand, skin conductance at the hand (a measure of sweating of the psychologically sensitive eccrine glands—used in lie detection), and gross motor movement on our "jiggle-ometer." All these time series were synchronized to the video time code. The data we collected are illustrated in Figure 11.1.

In this chapter I will stick to the behavioral time series, which we created through a weighting of our observational data. We then assigned point values to the codes of the SPAFF coding system based on their ability to predict divorce, with greater weights for the better predictors. Then we cumulated the weighted data over each 6-second time block, giving us 150 data points for every 15-minute interaction (900 seconds).

In our *Math of Marriage* book we actually modeled all three sources of data and examined their interrelationships. But here I will primarily examine the behavioral time series that come from coding the videotapes.

At this stage we're still talking about the data. Sometimes we cumulated the behavioral data so we could quickly see where the data were heading. This gave me the first inkling that the ratio of positive-to-negative interaction was a key predictor. In Figure 11.2 you can see that

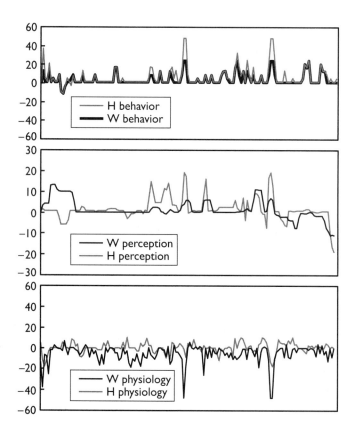

Figure 11.1   The basic data for our math modeling

there are three sets of cumulated graphs (the solid line is the wife's cumulative plot and the dotted line is the husband's). We discovered that happy couples have cumulative curves that go up; unhappy couples who divorce approximately 5.6 years after the wedding have curves that generally go down. This latter group has escalated conflict characterized by the four horsemen of the apocalypse (criticism, defensiveness, contempt, and stonewalling). A third group of couples, those who were later-divorcing, did not escalate conflict using the four horsemen, but they had low levels of positive affect during conflict.

The fs

Let's get back to the fundamental question the Murray group started with. What were the **fs**? I knew roughly what I wanted. To write down the equations on the right-hand side of the equals sign, I knew that

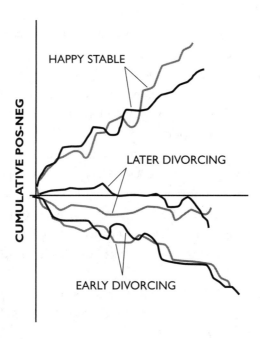

Figure 11.2   **Positive-to-Negative Interaction Graphs
for Three Couple Groups**

we needed to think about power and social influence in relationships. Power and influence are what link the two partner's equations. If we were to just write the wife's equations with only terms from her own time series, her equation and her partner's equation wouldn't be linked together, and then we would have no social influence whatsoever—no way of thinking about power. Linking the equations was going to be a theoretical statement about power. I wanted to be able to measure power asymmetry in relationships, because that seemed to be the basis that many feminists claimed was the source of unhappiness in relationships. Others had claimed that a dominance structure in relationships leads to *less* conflict and is more functional.

Our study of gay and lesbian couples and the literature on same-sex relationships suggested that equality was a major concern of these couples. So I wanted our equations to be able to measure power and influence, and imbalances in power. Therefore the two equations had to be linked.

When a person is relatively powerless in a relationship, there is no chance for respect to build in that relationship. Without respect, the quality of intimacy and trust must necessarily be compromised. Therefore, intuitively we would expect that an asymmetry in power would imply the erosion of trust and the building of betrayal.

I also thought that people's personality and the couple's history with each other needed to be in the equations. The right-hand side of the equation was therefore divided into two parts: (1) a self-influence part, and (2) a partner influence part that would link the two equations. One part described how people influenced *themselves* and what they brought to the interaction that was probably a part of both their personality and their history together. We were, after all, only getting one slice of a couple's relationship, what Malcolm Gladwell called a "thin slice."[28] So in our model we included a *self-influence* part. We decided to make that part linear.

One part of the model therefore was a straight line that had two terms: a constant term that represented how much goodwill (positivity or negativity) each person brought to the interaction, and a second term that told us how much that negativity or positivity *persisted within a person* over time (we called it "emotional inertia"). That last part took us 4 years to add. Murray didn't like it, but his students, especially Julian Cook,[29] and I added that constant when James went on vacation for a week, and the constant made the model fit the data very well. When James got back it was too late for him to object. The emotional inertia of each person assessed how long the emotional state of each person would persist by itself until it declined exponentially over time. We found that couples who were more unhappily married had: (1) a much more negative constant term, and (2) more emotional inertia (especially wives) than happy couples. So that self part of the model added to our knowledge a great deal. Even before influence processes began, we discovered that the unhappily married couples started more negatively and had less emotional regulation than happy couples.

The second and final part of the **f** function, which was added to the first self part, was the power part. It was the *influence* the partner had at any time point. Here was the idea: I am influenced by what *I* am feeling. That's the first part of the **f**. I am also influenced by my partner. That's the second part of the **f**. That second part of **f** interlocked the two equations. I'm influenced by what my partner is feeling and expressing, which, in turn, influences what my partner does, which, in turn influences me. Like two mirrors facing each other, we are reflected in each other's mirrors in infinite recess and repetition, but with some distortion. That's what the two interlocked equations simulate.

That power, or influence functions, was described by *two* straight lines of different slopes. That's what made the initial model nonlinear. The two slopes were a function of whether the affect was positive or negative. The theory was that in human relationships, negativity has more power to hurt than positivity has to heal. Negativity stops us and makes us think about how to avoid that mini-shock. Positivity only accelerates whatever we're doing. In most languages on the planet there are more words for negative emotions than there are for positive emotions. We give a lot more thought to the negative than we do to the positive, because it has a bigger impact on us. In the model, that is reflected mathematically in a steeper influence slope for negativity

than for positivity. If the affect was negative this means that the influence line had a steeper slope (was more powerful) than if the affect
was positive. Because we needed two lines to describe these influence
functions, we called this theory the "bilinear" model of social influence.

That's all the "theory" I could come up with, and even that took me 4
years to think of. It's not much of a theory, but it's all we had. Note that
we could always modify this theory if we wanted to, but we had to start
somewhere. That start seemed to fit a lot of the data that observational
researchers had been collecting all over the world.

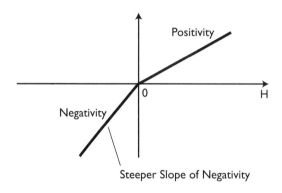

Figure 11.3   Influence of Husband on Wife

Figure 11.3 illustrates our bilinear theory about the interlocking influence process, or how people exert power on each other in a relationship.
The vertical axis is the amount of influence the husband has on the wife
and the horizontal axis shows how that influence varies as a function of
the husband's affect. For positive affect it has a less steep slope than for
negative affect.

I eventually grew uncomfortable with that bilinear theory, because
it was so grim. So I changed it so that there was an additional "repair"
term. That made the theory more satisfying to my clinical side. What
I wanted was that, after a certain threshold of negativity (which was
now a new parameter in the model), there could be a repair boost
that a couple could exert. The size of the boost and the "threshold"
at which the boost came in became two new interesting parameters

of the modeling. Psychologists have been fond of thresholds since the 19th century. I also added a "damping" term that down-regulated positivity, thinking that, unlike repair, damping might not be a good thing at all.

Now graphically, in phase space plots, we could draw the components of my new influence functions, and fit these to real data. In Figure 11.4 we used only data obtained from coding the interaction. The figure represents this new theory of the influence function, with repair and damping terms added. The points on the graph show how we fit that curve to the data, with varying degrees of success. Notice that the dotted line represents how the slope lines would have gone without the repair or damping terms.

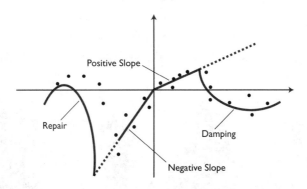

Figure 11.4   **Complete Influence Function Fit to Data**

Now the model was very cool theoretically to me. When we first started applying this new theoretical influence function, we discovered that for our newlywed sample, the couples who wound up divorced 6 years after the wedding had a more negative threshold for repair than couples who stayed married. That is, the couples who stayed together started their repair process before the interaction became too negative. The effectiveness of their repair was also greater than it was for couples who waited until the interaction became too negative. The damping term did nothing in discriminating the divorced from the stable couples. But those first results were a vindication for adding the repair term to the influence function. Repair was important to me theoretically, and when we did computations with repair in the model, we got some very interesting results. Murray was delighted. He said that a model is a good model if it leads you to ask some new questions. New findings make it even a better model.

Explaining What Phase Space Really Is

If we look at Figure 11.5 we can see the time series of the point graphs we created from the coding. I have illustrated the data in two places, one where she is positive but he is negative, and one where they are both negative.

The place we had to understand next was called "phase space." Recall that we can describe our "null-cline" lines for each equation. These are the lines where nothing changes for each partner.

Where the null-clines intersect in phase space are the steady states of the couple system. Let's first take an intuitive look at phase space.

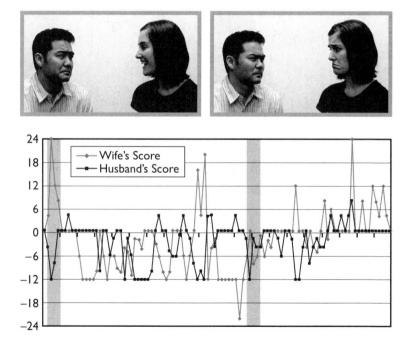

Figure 11.5   **Illustrating the SPAFF behavioral time series data**

Figure 11.6 illustrates the four quadrants of phase space. The woman on the right is my niece, Kathryn Schwartz, and the man on the left is Dan Yoshimoto. In the top right quadrant they are both positive. In the bottom left they are both negative. The upper left quadrant and lower right quadrant are mismatches in affect; one is positive and the other is negative.

When we plot the data in phase space, we are searching for a stable steady state. Figure 11.7 illustrates what data might look like of they lead us to gradual steady state that was negative. In Figure 11.8 we see the usual configuration with the bilinear model, a situation of two steady states, one negative and one positive.

We call each stable steady state an "attractor." They are the points to which all the couple's interaction is drawn. There will be two stable steady states with the bilinear model. That was illustrated in Figure 11.8.

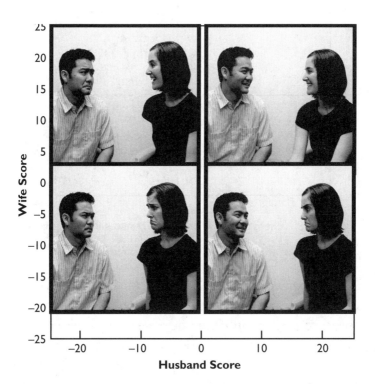

Figure 11.6   Illustrating the four quadrants of phase space

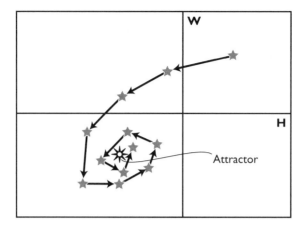

Figure 11.7   Motion in phase space toward a negative attractor

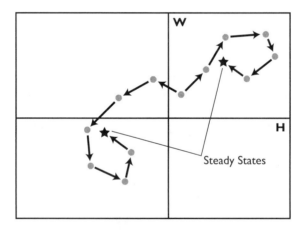

Figure 11.8   There are usually two steady states in phase space

Figure 11.9 shows way of illustrating the dramatic difference between the positive-positive quadrant (happy vacationing bunnies at the beach) and the negative-negative quadrant (the same bunnies getting rained out by storm). This figure shows that it is good to have a stable steady state in the upper right (positive-positive) quadrant of phase space, and not so good to have a stable steady state in the lower left (negative-negative) quadrant of phase space.

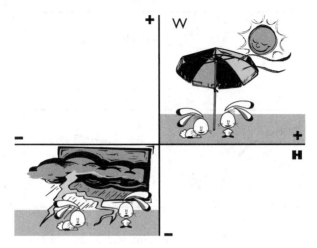

Figure 11.9   Illustrating the positive-positive and the negative-negative
quadrants with bunnies at the beach and bunnies in a storm, respectively

These figures are designed to give you an idea of what phase space is all about. The actual mathematical identification of the steady states, however, comes from the intersections of the null clines. With the repair and damping terms, these null clines and their intersections can become very complex, with as many as five steady states. The steady states alternate in being either stable (attractors) or unstable (repellors). Recall that a null cline is the curve in phase space where the equations for each partner do not change. Where the null clines intersect are the influenced steady states for that couple. We can mathematically derive the exact shape of the null clines. They turn out to be the influence functions stretched and translated a bit.

One confusing thing about phase space that took us a long time to get used to is that the husband and wife null clines get plotted as kind of mirror images of each other. That's because each null-cline line each refers to its own axis, with one axis for each partner. Where they intersect are the influenced steady states of the couple's system. The S in Figure 11.10 refers to the steady state as "stable" and the U refers to the steady state as unstable. Julian Cook proved that the stable and unstable steady states alternate as shown in the figure.

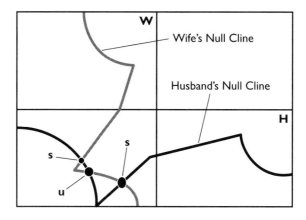

Figure 11.10   **Stable and Unstable Steady States**

The Couple's "Force Field"

Once we write down our two equations in phase space, they don't simply define the points of intersection of each null cline. Actually, each
point in phase space has not only a value determined by the equations
but also a *vector*, which has a magnitude and a *direction*. Like the iron
filings poured over a piece of paper placed on top of a magnet, the vec-
tors define the lines of force that move the couple's interaction in phase
space. These lines of force are especially important around a steady state.
Notice in Figure 11.11 the field of force lines repelling the interaction
around the region of an unstable attractor and pulling it toward the
attractor in the region of a stable attractor.

We can actually compute the strength of attraction or repulsion
around each steady state by a method called "the Jacobian" of the equations around each steady state.

Why do we care that we have a vector field? Because now the equations can *explain* the couple's behavior, not merely model it. The equations
define the force field that moves a couple through their conversations.
This use of the term "force field" isn't science fiction ("May the Force Be
With You!") but real science that comes directly from the mathematics.

Of course, we need to be skeptical. But that's okay, because one of
the great things about this representation in vector space is that we can

now *simulate* the couple's interaction as we vary the parameters of the model. That is, we can decide ahead of time how we want to change this couple so that their interaction will look more like a happy, stable relationship. We do this by manipulating the parameters of the math model and seeing what we get. Then we can then imagine the minimum therapeutic intervention that could accomplish these results. Simulation was never possible before the math model. With a math model, the model seems to cry out for simulation and experiment. The goal now becomes: Change the interaction so that the model gives us a different kind of vector space. What do we want? We might want the uninfluenced steady state to become more positive. We might want there to be less emotional inertia. We might want the influenced steady state to be more positive *than* the uninfluenced steady state. We might want there to be a positive influenced stable steady state, with lots of gravitas. We might want more equality between influence patterns. We might want the strength of the negative attractor to be far smaller than the strength of the positive attractor.

In fact, our research showed us that we want *all* of these things. The best thing is that the math model has given us a language for what we want to accomplish in couple therapy. It has also made it possible to create a theory for understanding and explaining couple's interaction.

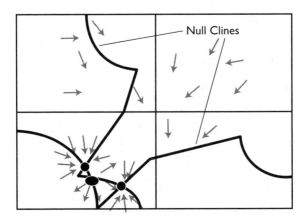

Figure 11.11   **Vector Field in Phase Space**

To summarize, the math proceeds from understanding the interaction-dependent variables by breaking each variable into the "uninfluenced" and "influenced" part of our theory of how the dependent variable may change over time. The fs will be decomposed into components that suggest a mechanism for the successful prediction of relationship stability or dissolution. Our "theory" of interaction will automatically give us the forces and the whole force field that attempt to explain why the couple interacts in this particular fashion.

Our mathematical equations are a theory because we have decided on a particular shape for the influence-power function. The vector force field we get from the mathematics is then an *explanation* of the dynamics of the couple, based on the theory of the shape of power (influence functions).

Note that the "qualitative" and *theoretical* portion of writing down our equations lies in writing down the mathematical form of the *influence functions*. An influence function is used to describe the part of the couple's interaction where they directly affect each other. The mathematical form of the influence functions are represented graphically, with the x-axis as the range of values of the dependent variable (positive minus negative at a turn of speech) for one spouse and the y-axis the average value of the dependent variable for the other spouse's immediately following behavior, averaged across turns at speech. This latter point is critical, and the math suggests social-influence ideas unfamiliar to non-mathematical social science: The influence functions represent averages across the whole interaction.

The Parameters of Power

The *slopes of the bilinear influence functions* in the two regions are the important parameters of power for the bilinear form of the influence functions. *These two slopes measure each person's power on the partner with either positive or negative affect.* In the bilinear model two parameters are obtained for each spouse's power, or influence, on the partner. Asymmetry in power is assessed by two numbers that measure the differences in each partner's slope in the positive and negative affect regions.

Other Parameters of the Model

Using the existing research on marital interaction, another parameter we decided that was important to include was the *emotional inertia* (positive or negative) of each spouse, which is each person's tendency to remain in the same state for a period of time. The greater the emotional inertia, the more likely the person is to stay in the same state for a longer period of time. It is a measure of emotion regulation: The higher the emotional inertia, the less emotion regulation. It has been consistently found, in marital interaction research, that the reciprocation of negativity is more characteristic of unhappy couples than of happy couples. This finding has held cross-nationally as well as within the United States. Surprisingly, the tendency to reciprocate *positive* affect may also be greater in unhappy than in happy couples.[30] One way of summarizing this result is to say that there is generally more time linkage or temporal structure in the interaction of distressed marriages and families. That was a classic finding made by Jay Haley about troubled families in the 1960s.[31] Another way of stating this finding is to say that there is more new information in every behavior in well-functioning family systems. The system is also more flexible because it is less time-locked. A high-inertia spouse is also less open to being influenced by the partner. Emotional inertia came from including the autocorrelation (self-correlation) component of human behavior.

Another parameter we added after 4 years of working on the model was a *constant* term. That constant represented the initial starting values of the conversation—a result, in part, of the partners' history together. A derived parameter from knowing both this starting value and the emotional inertias of both people (one that emerged from solving the equations) was the couple's *uninfluenced steady state*, which is their average level of positive minus negative when their spouse did not influence them (that is, when the influence function was zero). We decided that this state of affairs was most likely when the affect was most neutral or equally positive and negative. We think of this parameter as what each spouse brings into the interaction before being influenced by the partner. Clearly this uninfluenced set point may be a function of the past history of the couple's interactions. The constant term may also be a function of individual characteristics of each spouse, such as a tendency toward pessimism or optimism. We used to estimate the uninfluenced portion in two steps using a method developed by Julian Cook. We can now derive these uninfluenced parameters in one step along with the influence functions, thanks to Ellen Hamaker's method of estimation.[32]

Another derived parameter was *the influenced steady state* of the interaction, which is a steady state of the system after influence processes set in. One way of thinking about the influenced set point is to see it as a sequence of two scores (one for each partner) that would be repeated ad infinitum if the theoretical model exactly described the time series; if such a steady state is stable, then sequences of scores will approach the point over time. In a loose sense it represents the average score the theoretical model would predict for each partner. We also thought it might be interesting to examine the difference between influenced and uninfluenced set points. We expect that the influenced set point will be more positive than the uninfluenced set point in marriages that are stable and happy; that is, we asked the question: Did the couple's interaction pull the individual in a more positive or a more negative direction? This was an additional derived parameter in our modeling.[33]

Simulating Change

As mentioned earlier, a good model, according to James Murray, is one that leads us to ask interesting questions. It changes how we think about the phenomenon we are studying. Let's think of how this math modeling changes how we think about relationships conceptually. As I mentioned, a big contribution of the math is that the model makes it possible to imagine *simulations* of how a couple might be, merely by changing parameter values. Imagine if you could take a client couple and get the equations and simulate what the couple might be like if you changed certain key parameters of their interaction. We have learned that without actually changing the system's basic operating principles of influencing each other, we can have a dramatic effect on the couple.

Real Force Field Results

What, in fact, are the vector spaces like for couples who at first, at Time-1, when we first studied them, eventually turned out to be happy and

stable over time, for couples who eventually turned out to be unhappy
but stable over time, and for couples who eventually divorced? It turns
out that the vector spaces of these three groups of couples were very different from one another even way back when we first started studying
them. Figure 11.12 illustrates those results.

The couples who eventually wound up happy and stable had, at
Time-1, a phase space force field with only one positive stable attractor. The forces in that field impelled them to have a positive outcome of
their conflicts. No matter where in phase space they started the interaction, the forces would eventually move them to a positive place in phase
space. The couples who eventually stayed together but were unhappily
married had, at Time-1, a phase space force field with only one negative
stable attractor. The forces in that field impelled them to have a negative

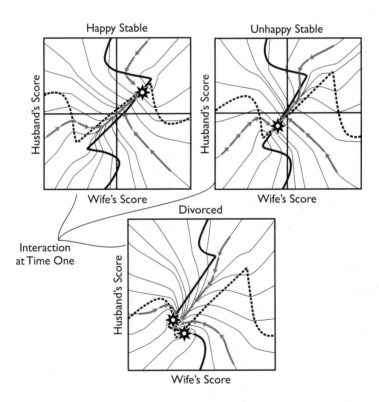

Figure 11.12   **Vector flow diagrams for three groups of couples,
based on initial (Time-1) interactions.**

outcome of their conflicts. No matter where in phase space they started the interaction, no matter how positively they began, unfortunately, the forces would eventually move them to a negative place in phase space. The couples who eventually stayed divorced had, at Time-1, a phase space force field with three negative attractors, two stable and one unstable. The forces in that field impelled them to have a complex variety of all negative outcomes of their conflicts. No matter where in phase space they started the interaction, no matter how positively they began, unfortunately, the forces would eventually move them to one of three negative places in phase space. Therefore, the force fields were not only predictive of the long-term outcomes of these relationships, but explanatory as well. That is a huge theoretical advance.

We worry that a couple's positivity may wear out over time. If it does, the couple is in trouble. We like to see more "systemic" and lasting changes. We want to also reduce the emotional inertial of both people, and make their influence functions different, so that they have more buffers against losing that positive steady state we have worked so hard to create.

Catastrophes

Sometimes couples change suddenly. They may suddenly improve or, more commonly, they may suddenly become significantly worse. A sudden change that happens after a parameter slowly changes and then a threshold value (for better or for worse) is called a "catastrophe" by mathematicians. (As noted earlier, in mathematics a catastrophe need not be a horrible event, which is its meaning in standard English.)

It became possible to model catastrophes with the math model. For example, with the math model it is possible for a couple's interaction to deteriorate over time so that they actually totally *lose* their positive attractor. Gradually their uninfluenced steady state can become so negative that after they cross a critical threshold, there is no longer a positive steady state. What would that mean? What would then happen?

The answer is that now, seemingly inexplicably, all the couple's conflict resolution discussions degenerate into an aversive and negative experience. They are now always drawn to their negative attractor, because the positive attractor no longer exists. This is a literal catastrophe, and we would predict divorce (or continued stable misery) as inevitable for this unfortunate couple. This is consistent with my 1994 report that when that happens the couple enters a series of cascades that results in increasing flooding, diffuse physiological arousal, arranging their lives in parallel so that partners have less interaction, and becoming increasingly lonely and vulnerable to other relationships. To the couple the change is inexplicable. They have weathered many stresses in the past and succeeded in staying together. But now every disagreement heads south toward the negative attractor. That is because there has been a qualitative change: There's no longer a positive attractor.

This kind of catastrophe also could explain the relapse that often unfortunately accompanies successful couple therapy. Here, then, we have an explanation for a very gradual trend during which the couple often thinks that they are simply adapting to increasing stresses in their lives, getting used to seeing less of each other, and experiencing more fighting, but fully expecting that things will get better eventually. However, sometimes this gradual change makes them vulnerable to losing their positive stable influenced steady states in which case we would predict a real relationship catastrophe. The gradual changes would change the marriage suddenly and then it would qualitatively become an entirely different relationship.

Although the model predicts this sudden catastrophic change under these conditions, it also predicts a phenomenon called "hysterisis," which means that this state of affairs is potentially reversible. However, clinical experience suggests that, for longer time spans, this reversibility is probably not the case when the relationship has been neglected for long enough. For example, one study reported that the average wait time for couples to obtain professional help for their marriage after they have noticed serious marital problems is about 6 years.[34] This problem of high delay in seeking help for an ailing relationship is one of the great mysteries in this field of inquiry. It may very well be related to another great unsolved mystery, which is the problem of relapse in couple therapy. Recently some of our best scholars have contended that couples' therapy has relapse rates so high (30 to 50% within a year after marital therapy ends) that the entire enterprise of marital treatment may be in a state of crisis.[35] Consistent with these conclusions, the recent Consumer Reports study of psychotherapy reported that marital therapy received the lowest marks from psychotherapy consumers.[36] Marital therapy may be at somewhat of an impasse because it is not based on a process model derived from prospective longitudinal studies of what real couples do that predicts that their marriages will wind up happy and stable, unhappy and stable, or end in divorce.

After so long a delay before getting help, it makes some sense to propose that a positive hysterisis journey (back to a positive attractor existing) may be less likely than a negative one. Also, some key life transitions may make going back to the more positive way things were less likely. This is particularly true for the transition to parenthood. Half of all the divorces occur in the first 7 years of marriage, and a great deal of stress is associated with the transition to parenthood. There are other vulnerable transition points for marriages in the life course. The low point crossnationally for marital satisfaction is when the first child reaches the age of 14, although this phenomenon is not well understood. Retirement is also such a delicate transition point. If these speculations are true, the model would have to be altered to accommodate these asymmetrical phenomena.

It does seem likely that there is something like a second law of thermodynamics for couple relationships, meaning that things fall apart unless energy is supplied to keep making the relationship alive and well. At this time in the history of Western civilization, marriages seem more likely to fall apart than to stay together. Hence, the hysterisis property of the model may turn out to be incorrect. However, our recent research with long-term first marriages paints a far more optimistic picture, one that suggests that some marriages mellow with age and get better and better.[37]

It should be pointed out that the model is designed to obtain parameters from just a 15-minute interaction, and one useful way of extending the model is to attempt to model two sequential interactions, in which the parameters of the second interaction are affected by the first interaction. What is very interesting about the catastrophic aspect of the model is that it does tend to fit a great deal of our experience, in which we have observed that many marriages suddenly fall apart, often after having successfully endured a period of high stress.

Implications of the Modeling

One of the interesting implications of the mathematical model is that even in the best of marriages, *it is likely that there will be both a positive and a negative stable steady state*. This means that, depending entirely on starting values, there will be times that the couple will be drawn toward a very negative interaction. This may not happen very often in a satisfying and stable marriage, but the model predicts that it *will* happen. To some extent these events are minimized if the strength of the negative steady state (or "attractor") is much smaller than the strength of the positive steady state.

The old concept of family homeostasis has to be modified: There are usually at least two homeostatic set points in a family, one more positive than the other. This concept may do a great deal toward ending what Dan Wile called the "adversarial" approach of family systems therapy.[38] Here the therapist struggles gallantly against great odds as the family's homeostasis holds on to dysfunctional interaction patterns. However, if there are *two* homeostatic set points, one more positive and one more negative, then the therapist can align with a family toward making their occupation time greater in the more positive homeostatic set point than in the more negative homeostatic set point.

Another implication of this two-homeostatic-set-point theory is that a negative steady state may have some positive functions in a relationship; the therapist ought not make war on negative effect, for example. Negativity might be useful in a relationship for a variety of reasons. One is that in any real close relationship our legacy is the full repertoire of emotions (they are controlled in more formal and more casual relationships).It would not be very intimate if some emotions were expurgated from the full repertoire of emotions that is our legacy as homo sapiens; in fact, a relationship with only positive emotions might actually be a living hell. Second, negative affects may serve the function of culling out behaviors that do not work in the relationship, continually fine tuning the relationship over time so that there is a better and better fit between partners. Third, negativity might serve the function of continually renewing courtship over the course of a long relationship; after the fight there is greater emotional distance, which needs to be healed with a re-courtship.

The model has accomplished a great deal just by dismantling our dependent variable into components and parameters. This has created *a new theoretical language for describing interaction.* Instead of having just a variable that predicts the longitudinal course of marriages, we now can speak theoretically about the *mechanism* of this prediction. We can expect that compared to happy, stable marriages, what happens in marriages headed for divorce is that:

- There is more emotional inertia.
- Even before being influenced, the *uninfluenced set point is more negative.*
- When interaction begins, the couple influences each other to become even more negative rather than more positive.
- Over time, as these negative interactions continue and become characteristic of the marriage, the couple may catastrophically lose its positive stable steady state.

The model also suggests one possible integration of the concepts of affect and power in relationships, which has haunted the field since its inception. The integration is that power or influence is defined as one person's affect having an influence over the other person's immediately following affect.

The integration of power and affect also suggest a greater order of complexity to the concept of power. Who is more powerful in the relationship may be a function of the level of affect, and how positive or negative it is. In one relationship, for example, a wife might be more powerful than her husband only with extreme negative affect, whereas her husband might be more powerful only with mild positive affect. We may also discover that the very shape of the influence function is different for couples heading for divorce, compared to happy, stable couples.

Therefore, unlike prior general systems writings, which remained at the level of metaphor, the mathematical model has given birth to a new theoretical language about the mechanism of change. In the marital research area we did not have such a language before the model was successfully constructed. The model provides the language of set point theory, in which a number of quantities, or parameters, may be regulated and protected by the marital interaction. It also provides a precise mechanism for change. The model itself suggests variables that can be targeted for change using interventions. In short, the model leads somewhere. It helps us raise questions, helps us wonder what the parameters may be related to, and why. It raises questions of etiology. Why might a couple begin an interaction with a negative uninfluenced set point? Why and how would they then influence each other to be even more negative?

One contribution of the model is the theoretical language and the mathematical tools it provides. It will give us a way of thinking about marital interaction that we never had before. Previous experience in the biological and physical sciences suggests that any model that accomplishes these things will probably be useful. The model also gives us insight about its own inadequacy. It is a very grim model. Where a couple begins the interaction in phase space will usually determine its outcome. Did it make sense to have a model in which there is a possibility of *repair*? Most of the time the repair component of the model wasn't very important in discriminating happy from unhappy couples. Unfortunately, when we examined our interactive data we found that only 4% of the couples who began the interaction negatively were able to significantly turn the interaction around so that it eventually became more positive than negative! Hence, even though major repair is a rare phenomenon, we thought that the model should have such a repair term in it. Couples would then vary in the extent to which they were able to repair the interaction. Perhaps in more effective couple therapy this repair term becomes strengthened.

We discovered new things with the model, things we never expected to find. We reported the discovery that different types of marriages have different types of influence functions,[39] and that divorce is only predicted by fundamental mismatches in influence function shape. Julian Cook also showed that there is an optimal balance between influence and inertia. Cook's analysis of the stability of the steady states of the marriage model shows that there is a dialectic between the amount of influence each spouse should have on the partner and the level of emotional inertia in each spouse's uninfluenced behavior for the steady state to be stable. Steady states tend to be stable when they have a lower level of influence and a lower level of inertia. Another way of saying this is that if a marriage is going to have high levels of mutual influence, for stability of (say) the positive steady state, there needs to be lowered inertia.

Our work with James Murray and his students put the study of personal relationships on a mathematical footing. We have only begun to explore the utility of this mathematics as we have begun to do proximal change experiments. After pilot-testing these proximal change experiments for 3 years, my wife and I began writing a monthly column with the *Reader's Digest* magazine in which once a month a couple came to our laboratory, we did an assessment (with a pre-intervention conversation that we model), and then we performed an intervention, and evaluated the intervention with our mathematical modeling of a post-intervention conversation. At the time of this writing we have successfully worked with 10 couples. These experiments are slowly building a library and a technology of what we call "proximal relationship change" intervention. That means that the interventions are designed only to make the second of two conflict conversations look less dysfunctional than the first conversation.

This dream of a mathematics for human social relationships is not new. The work we have done is reminiscent of Isaac Asimov's classic science fiction series of books called *The Foundation* series.[40] In that series a fictional mathematician named Hari Seldon creates a set of equations for predicting the future of the entire human species, a new branch of study he calls "psycho-history." Later in the books another mathematician creates a new set of equations, considered much harder to accomplish, for "micro-social-history," which is about accurate prediction of the fate of smaller social units. I believe that's exactly the enterprise that we've begun with the mathematical modeling of relationship interactions. Just two equations for each couple, with some general principles. The best part of this enterprise using methematics is that it is no longer science fiction, it's just science.

A Woman's Power With Negative Affect is Her Safety From Betrayal

Finally, what does the math model tell us about trust, betrayal, and asymmetries in power in marriages? Considering that equal power for women in love relationships appears to be one of the major goals of feminists throughout the world, and considering that in many countries the greater power of men is associated with increased levels of domestic violence toward women, this aspect of relationships is worth investigating. Recall that it was the motivating force for including this chapter in this book, and for studying the mathematics of relationships in the first place.

When he had more power with negative affect than she did. When there was asymmetry in power, and only for negative affect, there were the following consequences: (1) the marriage had more gender stereotypy on our OHI, so the roles of husband and wife were more traditional, (2) she had significantly more emotional inertia during conflict, (3) he had significantly more emotional inertia during conflict, (4) they had a less positive influenced steady state, (5) his maximum score was significantly less positive, (6) she was significantly less effective at damping down positive affect, (7) he was significantly less effective at repair, (8) she was significantly less positive when there was a stable influenced steady state, (9) there were significantly more negative-negative influenced steady states, and (surprisingly) (10) she was significantly more effective at repair. Hence, aside from the latter result, there are serious negative consequences of the husband having more power with negative affect than his wife.

Her power, not relative to him. Since negative affect is a major mechanism for repair, an index of her sheer power, not her relative power, may also be important. Here I am not examining asymmetry in power, but only her sheer power. That is, I am examining her ability to be able to influence her partner by expressing her negative affect may be important. We therefore are asking the question, is her power with negative affect (slope of her influence function in the negative affect ranges) related to our betrayal metric? Indeed it was significantly negatively correlated with the betrayal metric ($r = -.54$, $p < .001$).

What might be other interesting correlates of her sheer power with her negative affect? I found that to the extent that she was powerful with negative affect: (1) her husband was significantly more likely to be looking out for her interests in a conflict (high wife trust metric), (2) the conflict was significantly more cooperative and not a zero-sum game (low husband betrayal metric), and, (3) using the Tabares untrustworthiness detector, he was significantly more positive when they did the exercise using the Negative Adjectives Checklist.

We can conclude from these analyses that mistrust and betrayal are more likely to occur in marriages in which the husband has more power than his wife, specifically with negative affect, and in which she does not have very much power to influence him with her negativity.

Epilogue

What are we left with after this excursion into trust, trustworthiness, betrayal, and power? There are a baker's dozen contributions.

- First, I showed that trust, trustworthiness, and betrayal metrics can be reliably and validly measured in any interaction that uses the Levenson-Gottman paradigm, and game theory can be applied to the study of intimate relationships.
- Second, I showed that the rationality game-theory assumption holds for neutral-neutral and positive-positive, but not for negative-negative, conflict interaction.
- Third, I discovered that this is true because negative-negative interactions become an absorbing state for unhappy couples—they check into this state, but they don't check out.
- Fourth, I showed that the absorbing state is a state of flooding and low trust.
- Fifth, I showed that there is a distinct physiology to high trust that involves slower blood flow and reduced baseline sympathetic nervous system drive to the heart.
- Sixth, I showed that the zero-sum betrayal metric predicted early husband death in our 20-year longitudinal study of older couples.
- Seventh, I presented data that showed that the predictions of the Sound Relationship House theory were supported.
- Seventh, I presented data that showed how couples build trust through emotional attunement in three contexts.
- Eighth, I presented data from a randomized clinical trial that showed that trust can be built using exercises and information based on the Sound Relationship House theory.
- Ninth, I extended the idea of attunement to *intimate trust* in the sexual, romantic, and passionate aspects of a love relationship.
- Tenth, I presented new work on the dynamics of repair during

conflict and how the ability to repair is essential for building trust and healing from inevitable regrettable incidents.

- Eleventh, I presented a theory of the dynamics of betrayal and the dynamics of loyalty that integrated our work with the work of Caryl Rusbult and her colleagues on interdependence theory.
- Twelfth, using our clinical work, I presented a three-phase model for healing from betrayal.
- Thirteenth, using nonlinear mathematics, I showed that power imbalances between partners seriously compromise trust in relationships.

Clearly, we are on a threshold in working on trust, trustworthiness, power, and betrayal *within one interaction*. From here we have the precision to continue to examine these vital aspects of any lasting relationship, and to know how we can avoid betrayal, and, failing that, heal from it.

Appendix

Computing the Trust Metric in Any Interaction (Chapter 2)

Mathematically, the jump from nasty-nasty to neutral-neutral is the first part of my trust metric:

For her the first part of the trust metric is: $(W_{22}-W_{11})/(W_{1\_}-W_{2\_})$; *this ratio measures the extent to which her payoffs increase from nasty-nasty to neutral-neutral interaction as a function of* his *changing his behavior.*

The second part of the trust metric for her is: $(W_{33}-W_{11})/(W_{1\_}-W_{3\_})$; *this ratio measures the extent to which her payoffs increase from nasty-nasty to nice-nice interaction as a function of* his *changing his behavior.*

For him the first part of the trust metric is: $(H_{22}-H_{11})/(H_{\_1}-H_{\_2})$; *this ratio measures the extent to which his payoffs increase from nasty-nasty to neutral-neutral interaction as a function of* her *changing her behavior.*

The second part of the trust metric for him is: $(H_{33}-H_{11})/(H_{\_1}-H_{\_3})$; *this ratio measures the extent to which his payoffs increase from nasty-nasty to nice-nice interaction as a function of* her *changing her behavior.*

To simplify matters we multiply these two numbers together for each partner to obtain an estimate of the final products that *define the trust metric:*

Her trust in him $= ((W_{22}-W_{11})/(W_{1\_}-W_{2\_}))\mathrm{x}((W_{33}-W_{11})/(W_{1\_}-W_{3\_}))$
His trust in her $= ((H_{22}-H_{11})/(H_{\_1}-H_{\_2}))\mathrm{x}((H_{33}-H_{11})/(H_{\_1}-H_{\_3}))$.

The trust metric is therefore the product of two ratios. Ratios are often problematic in computation because they create the possibility of dividing by zero, which produces missing data.

The Untrustworthiness (Potential for Betrayal) Metric in Any Interaction: Computations (Chapter 3)

I do this computation in two steps. First, in terms of the game-theory matrices, for him we can measure how much her variability in actual behavior moves her out of the negative-negative cell payoffs into the higher neutral-neutral payoffs. Second, for him we can also measure how much her variability in actual behavior moves her out of the negative-negative cell payoffs into the higher positive-positive payoffs. These are like two jumps that assess how much he can count on her to change her behavior for her own self-interest. We make the same computations for her.

Thus, we again arrive at two numbers for each partner, one for each step, and we then multiply these two numbers together to get the untrustworthiness and betrayal potential in two parts that jump the couple out of nasty-nasty exchanges. Mathematically, the jump from nasty-nasty to neutral-neutral is a ratio:

For her the first part of the untrustworthiness metric is:

$(W_{22}-W_{11})/(W_{-1}-W_{-2})$

Her second part of the untrustworthiness metric is:

$(W_{33}-W_{11})/(W_{-1}-W_{-3})$

For him the first part of the untrustworthiness metric is:

$(H_{22}-H_{11})/(H_{1}-H_{2})$

His second part of the untrustworthiness metric is: $(H_{33}-H_{11})/(H_{1\_}-H_{3})$

We multiply these two numbers together for each partner to obtain the final products. *The metric of untrustworthiness is:*

Her untrustworthiness metric $= ((W_{22}-W_{11})/(W_{-1}-W_{-2}))x((W_{33}-W_{11})/(W_{-1}-W_{-2}))$
His untrustworthiness metric $= ((H_{22}-H_{11})/(H_{1}-H_{2})x((H_{33}-H_{11})/(H_{1\_}-H_{3})).$

Endnotes

Chapter 1. Why a Book on Trust?

1. Gladwell, M. (2005). *Blink*. New York: Little Brown.

2. Gottman, J. M., Gottman, J. S., & DeClaire, J. (2006). *Ten Lessons to transform your marriage*. New York: Crown.

3. The Art and Science of Love manual workshop and DVDs are available on www.gottman.com.

4. Putallaz, M., & Gottman, J. (1981). An interactional model of children's entry into peer groups. *Child Development*, *52*, 986–994.

5. Levenson, R. W., & Gottman, J. M. (1985). Physiological and affective predictors of change in relationship satisfaction. *Journal of Personality and Social Psychology*, *49*, 85–94.

6. Guerney, B. G. (1977). *Relationship enhancement*. San Francisco: Jossey Bass.

7. Bach, G., & Wyden, P. (1965). *The intimate enemy*. New York: Avon.

8. Tavris, C. (1982). *Anger: The misunderstood emotion*. New York: Simon & Schuster.

9. Darwin, C. (2006). *The expression of emotions in man and animals*. New York: Penguin Classics.

10. Ginott, H. (1965). *Between parent and child*. New York: Avon.

11. Gottman, J. M., (1993). The roles of conflict engagement, escalation or avoidance in marital interaction: A longitudinal view of five types of couples. *Journal of Consulting & Clinical Psychology*, *61*(1), 6–15. Gottman, J. M. (1993). A theory of marital dissolution and stability. *Journal of Family Psychology*, *7*(1), 57–75.

12. Gottman, J. M., & Levenson, R. W. (1999). What predicts change in marital interaction over time? A study of alternative models. *Family Process*, *38*(2), 143–158. Gottman, J. M., & Levenson, R. W. (2000). The timing of divorce: Predicting when a couple will divorce over a 14-year period. *Journal of Marriage and the Family*, *62*, 737–745.

13. Driver, J. L., & Gottman, J. M. (2004). Daily marital interactions and positive affect during marital conflict among newlywed couples. *Family Process*, *43*(3), 301–314.

14. Weiss, R. L. (1980). Strategic behavioral relationship therapy: Toward a model for assessment and intervention. In J. P. Vincent (Ed.), *Advances in fam-*

ily intervention, assessment and theory Vol. 1 (pp. 229–271). Greenwich, CT: JAI Press.

15. Robinson, E. A., & Price, M. G. (1980). Pleasurable behavior in marital interaction: An observational study. *Journal of Consulting and Clinical Psychology*, *48*, 117–118.

16. Heider, F. (1958). *The psychology of interpersonal relations*. New York: Wiley.

17. Terman, L. M., Buttenweiser, P., Ferguson, L. W., Johnson, W. B., & Wilson, D. P. (1938). *Psychological factors in marital happiness*. Stanford, CA: Stanford University Press.

18. Raush, H. L., Barry, W. A., Hertl, R. K., & Swain, M. A. (1974). *Communication, conflict, and marriage*. San Francisco: Jossey-Bass.

19. Satir, V., & Baldwin, M. (1968). *Satir step by step*. Palo Alto: Science and Behavior Books.

20. Christensen, A. (1987). Detection of conflict patterns in couples. In K. Hahlweg & M. J. Goldstein (Eds.), *Understanding major mental disorder: The contribution of family interaction research* (pp. 250–265). New York: Family Process Press. Christensen, A. (1988). Dysfunctional interaction patterns in couples. In P. Noller & M. A. Fitzpatrick (Eds.), *Perspectives on marital interaction* (pp. 31–52). Avon, England: Multilingual Matters. Christensen, A. (1990). Gender and social structure in the demand/withdrawal pattern of marital conflict. *Journal of Personality and Social Psychology*, *59*, 73–81. Christensen, A. (1991). *The demand/withdraw pattern in marital interaction*. Paper presented at the annual meeting of the Association for the Advancement of Behavior Therapy, New York. Christensen, A., & Heavey, C. L. (1990). Gender and social structure in the demand/withdraw pattern of marital conflict. *Journal of Personality and Social Psychology*, *59*, 73–82.

21. Greenberg, L. S., & Johnson, S. M. (1988). *Emotionally focused therapy for couples*. New York: Guilford.

22. Gottman, J. M., & Levenson, R. W. (1999). How stable is marital interaction over time? *Family Process*, *38*(2), 159–165.

23. Carrere, S., Buehlman, K. T., Coan, J. A., Gottman, J. M., Coan, J. A., & Ruckstuhl, L. (2000). Predicting marital stability and divorce in newlywed couples. *Journal of Family Psychology*, *14*(1), 1–17.

24. Hahlweg, K., Revenstorf, D. & Shindler, L. (1982). Treatment of marital distress: Comparing formats and modalities. *Advances in Behavior Research and Therapy*, *4*(2), 57–74. Hahlweg, K., Revenstorf, D., & Schindler, L. (1984). Effects of behavioral relationship therapy on couples' communication and problem-solving skills. *Journal of Consulting and Clinical Psychology*, *52*(4), 553–566. Hahlweg, K., Schindler, L., Revenstorf, D., & Brengelmann, J. C. (1984). *The Munich relationship therapy study*. K. Hahlweg & N. S. Jacobson. New York, *Marital Interaction: Analysis and Modification*, pp. 3–26. Guilford Press.

25. Hahlweg, K., Markman, H., Thurmaier, F., Engl, J., & Eckert, V. (1998). Prevention of marital distress: Results of a German prospective longitudinal study. *Journal of Family Psychology*, *12*, 543–556.

26. Ball, F. L. J., Cowan, P., & Cowan, C. P. (1995). Who's got the power? Gender differences in partners' perception of influence during marital problem-solving discussions. *Family Process*, *34*, 303–321.

27. Gottman, J. M., & Levenson, R. W. (2000). Dysfunctional marital conflict: Women are being unfairly blamed. *Journal of Divorce and Remarriage*, *31*(3/4), 1–17.

28. Driver, J. L., & Gottman, J. M. (2004). Daily marital interactions and positive affect during marital conflict among newlywed couples. *Family Process*, *43*(3), 301–314.

29. Jacobson, N., & Gottman, J. (1998). *When men batter women: New insights into ending abusive relationships*. New York: Simon and Schuster.

30. Coan, J., Gottman, J. M., Babcock, J., & Jacobson, N. S. (1997). Battering and the male rejection of influence from women. *Aggressive Behavior*, *23*(5), 375–388.

31. Gottman, J., Murray, J., Swanson, C., Tyson, R., & Swanson, K. (2002). *The mathematics of marriage: Dynamic nonlinear models*. Cambridge, MA: MIT Press.

32. Gottman, J. M. (1994). *What predicts divorce?* Hillsdale, NJ: Lawrence Erlbaum.

33. Gottman, J. M., & Levenson, R. W. (2000). The timing of divorce: Predicting when a couple will divorce over a 14-year period. *Journal of Marriage and the Family*, *62*, 737–745.

34. Gottman, J. M., Coan, J., Carrere, S., & Swanson, C. (1998). Predicting marital happiness and stability from newlywed interactions. *Journal of Marriage and the Family*, *60*(1), 5–22.

35. Robert Levenson has found that humor reduces physiological arousal (personal communication, 2010). These results are as yet unpublished.

36. Gottman, J. M., & Levenson, R. W. (1992). Marital processes predictive of later dissolution: Behavior, physiology and health. *Journal of Personality and Social Psychology*, *63*, 221–233.

37. Gottman, J. M. (1993). The roles of conflict engagement, escalation or avoidance in marital interaction: A longitudinal view of five types of couples. *Journal of Consulting & Clinical Psychology*, *61*(1), 6–15. Gottman, J. M. (1993). A theory of marital dissolution and stability. *Journal of Family Psychology*, *7*(1), 57–75.

38. Yoshimoto, D. K. (2005). Marital meta-emotion, emotion coaching, and dyadic interaction. *Dissertation Abstracts International, Section B: The Sciences and Engineering*, 3448.

39. Levenson, R. W., & Gottman, J. M. (1985). Physiological and affective predictors in relationship satisfaction. *Journal of Personality and Social Psychology*, *49*, 85–94.

40. Gottman, J. M. (1999). *The marriage clinic.* New York: Norton.

41. Wile, D. (1988). *After the honeymoon.* Oakland, CA: Wile Publications.

42. Christensen, A., & Jacobson, N. S. (2000). *Reconcilable differences.* New York: Guilford.

43. Frankl, V. (2000). *Man's search for meaning.* Boston: Beacon.

44. Bowlby, I. (1980). *Loss: Attachment and loss.* New York: Basic.

45. Greenberg, L. S., & Johnson, S. M. (1988). *Emotionally focused therapy for couples.* New York: Guilford.

46. Rusbult, C. E., Johnson, O. J., & Morrow, G. D. (1986). Predicting satisfaction and commitment in adult romantic involvements: An assessment of the generalizability of the investment model. *Social Psychology Quarterly, 49,* 81–89.

47. Thibaut, J. W., & Kelly, H. H. (1969). *The social psychology of groups.* New York: Wiley.

Chapter 2. The Trust Metric

1. Putman, R. D. (2000). *Bowling alone: The collapse and revival of the American community.* New York: Simon & Schuster.

2. Halpern, D. (2008). *Social capital.* Cambridge, UK: Polity Press.

3. Zak, P. J., Knack, S. (2002). Trust and growth. *Economic Journal, 111,* 2–40.

4. Cottrell, C., Neuberg, S. L., & Li, N. P. (2007). What do people desire in others? Sociofunctional perspective on the importance of different valued characteristics. *Journal of Personality and Social Psychology, 92,* 208–231.

5. Coleman, J. S. (1966). Foundations for a theory of collective decisions. *American Journal of Sociology, 71,* 615–627.

6. von Neumann, J., & Morgenstern, O. (1944). *Theory of games and economic behavior.* Princeton, NJ: Princeton University Press.

7. Glimcher, P. W., Camerer, C. F., Fehr, E., & Poldrack, R. A. (Eds.). (2009). *Neuroeconomics: Decision making and the brain.* Amsterdam: Academic Press-Elsevier.

8. Erikson, E. (1963). *Childhood and society.* New York: Norton.

9. Mooney, C. G. (2010). *Theories of attachment: An introduction to Bowlby and Ainsworth.* St. Paul, MN. Redleaf Press.

10. Blum, D. (2002). *Love at Goon Park: Harry Harlow and the science of affection.* New York: Berkeley Publishing Group.

11. Couch, L. L., & Jones, W. H. (1997). Measuring levels of trust. *Journal of Research in Personality, 31,* 319–335. J. P. (1975). Interpersonal trust and construct complexity for positive and negatively evaluated persons. *Personality and Social Psychology Bulletin, 1,* 616–619. Gertman, M. B. (1992). Trust, distrust, and interpersonal problems: A circumplex analysis. *Journal of Personality and Social Psychology, 62,* 989–1002.

12. Yamagishi, T. (2001). Trust as a form of social intelligence. In K. S. Cook (Ed.), *Trust in society* (pp. 121–147). New York: Russell Sage Foundation.

13. Cacioppo, J., & Patrick, W. (2008). *Loneliness.* New York: Norton.

14. Rempel, J. K, Holmes, J. G., & Zanna, M. P. (1985). Trust in close relationships. *Journal of Personality and Social Psychology, 49,* 95–112.

15. Kelley, H. H. (1979). *Personal relationships: Their structures and processes.* Hillsdale, NJ: Lawrence Erlbaum.

16. Rusbult, C. E., Johnson, O. J., & Morrow, G. D. (1986). Determinants of exit, voice, loyalty, and neglect: Response to dissatisfaction in adult romantic relationships. *Human Relations, 39,* 45–63.

17. Murray, S. L., & Holmes, J. G. (2009). The architecture of independent minds: A motivation management theory of mutual responsiveness. *Psychological Review, 116,* 908–928. An effective intervention for low-self-esteem individuals is presented in: Marigold, D. C., Holmes, J. G., & Ross, M. (2010). Fostering relationship resilience: An intervention for low self-esteem individuals. *Journal of Experimental Social Psychology, 46,* 624–630.

18. Rapoport, A. (1975). *Fights, games, and debates.* Chicago: University of Chicago Press.

19. Axelrod, R. (1984). *The evolution of cooperation.* New York: Basic. Axelrod, R. (1997). *The complexity of cooperation.* Princeton, NJ: Princeton University Press.

20. Pfaff, R. (2007). *The neuroscience of fair play.* New York: Dana Press.

21. Siegel, D. (2008). *The neurobiology of we.* Boulder, CO: Sounds True.

22. Panksepp, J. (1998). *Affective neuroscience.* New York: Oxford University Press.

23. Important books are: Kramer, R. M., & Cook, K. S. (2004). *Trust and distrust in organizations.* New York: Russell Sage Foundation. Hardin, R. (2002). *Trust and trustworthiness.* New York: Russell Sage Foundation. Fukuyama, F. (1995). *Trust: The social virtues and the creation of prosperity.* New York: Simon & Schuster. Misztal, B. A. (1996). *Trust in modern societies.* Malden, MA: Blackwell. Ostrom, E., & Walker, J. (2002). *Trust and reciprocity.* New York: Russell Sage Foundation. Cook, K. S. (Ed.). (2001). *Trust in society.* New York: Russell Sage Foundation. Cook, K. S., Hardin, R., & Levi, M. (2005). *Cooperation without trust?* New York: Russell Sage Foundation. Ztompka, P. (1999). *Trust: A sociological theory.* New York: Cambridge University Press.

24. Kelley, H. H., Holmes, J. G., Kerr, N. L., Reis, H. T., Rusbult, C. E., & Van Lange, P. A. M. (2003). *An Atlas of Interpersonal situations.* New York: Cambridge University Press.

25. Camerer, C. F. (2003). *Behavioral game theory: Experiment in strategic interaction.* New York: Russell Sage Foundation. See also: Camerer, C. F., Lowenstein, G., & Rabin, M. (Eds.). (2004). *Advances in behavioral Economics.*

Princeton, NJ: Princeton University Press. Wilkinson, N. (2007). *An introduction to behavioral economics.* Houndmills, UK: Palgrave Macmillan. Glimcher, P. W., Camerer, C. F., Fehr, E., & Poldrack, R. A. (2009). *Neuroeconomics* London: Macmillan. Another fascination behavioral economics book is Ariely, D. (2008). *Predictably irrational.* New York: Harper Collins.

26. Devlin, K., & Lorden, G. (2007). *The numbers behind Numb3rs.* New York: Penguin.

27. Rapoport, A. (1966). *Two-person game theory.* Mineola, NY: Dover.

28. Kelley, H. H. (1979). *Personal Relationships: Their structures and processes.* Hillsdale, NJ: Lawrence Erlbaum.

29. Nasar, S. (1998). *A beautiful mind.* New York: Touchstone; Siegfried, T. (2006). *A beautiful math.* Washington, DC: Joseph Henry Press; and Kuhn, H. W., & Nasar, S. (2002). *The essential John Nash.* Princeton, NJ: Princeton University Press;

30. Gottman, J. M. (Ed.). (1996). *What predicts divorce: The measures.* New York: Lawrence Erlbaum.

31. Jacobson, N., & Gottman, J. (1998). *When men batter women: New insights into ending abusive relationships.* New York: Simon and Schuster.

32. Gottman, J. M., & Levenson, R. W. (1985). A valid procedure for obtaining self-report of affect in marital interaction. *Journal of Consulting and Clinical Psychology, 53,* 151–160.

33. Levenson, R. W., & Ruef, A. M. (2003). Empathy: A physiological substrate. *Journal of Personality and Social Psychology, 63,* 234–246.

34. Thibaut, J. W., & Kelly, H. H. (1969). *The social psychology of groups.* New York: Wiley.

35. Lederer, W. J., & Jackson, D. D. (1968). *The mirages of marriage.* New York: Norton.

36. Gottman, J. M., Coan, J., Carrere, S., & Swanson, C. (1998). Predicting marital happiness and stability from newlywed interactions. *Journal of Marriage and the Family, 60*(1), 5–22.

37. Personal communication, 2009, Robert W. Levenson.

38. Levenson, R. W., & Ebling, R. (2003). Who are the marital experts? *Journal of Marriage and the Family, 63,* 130–142.

39. Susan Johnson first identifies negative cycles that a particular couple engages in. Many of these cycles involve one person pursuing and the other person withdrawing emotionally. See: Johnson, S. (2008). *Hold me tight.* Boston: Little, Brown. Johnson, S. (2004). *The practice of emotionally focused couple therapy, second edition.* New York: Brunner Routledge/Taylor & Francis Group. Johnson, S., Bradley, B., Furrow, J., Palmer, G., Tilley, D., & Wooley, S. (2005). *Becoming an emotionally focused couple therapist: The workbook.* New York: Routledge. Johnson, S. (2002). *Emotionally focused couple therapy with trauma survivors.* New York: Guilford.

40. Camerer, C. F. (2003). *Behavioral game theory: Experiments in strategic interaction.* New York: Russell Sage Foundation.

41. Notarius, C. I., Benson, P. R., Sloane, D., Vanzetti, N. A., & Hornyak, L. M. (1989). Exploring the interface between perception and behavior: An analysis of marital interaction in distressed and nondistressed couples. *Behavioral Assessment, 11,* 39–64.

42. Gabriel, B., Beach, S. R. H., & Bodenmann, G. (2010). Depression, marital satisfaction and communication in couples: Investigating gender differences. *Behavior Therapy, 41,* 306–316.

43. Weiss, R. L., & Cerreto, M. C. (1980). Development of a measure of dissolution potential. *American Journal of Family Therapy, 8,* 80–85.

44. Arnold, V. I. (1986). *Catastrophe theory.* Berlin: Springer Verlag. Gilmore, R. (1981). *Catastrophe theory for scientists and engineers.* New York: Dover. Thom, R. (1975). *Stability and morphogenesis.* Reading, MA: Benjamin.

45. Sztompka, P. (1999). *Trust: A sociological theory.* New York: Cambridge University Press.

Chapter 3. The Metrics of Untrustworthiness and Betrayal

1. von Neumann, J. (1955). *Mathematical foundations of quantum mechanics.* Princeton, NJ: Princeton University Press.

2. Macrae, N. (2000). *John von Neumann: The scientific genius who pioneered the modern computer, game theory, nuclear deterrence, and much more.* New York: Pantheon/Random House.

3. Kuhn, H. W., & Nasar, S. (2002). *The essential John Nash.* Princeton, NJ: Princeton University Press.

4. Pascal, B. (2007). *Pascal's Pensées.* New York: BiblioBazaar.

5. George Carlin Saturday Night Live, October 11th , 1975. Also in Carlin, G. (1997). Brain Droppings (pp 50–53). N.Y. Hyperion.

6. Pascal, B. (2008). *Pensées and other writings.* (H. Levi, trans.) New York: Oxford.

7. Smith, A. (1994). *An inquiry into the nature and causes of the wealth of nations.* New York: Modern Library.

8. Rapoport, A. (2000). *Certainties and doubts.* Montreal: Black Rose Books.

9. Brody, F., & Vámos, T. (1995). *The Neuman compendium.* Singapore: World Scientific Publishing Company.

10. Rapoport, A. (1960). *Fights, games, and debates.* Ann Arbor, MI: University of Michigan Press.

11. Kahn, H. (1984). *Thinking about the unthinkable in the 1980s.* New York: Simon and Schuster.

12. Rapoport, A. (2000). *Certainties and doubts.* Montreal: Black Rose Books.

13. Macrae, N. (2000). *John von Neumann:* The scientific genius who pio-

neered the modern computer, game theory, nuclear deterrence, and much more. New York: Pantheon/Random House.

14. Rapoport, A. (1960). *Fights, games, and debates*. Ann Arbor, MI: University of Michigan Press.

15. Richardson, L. F. (1980). *Statistics of deadly quarrels*. Chicago: The Boxwood Press/Quadrangle Books.

16. Schelling, T. G. (1980). *The strategy of conflict*. Cambridge, MA: Harvard University Press.

17. Macrae, N. (2000). *John von Neumann*: The Scientific genius who pioneered the modern computer, game theory, nuclear deterrence, and much more. New York: Pantheon/Random House.

18. Rapoport, A. (2000). *Certainties and doubts*. Montreal: Black Rose Books.

19. Ibid.

20. Ibid.

21. Ibid.

22. Source.

23. Ibid.

24. Blair, C. (1957, February 25). Passing of a great mind. *Life*, 89–105. See also Wikipedia entries on von Neumann.

25. Source. Heims, S. J. (1982). *John von Neumann and Norbert Wiener*. Cambridge, MA: M. I. T. Press.

26. Poundstone, W. (1992). *Prisoner's dilemma*. New York: Anchor/Random House.

27. Rapoport, A., & Chamman, A. M. (1965). *Prisoner's Dilemma: A study in conflict and cooperation*. Ann Arbor, MI: The University of Michigan Press.

28. Pfaff, D. (2007). *The neuroscience of fair play: Why we (usually) follow the Golden Rule*. New York: Dana Press.

Chapter 4. The Physiology of Trust and Betrayal

1. Ekman, P. (1984). Expression and the nature of emotion. In K. R. Scherer & P. Ekman (Eds.), *Approaches to emotion* (pp. 319–344). Hillsdale, NJ: Lawrence Erlbaum.

2. Selye, H. (2000). *The stress of life* (Rev. ed.). New York: McGraw Hill.

3. Gottman, J. M., & Silver, N. (1999). *The seven principles for making marriage work*. New York: Crown.

4. Gottman, J. M. (1996). *What predicts divorce?* Hillsdale, NJ: Lawrence Erlbaum.

5. Levenson, R. W., & Gottman, J. M. (1985). Physiological and affective predictors of change in relationship satisfaction. *Journal of Personality and Social Psychology, 49*, 85–94.

6. Tabares, A. A. (2008). How couples praise and complain: An examination

of two brief marital interventions. *Dissertation Abstracts International, SectionB: The Sciences and Engineering*, pp. 5596.

7. Gottman, J. M., & Krokoff, L. J., (1989). The relationship between marital interaction and marital interaction and marital satisfaction: A longitudinal view. *Journal of Consulting and Clinical Psychology, 57*, 47–52.

8. Siegel, D., & Hartzell, M. (2003). *Parenting from the inside out.* New York: Penguin Putnam.

9. Jacobson, N. S., & Gottman, J. M. (1999). *When men batter women.* New York: Simon & Schuster.

10. Porges, S. (2003). The polyvagal theory: Phylogenetic contributions to social behavior. *Physiology and Behavior, 79*, 503–513.

11. See www.heartmath.org and www.resperate.com.

12. Kiecolt-Glaser, J. K., Loving, T. J., Stowell, J. R., Malarkey, W. B., Lemeshow, S., Dickinson, S. L., & Glaser, R. (2005). Hostile marital interactions, proinflammatory cytokine production, and wound healing. *Archives of General Psychiatry, 62*, 1377–1384. Kiecolt-Glaser, J. K., Bane, C., Glaser, R., & Malarkey, W. B. (2003). Love, marriage, and divorce: Newlyweds' stress hormones foreshadow relationship changes. *Journal of Consulting and Clinical Psychology, 71*, 176–188.

13. Rowell, L. B. (1993). *Human cardiovascular control.* New York: Oxford University Press.

14. Coan, J. A., Schaefer, H. S., & Davidson, R. J. (2006). Lending a hand: Social regulation of the neural response to threat. *Psychological Science, 17*, 1032–1039.

15. Bennett, D. (2008, August 17). Confidence game. *The Boston Globe*, p.1.

16. Ibid.

17. Shamay-Tsoory, S. G., Fischer, M., Dvash, J., Harari, H., Perach-Bloom, N., & Levkovitz, Y. (2009). Intranasal administration of oxytocin increases envy and schadenfreude (gloating). *Biological Psychiatry, 66*, 864–870.

18. Carter, S. (1998). Neuroendocrine perspectives on social attachment and love. *Psychoneuroendocrinology, 23*(8), 779–818.

19. Gobrogge, K. L., Liu, Y., Young, L. J., & Wang, Z. (2009). Anterior hypothalamic vasopressin regulates pair-bonding and drug-induced aggression in a monogamous rodent. *PNAS, 106*, 19144–19149.

20. Kosfeld, M., Heinrichs, M., Zak, P. J., Fischbacher, U., & Fehr, E. (2005). Oxytocin increases trust in humans. *Nature, 435*, 637–676.

21. Huber, D., Veinante, P., & Stoop, R. (2005). Vasopressin and oxytocin excite distinct neuronal populations in the central amygdala. *Science, 308*(5719), 245–248.

22. Grewen, K. M., Girdler, S. S., Amico, J., & Light, K. C. (2005). Effects of partner support on resting oxytocin, cortisol, norepinephrine, and blood

pressure before and after warm partner contact. *Psychosomatic Medicine, 67,* 531–538.

23. Dalton, K. M., Nacewicz, B. M., Johnstone, T., Schaefer, H. S., Gernsbacher, M. A., Goldsmith, H. H., Alexander, A. L., & Davidson, R. J. (2005). Gaze fixation and the neural circuitry of face processing in autism. *Nature and Neuroscience, 8*(14), 19–26.

24. Ditzen, B., Schaer, M., Gabriel, B., Bodenmann, G., Ulrike, E, & Markus, H. (2009). Intranasal oxytocin increases positive communication and reduces cortisol levels during couple conflict. *Biological Psychiatry, 65,* 728–731.

25. Cushin, B. S., & Carter, C. S. (1999). Prior exposure to oxytocin mimics the effects of social contact and facilities sexual behavior in females. *Journal of Neuroendocrinology, 11,* 765–769. Chang, C. K. (2001). Oxytocinergic neurotransmission at the hippocampus in the central neural regulation of penile erection in the rat. *Urology, 58*(1), 107–112.

26. Carmichael, M., Warburton, V., Sixen, J., & Davidson, J. (1994). Relationships among cardiovascular, muscular, and oxytocin responses during human sexual activity. *Archives of Sexual Behavior, 23,* 59–79.

27. Ahern, T. H., & Young, L. J. (2009). The impact of early life family structure on adult social attachment, alloparental behavior, and the neuropeptide systems regulating affiliative behaviors in the monogamous prairie vole (Microtus ochrogaster). *Frontiers in Behavioral Neuroscience, 3,* 17.

28. Turner, R. A., Altemus, M., Enos, T., Cooper, B., & McGuiness, T. (1999). Preliminary research on plasma oxytocin in cycling women: Investigating emotion and interpersonal distress. *Psychiatry, 62,* 97–113.

29. See www.VeroLabs.com.

30. Shamay-Tsoory, S. G., Fischer, M., Dvash, J., Harari, H., Perach-Bloom, N., & Levkovitz, Y. (2009). Intranasal administration of oxytocin increases envy and schadenfreude (gloating). *Biological Psychiatry, 66,* 864–870.

31. Bos, P. A., Terburg, D., & van Honk, J. (2010). Testosterone decreases trust in socially naïve humans. *PNAS Proceedings of the National Academy of Sciences of the United States, 107,* 5.

32. House, J. S. (1981). *Work stress and social support.* Reading, MA: Addison-Wesley.

33. Berkman, L. F. & Syme, S. L. (1979). Social networks, host resistance, and mortality: A nine-year follow-up of Alameda County residents. *American Journal of Epidemiology, 109,* 186–204. Berkman, L. F., & Kawachi, I. (Eds.). (2000). *Social epidemiology.* New York: Oxford University Press.

34. Cacioppo, J., & Patrick, W. (2008). *Loneliness: Human nature and the need for social connection.* New York: Norton.

35. Ibid.

36. Grewen, K. M., Girdler, S. S., Amico, J., & Light, K. C. (2005). Effects of partner support on resting oxytocin, cortisol, norepinephrine, and blood pressure before and after warm partner contact. *Psychosomatic Medicine, 67*, 531–538.

37. See, for example, Levenson, R. W., Carstensen, L. L., & Gottman, J. M. (1993). Long-term marriage: Age, gender and satisfaction. *Psychology and Aging, 8*(2), 301–313.

38. Derogatis, L. S. (2000). SCL-90R. In A. E. Kazdin (Ed.), *Encyclopedia of psychology* (pp. 192–193). Washington, DC: American Psychological Association, Oxford University Press.

39. Weider, A. B., Keeve, M., Bela, W. D., & Wolff, H. G. (1946). The Cornell Index. *Psychosomatic Medicine, 8*, 411–413.

40. Ornish, D. (1998). *Love and survival.* New York: Harper Collins.

41. Lewis, T., Amini, F., & Lannon, R. (2000). *A general theory of love.* New York: Vintage.

42. LeDoux, J. (1996). *The emotional brain.* New York: Touchstone.

43. Schwartz, G. E., & Russek, L. G. (1998). Family love and lifelong health? A challenge for clinical psychology. In D. K. Routh (Ed.), *The science of clinical psychology: Accomplishments and future directions* (pp. 121–146). Washington, DC: American Psychological Association.

Chapter 5. When It's Time to Bail Out of a Relationship

1. Kluckhohn, F., & Strodtbeck, F. L., (1961). *Variations in value orientations.* Evanston, IL: Row Peterson.

2. Lewis, T., Amini, F., & Lannon, R. (2000). *A general theory of love.* New York: Random House.

3. Buehlman, K., & Gottman, J. M. (1996). The oral history interview and the oral history coding system. In J. M. Gottman (Ed.), *What predicts divorce: The measures.* Hillsdale, NJ: Lawrence Erlbaum.

4. Buehlman, K., Gottman, J. M., & Katz, L., (1992). How a couple views their past predicts their future: Predicting divorce from an oral history interview. *Journal of Family Psychology, 5*(3–4), 295–318.

5. Laurie Abraham, in her book *The Husband and Wives Club*, and in an article in *Slate*, reasoned illogically and confused this issue. Her illogical writing even led the *New York Times* to fallaciously declare that my divorce prediction results were wrong. The problem Abraham had was a lack of knowledge of both research logic and elementary probability and statistics.

6. Martin, T. C., & Bumpass, L. (1989). Recent trends in marital disruption. *Demography, 26*, 37–51.

Chapter 6. How Couples Build Trust With Attunement

1. Gottman, J. M., Katz, L. F., & Hooven, C. (1997). *Meta-emotion: How families communicate emotionally-links to child peer relations and other developmental outcomes.* Hillsdale, NJ: Lawrence Erlbaum.

2. Ekman, P. (2003). *Emotions revealed.* New York: Owl Books. Ekman, P., & Friesen. W. V. (1978). *Facial action coding system.* Palo Alto, CA: Consulting Psychologist Press. Ekman, P., Friesen, W. V., & Simons, R. C. (1985). Is the startle reaction an emotion? *Journal of Personality and Social Psychology, 49,* 1416–1426. Izard, C. E., Kagan, J., & Zajonc, R. (Eds.). *Emotions, cognition, and behavior.* New York: Cambridge University Press.

3. Levenson, R. W., Ekman, P., Heider, K., & Friesen, W. V. (1992). Emotion and autonomic nervous system activity in the Minangkabau of West Sumatra. *Journal of Personality and Social Psychology, 62*(6), 972–988.

4. Katz, D. (1994). *Fathers and sons: 11 great writers talk about their dads.* New York: Esquire.

5. Nahm, E. Y. (2007). A cross-cultural comparison of Korean American and European American parental meta-emotion philosophy and its relationship to parent-child interaction. *Dissertation Abstracts International: Section B; The Sciences and Engineering,* 4136.

6. Kahen, V. (1994). *Parent-child affect and interaction in a teaching situation.* Unpublished undergraduate honors thesis, University of Washington, Seattle.

7. Havighurst, S., Wilson, K. R., Harley, A. E., & Prior, M. R. (2009). Tuning into kids: An emotion-focused parenting program—initial findings from a community trial. *Journal of Community Psychology, 37,* 1008–1023.

8. A remarkable story of the effectiveness of emotion coaching is Dr. Christina Choi's Boystown-orphanages experiments on emotion coaching in Seoul and Busan, with approximately 2,000 children. Both orphanages were beset with severe oppositional defiant behavior by children (K through 12), and teachers were using corporal punishment with the children. Dr. Choi developed a zero-tolerance policy on physical punishment of children and instead used emotion coaching, teaching nuns and teachers the skills. The children's behavior dramatically reversed and they became cooperative and productive within one year (Personal Communication, 2010).

9. Gottman, J. M., & DeClaire, J. (1999). *Raising an emotionally intelligent child* New York: Simon & Schuster. Gottman, J., & Talaris Research Institute. (2004). *What am I feeling?* Seattle, WA: Parenting Press. The DVD *Emotion Coaching* is available from www.talaris.org.

10. Yoshimoto, D. K. (2005). Marital meta-emotion, emotion coaching, and dyadic interaction. *Dissertation Abstracts International, Section B; The Sciences and Engineering,* p. 3448.

11. Ginott, H. (2003). *Between parent and child* (Rev. ed). New York: Three Rivers Press.

12. Driver, J. L., & Gottman, J. M. (2004). Turning toward versus turning away: A coding system of daily interactions. In P. K. Kerig & D. H. Baucom (Eds.), *Couple observational coding systems* (pp. 209–225). Hillsdale, NJ: Lawrence Erlbaum.

13. Driver, J. L. & Gottman, J. M. (2004). Daily marital interactions and positive affect during marital conflict among newlywed couples. *Family process*, 43(3), 301–314.

14. Carlin, G. (1997). *Brain droppings*. New York: Hyperion.

15. Zeigarnik, B. (1984). Kurt Lewin and Soviet psychology. *Journal of Social Issues*, 40, 181–192.

16. Deutch, M. (1968). Field theory in social psychology. In *The handbook of social psychology*, G. Lindzey & E. Aronson (Eds.) pp. 412–487. Reading, MA: Addison-Wesley. chapter in the old Handbook of Social Psychology.

17. Siegel, D. (1999). *The developing mind*. New York: Guilford.

18. Tavris, C., & Aronson, E. (2007). Mistakes were made (but not by me). New York: Harcourt, Inc.

19. The distance and isolation cascade is discussed in Gottman, J. M. (1994). *What predicts divorce?* Hillsdale, NJ: Lawrence Erlbaum.

20. Gordon, T. (2000). *Parent effectiveness training*. New York: Three Rivers Press.

21. Wile, D. (1993). *After the fight*. New York: Guilford.

22. Heider, F. (1958). *The psychology of interpersonal relations*. New York: Wiley.

23. Vonnegut, K. (1999). *Slaughterhouse five*. New York: Dial.

Chapter 7. How Couples Build Intimate Trust

1. Yalom, M. (2001). *A history of the wife*. New York: Perennial/Harper Collins.

2. Hatfield, E., & Rapson, R. (1986). *Love and sex: Cross cultural perspectives.* New York: Allyn and Bacon. Walster, E., & Berscheid, E. (1971). Adrenaline makes the heart grow fonder. *Psychology Today*, 5, 62. Tenov, D. (1999). *Love and limmerance*. Lanham, MD: Scarborough House.

3. Lewis T., Amini, F., & Lannon, R. (2001). *A general theory of love*. New York: Vintage.

4. Perel, E. (2006). *Mating in captivity*. New York: Harper.

5. Kerr, M. E., & Bowen, M. (1988). *Family evaluation*. New York: Norton.

6. Schnarch, D. (1997). *Passionate marriage*. New York: Norton.

7. Papero, D. V. (1995). Bowen family systems and marriage. discoverma-

zine.com. In N. S. Jacobson & A. S. Gurman (Eds.) *Clinical Handbook of Couple Therapy* pp. 11–30. New York: Guilford.

8. Maddox, B. (2010) "The Body Shop: Where Life-like androids are born"

9. See: www.manifestation.com/neurotoys/eliza.php2.

10. Hedges, C. (2009). *The empire of illusion.* New York: Nation Books.

11. Frankl, V. E. (2000) *Man's Search for ultimate meaning.* New York: Perseus Book.

12. B. Zilbergeld (personal communication, 1995). Zilbergeld, B. (1999). *The new male sexuality.* New York: Bantam.

13. Piaget, J. (1962). *Play, dreams, and imitation in childhood.* New York: Norton.

14. Gendlin, E. (2007). *Focusing.* New York: Bantam.

15. Masters, W. H., & Johnson, V. E. (1965). *Human sexual response.* New York: Little, Brown. Masters, W. H., & Johnson, V. E. (1970). *Human sexual inadequacy.* New York: Little, Brown.

16. Hite, S. (1976). *The Hite Report: A nationwide study of female sexuality.* New York: Sever Stories Press.

17. Cupach, W. R., & Comstock, J. (1990). Satisfaction with sexual communication in marriage: Links to sexual satisfaction and dyadic adjustment. *Journal of Social and Personal Relationships, 7,* 179–186. Cupach, W. R., & Metts, S. (1991). Sexuality and communication in close relationships. In K. McKinney & S. Sprecher (Eds.), *Sexuality in close relationships* (pp. 93–110). Hillsdale, NJ: Lawrence Erlbaum. Cupach, W. R., & Metts, S. (1986). Accounts of relational dissolution: A comparison of marital and non-marital relationships. *Communication Monographs, 53,* 311–334. Cupach, W. R., & Metts, S. (1995). The role of sexual attitude similarity on romantic heterosexual relationships. *Personal Relationships, 2,* 287–300.

18. Jourard, S. M. (1971). *The transparent self.* New York: Van Nostrand.

19. Field, T. (2001). *Touch.* Cambridge, MA: MIT Press. Field, T. (1991). *Touch therapy.* New York: Churchill Livingstone. Montague, A. (1986). *Touching.* New York: Harper & Row.

20. Shackelford, J. (2003). *William Harvey and the mechanics of the heart.* New York: Oxford University Press.

21. Clarkson, M. R., Magel, C. N., & Brewer, B. M. (2010) *Pocket companion to Brenner & Rector's The Kidney, 8th Edition.* Philadelphia, PA: Elsevier.

22. Comfort, A. (2002). *The joy of sex.* New York: Octopus/Crown.

23. Gottman, J. M., Levenson, R. W., Gross, J., Fredrickson, B., McCoy, K., Rosentahl, L., Ruel, A., & Yoshimoto, D. (2003). Correlates of gay and lesbian couples' relationship satisfaction and relationship dissolution. *Journal of Homosexuality, 45*(1). 23–43. Gottman, J. M., Levenson, R. W., Swanson, C., Swanson, K., Tyson, R., & Yoshimoto, D. (2003). Observing gay, lesbian and

heterosexual couples' relationship: Mathematical modeling of conflict interactions. *Journal of Homosexuality*, 45(1), 65–91. Gottman, J. M., Gottman, J. S., DeClaire, J. (2006). *Ten lessons to transform your marriage*. New York: Crown.

Chapter 8. The Importance of Repairing Negativity During Conflict

1. Gianino, A., & Tronick, E. Z. (1988). The mutual regulation model: The infant's self and interactive regulation and coping and defensive capacities. In T. M. Field, P. M. McCabe, & N. Schneiderman (Eds.), *Stress and coping across development* (pp. 47–70). Hillsdale, NJ: Lawrence Erlbaum.

2. Brazelton, T. B. (1983). *Infants and mothers*. New York: Dell.

3. Tronick, E. Z. (2003). Things still to be done on the still-face effect. *Infancy*, 4, 475–482.

4. Dreyfus, N. (2009). *Talk to me like I am someone you love*. New York: Tarcher/Penguin.

5. Ball, F. L. J., Cowan, P., & Cowan C. P. (1995). Who's got the power? Gender differences in partners perception of influence during marital problem-solving discussions. *Family Process*, 34, 303–321. Oggins, J., Veroff, J., & Leber, D. (1993). Perceptions of marital interaction among Black and White, newlyweds. *Journal of Personality and Social Psychology*, 65, 494–511.

6. Gottman, J. M. (1994). *What predicts divorce?* Hillsdale, NJ: Lawrence Erlbaum.

7. Wile, D. (1993). *After the fight*. New York: Guilford.

8. Carrere, S., & Gottman, J. M. (1999). Predicting divorce among newlyweds from the first three minutes of a marital conflict discussion. *Family Process*, 38(3), 293–301.

Chapter 9. The Dynamics of Betrayal

1. Buskens, V. (2002). *Social networks and trust*. Boston: Kluwer Academic Publishers.

2. Berkman, L. F., & Kawachi, I. (Eds.). (2000). *Social epidemiology*. New York: Oxford University Press. Ornish, D. (1998). *Love and survival*. New York: HarperCollins. Waite, L., & Gallagher, M. (2000). *The case for marriage*. New York: Doubleday/Random House. Nock, S. L. (1998). *Marriage in men's lives*. New York. Oxford University Press.

3. Friedman, H. S., Tucker, J. S., Schwartz, J. E., Tomilson-Keasey, C., Martin, L. R., Wingrad, R. L., & Criqui, M. H. (1995). Psychosocial and behavioral predictors of longevity: The aging and death of the "termites." *American Psychologist*, 50, 69–78.

4. Olsen, R. B., Olsen, J., Gunner-Svensson, F., & Waldstrom, B. (1991). Social networks and longevity: A 14-year follow-up Study among elderly in Denmark. *Social Science & Medicine, 33,* 1189–1195. Ornish, D. (1998). *Love and Survival.* New York: HarperCollins. Berkman, L. F., & Syme, S. L. (1979). Social networks, host resistance, and mortality: A nine-year follow-up of Alameda County residents. *American Journal of Epidemiology, 109,* 186–204.

5. Yamagishi, T. (2001). Trust as a form of social intelligence. In K. S. Cook (Ed.), *Trust in society* (pp. 121–147). New York: Russell Sage Foundation.

6. Berkman, L. F. & Syme, S. L. (1979). Social networks, host resistance, and mortality: A nine-year follow-up of Alameda County residents. *American Journal of Epidemiology, 109,* 186–204.

7. Verbrugge, L. M. (1979). Marital status and health. *Journal of Marriage and the Family, 41*(2), 267–285. Verbrugge, L. M. (1985). Gender and health: An update on hypotheses and evidence. *Journal of Health and Social Behavior, 26,* 156–182. Verbrugge, L. M. (1989). The twain meet: Empirical explanations of sex differences in health and personality. *Journal of Health and Social Behavior, 30,* 282–304.

8. Ornish, D. (1998). *Love and survival.* New York: HarperCollins. House, J. S. (1981). *Work stress and social support.* Reading, MA: Addison-Wesley.

9. Waite, L., & Gallagher, M. (2000). *The case for marriage.* New York: Doubleday/Random House.

10. Nock, S. L. (1998). *Marriage in men's lives.* New York: Oxford University Press.

11. Terman, L. M., Buttenweiser, P., Ferguson, L. W., Johnson, W. B., & Wilson, D. P. (1938). *Psychological factors in marital happiness.* Stanford, CA: Stanford University Press.

12. Friedman, H. S., Tucker, J. S., Schwartz, J. E., Tomilson-Keasey, C., Martin, L. R., Wingrad, R. L., & Criqui, M. H. (1995). Psychosocial and behavioral predictors of longevity: The aging and death of the "termites." *American Psychologist, 50,* 69–78.

13. Yamagishi, T. (2001). Trust as a form of social intelligence. In K. S. Cook (Ed.), *Trust in society* (pp. 121–147). New York: Russell Sage Foundation.

14. Geller, J. D. (1968). Some personality and situational determinants of interpersonal trust. *Dissertation Abstracts International,* 4755. See also: Hamsher, J. H., Geller, J. P., & Rotter, J. B. (1968). Interpersonal trust, internal-external control, and the Warren Commission Report. *Journal of Personality and Social Psychology, 9,* 210–215.

15. Ostrom, E., & Walker, J. (2002). *Trust and reciprocity.* New York: Russell Sage Foundation.

16. Berg, J., Dickhaut, J., & McCabe, K. (1995). Trust, reciprocity, and social history. *Games and economic behavior, 10,* 122–142.

17. Buchan, N. R., Croson, R. T. A., Johnson, E. J., & Iacobucci, D. (2004). When do fair beliefs influence bargaining behavior? Experimental bargaining in Japan and the United States. *Journal of Consumer Research, 31*, 181–190.

18. Unoka, Z., Seres, J., Aspan, N., Bodi, N., & Keri, S. (2009). Trust game reveals restricted interpersonal transactions in patients with borderline personality disorder. *Journal of Personality Disorders, 23*, 399–409. For brain activity with respect to this disorder, see: Meyer-Lindberg, A. (2008). Trust me on this. *Science, 321*, 778–780.

19. Caryl Rusbult was a prolific researcher and writer. Here are some important papers by her and colleagues: Drigotas, S. M., & Rusbult, C. E. (1992). Should I stay or should I go? A dependence model of breakups. *Journal of Personality and Social Psychology, 62*, 62–87. Drigotas, S. M., Safstrom, C. G., & Gentilia, T.(1999). An investment model prediction of dating infidelity. *Journal of Personality and Social Psychology, 77*, 509–524. Drigotas, S. M., Rusbult, C. E., & Verette, J. (1999). Level of commitment, mutuality of commitment, and couples well-being. *Personal Relationships, 6*, 389–409. Finkel, E. J., Rusbult, C. E., Kumashiro, M., & Hannon, P. A. (2002). Dealing with betrayal in close relationships: Does commitment promote forgiveness? *Journal of Personality and Social Psychology, 82*, 956–974. Johnson, D. J., & Rusbult, C. E. (1989). Resisting temptation: Devaluation of alternative partners as a means of maintaining commitment in close relationships. *Journal of Personality and Social Psychology, 57*, 967–980. Rusbult, C. E., Johnson, O. J., & Morrow, G. D. (1986). Predicting satisfaction and commitment in adult romantic involvements: An assessment of the generalizability of the investment model. *Social Psychology Quarterly, 49*, 81–89. Rusbult, C. E., Johnson, O. J., & Morrow, G. D. (1986). Determinants of exit, voice, loyalty, and neglect: Response to dissatisfaction in adult romantic relationships. *Human Relations, 39*, 45–63. Rusbult, C. E., Verette, J., Whitney, G. A., Slorik, L. F., & Lipkus, I. (1991). Accomodation processes in close relationships: Theory and preliminary empirical evidence. *Journal of Personality and Social Psychology, 60*, 53–78. Rusbult, C. E., Martz, J. M., & Agnew, C. R. (1998). The investment model scale: Measuring commitment level, satisfaction level, quality of alternatives, and investment size. *Personal Relationships, 5*, 357–391. Rusbult, C. E., VanLange, P. A. M., Wildshutt, J., Yovetich, N. A., & Verette, J. (2000). Perceived superiority in close relationships: Why it exists and persists. *Journal of Personality and Social Psychology, 79*, 521–545.

20. The Hebrew Tanach, Proverbs 30. Eyshet Chayil. (1997). *The Jerusalem Bible*. Jerusalem: Koren Publishers.

21. Bowlby, J. (1980). *Loss: Attachment and loss*. New York: Basic.

22. For an excellent review of Harlow's work, see: Blum, D. (2002). *Love at Goon Park*. New York: Berkley Publishing Group.

23. Mikulincer, M., & Goodman, G. S. (2006). *Dynamics of romantic love:*

Attachment, caregiving, and sex. New York: Guilford. See also: Rholen, W. S., & Simpson, J. A. (2004). *Adult attachment.* New York: Guilford.

24. Glass, S. P., & Staeheli, J. C. (2003). *Not just friends.* New York: Simon & Schuster.

25. (r = .56, p<.001)

26. As assessed by low–frequency spectral power in the heart period spectrum, below the respiratory range.

27. Weiss, R. S. (1990). *Staying the course: The emotional and social lives of men who do well.* New York: Free Press.

28. Brown, M., & Auerback, A. (1981). Communication patterns in the initiation of marital sex. *Medical Aspects of Human Sexuality, 15,* 101–117.

29. Clark, R. D., & Hatfield, E. (1989). Gender differences in receptivity to sexual offers. *Journal of Psychology and Human Sexuality, 2,* 39–55.

30. Clark, R. D. (1990). The impact of AIDS on gender differences in the willingness to engage in casual sex. *Journal of Applied Social Psychology, 20,* 771–782.

31. Kennedy-Moore, E., & Watson, J. C. (1999). *Expressing emotion.* New York: Guilford.

32. Johnson, R. M. (2009). *Why men fear marriage: The surprising truth behind why so many men can't commit.* New York: Pocket Books/Simon & Schuster.

33. Stanley, S. M. (2002). *What is it with men and commitment, anyway?* Keynote address to the 6th annual Smart Marriages Conference, Washington, D.C.

34. Blumstein, P. & Schwartz, P.(1983). *American Couples.* New York: Morrow.

35. Fisher, H. (2009). *Why him? Why her?* New York: Henry Holt. Fisher, H. (2004). *Why we love.* New York: Henry Holt. Buss, D. M. (1994). *The evolution of desire.* New York: Basic.

Chapter 10. Healing From Betrayal

1. Tabares, A. A. (2008). How couples praise and complain: An examination of two brief marital interventions. *Dissertation Abstract International, Section B: The Sciences and Engineering,* p. 5596.

2. Tabares, A. (2006). *Praise and complain coding system.* Seattle, WA: University of Washington and the Relationship Research Institute.

3. The repeated Prisoner's Dilemma player begins with cooperation and stays there, unless there is unilateral betrayal. He or she is then considered "content." If the player becomes a victim of betrayal while in the being content strategy, the other player then becomes "provoked," and defects to betrayal until a cooperation from the partner causes him or her to become content again. If he or she betrays while content, he or she then becomes contrite and, of course, subsequently cooperates. Axelrod wrote in *The Evolution of Cooperation:* "Genorosity was effective at stopping the continuing echo of a single error. . . . The problem

is that generosity requires a tradeoff between the speed of error correction and the risk of exploitation" (p. 37).

4. Axelrod, R. (1997) *The complexity of cooperation.* Princeton, NJ: Princeton University Press.

5. Axelrod, R., & Cohen, M. D. (2000). *Harnessing complexity.* New York: Basic Books.

6. Marton, K. (2001). *Hidden power.* New York: Anchor.

7. Buskens, V. (2002). *Social networks and trust.* Boston: Kluwer Academic Publishers.

8. Schimmel, S. (2002). *Wounds not healed by time.* New York: Oxford University Press.

9. Gordon, K. C., & Baucom, D. H. (2003). Forgiveness and marriage: Preliminary support for a measure based on a model of recovery from a marital betrayal. *American Journal of Family Therapy, 31,* 179–199. Snyder, D. K., Baucom, D. H., & Gordon, K. C. (2008). An integrative approach to treating infidelity. *The Family Journal, 16,* 300–307. Christensen, A., Jacobson, N. S., & Babcock, J. C. (1995). Integrative A. S. Gurman (Eds.) *Clinical Handbook of Couple Therapy,* pp. 31–64. New York: Guilford.

10. Stanley, S. M., Rhoades, G. K., & Markman, H. J. (2006). Sliding versus declining: Inertia and the premarital cohabitation effect. *Family Relations, 55,* 499–509.

11. Ibid.

12. Murray, S. L., Holmes, J. G., & Pinkus, R. T. (2010). A smart unconscious? Procedural origins of automatic partner attitudes in marriage. *Journal of Experimental Social Psychology, 46,* 650–656.

13. Hart, J. J. E. (2007). More evidence for a security system model of attachment, self-esteem and worldviews: The effects of security boosts on defensiveness. *Dissertation Abstracts International, Section B: The Sciences and Engineering,* 4759. Hart, J., Shaver, P. R., & Goldenberg, J. L. (2005). Attachment, self-esteem, worldviews, and terror management: Evidence for a tripartite security system. *Journal of Personality and Social Psychology, 88,* 999–1013. Marigold, D. C., Holmes, J. G., & Ross, M. (2010). Fostering relationship resilience: An intervention for low self-esteem individuals. *Journal of Experimental Social Psychology, 46,* 624–630. Murray, S. L., Holmes, J. G., & Pinkus, R. T. (2010). A smart unconscious? Procedural origins of automatic partner attitudes in marriage. *Journal of Experimental Social Pyshcology, 46,* 650–656. Murray, S. L., Leder, S., MacGregor, J. C. D., Holmes, J. G., Pinkus, R. T., & Harris, B. (2009). Becoming irreplaceable: How comparisons of the partner's alternatives differentially affect low and high self-esteem people. *Journal of Experimental Social Psychology, 45,* 1180–1191.

14. Booth-LaForce, C., Oh, W., Kim, A. H., Rubin, K. H., Rose-Krasnor, L., & Burgess, K. (2006). Attachment, self-worth, and peer group functioning in middle-childhood. *Attachment and Human Development, 8,* 309–325.

15. Curseu, P. L., & Schruijer, S. G. L. (2010). Does conflict shatter trust or does trust obliterate conflict? Revisiting the relationships between team diversity, conflict, and trust. *Group Dynamics, 14,* 66–79.

16. Levin, D., Whitener, E., & Cross, R. (2006). Perceived trustworthiness of knowledge sources: The moderating effects of relationship length. *Journal of Applied Psychology, 91,* 1163–1171.

17. Rusbult, C. E., Kumashiro, M., Finkel, E. J., & Wildschut, T. (2002). The War of the Roses: An interdependence analysis of betrayal and forgiveness. In P. Noller & J. A. Feeney (Eds), *Understanding marriage: Developments in the study of couple interaction* (pp. 251–281). New York: Cambridge University Press.

18. a. Fincham, F. D., Stanley, S. M., Beach, R. H. (2007). Transformative processes in marriage. An analysis of emerging trends. *Journal of Marriage and Family, 69,* 275–292

b. Van Lange, P. A. M., Rusbult C. E., Drigotas S. M., Arriapa, X. B., Witcher, B. S., & Cox, C. L. (1997). Willingness to sacrifice in close relationships. *Journal of Personality and Social Psychology, 72,* 1373–1395.

19. www.menstuff.org/issues/byissue/infidelitystats.html

20. Vaughan, P. (2002). *Help for therapists and their clients in dealing with affairs: Based on results of a survey with 1,083 people whose spouses had affairs.* San Diego, CA: Dialog Press.

21. Gottman, J. S. (2004). *The marriage clinic casebook.* New York: Norton.

22. Zillmann, D., & Bryant, J. (Eds.). (1989). *Pornography: Research advances and policy considerations.* Hillsdale, NJ: Lawrence Erlbaum.

23. Hedges, C. (2009). *The empire of illusion.* New York: Nation Books. Dworkin, A. (1981). *Pornography: Men possessing women.* New York: Plume.

24. Maltz, W., & Maltz, L. (2010). *The porn trap.* New York: Harper.

25. Wolak, J., Mitchell, K. & Finkelhor, D. (2007). Unwanted and wanted exposure to online pornography in a National Sample of Youth internet users. *Pediatrics, 119,* 247–257.

26. Maltz, W., & Maltz, L. (2010). *The porn trap.* New York: Harper.

27. Ibid.

28. Carnes, P. (2001). *Out of the shadows: Understanding sexual addiction.* Center City, MN: Hazelden.

Chapter 11. The Mathematics of Relationships:
Power Imbalance, Trust, and Betrayal

1. Hardin, R. (2002). *Trust and trustworthiness.* New York: Russell Sage Foundation.

2. Broderick, C. B. (1993). *Understanding family process.* Newbury Park, CA: Sage.

3. Vuchinich, S. (1980). Logical relations and comprehension in conversation. *Journal of Psycholinguistic Research, 9*, 473–501. Vuchinich, S., Wood, B., Angelelli, J. (2005). Coalitions and family problem solving in the psychosocial treatment of preadolescents. In E. D. Hibbs & P. Jensen (Eds.), *Psychosocial treatments for child and adolescent disorders* (pp. 497–518). Washington, DC: American Psychological Association. Patterson, G. R., Crosby, L., & Vuchinich, S. (1992). Predicting risk for early police arrest. *Journal of Quantitative Criminology, 8*, 335–355. Vuchinich, S., & Teachman, J. (1994). Influences on the duration of wars, strikes, riots and family arguments. *Journal of Conflict Resolution, 38*, 586.

4. Aries, E. (1996). *Men and women in interaction.* New York: Oxford University Press.

5. Kenkel, W. F. (1963). Observational studies of husband-wife interaction in family decision-making. In M. B. Sussman (Ed.), *Sourcebook in marriage and the family* (pp. 144–156). Boston: Houghton-Mifflin.

6. Gottman, J., Murray, J., Swanson, C., Tyson, R., & Swanson, K. (2002). *The mathematics of marriage: Dynamic nonlinear models.* Cambridge, MA: MIT Press.

7. von Bertalanffy, L. (1968). *General system theory.* New York: George Braziller.

8. Wiener, N. (1961). *Cybernetics.* Cambridge, MA: MIT Press.

9. Shannon, C. E., & Weaver, W. (1963). *The mathematical theory of information.* Chicago: University of Illinois Press.

10. Cannon, W. B. (1932). *The wisdom of the body.* New York: Norton.

11. Charlton, N. G. (2008). *Understanding Gregory Bateson.* Albany, NY: State University of New York Press.

12. Ray, W. A. (2009). *Don D. Jackson: Interactional theory in the practice of therapy.* Phoenix, AZ: Zeigh-Tucker.

13. Watzlawick, P., Weakland, J., & Fisch, R. (1974). *Change.* New York: Norton.

14. Satir, V. (1964). *The new peoplemaking.* Palo Alto, CA: Science and Behavior Books.

15. Minuchin, S. (1974). *Families and family therapy.* Cambridge, MA: Harvard University Press.

16. Fivaz-Depeursinge, E., & Corboz-Warnery, A. (1999). *The primary triangle.* New York: Basic.

17. Shapiro, A. F. (2005). Examining relationships between the marriage, mother-father-baby interactions and infant emotion regulation. *Dissertation Abstracts International, Section B: The Sciences and Engineering,* 3750. Christianson, G. E. (1984). *In the presence of the creator.* New York: Free Press.

18. Newton and Liebnitz The Calculus Wars, & bio of Newton Bordi, J. S. (2006). *The calculus wars.* New York: Avalon.

19. Gleick, J. (1988). *Chaos*. New York: Penguin.

20. Murray, J. (2001). *Mathematical biology* (2nd ed., Vols. 1–2). Berlin: Springer-Verlag.

21. Edelstein-Kesher, L. (2005). *Mathematical models in biology*. New York: SIAM.

22. Strogatz, S. H. (1994). *Nonlinear dynamics and chaos*. New York: Addison-Wesley.

23. Mahon, B. (2003). *The man who changed everything: The life of James Clerk Maxwell*. New York: Wiley.

24. Einstein, A., & Infeld, L. ((1938). *The evolution of physics*. New York: Touchstone.

25. Personal communication, 2010.

26. Kattan, P. I. (2010). *MATLAB for beginners: A gentle approach*. Self-published by Kattan Books.

27. Gottman, J. M., Kahen, V., & Goldstein, D. (1996). The Rapid Couples Interaction Scoring System (RCISS). In J. M. Gottman (Ed.), *What predicts divorce: The measures* (pp. 170–238). Hillsdale, NJ: Lawrence Erlbaum.

28. Gladwell, M. (2005). *Blink*. New York: Little, Brown.

29. Cook, J., Tyson, R., White, J., Rushe, R., Gottman, J., & Murray, J. (1995). The mathematics of marital conflict: Qualitative dynamic mathematical modeling of marital interaction. *Journal of Family Psychology*, 9(2), 110–130.

30. Gottman, J. M. (1979). *Marital interaction: Experimental investigations*. New York: Academic Press.

31. Haley, J. (1964). Research on family patterns: An instrument measurement. *Family Process*, 3, 41–76.

32. Hamaker, E., Zhang, Z., & van der Maas, H. L. J. (2009). Using threshold autoregressive models to study dyadic interactions. *Psychometrika*, 74,727–745.

33. Amazingly, it is possible to show that if we have the general differential equation, it turns out that a state is a stable state if the rate of change of the function **f** is negative at a point and unstable if the rate of change of **f** is positive at a point. Graphically to find stable states we can look at the slope of **f** where it crosses the x-axis; each point where it is zero (crosses the x-axis) is where the rate of change (also called the "derivative") on the right-hand side of the equation is zero, so it's a null cline. Each point of *negative slope* where **f** crosses the x-axis represents a stable steady state, while each point of *positive slope* for **f** implies an unstable steady state. Recall the function **f** is given by each of our equations, once we know how to write them down. There it is. The math makes stability precise and well defined. I loved that precision. Mathematically, it is easy to show that the uninfluenced steady state is $a/(1-r_1)$ for the wife and $b/(1-r_2)$ for the husband.

34. Notarius, C., & Buongiorno, I. (1992). [Wait time until seeking couples'

therapy or any other couples intervention.] Unpublished study, Catholic University of America.

35. Jacobson, N. S., & Addis, M. E. (1993). Research on couple therapy: What do we know? Where are we going? *Journal of Consulting and Clinical Psychology, 61*(1), 85–93.

36. Seligman, M. E. P. (1996). A creditable beginning. *American Psychologist, 51,* 1086–1088.

37. Levenson, R. W., Carstensen, L. L., & Gottman, J. M. (1993). Long-term marriage: age, gender and satisfaction. *Psychology and Aging, 8*(2), 301–313. Carstensen, L. L., Gottman, J. M., & Levenson, R. W. (1995). Emotional behavior in long-term marriage. *Psychology & Aging, 10*(1), 140–149.

38. Wile, D. (1993). *Couples therapy: A nontraditional approach.* New York: John Wiley.

39. Cook, J., Tyson, R., White, J., Rushe, R., Gottman, J., & Murray, J. (1995). The mathematics of marital conflict: Qualitative dynamic mathematical modeling of marital interaction. *Journal of Family Psychology, 9*(2), 110–130.

40. Asimov, I. (1951). *Foundation.* New York: Ballantine.

Additional Readings on Specialized Topics on the Mathematics of the Science of Trust

Game Theory Mathematics

Auman, R. J., & Maschler, M. B. (1995). *Repeated games with incomplete information.* Cambridge, MA: MIT Press.

Beasley, J. D. (2006). *The mathematics of games.* Mineola, NY: Dover.

Binmore, K. (2007). *Game theory: A very short introduction.* New York: Oxford University Press.

Dresher, M. (1981). *The mathematics of games of strategy.* Mineola, NY: Dover.

Gibbons, R. (1992). *Game theory for applied economists.* Princeton, NJ: Priceton University Press.

Gintis, H. (2009). *Game theory evolving.* Princeton, NJ: Princeton University Press.

Gintis, H. (2009). *The bounds of reason.* Princeton, NJ: Princeton University Press.

Hendricks, V. F., & Hansen, P. G. (2007). *Game theory: 5 questions.* New York: Automatic Press.

Isaacs, R. (1965). *Differential games.* Mineola, NY: Dover.

Karlin, S. (1959). *Mathematical methods and theory in games, programming, and economics.* Mineola, NY: Dover.

Kuhn, H. W. (Ed.). (1997). *Classics in game theory.* Princeton, NJ: Princeton University Press.

Luce, R. D., & Raiffa, H. (1957). *Games and decisions.* New York: Wiley.

Meyerson, R. B. (1991). *Game theory: Analysis of conflict.* Cambridge, MA: Harvard University Press.

Osborne, M. J. & Rubenstein, A. (1994). *A course in game theory.* Cambridge, MA: MIT Press.

Owen, G. (1968). *Game theory.* Philadelphia: W. B. Saunders.

Hidden Markov Models Mathematics

Cappe, O., Moulines, E., & Ryden, T. (2005). *Inference in hidden Markov models.* Berlin: Springer.

Elliott, R. J., Aggoun, L., & Moore, J. B. (1995). *Hidden Markov models: Estimation and control.* Berlin: Springer.

Fraser, A. M. (2008). *Hidden Markov models and dynamical systems.* Philadelphia: SIAM.

Iosifescu, M. (1980). *Finite Markov processes and their applications.* Mineola, NY: Dover.

Zucchini, W., & MacDonald, I. L. (2009). *Hidden Markov models for time series: An introduction using R.* New York: CRC Press/Taylor & Francis Group.

Behavioral Economics and Trust Research Mathematics

Bachman, R., & Zaheer, A. (2006). *Handbook of trust research.* Cheltenham, UK: Edward Elgar.

Glimcher, P. W. (2003). *Decisions, uncertainty, and the brain.* Cambridge, MA: MIT Press.

Kagel, J. H., & Roth, A. E. (1995). *The handbook of experimental economics.* Princeton, NJ: Princeton University Press.

Index

[Page numbers followed by *f* or *t* refer to figures or tables, respectively.]